The Economic History of Britain since 1700

Volume 1: 1700–1860

The Economic History of Britain since 1700

Edited by
RODERICK FLOUD *and* DONALD McCLOSKEY

Volume 1: 1700–1860

Cambridge University Press

Cambridge
London   New York   New Rochelle
Melbourne   Sydney

Published by the Press Syndicate of the University of Cambridge
The Pitt Building, Trumpington Street, Cambridge CB2 1RP
32 East 57th Street, New York, NY 10022, USA
296 Beaconsfield Parade, Middle Park, Melbourne 3206, Australia

First published 1981

Printed in Great Britain at the University Press, Cambridge

British Library Cataloguing in Publication Data
The economic history of Britain since 1700.
Vol. 1: 1700–1860
1. Great Britain – Economic conditions
I. Floud, Roderick   II. McCloskey, Donald Nansen
330.9′41′07   HC255   79-41645

ISBN 0 521 23166 3 hard covers
ISBN 0 521 29842 3 paperback
Vol. 2 ISBN 0 521 231671 hard covers
        ISBN 0 521 298431 paperback

To Lydia, Sarah, Daniel and Margaret

Contents

viii

Tables

Figures

Introduction

R. C. FLOUD & D. N. McCLOSKEY

Economic history is an exciting subject, a subject full of problems and controversy. It is exciting because in economic history one is constantly forced to ask the question – why? Why were steam engines brought into use at a particular point during the industrial revolution? Why did so many millions brave great dangers to emigrate to the new world? Why were so many unemployed in the depression of the 1930s? Why do parents today have fewer children than parents two hundred years ago? Economic history is not, therefore, a story – still less a chronological story, for most events in economic history cannot be neatly dated. Instead it is a list of questions; some can be answered, some cannot, but it is the search for answers, and for the best way to seek answers, which gives the subject both its justification and its interest. 'Economic history concerns the dullest part of human life. Sex, art, aberrant behaviour, politics, bloodshed – it is largely devoid of these' (Parker 1971). Yet it is concerned instead with how people live most of their lives, how many people are born and how they die, how they earn and how they spend, how they work and how they play.

At the same time, economic history can be hard, boring and frustrating, both to write and to learn. Simply because it is concerned with how people have commonly lived, and why they have commonly behaved in a particular way, it is often difficult to discover relevant evidence; people, certainly most people, do not record in great detail for posterity what they buy or what they do at work, nor even how many children they have. The historian has to reconstruct the details of such behaviour from scattered and ambiguous evidence, and his reconstruction can often only be imprecise; few of the statements made in this book are, for that reason, entirely free from the possibility of error, and many represent only guesses. They are the best guesses made, when the book was written, by economic historians expert in their subject, but guesses nonetheless. Indeed, part of the fascination of economic history, although also one of the main causes of the controversies which rumble on for years in the scholarly journals of the subject, lies in making new guesses, and in working out what the effect on our knowledge of the past might be if we made different, but still sensible, guesses about the interpretation of evidence.

Even when we know, at least approximately, whether people ate white or

xi

brown bread, or at what age they married, they are very unlikely to have
recorded for posterity why they ate white bread when their parents ate brown,
or why they married at 27 when their parents married at 24. Even if they did
so, their records would be inconclusive, for two reasons: first, people are poor
at self-analysis; second, the factor which they choose as 'the' reason why is
usually one among many joint reasons. In any case, the economic historian's
interest is not normally in the behaviour of individuals, except as exemplars of
the behaviour of society, or large groups within society, as a whole. While a
political historian can reasonably hope to understand something of the political
history of the nineteenth century by studying the life and thoughts of Queen
Victoria or of Abraham Lincoln, the economic historian knows that the
behaviour of any one individual has very little or no effect upon, and may even
be totally different from, the observed behaviour of society as a whole. The fact
that the marriage age in a parish is observed to have fallen from an average of
27 in one generation to an average of 24 in the next does not show that all those
who married did so at the age of 24; nor, conversely, does the fact that two people
married at 29 invalidate the fact of the fall in the average.

The answer that we give to a question such as 'why did people marry at an
earlier age than their parents' cannot therefore stem directly from the memories
or writings of those who were doing the marrying. It can stem partly from such
evidence, but only because such evidence helps to build up a set of the many
possible reasons why people might have decided to marry earlier. This set of
reasons, based partly on evidence from those who married and partly on the
knowledge and common sense of the historian, is a necessary beginning to the
task of explanation. Armed with it, the historian can begin to explore the
evidence, and to see to what degree the behaviour which he observes fits best
with one reason rather than another. He might begin, for example, with the belief
that people are likely to marry if they are richer and can afford to set up house
at an earlier age than their parents; if he finds after seeking for evidence of
changes in income levels that on the contrary income levels fell at the same time
as marriage became earlier, then that belief seems unlikely to be helpful, and
another possible reason must be explored.

In other words, the historian uses evidence of the behaviour of individuals to
help him to build up an expectation of how people might have behaved, against
which he can contrast his observations of how they actually seem to have
behaved. The expectation, or model as it is often called, is founded on
assumptions about human behaviour, and therefore about the likely response
of groups of individuals to changes in their circumstances. At its most simple,
for example, the expectation might be that in general people buy less of a
commodity as it becomes more expensive. The expectation may not always be
correct for each individual, but it serves in general.

We need to have such expectations, or models, if we are to organise our thoughts and assumptions and apply them to the elucidation or solution of problems about what happened in history. If we do not, then we can only flounder in a mass of individual observations, unaware whether the individual behaviour which we observe is normal or aberrant. Models, therefore, cut through the diversity of experience and behaviour which we all know to characterise any human activity, and embody our judgement as to why people are likely to have behaved as they did.

If the models of historians are to be useful in analysing the past, then they must be carefully chosen. The economic and social historian deals in his work on past societies with subjects which are the concern of many analysts of contemporary society: economists, geographers, sociologists, political scientists. It is sensible for the historian to consider whether he may use their models to aid him in his work. In making the choice he must always be conscious that contemporary society is different from past society, and that a model may either have to be adapted to the requirements of historical analysis or, at the extreme, rejected as entirely inappropriate. But if the adaptation can be made then the historian is likely to gain greatly in his work from the insights of contemporary social scientists; these insights help him to expand and refine his model of the past.

These assertions are controversial. Not all historians accept that it is useful to apply models drawn from the social sciences to historical analysis. Not all, even today, would accept that the primary task of the historian is to explain; they would hold, instead, that description, the discovery of the record of what happened in the past, should be given pride of place. Most frequently, critics of the use of models and of the statistical methods which often accompany them claim that models cannot cope with the rich diversity of human behaviour in the past, that they simplify and therefore distort. Even mere statistical description – counting heads and calculating averages – has been attacked for dehumanising history and for replacing people by numbers.

Such attacks are based largely on misunderstanding. It is certainly true that models of human behaviour must simplify; indeed, that is their purpose, to enable the historian to concentrate on a restricted set of possible explanations for that behaviour, rather than being distracted by the diversity of individual deeds. It is also true that models concentrate on expectations of normal or average behaviour; again, this is deliberate and necessary if the normal is to be distinguished from the aberrant. The historian who uses models does not forget that diversity exists; indeed he makes use of that diversity, those different reactions to different circumstances, to help him to frame and then to improve his model. In some circumstances, no doubt, the diversity of the past may defeat the simplifying powers of the historian and the most complex of models, but such circumstances, are no grounds for rejection of the use of models as a whole.

A more reasonable criticism of models and their application to history is that they are often themselves too simple, and that they embody unjustifiable assumptions about human behaviour. In later chapters of this book, for example, we make use of models which assume the existence of full employment, or of perfect mobility of labour; such models may lead to misleading results if such conditions do not obtain. Yet to criticise the use of one model in one set of circumstances does not show that all use of models is wrong. It shows simply that the historian, and the reader of this or any book, should be alert and critical and should not make silly errors; the same could be said of any scholarly work.

A third ground of criticism of the use of models and of statistical methods in history is better founded. Many social scientists use mathematical language to express their ideas and to formulate their models, while most historians, and even many social scientists, are not sufficiently familiar with mathematics to understand what is written. They do not appreciate that mathematics is often used merely as a shorthand, and are even less likely to appreciate that it is sometimes used merely to impress the unwary. Very reasonably, someone who does not understand may reject the ideas along with the language by which they are veiled, even though, in truth, the models can almost always be expressed in a language which is comprehensible to non-mathematicians.

This book has been written by economic and social historians who are expert in the use of models and of statistical methods in history, but are conscious of the fears, doubts and misunderstandings which such usage evokes. They wish to show that economic and social history is not diminished thereby but augmented, and that the results can be understood by anyone interested in historical problems. The economic and social history which they write, and which is discussed in this book, is sometimes called the 'new' economic and social history. The novelty of applying the methods of social science to history is by now about a quarter of a century old; it is often 'new' not so much in its aim nor even in its methods, but merely in the language which it uses. The results, however, are of great interest, and for this reason the authors have expressed their ideas in a language which any student of the subject can understand; where they have used a model or a statistical method which may be unfamiliar, it has been explained.

Together, the chapters in this book make up an economic history of England and Wales since 1700. The basic chronology and the evidence on which it is based are discussed, and the book as a whole provides a treatment of the most important themes in English social and economic history during the period of industrialisation and economic growth. Much has been left out, for the authors and editors have chosen to concentrate on the topics which are most problematical and yet where solutions to problems may be attainable. The book is divided into five overlapping chronological divisions, corresponding to the periods from 1700 to 1800, from 1780 to 1860, from 1860 to 1914, from 1900 to 1945, and from 1945 to the present day. Each division except the last begins with a general survey of the period, which is followed by a number of chapters which consider the main problems which have arisen in the historical interpretation of that period; each division except the first and last concludes with a chapter dealing with the social history of the period in relation to the economic changes which have been considered. The period since 1945 is treated as a whole in one, final, chapter. The book is divided into two volumes, with the break at 1860, although a number of chapters in both volumes bridge the break. Each volume has its own index and glossary, and its own bibliography; frequent references to sources and to further reading are given in the text, making use of the 'author–date' system of reference. In this system, books or articles are referred to in the text simply by the name of the author and the date of publication, for example (Keynes 1936); the bibliography is an alphabetical list of authors, with the date of publication immediately following the author's name. Thus (Keynes 1936) in the text has its counterpart as Keynes, J. M. 1936 *The General Theory of Employment, Interest and Money* in the bibliography.

The book has been planned and written by many hands. The Social Science Research Council of Great Britain generously made funds available both for an initial planning meeting and for a conference at which the first drafts of the chapters were discussed. The authors and editors are grateful to the SSRC for its generosity, and to Donald Coleman, Philip Cottrell, Jack Dowie, Malcolm Falkus, Jordan Goodman, Leslie Hannah, Max Hartwell, Brian Mitchell, Leslie Pressnell, John Wright and Tony Wrigley for attending the conference and making many helpful comments. Annabel Gregory, Alan Hergert, Nigel Lewis, and Ali Saad gave invaluable help in preparing the manuscript for publication.

1

The eighteenth century: a survey

N. C. R. CRAFTS

1. The key changes

The story opens with Britain among the richest countries in Europe, but rich – as the rest were – by a traditional definition: productive if unscientific agriculture, busy if unmechanised industry, and vigorous if narrow commerce. The eighty years before 1780 are years of traditional success introducing two centuries of breaking and rebreaking of tradition.

Any approach to the subject must simplify, as does what follows, by taking a few classes of facts about Britain before industrialisation and studying their links. Even so 'simple' an economy as Britain's in the eighteenth century, after all, was the mutual interplay of seven million souls. The economic approach merely makes the simplification explicit, displaying its simplicity in a fascination with simple statistics. Naturally the statistics we have on the eighteenth century economy are imperfect, and those used here should be regarded as 'best guesses' with a substantial margin for error. All recent work on the century relies heavily on the pioneering guesses of Deane and Cole (1966); as we shall see, even their's are doubtful in some respects. In any event, they give a picture of a two-stage acceleration in economic growth, with the first coming in the middle of the century and the second – the usual date of the 'take-off' (Rostow 1960: 38) – in its last two decades. The picture, which represents the state of quantitative knowledge until very recently, is summarised in table 1.1. More recent work has suggested alternative estimates for at least the first half of the century. The revised estimates of table 1.2 following, then, are probably preferable to those of table 1.1, but should themselves be treated with caution.

Table 1.2 and the last two columns of table 1.1 make several points. Growth of real output (i.e. corrected for price changes) was considerably faster at the end of the eighteenth century than it had been at the beginning, although it was still a little below what it was to be in the nineteenth century. The growth of both total output and output per person appears to have been sustained throughout the century prior to the 'take-off'. That is, the big acceleration in industrial output growth at the end of the century was preceded by a long period of steady growth in both workshop and farm.

The faster population growth after 1740 was matched by faster output growth,

1

2

Table 1.1. *Growth rates of output and output per head according to Deane and Cole*

	(per cent per annum)		
	1710–40	1740–80	1780–1800
Real output	0.2	1.0	2.0
Real output/head	0.2	0.3	1.0
Population	0.0	0.7	1.0
Industrial output	0.7	0.9	2.8
Agricultural output	0.0	0.5	0.6

Source: Derived from Deane and Cole (1967: table 19).

Table 1.2. *Revised growth rates of output and output per head according to Crafts and Lee*

	(per cent per annum) 1710–40		(per cent per annum) 1710–40
Real output	0.6	Industrial output	0.7
Real output/head	0.3	Agricultural output	0.9
Population	0.3		

Source: Derived using Lee's new estimates of population, see ch. 2, according to the method described in Crafts (1976).

Note: Two corrections underlie the revised estimates of table 1.2. First, Deane and Cole used population figures that are now thought to underestimate its growth in the early eighteenth century. Second, agricultural prices were falling during the early decades which, since demand was certainly growing, implies that agricultural output was growing rather than stagnating (as Deane and Cole assume).

leaving the growth rate of output per head unchanged at a low level until the last decades of the century. In the second half of the century, however, unlike the first half, there was a tendency for population to grow faster than agricultural output and for agricultural prices to rise relative to other prices. The overall growth rates of output in the eighteenth century were not high by twentieth century standards, but population growth rates were much below the $2\frac{1}{2}$ per cent or so common in today's developing countries (World Bank 1974: 1–38).

Some industries grew much faster than the average. Among these were, of course, cotton and iron. Raw cotton consumption rose from 1.2 m. lb. in 1760 to 6.5 m. lb. in 1780 and 51.6 m. lb. in 1800 (Mitchell and Deane 1962: 177–8). Pig iron output rose from 28 th. tons in 1750 to 54 th. tons in 1780 and 250 th. tons in 1805 (Hyde 1973: 408). According to Deane and Cole's indices real output of industries orientated to foreign trade rose by 444 per cent during the eighteenth century (by 146 per cent up to 1780), whilst industries orientated to domestic industry rose by 52 per cent (23 per cent to 1780).

By the end of the eighteenth century it is clear that a substantial 'structural' change was also taking place. The relative importance of industry and commerce in output and employment was increasing and that of agriculture was falling. Deane and Cole suggest that agriculture accounted for perhaps 45 per cent of output in 1700 compared with only 33 per cent in 1800, most of the decline coming in the last quarter of the century, whilst industry and commerce rose from 30 per cent of output in 1700 to 40 per cent in 1800 (1967, 78–9). Employment is more elusive, for by the end of the eighteenth century industrial employment was much more a full time occupation than the supplementary activity for rural workers it had often been in earlier times. The economy was adopting a factory system of enterprise and the old rural by-employments in cottage industry were declining in relative importance as specialisation gathered pace.

The crux of the industrialisation problem for an economy like eighteenth-century Britain is as follows. Suppose agriculture is characterised by diminishing returns to labour. Suppose also that food demand grows at the same rate as population. Then if the relative share of labour in agriculture is to fall, it is necessary that the growth rate of the labour force in agriculture be less than the growth rate of population and the labour force overall. This appears to pose problems, for whilst the demand for food grows with population the food supply grows less rapidly even if all the extra labour is used in agriculture (which would, of course, amount to deindustrialisation). Clearly, to home feed all the extra population and also industrialise it would be necessary to have output per man in agriculture rising. Obviously, if demand were growing faster than population, the preceding arguments hold, a fortiori. Since it is supposed there are diminishing returns to labour in agriculture, industrialisation requires some other force such as technical progress or capital accumulation to raise output per man in agriculture.

This is what happened during 1700–60, when neither food imports nor price changes disrupt the picture. The best estimates we have suggest that for this period agricultural output grew at 0.70 per cent per year, whilst the agricultural labour force grew at 0.13 per cent and the population at 0.44 per cent. The trend rate of growth in agricultural labour productivity from investment and innovation together was 0.65 per cent (Crafts 1978).

Agriculture, in other words, was emphatically not a declining enterprise – indeed, in the second half of the century the much greater pressure of demand on its limited supplies drove up agricultural relative to industrial prices. The last stages of the agricultural revolution (see chapter 4) made it possible for agriculture to grow relatively more slowly than industry, yet still supply food to the growing nation.

The estimate of 45 per cent for the share of output derived from agriculture in 1700 fits the economist's stereotype of an 'underdeveloped country': a similar share characterises the poorest countries of the post 1945 era. But the impression is wrong, for income per head was much higher than in such countries. Maddison gives a speculative figure of about $200 (1965 US) for England in 1700, while as late as 1965 the average for Africa was only $130 (1965 US) (1967: 308). Moreover, the economy was already exhibiting signs of increasing integration of markets (Granger and Elliot 1967), and (as befits an international trading economy) possessed a superstructure of financial markets and institutions topped by the Bank of England.

The growth of productive potential in the eighteenth century can be thought of as the result of on the one hand, increased amounts of the factors of production, labour, land, and capital and, on the other, a greater output per unit of input (higher productivity). The increases which occurred in the growth of population are a good first estimate of the growth of labour (see chapter 2). We can regard the rate of growth of land as zero, i.e. we can consider land as a fixed factor of production (see chapter 4).

Measures of the rate of growth of the amount of tools, buildings, and other equipment – the 'capital stock' – are unavoidably very shaky. Deane and Cole (1967: 261–3) thought that the capital stock grew at about the same rapid pace as output during the century; and this is consistent with Deane's evidence that the ratio of capital to output was about the same in the late seventeeth and early nineteenth centuries [1973: 355]. The rapid growth of the capital stock required a higher share of national output to be used for making new capital: Deane and Cole suggested that new capital ('net investment') accounted for perhaps 3 per cent of output in 1700, rising to perhaps 5 or 6 per cent in the 1770s and perhaps 7 per cent by 1800 (1967: 263). There were notable changes in the composition of the capital stock. According to Feinstein (1978: table 8; see chapter 7) the proportion devoted to industry and commerce rose from 12 per cent in 1760 to 22 per cent in 1800, and in the same period the share used in transport rose from 12 to 17 per cent (this being the era of the construction of the canal network). A number of features of the economy aided fixed capital formation. It has been argued that population growth was restrained by a number of 'preventive checks' on fertility (e.g. delayed marriage), which prevented population size from reaching the maximum consistent with subsistence and thus allowed a surplus to exist which might be used for investment in industry (Wrigley 1969: chs. 3–4). The surplus, moreover, was distributed very unequally, as it is in most economies. In 1968 the top 5 per cent of the population received about 25 per cent of income. Beginning much earlier but becoming evident in the eighteenth century were new financial institutions, such as the country banks (Pressnell 1956) or mercantile credit from foreign trade or the new government debt, which expedited the channelling of the surplus into capital formation.

A key point, however, is not so much that capital was able to grow, but that its growth alone is not the whole story. The rise in output from the invention of better machines (a proxy for all capital) as distinct from the making of more machines was important, though difficult to measure. The eighteenth century witnessed increasing inventive activity. The number of patents granted rose from 4 in 1740 to 33 in 1780 and 96 in 1800 (Mitchell and Deane 1962: 268). From qualitative sources we know of a number of famous inventions made in the period between 1700 and 1780; in iron there was Abraham Darby's coke smelting process (1709), in power James Watt's steam engine (1763), and in cotton textiles James Hargreaves's jenny (1768), Richard Arkwright's waterframe (1769) and Samuel Crompton's mule (1779). In agriculture improved crop rotations were coming into more widespread use and from about 1730 the parliamentary enclosure movement gained momentum.

The separation of this inventive activity from simple increases in machines and men is the next object. For the moment it should be noted that, however they are separated, the upturns in the growth rates of inputs and innovation occurred well before the end-century date of the 'industrial revolution'. It might be said that the middle decades of the century saw the initiation of changes in the economy (for example, in textiles and in transport) that came to fruition in the decades following. The economy before 1780 was developing, although the differences between 1780 and, say, 1820 were much bigger and more obvious than those between 1700 and 1780.

In 1780 the factory system was still in embryo, the improved steam engine scarcely diffused at all, iron output in absolute terms not much above 1720, and cotton still a small activity relative to the economy as a whole. The growth of the economy prior to 1780, moreover, was similar to that of other areas of Europe – France, for example (Rostow 1975: 168; O'Brien and Keyder 1978; Roehl 1976). If the metamorphosis of the economy to the 'workshop of the world' is seen as the outcome of the application of new types of energy and capital equipment (coal and iron replacing water and wood), the major transformation had still to come. Yet by 1780 a beginning had been made.

2. The sources of economic growth

An examination of the time series for the economy of England and Wales in the eighteenth century prompts a subtle but central question: how was the economy able to increase the rate of economic growth and begin the industrial revolution with apparently so little change in the rate at which new capital was created, the investment rate? From Aristotle to the Agency for International Development, the usual explanations of economic growth or its lack have depended on the investment rate. Yet on a first look the evidence runs against this view.

One crude way of measuring the contribution of capital and other inputs is as follows. The growth rate of output is regarded as the outcome of the growth rate of inputs on the one hand and the growth rate of the productivity of those inputs on the other hand. The total growth of factor inputs is measured in terms of a *weighted average* of the growth rates of the factors of production, land, labour and capital. The weights must reflect the 'importance' of the particular input in the productive process, and a convenient measure of importance is the input's share in costs – for labour this is the share of wages in national income, for land the share of rents, and for capital the share of profits. Thus we have the expression for the proportional change in output:

$$\frac{\Delta Y}{Y} = \alpha \frac{\Delta K}{K} + \beta \frac{\Delta L}{L} + \gamma \frac{\Delta T}{T} + r^* \tag{1}$$

Or, in other words:

| Proportional change in output | equals | Contribution of capital | plus | Contribution of labour |

| plus | Contribution of land | plus | Contribution of productivity change |

Where Δ represents 'the change in' and hence $\Delta Y/Y$ (for example) is the proportional growth rate of output. Y is output, K is capital, L is labour, T (terre) is land and α, β and γ are the shares of profits, wages and rents in national income. The growth rate of output per unit of all inputs together ('total factor productivity' to distinguish it from 'partial' or 'single factor' productivities such as output per man or per acre) is r^*. Equation (1) says, in words, that the rate of growth of output is the rate of growth of the capital stock times the share of profits in national income plus the rate of growth of the labour force times the share of wages in national income plus the rate of growth of land times the share of rent in national income plus the rate of growth of total factor productivity, r^*.

Equation (1) only seems to achieve half the object in the search for the sources of growth in eighteenth-century Britain, for it still does not give a measure of the rate of growth of productivity. If we had data on all the variables in this equation other than r^*, however, we could use the equation to deduce r^*, and would thus be able to measure both the contribution of labour, capital, and land, and the growth rate of total factor productivity. That is, r^* is found as a residual, which is what it is sometimes called.

The facts presented in section 1 provide all that is necessary, except data on factor shares needed to fill in α, β and γ. Deane and Cole give information on factor shares, reproduced in table 1.3.

Table 1.3. *Distribution of incomes: factor shares (per cent)*

	Employment incomes	Rents	Profits, interest and mixed incomes
1688 (England and Wales)	25–39	27	34–48
1801 (Great Britain)	44	20	37

Source: Deane and Cole (1967: table 80).

The categories do not quite correspond to the ideal. The major problem is inevitable, namely that in a pre-industrial economy like that of eighteenth-century Britain many incomes were really 'mixed incomes', so that even in 1801 'rents' probably includes some returns to capital and 'profits, interest and mixed incomes' certainly includes some returns to labour. The values for α, β and γ are therefore unavoidably arbitrary. The choice made for the results presented in table 1.4 is for $\alpha = 0.35$, $\beta = 0.50$ and $\gamma = 0.15$. The 1801 figure (under-estimated, remember, by the labour part of mixed incomes) for labour's share was 0.44, and, since there is a good case for believing that labour's share was if anything lower at the end than at the beginning of the century (see chapter 2), a value of 0.5 (adding in some mixed incomes) is probably reasonable for the eighteenth century as a whole. The division of non-labour income into rent and profits was made arbitrarily on the basis of the 1801 figures.

Table 1.4 brings together the data necessary for the application of equation (1) to impute the sources of growth and to uncover the 'residual'. For example, for 1740–80 the growth rate of output was given in table 1.1 as 1.0 per cent per year. The contributions to that growth are as follows: $(0.35 \times 1.0) = 0.35$ per cent per year to growth of capital; $(0.5 \times 0.7) = 0.35$ per cent per year to growth of labour; and – unsurprisingly, since it is fixed in amount – $(0.15 \times 0.0) = 0.0$ per cent per year to the land. The sum of growth from factor inputs is then $(0.35 + 0.35 + 0.0) = 0.7$ per cent per year. We then deduce as 'the residual' that 0.3 per cent per year growth came from increased productivity. The calculations for other periods are done in like fashion.

We can now obtain a tentative answer to the question of how the acceleration in economic growth took place. For the decades of most violent acceleration, 1780–1800, 0.7 per cent per year growth in output is attributed to growth in capital and 0.5 per cent to growth in labour leaving 0.8 per cent as the residual. Of the rise of 1 per cent in the growth rate of output experienced 1780–1800 over that experienced 1740–80, 0.5 per cent can be attributed to productivity growth, 0.35 per cent to a faster growth of capital and 0.15 per cent to a faster growth of labour. It should be noted that, although the rise in the investment rate was not (according to Deane and Cole) dramatic, nevertheless it was associated with

Table 1.4. *The 'sources of economic growth'*

	Growth rate of income	Contributions of:			
	($\%$/yr) $(\Delta Y/Y)$	capital $\alpha \times (\Delta K/K)$	labour $\beta \times (\Delta L/L)$	land $\gamma \times (\Delta T/T)$	productivity r^*
1710–40	0.6	0.35×0.6	0.5×0.3	0.15×0.0	0.24
1740–80	1.0	0.35×1.0	0.5×0.7	0.15×0.0	0.30
1780–1800	2.0	0.35×2.0	0.5×1.0	0.15×0.0	0.80

a faster growth in the capital stock and was important in bringing about the acceleration in economic growth during the eighteenth century. If we similarly compare 1740–80 and 1710–40 an interesting difference emerges. The increased growth of output between these periods seems much more due to faster growth of factors of production than to greater productivity growth. Only 0.06 per cent out of the 0.4 per cent rise in the growth rate is due to the higher value of the residual.

These results are of interest in that over some years there have been lengthy, though largely non-quantitative, discussions about the relative importance of capital formation and technological progress in eighteenth-century economic growth (Crouzet 1972: introduction). The quantitative exercise in table 1.4 suggests one reason for the controversy, and suggests its resolution. Estimates of 'the residual' are highly sensitive to errors in the measurement of the other components of equation (1). As the discussion has stressed, errors of measurement are likely, yielding a 'best guess' rather than a definitive account. This best guess suggests that at the century's end the change in productivity was rather more important as a source of faster growth than capital formation, whereas earlier the change in productivity played a relatively minor role.

To fill out the picture we need to relate the growth of the capital stock to the changes in the share of output going to capital formation. A simple identity exists between the rate of growth of the net capital stock and the ratio of net investment to income. The net investment rate (s) divided by the ratio of capital to output ($K/Y = v$) necessarily equals the growth rate of the capital stock ($\Delta K/K$), $g = s/v$.[1] The value put by Deane (1973) and Kuznets (1974) on the net capital to output ratio, v, is about 2.5.[2] Using the relationship just established, then, it is clear

---

[1] This is easily seen. $\Delta K =$ Net investment $= sY$; $K/Y = v$ and so $K = vY$. Hence $\Delta K/K = sY/vY = s/v$.

[2] The reader who has also read chapter 10 or Feinstein (1978) may be puzzled by the difference between the capital output ratio of 2.5 suggested here and that of over 7 shown in Feinstein. The important point to note is that Feinstein's figure is for the gross capital to output ratio, that given

that the rise of 1.4 per cent per year in the growth rate of the capital stock that occurred during the century required a rise of $(2.5 \times 1.4) = 3.5$ per cent in the ratio of net investment to output (a change in g, given v, required a change in s of v times the change in g, since $s = gv$). This change in the ratio (which is in other words the saving rate) is much smaller than would have been required in a more capital-intensive development, i.e. with a higher capital to output ratio. For example, had v been 4.8, as in nineteenth-century Germany (Kuznets 1974: 132), the required rise in the net investment rate would have been $(4.8 \times 1.4) = 6.7$ per cent.

In short, the acceleration in economic growth was achieved without a massive rise in the investment rate for two reasons. The capital to output ratio was not high and the productivity increase was high.[3]

3. Interactions in growth

The preceding section gave a very general statement of the sources of economic growth in eighteenth-century England and Wales. But the model is a very simple one. The rates of growth of factors of production and productivity change were treated as if they were independent of each other, and interactions between them were ignored. Growth is 'accounted for' but there is no answer to questions such as what explains changes in the amount of innovation or the growth of capital in the economy.

It is desirable to turn to richer models, that is, models in which more variables have their values determined within the model itself and in which interactions can be considered. For example, a popular way of looking at the problems of countries trying to develop is to argue that they can get trapped in a 'vicious circle' of under-development. There are many variants of this argument, but a fairly typical one is: low income levels imply low savings rates which imply low rates of capital accumulation and productivity growth which imply low growth of incomes inadequate to outweigh rapid population growth which implies, to return to the beginning, low income levels.

here for the net ratio. For a lower growth economy such as mid-eighteenth-century England, such a gap between the gross and net ratio is to be expected as Kuznets shows (1974: 150–1) and the two figures are more or less consistent with each other. Kuznets' examples also point to the fact that the gross investment rate probably changed very little over the century as a whole.

[3] It should be noted that Deane's figure of about 2.5 for the capital to output ratio implies, given the capital stock growth rate figures of table 1.4, a net investment share of 1.5 per cent 1710–40, 2.5 per cent 1740–80, and 5 per cent 1780–1800. This is rather below Deane and Cole's estimates of 3, 5 and 7 per cent respectively. The most likely implication is that Deane and Cole have overestimated the net investment rate. In any event Deane's figure for the capital to output ratio and Deane and Cole's figures for the net investment rate and growth rate of the capital stock are not consistent as they stand. (For example, the Deane and Cole figures imply a capital to output ratio of 5, not 2.5 for 1710–40.)

It is easy to point to several reasons why England in the early eighteenth century was already in a position where the vicious circle was not particularly vicious. As we saw in section 1 incomes per head were high for a preindustrial economy: and population growth was low enough to permit a sizeable investible surplus. Indeed, there seems to be widespread agreement that England had a capacity to save considerably greater than the amount actually devoted to investment. It thus appears likely that the availability of attractive investment outlets was the major requirement for raising the investment rate. Agricultural output was growing and there was no reason to expect an imminent subsistence crisis at the prevailing rate of growth of population.

The growing living standard, however, might itself be an inducement to faster growth of population, which could in turn reverse the rise in living standards. Such a prophecy was later associated with Thomas Malthus, and this version of the vicious circle argument is therefore referred to as the 'Malthusian Trap'. To be sure, as section 1 indicated, the rising living standard was soon challenged by the faster population growth of the mid-eighteenth century. How, then, did the economy avoid the Malthusian Trap?

The rise in the growth of population in England in mid-century was 0.4 per cent. To achieve a corresponding rise in the growth of the capital stock – as the economy apparently did – required therefore a rise in the net investment rate of 0.4×2.5 (the capital to output ratio), i.e. 1 per cent (compare the similar calculation above). The pressure on the net investment rate would obviously have been greater had population growth risen more or had the capital to output ratio been higher, but by twentieth-century standards this mid-century pressure on the investment rate was quite gentle. That is to say, the difficulty of equipping the rising population with buildings, machines, fences, roads, and other capital was slight, and the Malthusian threat on this score correspondingly small.

There remains the Malthusian threat arising from a factor of production whose amount (unlike capital) cannot be increased, namely land. A fixed factor of production creates a problem of which the classical economists such as Ricardo were only too well aware, i.e. the bogey of diminishing returns. The fear was that increases in population, by reducing the amount of land per head, would reduce incomes per head. The fear was logically cogent but incomplete, for the problem can be and was overcome by technological progress. The possibility and reality can be made precise with a little secondary-school algebra. In the long run there are good reasons for believing that the growth rate of the capital stock will tend to a rate equal to that of output – as happened apparently in the eighteenth century. Using this equality and isolating $\Delta Y/Y$ on one side of equation (1) above yields:

$$\frac{\Delta Y}{Y} = \frac{\beta \Delta L/L + \gamma \Delta T/T + r^*}{(1-a)} \tag{2}$$

But we are thinking of the British economy of the eighteenth century for which we have supposed there was little or no land growth ($\Delta T/T = 0$), and so

$$\frac{\Delta Y}{Y} = \frac{\beta \Delta L/L + r^*}{(1-a)} = \left(\frac{\beta}{1-a}\right)\left(\frac{\Delta L}{L}\right) + \frac{r^*}{1-a} \qquad (3)$$

A technologically stagnant economy of the sort the classical economists predicted would have $r^* = 0$, leaving the growth of output less than population growth if β was less than $(1-a)$. It was, as table 1.3 indicates. Output would not have kept pace with population if technology had not progressed. In truth, the idea is easy to believe without the algebra, and was in fact believed by Ricardo and his followers in verbal form. The advantage of the algebra is that it measures the quantitative weight of the idea. Given $\beta = 0.5$ and $(1-a) = 0.65$ (the values suggested above), equation (3) asserts that to avoid a fall in output per head, a growth rate of population of 0.7 per cent per year required a rate of growth of total factor productivity of 0.10 per cent per year. That is a low rate, well below the rate actually achieved. The Malthusian Trap was shallow, and held no fear for an economy as dynamic as Britain's in the eighteenth century.

Although the economy was probably not trapped in a desperate vicious circle, it remains of considerable interest to ask what forces were promoting investment and innovation. Thus far we have treated them both as independent of the economic system and examined the consequence of changes in capital stock growth and total factor productivity growth. The literature of economic history, however, has of late argued that the economy itself influences investment and innovation.

As far as innovation is concerned the rationale is simple: 'This is not a story of sophisticated inventions breaking through some technological barrier, and so creating the conditions for expansion. Developments that were technically so simple can only be responses to social and economic conditions' (Lilley 1973: 195). Some have seen British society in the eighteenth century as an especially rich soil for innovation (Landes 1969: chapters 1–3; Wilson 1965), but here we will deal only with the strictly economic hypotheses. They are two: the fuel shortage and the demand bottleneck. The first alleges that the growth of output and the capital stock was tending to outrun the growth of the labour supply and natural resources (notably wood), and that the resultant changes in relative prices were a powerful incentive to innovations vital to the industrial revolution (Crouzet 1966; 168, Landes 1969: Chapter 2). The idea is that an energy crisis of the eighteenth century generated its own solution through the price mechanism: expensive wood led to exploiting cheap coal, and then to steam. The second hypothesis alleges more generally that growth increased demand along a wide front, putting pressure on sources of supply and eliciting a vigorous innovative response (Lilley 1973: 216); more particularly, Cole has argued that faster population growth, from the 1740s on, ultimately *stimulated* growth of incomes per head – in sharp contrast with the Malthusian prediction – because greater demand pressure led to induced innovations more than sufficient to offset diminishing returns (1973: 348).

Certainly one of the major successes of the eighteenth century was to find a solution to the pressing energy problem. Nevertheless the impact of steam power was not large straightaway (see chapter 8) and even in cotton was delayed until the mid 1790s (Chapman 1972: 23). Similarly there were delays before the two major developments of the century in iron, the use of coal in the blast furnace and the refinery, were widely adopted. Coke smelting achieved by Darby in 1709 was not widely taken up until the 1760s and 1770s and the puddling process of making wrought iron achieved in 1779 was similarly not widely taken up until about 1800 (Hyde 1977). The diffusion of these improvements has been shown to be largely conditioned by the impact of relative prices and market demand on the profitability of the processes concerned and by the time needed to improve on the basic inventions (Chapman 1971a; Hyde 1973; 1974).

The argument that productivity increase was induced by economic events rather than being wholly autonomous is sensible. The evidence, however, points to economic factors in the subsequent diffusion of steam and mechanisation more than to economic factors in the original inventions. Although the search for improvements was doubtless encouraged by prospects of profit, the success of such a search was uncertain. Therefore, connecting factors such as the growth of population to the inventions central to the industrial revolution has proven difficult. It may be wrong to look for something special about the mid-eighteenth-century economy to mark it out beforehand as more likely to embark on rapid industrialisation than the economy of, say, fifty years earlier – there was an element of randomness in the timing of particular inventions (Crafts 1977b).

The inconclusiveness here, by the way, illustrates an important point of method. Cole's argument predicts that faster population growth would have tended to generate rises in living standards, whereas the Malthusian model examined earlier yields the opposite prediction. The two arguments reach different historical conclusions because they differ on the (unobservable) 'counterfactual' situation, i.e. what would have happened if population growth had *not* increased. A case can be constructed for either argument in logic, although based, of course, on different assumptions. Since economic history does not have the controlled experiments of the laboratory and since no way has yet been found to refute either argument conclusively, either can still be entertained. He who seeks conclusiveness should flee from British economic history in the eighteenth century.

So much (or so little) for the determinants of innovation. Relatively little has been written on the determinants of investment. The tendency of the recent literature has been to look for factors that raised the profitability of investment (its demand) rather than those which increased the flow of saving (its supply).

Ashton (1948) argued that falls in the rate of interest were an important stimulant of investment, a difficult hypothesis to test in the absence of statistics on investment expenditure, but which has met much scepticism (Dickson 1967: 452–3), not all of it well placed. The more usual notion stresses the role of increased demand for final goods, reacting back on the demand for (profitability of) investment. The notion raises two important issues. The first is one of controversy between different schools of economists. One school maintains that for the economy as a whole there can be no independent role for demand; that in the long run supply creates its own demand, and an examination of the supply side of the economy is sufficient for an understanding of economic growth at the aggregate level. A recent exponent of this point of view is Mokyr (1977). The rival school (of 'Keynesians') disputes this claim, maintaining that in the short run supply does not automatically create its own demand and that the level of output depends on the level of aggregate demand, which may not be that which achieves full employment. Levels of demand that push the economy towards full employment in the short run might elicit greater investment and productivity increase, thereby enhancing the growth rate of the productive potential. The long run is made up of a large number of these short-run spells, and so the economy's rate of growth will depend on levels of demand. The majority of recent English economic historians of the eighteenth century have (possibly unconsciously) written in this vein. Which view gives greater insight into the period remains unclear.

The second issue, which has much interested the demand school, concerns the importance of different sources of demand, in particular whether home or foreign markets imparted more stimulus (Hartwell 1971: 152, Hobsbawm 1968: chapter 2). The major investigation of this issue is conducted in chapter 3 at a disaggregated level, but in view of demand's prominence in discussions of innovation and investment an introduction to the broad evidence is given now.

A model of growth in aggregate demand looks in the first instance to growth in 'autonomous expenditure', i.e. items of expenditure which are not themselves functions of the level of income, such as government expenditures on war or investment booms based on optimism. Increases in the level of effective demand consist of increases in autonomous expenditure times the 'multiplier': the increases in autonomous expenditure generate higher output and income which in turn generate spending out of these higher incomes, yielding still higher incomes, etc. For the eighteenth century the multiplier would be about 2.25.[4]

[4] Y will equal $Z(1)/(1-c+ctd+te+m)$, where Z is the level of autonomous expenditure and $1/(1-c+ctd+te+m)$ is the multiplier, which will have a value greater than 1. In this expression c is the marginal propensity to consume out of disposable income, td is the direct tax rate, te the indirect tax rate and m is the marginal propensity to import. For 1750 the parameters underlying the multiplier might have been about $c = 0.9$, $td = 0.03$, $te = 0.15$ and $m = 0.2$, giving a multiplier of 2.25. The derivation of multipliers is shown in any book on elementary economics, such as Lipsey, or Samuelson, *Economics*. The level of c was guessed from Deane and Cole (1967: table 1); td and te were based on comparison of the public finance figures of Mitchell and Deane (1962:

Table 1.5. *Some components of national expenditure (£m. current prices)*

	(1) Aggregate expenditure[a]	(2) Exports[b,e]	(3) Government expenditure[c,e]	(4) Transfers spent[d,e]	(5) Government transfers, and the implied domestic autonomous expenditure (if multiplier = 2.25)[e,f]
1740	49.0	5.6	4.8	1.1	16.2
1750	51.6	7.3	5.8	1.4	15.6
1760	66.3	9.9	10.5	1.8	19.6
1770	63.0	10.4	5.4	2.4	17.6
1780	84.0	10.3	14.3	3.2	27.0

Notes:

[a] Deane and Cole's real output index (1967: 78) converted into money terms by taking Y in 1801 = £232m. (Deane and Cole 1967: 282) and allowing for price changes using the Schumpeter–Gilboy price index (Mitchell and Deane 1962: 469).

[b] Exports obtained following the method outlined in McCusker (1971).

[c] Government expenditure is net public expenditure minus debt charges (Mitchell and Deane 1962: 389–91).

[d] Transfers are debt charges (Mitchell and Deane 1962: 389–91); the marginal propensity to consume out of these is assumed to be 0.5.

[e] These variables are 11 year averages centring on the year in question.

[f] Thus, in 1740, the total income of £49m. was the consequence (so to speak) of the multiplier (= 2.25) multiplied by the sum of exports (col. 2). government expenditure (col. 3), transfers spent (col. 4), and some unknown A, domestic expenditure. That is, $49 = (2.25)(11.5 + A)$, from which one can find A to be 10.3 and column (5) therefore $4.8 + 1.1 + 10.3 = 16.2$.

In looking at a demand-based theory of expansion, then, our attention is directed towards increases in the components of 'autonomous expenditure' during the eighteenth century. For our purposes, autonomous expenditure is government spending on final goods and services, transfer payments by government multiplied by the marginal propensity to consume out of them, other autonomous domestic expenditure (including replacement investment), and exports. For the mid-eighteenth century we have estimates of all these except 'other domestic autonomous expenditure'. Given the known variables and the value of the multiplier we can deduce an estimate for the unknown variable.

Table 1.5 shows that over the long run both exports (col. 2) and total domestic autonomous expenditure (col. 5) were rising, with exports rising slightly faster in percentage terms, domestic spending slightly faster in absolute terms. Both components of spending, however, rise erratically – exports are very strong

389–91) with the national expenditure estimates given here in table 1.5; m was guessed by taking $M/Y = 12$–14 per cent for the mid-century and noting that imports were tending to grow a little faster than income.

Table 1.6 *Impact of the government* (£m. *current prices*)[a]

1740	−3.9	1770	−4.3
1750	−0.7	1780	+18.1
1760	+9.1		

[a] 11-year averages centred on the year in question.

Source: In the notation of note 4 above, the income *with* the government is the multiplier times autonomous expenditure, or

$$Y_G = \left(\frac{1}{1-c+ctd+te+m}\right)(G+c'Tr+A+X).$$

where $c'Tr$ is the marginal propensity to consume out of transfer payments, and X is exports.

Without the government – i.e. without any taxing or spending activity by it – the corresponding income would be

$$Y_{NG} = \left(\frac{1}{1-c+m}\right)(A+X).$$

The measure of the impact of the government is $Y_G - Y_{NG}$, using the data underlying Table 1.5.

between 1740 and 1760, domestic spending between 1770 and 1780. In other words, the relative importance of home and foreign markets depends on which period is under discussion.

The volatility of domestic spending derives particularly from changes in the fiscal stance of the government. Such changes were substantial because of periodic wars financed mainly by budget deficits. For example, government revenue was £7m. in 1750 and only £8.8m. in 1760, whilst government spending $(G+TR)$ had risen by £5.5m. (not $8.8-7 = 1.8m.$). A crude measure of the impact of the government on the economy comes from the multiplier argument. Table 1.6 tabulates the multiplier effects, positive and negative, of the existence of the government. Clearly government's impact on the economy varied a great deal. The estimates in this and table 1.5, to be sure, are highly speculative. But if the assumption of less-than-full employment is correct, then their main message is robust, despite the crudeness of the model and likely errors in both the expenditure figures and the multiplier. The message is that if one looks to increases in autonomous expenditure as a dynamic force behind economic growth, then foreign and home spending were both important at different times. For example, according to the figures of table 1.5 the multiplied effects of changes in exports account for about 56 per cent of the change in income between 1740 and 1760 $(2.25)(4.3)/(17.3)$, but only about 5 per cent $(0.9/17.7)$ of the income change between 1760 and 1780. This is partly because of the retardation in the growth of exports during the American War of Independence, but also, as table 1.6 indicates, because of marked changes in government spending (itself caused by war).

In sum, then, the possible reasons for economic growth in the eighteenth century are many. The acceleration of productivity change (calculated in section 2) appears to have been more important than the acceleration of saving and investment. Yet productivity change does not fall from heaven. It can itself be, as argued here, a consequence of economic growth, especially of (if it were known for sure that the economy was at less-than-full employment) demand. And demand had many sources. With this array of possibilities in mind, we turn in the chapters following to the details of the story.

2

British population in the eighteenth century

R. D. LEE & R. S. SCHOFIELD

The evidence

At the beginning of the eighteenth century the economy of Britain, still predominantly agricultural, was subject to sharply diminishing returns to labour. Population increase at more than a modest pace would send real wages tumbling, as it had in the sixteenth and seventeenth centuries. A doubling of population had then depressed real wages to perhaps 40 per cent of their previous level (Phelps-Brown and Hopkins 1956; Lee 1973 and forthcoming). By the early nineteenth century, however, British population was growing at an unprecedented rate, and the economy was able to absorb the expanding labour force with little change in living standards. Were these accelerations in the growth of population and the demand for labour coincidental? Did population grow in response to the demands of an expanding economy, or was the economy stimulated by the demands of increasing populations? After more than a century of research, these still remain the major interpretive issues of eighteenth-century British population history.

Part of the difficulty in resolving the issues stems from the shakiness of the available data; the first task, therefore, must be a review of the facts and their sources. The sources, and the information which they give, relate either to England and Wales or to Scotland. We shall concentrate in this chapter on England and Wales, since Scotland has been fully discussed in Flinn et al. *Scottish Population History* (1978). For comparison, however, the first British census in 1801 after some adjustment gives a population size for England and Wales of 9.16 million, and for Scotland 1.60 million. For the beginning of the eighteenth century we are on less solid ground. For Scotland, Deane and Cole (1967: 6) give figures of 1.04 million in 1701 and 1.25 million in 1751, but these are based on a venerable source, Sir John Sinclair, *Analysis of the Statistical*

[1] Acknowledgements: Ronald Lee's share of this research was funded by NICHD Grant 2R01 HD08686-03. We are grateful to the Cambridge Group for the History of Population and Social Structure for making this preliminary version of the aggregate parish data set available to us. John Knodel, E. A. Wrigley and Donald McCloskey made helpful comments on earlier drafts. Tom Fraker rendered valuable research assistance.

17

Account of Scotland (1825: 149); Flinn et al. discuss their accuracy but do not provide alternatives. For England and Wales, Gregory King estimated the population of 1695 to be 5.5 million, based on hearth tax returns. Glass reanalysed the available portions of King's data and arrived at the lower figure of 4.9 million (Glass 1965a: 203). Taking this as a lower bound, he then suggested 5.2 million as a plausible revision of King's estimate. Hollingsworth (1969) and Chambers (1972) have concurred that 5.2 million, or perhaps less, is a reasonable figure.

These enumerations provide benchmarks for the beginning and end of the eighteenth century. For the intervening period, historians have had to rely principally on the 'parish registers', which are lists of baptisms, burials and marriages maintained by the clergy. The way these have been used, and the attendant difficulties, have been the subject of detailed scholarship, but the main outlines are as follows.

John Rickman, director of the British censuses from 1801 to 1841, arranged for all parishes in England and Wales to report to him the numbers of baptisms, burials and marriages recorded in their registers for certain dates: for baptisms and burials, 1700, 1710, 1720, 1730, 1740, 1750, 1760, 1770, 1780 and every year thereafter; for marriages, every decade as above, but annually from 1754 on. If net migration in or out of England and Wales was negligible, if Rickman's count of baptisms and burials accurately reflected the numbers of births and deaths, and if the decadal years were demographically representative, one could (as many have) estimate eighteenth-century population by counting back from the census of 1801: to find the population in 1800, subtract births and add deaths occurring in 1800; to find the population in 1799, subtract the births and add the deaths from 1799 to the estimate for 1800; and so on. Earlier in the century, one multiplies each isolated figure of births and deaths by ten. All estimates of population in the eighteenth-century have been obtained in essentially this way, but only after some adjustment to overcome the deficiencies of Rickman's raw numbers.

There are four possible deficiencies: (1) the decadal years chosen by Rickman may be atypical; (2) baptisms and burials may have gone unregistered; (3) parishes may have failed to respond, or their records may have been lost or inaccurately summed by Rickman's clerks; (4) the growth of nonconformity at the end of the eighteenth century may have led to an increasing amount of under-registration of deaths by the Anglican registers (see Krause 1965). Recent work by Razzell (1972) and Wrigley (1975 and 1976a) goes far towards resolving points (2) and (3). Points (1) and (4) will be dealt with below.

For the past 175 years the study of eighteenth-century population at the national level has depended on Rickman's evidence, deficiencies and all. In recent years, the reworking of it by Brownlee has been most widely accepted. For informative surveys of work on eighteenth-century population based on Rickman's series, the reader is referred to Glass (1965b), Tranter (1973a), Flinn (1970), Wrigley (1976a), Ohlin (1955), and several articles in Drake (1969). Brownlee's work provides estimates of population size and crude vital rates (numbers of births, deaths and marriages per 1000 population). Yet the most useful demographic estimates have remained unavailable: the size of each age group, the age-specific fertility rates and mortality rates, and summary measures such as total fertility rates and life expectancy.

New evidence, fortunately, is at hand, assembled since 1964 by the Cambridge Group for the History of Population and Social Structure with the help of hundreds of local volunteers. Their efforts have led to the collection of data from 404 parishes with registers of good quality, representing about one sixteenth of the total population. Some of the registers span the entire period from 1538 (when Thomas Cromwell ordered their compilation) to 1840 (when civil registration of vital events became effective). Most of the parishes covered began registration by 1560, 90 per cent by 1610, and all by 1662. The work which has been done with this material is important in itself and as an example of demographic study, and it is therefore worth recounting in detail.

Each parish register was first scanned for obvious short-term gaps and registration deficiencies, and these were made good by interpolation. Since the 404 parishes were not drawn as a strictly random sample, their distributions across a number of standard social and economic characteristics were compared to the distributions obtained from a stricly random sample of parishes. The 404 parishes turned out to be representative of most characteristics – for example geographical spread and the proportions of the populations employed in agriculture, manufacturing and commerce as defined in the 1831 census. However, they were found to include too many parishes with large populations and too few with small ones. In order to avoid any consequent bias from this source, the parishes were divided into a number of population size-groups and the total numbers of baptisms, burials and marriages ('vital events' or simply 'events') recorded in each size-group were re-weighted to correct for the biased size-distributions of the parishes before being aggregated together to form an overall total. These overall totals were then corrected for under-registration in two ways. First the numbers of baptisms and burials that were missing because children died very young (before they could be baptised) were estimated from studies of infant mortality and from the results of 'family reconstitution' by which all possible family trees in a single community are reconstructed from the parish registers. Second, the numbers of events missing for other reasons, for example because of nonconformity or poor registration, were estimated for the early nineteenth century by adjusting the national totals of births, marriages and deaths as recorded in Rickman's survey of all parish registers using the totals implied by the age information contained in the early nineteenth-century censuses. While the under-registration due to late baptism can be estimated

use briefly in intro.

independently at all dates, this second catch-all category of under-registration can only be estimated directly for the early nineteenth century. For earlier periods the levels estimated for around 1800 were tapered off back through the eighteenth century following the curve described by the numbers of events recorded in nonconformist registers during this period. Finally the vital events recorded in the set of 404 parishes, adjusted in the ways just described, could be inflated to produce 'national' totals because they were found to comprise a constant proportion of the national totals of events collected by Rickman for sample years in the eighteenth century, producing a ratio which matched the ratio between the total population of the 404 parishes and the national population enumerated in the 1811 Census. A further adjustment was made to take account of changes in the proportion of the national total of events contributed by London, which was not represented in the set of 404 parishes and which had a very different ratio between baptisms and burials.

Thus the frequencies of baptisms, burials and marriages as originally recorded in the parish registers have passed through several stages of correction, each of which involves a risk of error. Nonetheless, the new estimates enable us to push our knowledge of population back on a continuous basis about two centuries further than is currently possible for any other country.

The dimensions

Population size

Because the new data give baptisms and burials for every year while Rickman's series gave them for only one year in each decade, the new data series can be used to check the representativeness of the years for which Rickman's data are available. Let us suppose, for the moment, that the new series provided data only for the Rickman years (1700, 1710, etc.), and that we based a population estimate upon it. Assuming these years were typical, we would conclude that between 1700 and 1740 population actually *declined* by about 215000. If we now calculate the population change using *all* the available years, we find a population increase of about 660000 people over this same forty year period, 1700 to 1740. The years chosen by Rickman, in other words, had atypically low growth, and treating them as representative leads to a very substantial underestimate of population growth for the first half of the eighteenth century

Figure 2.1 plots estimates of population size based on the new data (with the older estimates by Brownlee) for the years 1695 to 1801. The actual estimates are given in table 2.1. Clearly the agreement is very close from 1740 to 1840, but as indicated above, the Brownlee estimates show stagnation while the new estimates show growth for 1701 to 1740. Thus, while Brownlee puts the figure for 1701 at 5.83 million, the new estimate has it as 5.29 million. For 1695, the new data suggest a figure of 5.18 million, which agrees very well with the contemporary reappraisals discussed above of Gregory King's estimate.

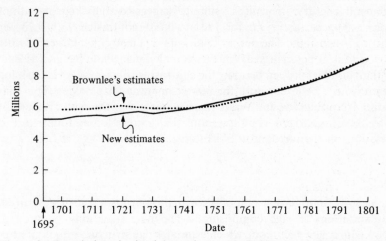

Figure 2.1 Population size in eighteenth-century England and Wales. Source: See text.

Table 2.1. *Estimates of population size and growth for England and Wales 1695–1801*

Date	Population size (millions)		Growth rate since preceding date (% year)	
	Brownlee	New estimates	Brownlee	New estimates
1695	—	5.18	—	—
1701	5.826	5.29	—	0.35
1711	5.981	5.51	0.26	0.41
1721	6.001	5.66	0.03	0.27
1731	5.947	5.59	−0.09	−0.13
1741	5.926	5.94	−0.04	0.62
1751	6.140	6.20	0.35	0.42
1761	6.569	6.62	0.68	0.66
1771	7.052	6.97	0.71	0.51
1781	7.531	7.57	0.66	0.83
1791	8.247	8.21	0.91	0.82
1801	9.156	9.16	1.05	1.08

Source: For Brownlee's estimates, Deane and Cole (1967: 6). The new estimates are derived from a preliminary version of the Cambridge Group's aggregate data, and are subject to revision; for details, see text.

The revision of the population estimates for the first half of the eighteenth century may seem inconsequential, but it is not. The widely accepted view that population stagnated during this period has played an important role in the construction of other statistics and in the interpretation of economic changes in the eighteenth century. Brownlee's estimates suggested an average growth of population of 0.05 per cent/year for 1701 to 1740, contrasted with 0.73 per cent/year for 1741 to 1800. The new estimates suggest 0.30 per cent/year for the first period, and 0.71 per cent/year for the second. Thus, while the growth rate did more than double between periods, the contrast is considerably less striking than was previously believed. Both the new estimates and the old assume that net migration from England and Wales was negligible over the century. Current research by the Cambridge Group questions this assumption and may lead to further revisions of the population estimates.

Age structure

The total size of a population is useful for many purposes, but it may mask important variations in age composition. The new data may be used in conjunction with a new technique which estimates age structure and vital rates (the numbers of births, deaths and marriages in relation to the number in the population in which they took place) from series of births and deaths (see Lee 1974, and Brunborg 1976). The combination of data and technique makes it possible to provide quinquennial estimates of age-group size, total fertility rates, and life expectancy for eighteenth-century England. Using the new method it is possible to estimate the population in each age group at five year intervals throughout the eighteenth century, based on the observed flows of births and deaths into and out of the population. The estimated age structures are conveniently portrayed by 'population pyramids'. Figure 2.2 shows these for 1700, 1750, and 1815, along with a pyramid for England and Wales in 1973 for purposes of contrast. The left and right hand sides of the pyramids show the male and female populations with the proportionate size of the age-group indicated by the length of the horizontal bar. For the eighteenth century it is assumed that half the population at each age was female; for 1973, the actual age–sex distribution is shown.

A comparison of the 1973 age pyramid with the others indicates that the early populations had relatively many young people and few old ones. This is a characteristic feature of preindustrial populations, primarily reflecting their higher birth rates, and not, as one might expect, their higher death rates. The pyramids also show that the population was considerably younger in 1815 than in 1700 or 1750, again a consequence of fertility differences. The economic implications of these age structures will be discussed later.

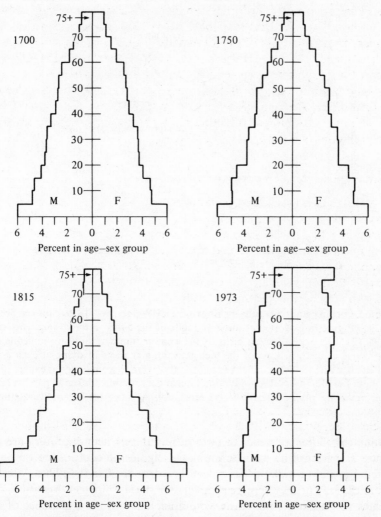

Figure 2.2 Population pyramids for England and Wales. Source: See text.

Mortality

As well as the population size, age structure and rate of growth, it is also of great interest to know the vital rates. Although it is easiest to calculate what are called 'crude' rates, by dividing vital events by the total population size, these rates depend very much on the age structure of that population; 10 or 60 year old males, for example, sire few children. It is therefore worth calculating measures which are pinned to a particular age, such as life expectancy at birth, or the marriage rate of 20 year olds; these are known as 'age-specific' rates.

24

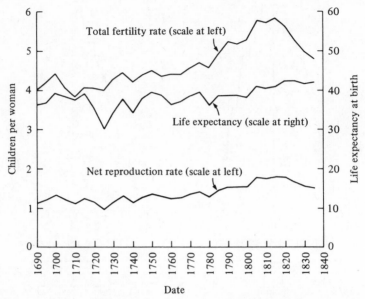

Figure 2.3 Fertility and mortality in England and Wales 1690–1839. Source: See text. Notes: (1) Figures are plotted at the initial date of the 5-year interval; e.g. 1690 means 1690–94. (2) 'Life expectancy at birth' is the average numbers of years someone could expect to live at birth in view of the then prevailing chances of dying at each age. (3) 'Total fertility rate' is the number of children the average woman could expect to have throughout her life. (4) 'Net reproduction rate' is the ratio of children to parents implied by the prevailing rates of fertility and mortality. A rate over 1.0 indicates that the population is growing.

Estimates of life-expectancy at birth during the eighteenth century are given in figure 2.3. According to these estimates, eighteenth-century life expectancy stayed in the mid-to-high thirties except for a drop to 30 in the 1720s. After 1800 it rose to the low forties where it remained until the late nineteenth century. These estimates are tentative; nonetheless, comparison with the experience of other national populations suggests that they are unlikely to be far wrong either in levels or in the timing of change. Figure 2.4 plots the results for England and Wales together with decennial estimates for France, 1740–1830, and quinquennial estimates for Sweden, 1750–1830. Aside from some specifically Swedish crises, such as the Finnish War of 1808–9 and ensuing epidemics, the level and trend of the English and Swedish life expectancies agree remarkably well. Similarly, although the level of life expectancy for French females is consistently about five years lower, the trend is nearly identical to England's. These comparisons show that there is nothing bizarre about the mortality estimates for eighteenth- and early-nineteenth-century England.

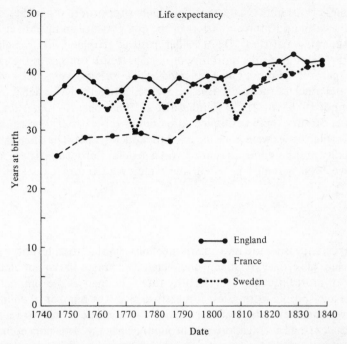

Fig. 2.4 Life expectancy in France, Sweden, and England 1740 to 1840. Note: French data are for females only; English and Swedish data are for both sexes. Observations are plotted on the midpoint of each interval. Source: France (Blayo, 1975; 141) ; Sweden (Bolander *et al.*, 1970: 81, 84); England (see text).

There were large variations in mortality over time. Preindustrial populations were afflicted by 'demographic' crises, that is, sharp rises in mortality and falls in conceptions and marriages. In earlier centuries such crises were often connected with harvest failures, as they continued to be in eighteenth-century France; but by the same period in England they were more usually the result of epidemics and thus largely independent of the state of the economy (Chambers (1972: 77–106; Wrigley, 1969: 62–76). The English population experienced two such crises in the first half of the eighteenth century: one from 1727 to 1730, with deaths peaking at 80 per cent above normal in 1729; another in 1740 to 1742, with deaths peaking in 1742 at about 40 per cent above normal. Although in both instances grain prices were high, they were not strikingly so, and neither of these was a pure 'subsistence' crisis of the old type. Contemporary medical observers reported a wide variety of diseases, almost all of which were airborne infections, including all manner of fevers, smallpox, chickenpox and whooping cough (Short 1967: 84). The epidemics lasted considerably longer than was usually the case with an epidemic caused by a single disease, and in those areas where epidemics occurred they affected a far higher proportion of parishes than was usually the case, up to three-quarters of the city parishes and just over one half of the country parishes. On a wider canvas, Holland like England experienced the worst epidemic mortality of the eighteenth century in the same years, some parts of France were affected while others were not, while Scandinavia and much of the rest of Europe escaped altogether (van der Woude 1972: 205; Imhof 1976, vol. I: 77; Reinhard et al. 1968: chs. 10–13). After the first half of the century there continued to be minor crises from time to time, but the catastrophic crises were gone for good (Schofield 1972). The attenuation of crisis mortality in the eighteenth century was a general European pattern, and may well have been a major factor in the widespread improvement of life expectancy.

Fertility

Just as life expectancy is a pure measure of mortality, so the 'total fertility rate' is a pure measure of fertility, relatively unaffected by changes in the population age structure or mortality. The total fertility rate is defined as the sum across all ages of the age-specific birth rates; it therefore gives the number of children the average woman would have if she survived to the age of forty-five and experienced the current average fertility throughout her life. It is conceptually close to 'completed family size', averaged over all surviving women, including spinsters, at the end of their reproductive years. Estimates of the total fertility rate are plotted in figure 2.3 above. They differ from Brownlee's estimates in suggesting less increase between 1700–39 and 1740–79, and more in the nineteenth century; they are consistent with the view (Krause 1965) that changes in the under-registration rates concealed the true demographic behaviour.

The naive view of fertility before modern contraception is that it was at the biological maximum. It was not. The biological maximum to the total fertility rate is about eleven children per woman, and fertility in eighteenth-century England amounted to less than half of this. The question is how society achieved limited fertility.

To answer this question we must distinguish between the effects of age, of marriage and of fertility within marriage. The new data from the Cambridge group do not allow us to do this directly, so we must turn to other methods. Information on age at marriage is available from two sources: marriage licences and family reconstitutions of individual parishes. Both have their drawbacks: the former are biassed in favour of high social status and education, while the latter generally only cover those who marry in the parish in which they were born. Yet some points stand out clearly in table 2.2. First, the average age at marriage of women was high, between 24 and 27 years, and thus on average women who married could have children (legitimately, at least) only during two-thirds of the

Table 2.2. *Age at first marriage* 1550–1849

Period	Males	Females
1550–1599	27.2	24.8
1600–1649	28.1	26.0
1650–1699	28.2	26.6
1700–1749	28.1	27.0
1750–1799	27.1	25.4
1800–1849	26.5	24.3

Note: The figures are unweighted averages of mean age at first marriage for a collection of 10 parishes (9 for 1550–99). The parishes are Alcester (Warwickshire), Aldenham (Hertfordshire), Banbury (Oxfordshire), Bottesford (Leicestershire), Colyton (Devonshire), Gainsborough (Lincolnshire), Hartland (Devonshire), Hawkshead (Lancashire), Shepshed (Leicestershire), Terling (Essex); Hawkshead was not included for 1550–99.
Source: Wrigley 1976b.

years during which they were potentially able to do so. In addition, about 10 per cent of women never married at all. Here England was entirely typical of most of northwest Europe: this 'West European marriage pattern' (Hajnal 1965) accounts for the relatively low levels of fertility to be found in preindustrial European communities compared with traditional societies elsewhere in the world.

Fertility in the preindustrial world was overwhelmingly marital, although eighteenth-century England did witness a striking increase in extra-marital fertility, from just under 2 per cent of all births around 1700 to 6 percent of all births around 1800 (see Laslett and Oosterveen 1973). Changes in the age of marriage would have had considerable impact on fertility levels. Information on changes in the age of marriage is difficult to acquire. For example, the marriage licences so far collected do not provide any information on ages at marriage for the same area at different dates, so changes over time cannot be inferred from them. The family reconstitution studies are some help, but so far few of these have been completed. Nevertheless, the 10 parishes which are listed in table 2.2 experienced a fall in the average age of marriage of women of about 2.7 years between the early eighteenth and the early nineteenth centuries. This is a very small number of parishes, but each of them experienced a fall in the age of marriage, although they differed greatly in location and economic characteristics. Moreover, an additional 2.7 years is easily enough to add one extra child to the four which the total fertility rate (figure 2.3) shows to have been the average at the beginning of the eighteenth century. It appears, therefore, that there was a fall in the age of marriage of women, and that this was an important factor in the increase in the total fertility rate.

Dimensions - mortality - summed up in Hudson -

Regional variations in population growth

We have so far concentrated on the national population trends, but there were important local variations. Mortality, for example, was much higher in towns than in the country, and seaports were particularly unhealthy (Wrigley 1969: 96–8); London required a perpetual stream of immigrants from rural areas to offset her deficit of births over deaths (Wrigley 1967). By contrast, fertility appears to have been higher in the industrialising north-west than elsewhere. Deane and Cole (1967: ch. 3) note that population growth was more rapid in industrial and commercial counties than in agricultural ones, and more rapid in the north-west than in the south-east. They also find that the more rapid growth of the industrial and commercial areas was caused not as one might suppose by migration, but rather by 'natural increase', i.e. the excess of births over deaths. The higher natural increase, in turn, was due to high birth rates rather than low death rates.

Appealing as these results are to historians interested in the connections between population trends and industrialisation, they must be regarded with caution until they are tested against better evidence. The estimates by Deane and Cole depend on the Rickman series in a particularly demanding way, subtracting one error-ridden series from another to infer migration. In addition, nonconformist religions were stronger in some areas, especially industrialising areas, than in others, causing differential underestimation of the true fertility and marriage patterns by figures, such as Rickman's, based on the statistics collected by the Anglican church. Migration itself affects the age structure and the vital rates in both the sending and the receiving areas (see chapter 21). Regrettably the Cambridge Group has as yet collected data for too few parishes to make a reasonable estimate of population for individual counties, though it may ultimately be possible to make estimates for broad regions or economic categories such as 'agricultural', 'industrial', or 'commercial'. In the meantime, the description and analysis of English population in the eighteenth century must remain largely based on national averages.

The effects of population growth

Real wages and the burden of children

The largest and most obvious effect of the sharp rise in population in the eighteenth century was on the national average wage of labour. Labour is one of the factors of production. When it grows in supply more rapidly than the others, its relative price (the real wage) will fall, unless productivity change is sufficiently rapid. The pace of innovation and capital formation was apparently high enough in eighteenth-century England to allow a growth rate of labour of the order of 0.4 to 0.6 per cent per year with constant real wages (Lee, 1979; compare chapters 1 and 7). Slower growth than this (as in the first half of the century) allowed real wages to rise; faster growth (as in the second half) depressed them sharply. The logic of the argument is reinforced by the truth of another of its implications. The increase in the labour force relative to agricultural land would have increased the value of land and increased rents. Prices of agricultural goods therefore would rise more than prices of manufactured goods, since agricultural production was relatively land intensive and manufacturing labour intensive. True to these predictions, in the first half of the century the ratio of industrial to agricultural prices rose and in the second half it fell (see Lee 1979). During the second half of the eighteenth century, then, population grew more rapidly and the evidence on wages (imperfect though it is) indicates a decline in the real wage of labour. At the same time, per capita income rose quite markedly (see chapter 1 and Deane and Cole, 1967: 78). On the face of it, these opposite trends suggest a redistribution of income away from labourers and towards landowners and capitalists. Whether a redistribution of family income actually occurred depends in part on whether the children and wives of labourers increased their work enough to offset the decline in wage rates (chapter 9).

The connections between population increase and wages therefore seem clear. But it must be remembered that not all members of the population are workers, although they are all consumers. In the long run, population size and labour supply move roughly together; in the short run, however, changes in the average age and in the work supplied at each age ('labour force participation') allow some divergence of the two. An unusually large number of births, for example, will increase population without affecting the labour force for about fifteen years. Estimates of age structure can be used to adjust population size for changes of this sort, and thereby to get a better indication of changes in the labour supply. In principle, each age group can be multiplied by a weight reflecting its contribution to production, that is, average hours worked times wages per hour. Such age-specific weights are usually expressed as a proportion of the productivity of a prime age adult. The sum of all population age groups, weighted in this way, is called the number of 'equivalent adult producers'. Unfortunately such weights are not available for eighteenth-century Britain, but a set of weights representative of a contemporary developing economy (see Mueller 1976) was used to calculate in a rough way the number of equivalent adult producers as a proportion of the total population at five-year intervals from 1700 to 1840. Since a fixed set of weights was used, changes in labour force participation are not taken into account; only changes in age structure can affect the outcome. The calculated proportions of equivalent adult producers are constant from 1700 to 1750 and thereafter begin to decline steadily. From their peak in 1730 to their trough in 1820 they decline by about 11 per cent. Because of rising fertility, that is, the number of children grew more rapidly than the number of workers.

Consumption does not grow in strict proportion to the population, of course, since children consume less than adults. To summarise the effect of change in the age structure on consumption, it is convenient to calculate the total number of 'equivalent adult consumers' just as for production. Fixed consumption weights representative of Western Europe around 1900 were used (Mueller 1976). The proportion of equivalent adult consumers in the total population declined by about 5 per cent from its peak in 1730 to its low point in 1820. Combining the results on consumption with those on production implies an increase in the ratio of consumers to producers of 11 per cent minus 5 per cent, or 6 per cent down to 1820. The upshot is that changes in the age structure of the population, due primarily to its higher fertility late in the century, did increase the consumption pressure on the typical worker. The increase, however, was small, and could easily have been swamped by the unmeasurable changes in participation in the labour force.

The level and composition of demand

The effect on labour supply is one side; the effect on the demand for goods is the other. As the population grows, so does aggregate income and aggregate demand, creating a buoyant and less risky environment for investors and entrepreneurs, and stimulating the demand for investment goods. Population growth may therefore encourage economic growth more than might be expected from the growth in labour supply alone (see e.g. Keynes 1937). A well-known economist has suggested that 'perhaps the whole Industrial Revolution of the last two hundred years has been nothing else but a vast secular boom, largely induced by the unparalleled rise in population' (Hicks 1939: 302n). The logic and evidence for this view were treated in chapter 1. Here we may mention the effect of population growth not on the aggregate level of consumption, but on the distribution of consumption between agricultural and industrial goods (John 1967a; Eversley 1967; Tranter 1973a). The influence, unfortunately, operates in two opposite ways: through changes in income per head and through changes in relative prices. Poor people spend a high share of their incomes on food. As income rises, the share falls: one says that the 'income elasticity' of expenditure on food is less than one, a proposition known as Engel's Law. As the share of food declines, the share spent on industrial commodities rises. The demand for industrial goods therefore depends not only on total national income but also on the number of consumers, i.e. on how many poor people there are. While population growth does raise total income and demand, it typically reduces real wages or average income. And because the allocation of demand between the industrial and agricultural sectors depends on average income, it may be that on this count the population growth of the eighteenth century diverted demand from the industrial sector rather than stimulating it.

On the other hand, as we have seen, by depressing wages and raising land rents population growth made manufactured goods (using labour intensively) cheaper in comparison with agricultural goods. On this count, people would have substituted manufactured for agricultural consumption. In short, the net effect of population growth on the demand for industrial commodities is unclear, and the question whether population growth increased or decreased the home demand for manufactured commodities in the eighteenth century remains unresolved (although see Ippolito 1975). The conclusion is by now familar: economic reasoning and statistical fact narrow the possible range of interpretation, but do not always end the debate.

Causes of population growth in the eighteenth century

As with the consequences, so with the causes. The historical debate has centred on whether eighteenth-century population growth was caused by economic growth or merely happened to coincide with it (Habakkuk 1965; Deane and Cole 1967). The debate has often degenerated into one over whether the rise in population was caused by a rise in birth rates or a fall in death rates, the notion being that one or the other was itself economic in cause. Many writers have realised that the demographic facts alone could not determine whether this notion was true (Marshall 1929; Habakkuk 1965; Deane and Cole 1967). Nevertheless, the behaviour of the demographic facts is a convenient place to start.

From 1700 to 1739, population grew at an average annual rate of 0.3 per cent; from 1800 to 1839, it grew at 1.45 per cent. The new estimates from the Cambridge Group assign a clearly dominant role to the birth rate, which accounts for about 70 per cent of the increase in population growth rates. If the birth rate had remained unchanged, the declines in the death rate would have boosted annual growth rates to about 0.7 per cent per year in the early nineteenth century, a significant increase but far short of the actual.

The arithmetic dominance of fertility is reinforced by a comparison with the rest of Europe, which was also increasing in population. Over the eighteenth century as a whole the growth rate of population in England and Wales was not notably high even if the frontier populations of Finland and Eastern Europe are excluded from the comparison. Only at the very end of the eighteenth century and the beginning of the nineteenth did the population of England and Wales grow distinctly more rapidly than those of other European countries away from the frontier (see Dupâquier 1976: 190; Wrigley 1969: 152–6; Tranter 1973a: 43). But it was precisely in these years that fertility, as we have seen (figure 2.3 above) increased dramatically. Fertility, then, not mortality, was the peculiar feature of England's experience.

Most writers have emphasised a decline in mortality rather than an increase in fertility as the cause of the eighteenth-century population rise, and have

32

assume rise in fertility + decrease in mortality

pointed to cheaper transport reducing the consequences of local harvest failure; fortunate improvements in climate; a reduction in the virulence of diseases; medical advances, especially the spread of smallpox vaccination (Razzell 1965); improved nutrition through new agricultural techniques and the spread of cheap food crops such as the potato. The few writers who emphasise an increase in fertility in the eighteenth century have pointed to the increased chances for marriage and subsistence that agricultural advance afforded, supplemented by earnings from 'proto-industry', or the development of cottage industry. Both sides of the debate tend to assume a smooth decline in mortality or a smooth rise in fertility. The new data complicate the issue. A hypothesis explaining the rise in fertility must now accommodate a decline in fertility after 1815; one explaining the fall in mortality must accommodate 50 years of ups and downs in the death rate between 1700 and 1750, followed by 50 years of stagnation, followed in the first 20 years of the nineteenth century by a rapid fall, followed again by a further half century of stagnation.

And in any case an 'explanation' of falling mortality or rising fertility must recognise that the connections of causation betwen population and other things (especially the economy) are mutual. The potato could make dense population possible, but dense population could make the potato necessary; the beginnings of industrialisation could cause early marriage and high fertility, but high fertility could provide the cheap labour for further industrialisation. The connections are complex, and require a simplified view of the main ones. The modern view among economists and demographers is a simplification of the thoughts of parson Malthus, built on three behavioural relationships and one truism about four variables: the wage (called w in what follows), the population (N, for 'numbers'), the birth rate (b), and the death rate (d) per thousand population. First, for familiar reasons, the wage falls when population rises. Second, since resistance to disease depended in part on nutrition, the death rate rises when the wage falls. Third, since in Western Europe couples did not in general marry without a sufficient livelihood, marriage and therefore the birth rate rise when the wage rises (Wrigley 1966; Lee 1973, 1974, 1978 and forthcoming). Finally as a truism, present population is (in the absence of migration) the result of past differences between the birth rate and the death rate.

The system which is comprised of these three relationships is portrayed in figure 2.5. The top panel shows the positive relation ($b(w)$) of the birth rate to wages, and the negative relation ($d(w)$) of the death rate to wages. At the intersection of these curves, the growth rate (equal to $b-d$) is zero, and the population has no tendency to change. The wage that corresponds to zero growth is the long-run equilibrium wage, or 'natural price of labour'; it is labelled w^* on the horizontal axis.

The lower panel of figure 2.5 shows – in the solid curve labelled $w(N)$ – the negative relation of wages to population; this curve represents the 'demand for

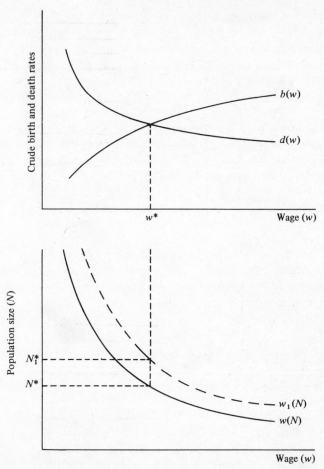

Figure 2.5 Demographic equilibrium before and after a shift in the demand for labour.

labour', or the amount of labour demanded at each real wage. There is a population size N measured on the vertical axis which corresponds to each wage on the horizontal axis; the exact correspondence is established by the curve $w(N)$; only if the population happens to be N^* will it be consistent with the zero-growth wage w^*, and therefore only when it is at N^* will the population have no tendency to change. If a society started with a population other than N^*, the population would rise or fall towards N^*. At a population below N^*, for example, the implied wage (read from $w(N)$) would be larger than w^*; in the top panel, this would imply that the birth rate would exceed the death rate, and population (in the bottom panel) would rise until the higher N^* and the lower w^* were achieved.

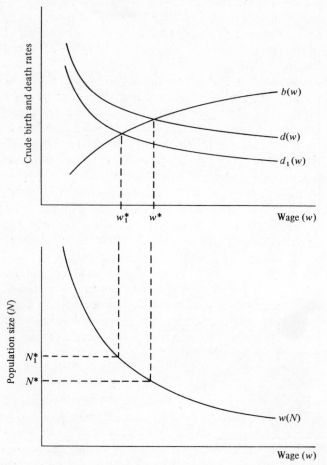

Figure 2.6 Demographic equilibrium before and after a shift in mortality.

Now consider the effect of an increase in the demand for labour, resulting, say, from investment in agriculture. This can be represented as an outward (i.e. away from the origin) shift in the curve in the lower panel, as indicated by the dotted line $w_1(N)$ in figure 2.5. The initial effect of such a shift is to raise wages, as the old population N^* intersects with $w_1(N)$ at a point further to the right than it intersects with $w(N)$, and thereby stimulate population growth. Note, however, that none of the relationships in the upper panel have changed, so the ultimate equilibrium wage is unaltered. We would expect that soon population would grow to its new equilibrium, N^*, and the wage would return to its old equilibrium, w^*. Even though the demand for labour has increased, the workers do not benefit in the end. This illustrates the 'iron law of wages' of the classical economists, and the circumstances of England before the industrial revolution. Only sustained economic growth, pushing the demand curve out again and again, can benefit the working population more than temporarily. Only the frenetic pace of economic life since the eighteenth century has prevented the iron law from taking effect.

Figure 2.6 shows the effect, within the same framework of relationships, of an autonomous fall in the death rate, such as appears to have occurred towards the end of the eighteenth century and at the beginning of the nineteenth. Look at the top panel. At each level of the real wage (measured along the horizontal axis) the death rate (measured along the vertical axis) is lower. The effect, therefore, of a fall in the death rate as shown by an inward movement of the curve from $d(w)$ to $d_1(w)$ is to lower the equilibrium wage to w_1; population size increases at the expense of wages, while fertility falls somewhat in response to the decline in wages. Note that in this case the system responds so as to bring birth rates and death rates back to equality, but at a level lower than before. The effect of an autonomous upward shift in the fertility curve would be similar, and closer to the events of the late eighteenth century.

The most important point which stems from this model is that a decline in the death rate or rise in the birth rate, if it were 'exogenous' or caused outside the system of relationships depicted here, would cause population growth, but not *sustained* population growth. With such exogenous shifts, the birth and death rates would converge to equality again at a lower wage, as in figure 2.6. But toward the end of the eighteenth century the two rates did not converge; instead they diverged, resulting in the population explosion of the early nineteenth century. Apparently the demographic changes were not purely exogenous. Yet neither were they purely 'endogenous' or determined within the system. Sustained economic growth would have increased the wage, leading (endogenously) to rising birth rates and falling death rates. But in fact wages did not increase markedly in the late eighteenth and early nineteenth centuries; indeed several wage series suggest a decline (Phelps Brown and Hopkins 1956; Deane and Cole 1967: 19–21; von Tunzelmann 1979; chapter 9 below).

Neither purely exogenous nor purely endogenous, the causes of population change were a mixture of the two. On the one hand, the schedules of birth and death rates (the top panel in the figures) moved apart, producing growth at the existing wage; on the other, the demand for labour (the bottom panel) moved out vigorously enough to keep wages from falling even though the population was growing. By such fortunate events did the nation avoid the immiseration that accompanied population growth among less fortunate neighbours (Ireland in particular) and in earlier times (Marshall 1929: 248; Deane and Cole 1967: 134; Lee 1978).

3

Factors in demand 1700–80

W. A. COLE

The problem of demand

The growth of the British economy in the eighteenth century, which was analysed in the first chapter of this book, was undoubtedly substantial in comparison with that of many preindustrial countries, but it was not unique. It appears that the economic growth of eighteenth-century France was as rapid as that of England, at least until about 1780 (Crouzet 1966); and it seems likely that the Dutch United Provinces had experienced a similar phase of relatively rapid growth in the century following their successful struggle for independence from Spain (North and Thomas 1973:116–17). What distinguished the experience of eighteenth-century England from that of its neighbours in western Europe, and, indeed, from all other countries in the world up to that time, was the fact that, in the last two or three decades of the century, it witnessed a surge of industrial growth and the onset of a rapid structural transformation of the economy; by the middle of the nineteenth century, this island had been turned into the world's first industrial nation.

Until recently, the role of demand in this momentous transformation had been little studied by historians. The early students of the industrial revolution drew attention to its commercial origins, and some of them acknowledged that, in addition to the remarkable expansion of Britain's overseas trade, there was also an increase in the demand of the population at home. But, as Dr Gilboy pointed out as long ago as 1932, the mechanism by which this increase in demand occurred was seldom analysed, and it was left to later historians to begin to repair the omission (Gilboy 1932). In more recent years, however, a substantial literature has begun to appear on the subject, and the growth of demand is now widely regarded as one of the essential elements in the transformation of the economy.

To a large extent this recent interest in demand simply reflects a change in the approach of economists and historians towards the problem of explaining economic development in general. So long as the investment and innovation which lie at the heart of the growth process were assumed to be determined independently of the economic system, there was little occasion for historians to concern themselves with the question of demand. But as soon as they came

36

to be regarded as products of economic and social conditions, it was natural that historians should begin to search for the changes in market demand and relative factor prices which could have induced them. There is, however, a particular reason why a consideration of changes on the demand side should bulk large in discussions of the industrial revolution. This is because the transition from small-scale domestic industry to relatively large-scale factory production, which was one of the features of that revolution, constitutes a classic example of what some economists call a 'developmental block', in which advance must take place on a wide front if it is to occur at all (Pollard 1958). For factory production implies the concentration of production, as opposed to its dispersal, and this in turn implies the existence of a developed transport network to bring raw materials to the point of production and to distribute the finished goods to distant markets. Moreover, factories need machines, the power to drive them and relatively large numbers of men to operate them; and these in turn imply the existence of an engineering industry to provide the machines, the exploitation of abundant sources of energy to provide the power, and a large-scale construction industry to build the factories and the houses for the people who run them. Now each of these developments requires a critical minimum level of investment if it is to be economically viable, and each depends for its success on all the others. Hence the problem is to explain not just the small, piecemeal investment outlays which were required for expansion under the domestic system, but the widespread investment in a series of inter-related fields which were required to sustain an industrial revolution. In a modern economy, in which a programme of industrialisation may be launched as a deliberate act of government policy, it may sometimes be possible to stimulate it as part of a centrally co-ordinated economic plan, or, in some cases, it may be undertaken by the government itself. But in the case of the first industrial revolution, it happened more or less spontaneously, as a result of the independent decisions of a large number of individuals, each seeking his own private profit. And it is, of course, this aspect of the process which has prompted one recent student of the subject to ask:

How did entrepreneurs come to see before them, not the modest if solid expansion of demand which could be filled in the traditional manner, or by a little extension and improvement of the old ways, but the rapid and limitless expansion which required revolution? A small, simple and cheap revolution by our standards, but nevertheless a revolution, a leap into the dark [Hobsbawm 1968: 26–7].

Not all students of the industrial revolution would accept the assumptions underlying this formulation of the problem, and the view that demand was a major factor in the transformation of the British economy has been strongly challenged (Mokyr 1977). Nevertheless, implicitly or explicitly it underlies a good deal of the recent literature on the eighteenth century. The answers which historians have given to the question, however, differ substantially in both their nature and emphasis. One school of thought attaches primary importance to exports in the development of a market for industrially produced goods (Berrill 1960; Habakkuk and Deane 1963), while another regards exports as of only minor significance (John 1961, 1965; Eversley 1967). Moreover, amongst those who have chosen to focus attention on the growth of home demand, there are, as we shall see, equally strong differences of opinion about how that demand was able to grow. In this chapter, therefore, we shall attempt to review some of these conflicting interpretations in an effort to give our own answer to the question of how demand was able to increase in eighteenth-century England and why, in particular it gave rise to the development of a mass market for industrially produced goods.

Home versus overseas demand?

Let us begin with the question of overseas trade. The role of overseas trade in the process of eighteenth-century economic growth will be examined in detail in chapter 5. But in view of the importance which has been attached to it by so many distinguished scholars in the past, it is clearly necessary to say something here about the effect of exports on both the composition and level of demand.

Whether or not we accept the view that there are compelling reasons 'for making the growth of exports a driving force in British expansion' (Whitehead 1964: 74) there can be little doubt that the foreign trade section grew distinctly faster than the economy as a whole in the eighteenth century. Moreover, Britain's involvement with overseas markets seems to have increased almost continuously throughout the period. According to Deane and Cole's estimates, the volume of domestic exports plus net imports was growing about three times as fast as total output in the first four decades of the eighteenth century, but thereafter the ratio fell to about 1.7:1 (Deane and Cole 1967: 310–11), which would suggest that there was quite a marked relative shift towards the home market in the latter part of the period. But it now seems probable that Deane and Cole considerably underestimated the increase in total output in the early part of the century, and the revised estimates of national product, which are reported in detail in the appendix to this chapter, indicate that the ratio remained fairly constant throughout the eighteenth century – except during the major depressions in international trade which were associated with some of the wars of the period, notably the War of the Austrian Succession (1739–48) and the War of American Independence (1775–83).

As we might expect, the relatively rapid growth of overseas trade was reflected in a fairly steady increase in the proportion of national output exported. Thus, at the beginning of the century, domestic exports (f.o.b.) probably accounted for about seven or eight per cent of the national income, fluctuated between 10 and 12 per cent during the middle decades, and then rose to a peak of 16 or 17 per cent at the end of the period. It is true that despite this progressive increase in the importance of overseas markets, exports were not, by themselves, large enough to account for much more than a fifth of the increase in the output of the economy as a whole. But overseas markets were of much greater importance to some sectors of the economy than others. During the first half of the century, England exported large and growing quantities of grain and other foodstuffs, and at their peak, around 1750, exports of grain were sufficient to feed a population the size of London at the time (John 1976). Yet even then they probably accounted for less than five per cent of the output of agriculture as a whole, and in the second half of the century England became a net importer of grain. In the industrial sector, which in the form of manufactured goods and industrial raw materials such as lead and tin nearly always accounted for 80 per cent, and usually for more than 90 per cent, of total domestic exports, the position was quite different; exports, always important, grew considerably and were an important component of demand for the products of many manufacturing industries. Ever since the late Middle Ages, English exports had been dominated by the trade in woollen cloth, and at the beginning of the eighteenth century the woollen industry was still easily the most important export industry, since it accounted for roughly 70 per cent of total domestic exports, and according to one estimate, its overseas sales usually represented more than 40 per cent of its total product (Deane 1957b). But in the course of the century, although some industries, such as leather and food processing, remained overwhelmingly dependent on the home market, many others, including non-woollen textiles (especially cottons), non-ferrous metals, glass and earthenware and iron and steel, all began to build up thriving export trades which accounted for a significant part of their total product.

What contribution did this expansion of exports make to the growth of industrial output as a whole? The estimates presented in table 3.1 indicate that in the eighteenth century industrial output nearly quadrupled and home consumption roughly trebled, while exports increased more than sixfold. They imply that the proportion of industrial output exported rose from about a fifth at the beginning of the century to more than a third at the end. The increase was not continuous, for in the second and third decades of the century, and again in the 1760s and 1770s, home consumption grew faster than exports. For the most part, these periods appear to coincide with years when the terms of trade were moving strongly in Britain's favour, and it is well known that such movements tend to raise real domestic incomes while making exports less competitive in international markets. However, the generally favourable trend in the terms of trade which occurred between 1760 and 1785 was interrupted by a sharp rise in import prices during the American War of Independence (1775–83); and since the home consumption of industrial goods continued to increase, while the volume of exports actually fell, there must have been other forces operating to maintain home demand during those years.

Despite these short-term variations, the size of exports and their long-run

Table 3.1. *Industrial output, exports and home consumption for England and Wales* (*at* c. 1697–1704 *prices*)

	Industrial output (£m.)	Of which: exports (£m.)	(%)	Home consumption (£m.)	Home consumption per capita (£)
1700	18.5	3.8	20.6	14.6	2.77
1705	19.3	4.2	22.0	15.0	2.79
1710	19.2	4.9	25.3	14.4	2.61
1715	20.4	5.1	24.8	15.3	2.75
1720	21.9	5.0	23.1	16.8	2.97
1725	22.6	5.6	22.6	17.4	3.10
1730	23.5	5.4	23.1	18.1	3.24
1735	24.8	6.0	24.2	18.8	3.26
1740	24.2	6.3	26.1	17.9	3.01
1745	24.3	6.7	27.7	17.5	2.89
1750	27.5	8.0	29.0	19.5	3.14
1755	30.4	9.2	30.1	21.2	3.31
1760	33.2	10.3	31.0	22.9	3.46
1765	35.5	10.9	30.8	24.6	3.62
1770	36.9	11.2	30.3	25.7	3.69
1775	36.5	10.6	29.1	25.9	3.56
1780	36.0	9.9	27.6	26.1	3.45
1785	42.4	11.7	27.6	30.7	3.89
1790	51.7	15.2	29.5	36.5	4.44
1795	58.9	19.0	32.2	39.9	4.59
1800	68.2	23.5	34.5	44.7	4.88

Sources and notes: All figures are decade averages, roughly centring on the years specified. The entries for industrial output are rough estimates of the gross value of final output and therefore include the cost of imported raw materials and inputs from other domestic sectors. The estimate for c. 1800 was derived from our estimate of English exports at the prices of 1697–1704 and Eden's estimates of the current value of gross (British) industrial output, exports and home consumption in Macpherson (1805: IV, 549); those for earlier decades were obtained by applying a slightly revised and expanded version of the index of industrial and commercial output in Deane and Cole (1967: 78) to the estimate for 1800. Although they are necessarily rather crude, these estimates should provide a more appropriate basis for comparison with the values of exports than those in the second column of table 3.2, which refer to the *net* product of both industry and commerce. The export figures are the official values of domestic exports from Deane and Cole (1967: 48, 319–22), adjusted to represent English exports only at the prices of 1697–1704 throughout, and excluding grain exports for the years of net exports before 1765 from John (1976: 49, 64). The population series underlying the figures of home consumption per head was derived from the new estimates of population presented in chapter 2 above.

tendency to outpace the growth of domestic consumption combined to ensure that they made a substantial contribution to the growth of the industrial sector of the economy; indeed, the estimates imply that they accounted for nearly 40 per cent of the increase in industrial output over the century as a whole. Moreover, in order to set their contribution in perspective, it is important to remember that exports represented, for the most part, a net addition to the home consumption of industrial goods. It is true that where there are exports there will be imports, and at the beginning of the eighteenth century nearly 30 per cent of net imports consisted of manufactured and semi-manufactured goods. But in the eighteenth century they gradually declined until by 1815 they were of negligible importance (Deane and Cole 1967: 32; Davis 1979: 33, 36), and there can be no doubt that the growth of England's export trade did involve a major extension of the market available to her traders and manufacturers.

The significance of this development, which will not be lost on anyone familiar with Adam Smith's famous passage in which he pointed out that the division of labour is limited by the extent of the market, can easily be illustrated by a simple calculation. The estimates of the national product reproduced in the appendix to this chapter indicate that, at the beginning of the eighteenth century, industry and commerce together accounted for about a third of the national income and agriculture for roughly 40 per cent, whereas a hundred years later these proportions has been almost exactly reversed. Now let us imagine what would have happened if England had been a closed economy which was entirely cut off from overseas markets and sources of supply in Europe, Africa, America and the Far East. In 1700 the manufactured goods which she imported from abroad, or substitutes for them, would no doubt have been produced at home, but the markets for the much larger quantities she sold abroad would have been lost, and home substitutes would have had to be provided for the foodstuffs and raw materials she imported, with the net result that industry and commerce might have accounted for only 27 per cent of her national income and agriculture for roughly 46 per cent. And if, in 1800, this situation had persisted, and all other things had remained equal, it seems clear that these proportions would have changed very little. In other words, England, instead of being well on the road to becoming an industrial nation, would not yet have begun the trip.

By making the appropriate changes in the assumptions which underlie this counter-factual exercise, it would, of course, be possible to suggest rather less striking conclusions about the contribution which the development of overseas markets made to Britain's economic development. But it is also clear that, in an important sense, the argument so far may actually understate the importance of overseas trade to the growth of her industrial economy, since it takes no account of the gains from trade. And if we assume that these gains were not entirely counter-balanced by the benefits which Britain might have derived from an alternative pattern of development, it would follow that, as a result of trade, she was richer than she might have been, and, in consequence, not only was the industrial market available to her augmented by the amount of her overseas sales, but the domestic market itself was larger than it would have been in the absence of trade. How much richer is, of course, a question, since no-one has yet attempted to measure the contribution made by overseas trade to economic growth in eighteenth-century England. If we may judge by the experience of England's neighbour France, in which trade expanded as fast as it did in England, but in which it also had a much smaller weight in the economy as a whole (Crouzet 1966: 146), it is certainly possible that she would not have been very much poorer; and it is noteworthy that even in the nineteenth century, though France did not enjoy Britain's dominating position in international markets and did not experience an industrial revolution on the British model, she nevertheless succeeded in raising the incomes of her people at roughly the same rate as her rival across the English Channel (Cole and Deane 1965: 11–12; O'Brien and Keyder 1978). But whatever the importance of trade in Britain's economic growth there seems little reason to doubt that it was a major, and perhaps decisive, factor in her early emergence as an industrial power.

So far we have considered the importance of overseas trade in widening the market for industrial goods and touched on its possible role as a factor in the growth of the economy as a whole. But we have not considered the reasons for the growth of trade itself, and these are of fundamental importance from the standpoint of a demand-based 'explanation' of the industrial revolution and economic growth. It is obvious that the extension of European commerce in the seventeenth and early eighteenth centuries by the opening up of new markets and sources of supply in other parts of the world, the growth of population and incomes in much of the European trading area, particularly from the 1730s and 1740s onwards, and the success of Britain in using her naval power to secure a major share of these new and expanding markets, were all factors which contributed to the growth of English trade; none of them can be regarded as merely a function of her own economic development. Indeed, it is possible to regard the growth of demand for British goods as a largely 'autonomous' development; if we do so it is not difficult to see that the resulting expansion of her export industries would be likely to stimulate the growth of other industries through their links with these other sectors, and that the spending out of the higher levels of income generated in the export sector might (if there was substantial unemployment) have multiplier effects in other parts of the economy. This would induce higher levels of investment, employment and income, and might also stimulate innovation which would make possible still higher levels of output and income in the long run. We saw in chapter 1 that, in spite of their limited size, the growth of exports in the decades between 1740 and 1770 might be sufficient to account for as much as 75 per cent of the increase in the national income as a whole during that period. It is true that in the period from 1760 to 1780 the use of the same model implies that exports were sufficient to account for only five per cent of the increase in income. But this was mainly because of the temporary collapse of exports during the American War of Independence; the experience of war years can scarcely be regarded as typical. Hence it is quite conceivable that an extension of the argument might suggest that the demand for exports was a major, and perhaps dominant, driving force which propelled the economy forward and upwards during most, if not quite all, of the eighteenth century.

The very simplicity of such a conclusion has attractions, but it is undermined by the fullness of employment (discussed in section 4) and by yet another difficulty. The model was based on the assumption that changes in incomes at home have no effect on the demand for exports and that the demand for exports in consequence is wholly autonomous. Although this assumption is appropriate for the purposes of short-term analysis, it could be highly misleading in the long run. For if an increase in the demand for exports tends to generate higher incomes at home, it is equally possible that an increase in the demand for imports will also raise incomes abroad, and part of the spending out of these additional incomes may well feed back into the domestic economy through an increased demand for exports. To the extent that this happens, of course, an expansion of exports may represent no more than a link in the growth of home demand (Eversley 1967: 221–2).

How important the feedback is will depend both on the values of the parameters underlying the multipliers at work in overseas markets, and on how those markets are organised. Thus, an increase in the demand for imports in Britain could have led to a considerable rise in incomes abroad, but if Britain's overseas customers had a low import propensity, or if they were free to meet their demand for imports from countries which, for one reason or another, were unwilling or unable to buy British goods, the feedback might have been small or even non-existent. It seems more likely, however, that Britain's colonial trade helped to ensure that in the case of her vitally important and rapidly growing triangular trades with Africa and the Americas at least, the demand for her exports was heavily dependent on the incomes of the planters in the West Indies and the southern colonies on the North American mainland who specialised in the production of cash crops for sale to the mother country. Hence it might conceivably be true, as Deane and Cole concluded, that the rate of expansion of British overseas trade mainly depended on the demand for imports in Britain (Deane and Cole 1967: 83–9).

As an explanation of the long-term factors underlying the growth of trade in the eighteenth century, Deane and Cole's approach may well contain an important element of truth, and it seems no less plausible than the alternative view that the forces which promoted growth were mainly external to the British economy. After all, as Coleman has recently reminded us, the expansion of commerce with America and Asia in the late seventeenth and eighteenth centuries was essentially an 'import-led' advance (Coleman 1977: 137). America was first discovered by Europeans in the course of their quest for a new route to the riches of the East and throughout the early modern period the Americas were valued less for the markets they provided for European goods than at first for the precious metals which filled the galleons of Spain, and later the tobacco, sugar, coffee, cotton and dyestuffs which the plantations supplied to the consumers and industries of England and other European countries. In order to pay for the new colonial commodities England developed an important re-export trade, and it was only at a comparatively late stage in the process, as the rising demand for them increased the income of the planters, that the colonies began to provide an expanding market for English manufactures (Davis 1954: 78–82).

Deane and Cole's analysis is, however, also open to the charge that it is too one-sided and therefore incomplete; it is certainly by no means clear that they were completely justified in their conviction that the impetus behind the accelerating growth of British trade in the second half of the eighteenth century was an increase in home rather than overseas demand. The analysis was based partly on the terms of trade which tended to move against Britain in the periods of most rapid commercial expansion between 1745 and 1760 and in the 1780s and 1790s. But the argument is inconclusive; first because the evidence for movements in both the gross barter terms of trade and the relative prices of imports and exports is seriously defective, and in the second half of the century as a whole the evidence which does exist suggests that the terms of trade moved in favour of Britain and not against her; secondly because, as Whitehead had pointed out (1964: 74), changes in the terms of trade tend to reflect short-term elasticities of demand and supply and provide only a poor clue to how demand and supply curves shift in the long run.

More recently, an attempt has been made to reinforce Deane and Cole's original argument by using the data on re-exports to construct an appropriately weighted index of the sales in export markets of goods which were also imported into Britain (Cole 1973). When this is compared with an index of retained imports it apparently tends to confirm the view that home demand was growing faster than that from abroad in both the periods of rapid commercial expansion. But the evidence is more persuasive for the end of the century than it is for the middle decades. This is because there are grounds for believing that in the earlier period the rapid expansion of British trade 'formed part of a spasm of growth which affected the commerce of Western Europe' as a whole (John 1965: 180–1; Cole 1973: 331–2) and the re-export data themselves suggest that overseas demand was growing more rapidly between 1730 and 1760 than at any other time in the eighteenth century. It is true that the official trade returns imply that the acceleration in the rate of growth of the combined volume of net imports and domestic exports was confined to the second half of this period, and that at that time home demand was growing faster than that from abroad; whereas in the first half of the period, home demand appears to have been relatively stagnant, even when an allowance has been made for the influence of smuggling on the official figures for imports. But the same allowance for smuggling would also suggest that the quickening tempo of commercial expansion which is apparent after 1745 in fact had its origins in the 1730s, before it was temporarily interrupted by the war of 1739–48. If that is so, it is possible that the impulse which initiated the upturn also had its origins abroad, and that by the time the increased overseas demand was translated into higher incomes at home, the resulting increase in the demand for imports encountered an adverse movement of the terms of trade, partly because of the effect of war on freight costs, and partly because of growing inelasticities of supply in some of Britain's overseas trading partners.

In short, both the evidence which has so far been collected and a little common sense might lead us to conclude that the impulses which promoted the expansion of Britain's trade in the eighteenth century came first from one side, then the other, and that in the long run both home and overseas demand were essential to the growth process. The debate about the relative importance of the two may well continue, but the attempt to determine which was primary could be both fruitless and misleading if it is allowed to distract attention from their mutual interaction (Thompson 1973: 93–103). Even if it could be established that the impulses to growth tended to come from one side rather than the other it would still be true that the response they evoked would depend on conditions of both demand and supply in the 'passive' partner. Thus, if the stimulus came principally from the British side, it is clear that the process of growth could not have continued if her demand for imports had encountered ineradicable inelasticities of demand and supply overseas which led to a massive and continuing deterioration in her terms of trade. Alternatively, if the stimulus came from overseas it is no less evident that the expansion of British exports would soon have been brought to a halt if Britain had been unable or unwilling to import goods from abroad in return. It is also true that foreign trade could not have been an engine of growth as its proponents believe, if the additional demand generated by an expansion of exports had simply been dissipated in extra imports by the limited export sector, for in that case there would have been little or no multiplier effect on the incomes of the population at large. Hence in order to explain why Britain did not suffer the fate of many 'enclave' economies in more recent times, but instead experienced industrial revolution and economic growth and development on a wide front, it would still be necessary to explain how and why the home market was able to grow; and it is to this problem that we must now turn.

The growth of the home market 1700–50

Although historians have recently begun to pay much more attention to the development of the home market, the study of the subject is still severely handicapped by the lack of adequate quantitative data. The growth path of both population and incomes has long been a matter of controversy, and we are even less certain about how the population spent their incomes. It is possible to derive a plausible picture at least of the composition of both total national and personal expenditure at the end of the seventeenth century from Gregory King's estimates for 1688 (Deane and Cole 1967: 2), but at present it is scarcely possible even to guess what the changes in overall expenditure patterns may have been in the course of the eighteenth century. Nor do we know much about the consumption habits of different regions and social groups. The family budgets collected by Davies and Eden at the end of the eighteenth century provide some of the details for the labouring poor (see Stigler 1954; Minchinton 1973: 16), but the basic research required to fill out the picture for society and the century as a whole has yet to be done.

It is not surprising that historians should differ in their interpretations of the growth of the home market, since it is often not clear precisely what it is that has to be explained. This is most obviously true in the case of the first half of the eighteenth century, for while some historians have tended to argue that the early eighteenth century, and particularly the second quarter, was a period of comparative stagnation or retardation in the home market (Deane and Cole 1967; Little 1976), others have suggested that it was a period of buoyancy and progress in which rising agricultural productivity laid the basis for accelerating industrialisation and economic growth later in the century (Jones 1965; John 1965). Thus, Deane and Cole argued that in the first half of the century an almost stationary population, coupled with unusually favourable climatic conditions, tended to depress agricultural prices, and that falling prices reduced agricultural incomes, discouraged agricultural investment, and were also associated with a decline in the demand for industrial goods. In particular, they believed that the long run of good harvests in the 1730s and 1740s, when the prices of grain were almost continuously low, was accompanied by a widespread agricultural depression, characterised by vacant holdings and the accumulation of arrears of rent, and by stagnation or even contraction in the home market for manufactured goods.

Both these propositions have been challenged by the John–Jones school. Jones has argued that there was no general depression in agriculture, because the sector was able to meet the challenge of falling prices by cost-reducing innovations, of which the most important was the introduction of fodder crops into the rotations. He admits that many farmers on the heavy clay soils of lowland England were unable to take advantage of the new techniques, and some of these were forced to abandon the land in favour of other pursuits. But farmers on the light, easily-worked soils of eastern England found that the new techniques enabled them both to produce more livestock products and to achieve higher yields of grain at lower unit costs, with the net result that the productivity of agriculture rose and farmers as a whole were able to maintain or increase their incomes even in the face of falling prices. But if farmers and landlords were in general no worse off as a result of falling prices, A. H. John argues that cheap food meant an increase in the real incomes of the mass of population, and that in consequence the demand for manufactures rose substantially in the first half of the eighteenth century. The section of the community which gained most from this period of low food prices was, of course, the labouring poor, for while foodstuffs accounted for only about 43 per cent of average personal expenditure, the Eden–Davies family budgets indicate that the proportion amongst wage labourers was as high as 70 per cent. It is John's case that it was precisely during the period of low prices in the early part of the century, when wage earners had a significant margin to spend on things other than food, that the foundations of a mass market for manufactured goods began to be firmly laid.

Deane and Cole's somewhat pessimistic view of the home market in the early part of the eighteenth century was strongly influenced by the nature of a turning-point which they thought they had detected in the rate of growth of total, if not per capita, output and incomes in the 1740s. Hence, in their approach to the early eighteenth century, they were more concerned to identify the obstacles which impeded growth than to explain the growth that did occur (Whitehead 1790: 4–5). Since, as we have seen, their estimates clearly implied that in the first four decades of the century foreign trade was expanding very much faster than the national income, their analysis was directed, in particular, at the obstacles to growth at home. But it is also apparent from the discussion in chapters 1 and 2 that Deane and Cole's estimates for the first half of the eighteenth century are in need of substantial revision in the light of more recent research. This is partly because their estimates of national output were heavily dependent on Brownlee's population estimates which are now thought to understate the increase in numbers during the early part of the century. In the absence of direct output statistics, Deane and Cole assumed that the consumption of food and the real incomes derived from the rent of housing, professional and domestic services varied directly with population; and since agriculture, rents and services accounted for about 60 per cent of total output at the beginning of the century, a revision of the population estimates is bound to make a significant difference to their estimates of national output. Moreover, Deane and Cole's assumption that the consumption of foodstuffs varied directly with population has also been strongly challenged. For the second half of the century, when both incomes and prices were rising, it is reasonable enough. But for the first half of the century, when average incomes were rising and food prices falling, it implies the further assumption that the income and price elasticities of demand for food were virtually zero which, as Crafts (1976, 1977a) has shown, is inconsistent both with the experience of developing countries today and with the empirical data for England in the late eighteenth and early nineteenth centuries, when the income elasticity of demand for food may have been as high as 0.74.

The implications of these considerations for our view of the course of economic growth in eighteenth-century England are far-reaching, and they are incorporated in the revised estimates given in the appendix to this chapter. Quite apart from the fact that they considerably soften the turning-point in the rate of growth of total output and incomes in the 1740s, they also imply that in the early part of the century agricultural output was expanding at roughly the same rate as the output of industry and the economy as a whole, in agreement with chapter 4. Moreover, although the rate of growth of population implied by the new estimates in chapter 2 may still seem modest in the light of later experience, it is not by the standards of most of the countries of Western Europe before the eighteenth century. Indeed, it is clearly above the long-term average suggested by the available estimates of the population of England and Wales in the six centuries or so from the time of Domesday Book onwards; and although it is probably below that achieved in the sixteenth century after the decline in numbers during the late Middle Ages, it is similar to J. C. Russell's estimates for twelfth- and thirteenth-century England, which has generally been regarded by historians as a period of relatively rapid population growth.

It follows that the new estimates of population and agricultural output also cast a somewhat different light on the fall in agricultural prices in the first half of the eighteenth century. For whereas Deane and Cole and, indeed, most other students of the subject have generally assumed that the fall was the result of the combination of stagnant demand with the bounty of nature, the new estimates suggest that, in fact, the demand for food from a growing population was increasing at a rate which, in many earlier periods, would have pushed prices up, but that the output of agriculture was growing even faster. How far that increase in output was due to the industry of man and how far to the vagaries of the weather must remain uncertain. But it is certainly tempting to speculate that improvements in farming were not simply the product of a process of adjustment to an independently determined fall in agricultural prices, but were themselves a significant cause of the price-fall. As E. L. Jones has suggested, the innovations which characterised the century before 1750 may have been initially stimulated by a change in the pattern of consumption and a consequent swing in the ratio of livestock to cereal prices which may have resulted from a temporary check to population growth in the seventeenth century. But it is likely that, once started, the process of agricultural improvement began to acquire life of its own, and that, by the early eighteenth century, it was producing cheaper food for a population which was once more able to grow.

Finally, whatever the truth of these speculations may be, the new estimates undoubtedly provide powerful quantitative support for the John–Jones view – which was largely derived from qualitative evidence – that rising agricultural productivity was the major factor in the growth of the economy as a whole in the early part of the eighteenth century.

In the first place, it seems likely that, in the first half of the century with which we are principally concerned here, the increase in output per head in agriculture was greater than in other sectors of the economy and it would appear that, in that period, rising agricultural productivity could indeed have accounted for most, if not all of the estimated increase in output and incomes per head of the population as a whole. Secondly, it seems probable that, after 1750, output per head in agriculture grew less rapidly than it had done earlier, particularly in the third quarter of the century; and although it recovered in the last two or three decades of the century, it is likely that by that time labour productivity was rising more rapidly outside agriculture than in it.

What was the significance of the increase in agricultural productivity in the first half of the eighteenth century for the development of the domestic market for industrial goods? If we assume that manufactures were a normal good, it follows that an increase in output per head in agriculture, by raising average real incomes, should have led to a higher demand for industrial goods. However, if productivity in agriculture rose faster than in other sectors of the economy, the effect on industrial demand may have been reduced by a relative decline in agricultural prices; this would probably tend to encourage consumers to spend rather more of their additional incomes on more and better food than would otherwise have been the case. The net effect on the demand for the products of industry would therefore depend on the relative magnitudes of the income and cross-price elasticities of demand for manufactured goods. Given the comparatively high income elasticity of demand for food indicated by Crafts' researches, it seems likely that, *ceteris paribus*, the income elasticity of demand for manufactured goods was not particularly high in eighteenth-century England; it was probably close to the figure of 1.25 suggested by Ippolito (1975). It is not surprising, therefore, that the estimates assembled in table 3.1 and in the appendix to this chapter imply that agricultural and industrial output rose at roughly the same rates in the first half of the eighteenth century, and that the consumption of food probably increased slightly more than the home consumption of manufactured goods. If the increase in incomes during the period was largely due to rising agricultural productivity, it seems equally clear that the modest increase of about thirteen per cent in the per capita consumption of manufactured goods over the period as a whole can be attributed to the same underlying cause.

At first sight, we might expect that, in the same way, good harvests would tend to stimulate industrial demand in the short term. Whether they really did so has been much debated. This is because the demand for foodstuffs in general, and cereals in particuar, tends to be relatively price inelastic; although this was probably less marked in eighteenth-century England than in some other places at other times, it is still probable that the average price elasticity of demand for food was less than unity. In consequence, the effect of the increase in output resulting from a good harvest would be a decline in the gross revenues of farmers and possibly landlords.

If we assume that in the long term supply and demand tended to be in equilibrium, a fall in prices of agricultural produce would not necessarily indicate a fall in the nominal and still less the real incomes of farmers and landlords, since relatively cheap food might, as suggested above, simply indicate that average costs of production were tending to fall faster in agriculture than in other sectors of the economy. This is probably what happened in the first half of the eighteenth century, since the productivity of agricultural labour seems to have risen by somewhere between 25 and 50 per cent at a time when the money wages of labourers in rural districts appear to have changed very little and the price of wheat seems to have declined by about 26 per cent in nominal, and 16 per cent in 'real' terms (Deane and Cole 1967: 91). It is true that a fall in labour costs per unit of output does not tell us what was happening to unit costs as a whole. But although the literary evidence does not suggest that inputs of land and capital declined in the period – and they probably rose (Jones 1970) – it is very unlikely that they increased at the same rate as agricultural output; there is certainly no warrant for assuming that the real incomes of farmers and landlords were lower at the end of the period than they had been at the beginning.

In the short run, agricultural costs were, for the most part, fixed in advance of the harvest, and indeed the only effect of an abundant harvest on production costs was to increase the amount of labour required to gather it. Hence, it is clear that, in the absence of large-scale imports or exports of foodstuffs, good harvests tended not only to decrease the gross receipts of the farming community but also to reduce their net disposable incomes. Admittedly, the decline in farmers' incomes involved a corresponding gain for food consumers; but since the gross receipts from the sale of agricultural produce must have been equal to gross purchases, the effect of this redistribution of incomes on industrial demand would have been precisely zero, unless there were significant differences in the marginal propensity of farmers and food consumers to buy manufactured goods (Ippolito 1975). But it is dangerous to assume that these differences were insignificant. The evidence we possess suggests, as we might expect, that agricultural labourers tended to spend more of their cash incomes on manufactured goods and less on food than their industrial counterparts (Stigler 1954: 97); it seems likely that the same may well have been true of farmers as compared with food consumers of similar levels of income. Moreover, Deane and Cole have argued that, in the early part of the eighteenth century, the wage labourers as a whole who gained most in relative terms from cheap food also had a high leisure preference; in consequence they tended to take out part of the benefits of increased real wages resulting from favourable harvests in the form of more leisure rather than higher real earnings (Dean and Cole 1967: 93). Hence it is quite possible that the income and distribution effects of good harvests pulled in opposite directions, and it is not surprising that there is no agreement as to the net effect on industrial demand. (See, *inter alia*, Ashton 1955; 1959; Habakkuk 1956; Mingay 1956; Gould 1962; John 1965; Deane and Cole 1967; Whitehead 1970; Ippolito 1975.)

It is even conceivable that at times the potentially adverse distribution effects of good harvests could have more than outweighted their positive income effects: a recent study of Asia in the late nineteenth and early twentieth centuries, for example, indicates that there may have been a positive relationship between rice prices and expenditure on imported cotton goods (Latham 1978: 144–7); Deane and Cole believed that a similar situation prevailed in early-eighteenth-century England. Whether this was indeed true in the English case may well be doubted. England, even in the eighteenth century, was not a poor agricultural country in which it is plausible to assume that relatively wealthy farmers, landlords and dealers in grain occupied a decisive position in the market for industrial goods. Moreover, as Whitehead (1970: 14) has pointed out, it is not easy to reconcile contemporary complaints of the scarcity and 'idleness' of labourers which Deane and Cole invoked in support of their leisure preference thesis with an actual decline in the demand for labour in periods of cheap food.

What is required to resolve the issue is a careful re-examination of the relationship between food prices and the consumption of manufactured goods. It would be desirable to construct indices of both food prices and total industrial output on an annual basis, preferably for harvest years, but this is impracticable. The estimates of industrial output in overlapping decades which were presented in table 3.1 are open to the objection that their behaviour may reflect medium-term adjustments to harvest fluctuations rather than the latter's immediate short-term effects. As it happens, however, a good deal of the controversy about the effects of harvest variations has been concerned with the consequences of successions of relatively good and bad seasons – particularly the long run of almost continuously low prices in the 1730s and 1740s – and it is of some interest, therefore, to see how far the behaviour of the series supports Deane and Cole's conclusions. What we have done, therefore, is to plot the percentage changes between overlapping decades of both wheat prices and the domestic consumption of industrial goods, with the results shown in figure 3.1.

It is immediately apparent from the diagram that, for the early part of the century, with which we are primarily concerned here, the relationship between wheat prices and the home consumption of industrial output was almost the exact opposite of that which Deane and Cole's interpretation of the data would lead us to expect. If attention is focused first on the upper part of the figure, which illustrates the movements in the actual prices of wheat and the total home consumption of industrial goods, it will be seen that there appears to be a fairly clear inverse relationship in the nine quinquennial intervals between 1700 and

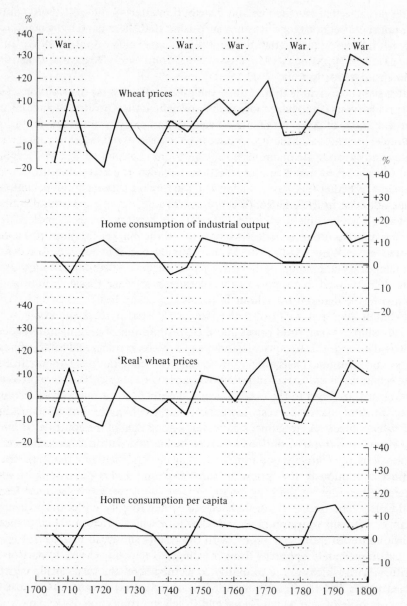

Figure 3.1 Fluctuations in wheat prices and the home consumption of industrial output (percentage changes between overlapping decades). Sources: Industrial output figures from table 3.1; wheat prices from table 23 in Deane and Cole (1967: 91).

1745. When the figures are adjusted to take account of changes in the general price level and the size of the population, the pattern is similar, except that in one of the intervals the relationship now appears to be positive: between 1730 and 1735 a fall in the price of wheat is accompanied by a fall in the rate of increase of home consumption per head of the population.

It is probable, however, that the exception was more apparent than real, since it appears likely that the increase in the volume of international trade, on which the estimates of industrial output heavily depend, is understated during this period as a result of a sharp increase in smuggling (Cole 1958), and this factor alone might well account for part of the discrepancy. Moreover, in the light of the discussion in chapter 2, it is probable that the estimates of the total population which have been used here to deflate the figures of home consumption, although reasonably acceptable as a means of discounting the long-term effects of population growth on the level of effective demand, may well be misleading when applied to short-term movements – particularly in the early part of the century, when fluctuations in the rate of population gave rise to quite significant changes in the dependency ratio. Thus, the apparent decline in the rate of increase in home consumption per head in the 1730s may indicate not so much a falling off in the level of effective demand per person employed, as an increase in the number of dependants supported by each worker.

Nevertheless, the data undoubtedly suggest that the home market was relatively depressed for much of the period between 1730 and 1750, although it is probable that this was the result of war rather than the generally good harvests of those years. Between 1735 and 1740, the outbreak of war was accompanied by a barely perceptible increase in wheat prices and the biggest fall in industrial demand in the course of the century; when wheat prices dropped again between 1740 and 1745 this served only to reduce the rate of decline in the home consumption of industrial goods. Eighteenth-century wars could, of course, affect the domestic economy in a variety of ways, but two are of particular importance in the present context. In the first place, it should be noted that in three of the major wars of the century – those of 1702–13, 1739–48 and 1775–83 – there was a sharp contraction in the volume of Britain's overseas trade, followed by a rapid postwar recovery; given the method of construction of the index of industrial production, these movements are bound to be reflected in our estimates of industrial output. Whether their impact was as great as the figures in table 3.1 suggest is, of course, another matter, but it would certainly be surprising if major disturbances in international trade had no effect at all on the level of economic activity at home.

There is, however, a second reason why most eighteenth-century wars had a particularly adverse effect on the home market. In each of the wars of the century, the terms of trade moved strongly against Britain, whereas in the intervals of peace the movement was usually favourable, particularly in the immediately postwar years when the cost of insurance and freight on the high seas might be expected to decline. This meant that incomes at home tended to be depressed in war-time and boosted in periods of peace irrespective of either the level of international trade or the state of the domestic harvest. The importance of this factor should not be underestimated. From the depths of the war-time depression *circa* 1710 to the 1730s, for example, import prices, relative to the prices of exports, probably fell by at least 40 per cent, whereas, in the same period the decline in the 'real' price of wheat was only about 20 per cent. It is true that agricultural produce probably accounted for roughly 40 per cent of domestic expenditure at this time, and imports for only about 10 per cent. Nevertheless, even if all agricultural prices declined at the same rate as the price of wheat during this period, these figures suggest that average real incomes may have risen by roughly eight per cent as a result of the fall in food prices (0.4 × 20) and by not less than four per cent because of the improvement in the terms of trade (0.1 × 40). Conversely, in the 1740s, when wheat prices were about the same as in the previous decade, but the terms of trade were about 28 per cent worse, this factor alone would have reduced real incomes at home by nearly three per cent.

If changes in the terms of trade could have potentially significant effects for good or ill on real incomes, and hence on the volume of industrial goods consumed at home, it should be remembered that they also tended to have the opposite effects on the volume of exports. The compensation was not necessarily complete, since it also appears to be true that in the eighteenth century as a whole Britain's trade balance usually tended to deteriorate in war-time, when the terms of trade were adverse, and to improve in peace, when the terms of trade were moving in her favour. But in the early part of the century the tendency for the domestic and export markets for industrial goods to fluctuate in opposite directions did mean that, although the overall pattern is similar, both the war-time depressions and the recovery boom after the first war of the century are rather less marked in the series for total industrial output than they are in the figures for home consumption which have been plotted in figure 3.1. In consequence, the strong negative relationship with the movement of wheat prices is even more pronounced in the former case than it is in the latter, so that it appears, somewhat paradoxically, that the state of the domestic harvest exerted a more powerful influence during this period on the demand for industrial output as a whole than it did on that portion of it which was consumed at home. The strength of the correlation is such that we may conclude that until 1745 the condition of the harvest was a major factor governing fluctuations in the demand for industrial goods in periods of war and peace alike. The breakdown of the decade averages of prices and output might modify the picture in detail. But within the limits considered here there seems little reason to doubt that, as Adam Smith suggested at the time, and others, notably T. S. Ashton have maintained since, cheap food did, on balance, stimulate rather than retard the growth of industrial demand.

After 1745, it seems at first sight much more difficult to establish a systematic connection between fluctuations in grain prices and industrial output; indeed, the graphs appear to suggest that the relationship was more often positive than negative. But on closer inspection it becomes clear that this was simply due to the fact that, whereas in the early eighteenth century the influence of wars and their aftermath usually reinforced the effect of harvest variations, in the middle decades of the century this was no longer true. Thus between c. 1745 and c. 1750, a recovery in international trade (and, in all probability a decline in smuggling), coupled with a favourable swing in the terms of trade at the end of the War of Austrian Succession, produced a sharp increase in recorded output for the home market, even though grain prices were rising at the time; on this occasion the trade balance improved so much that the increase in total industrial output was even larger. Similarly, the Seven Years' War of 1756–63 produced another, albeit minor, hiccough in the series. For although Britain's naval successes ensured that her overseas trade and industrial output continued to expand, the highly adverse terms of trade of the war years did lead to a noticeable dip in the production of goods for the home market, in spite of relatively favourable harvests at home. Finally, the virtual collapse of exports during the American War of Independence was accompanied by an apparent (if not an actual) decline in home output per head, and an even larger decline in total industrial output per head, notwithstanding the substantial fall in grain prices during the period; while the return of peace produced a virtual repetition in the period c. 1780–85 of the experience of c. 1745–50. On the other hand, if we ignore the temporary aberration produced by the Seven Years' War, in the course of the two decades between 1750 and 1770 the rates of increase of all the series for industrial output tended to fall steadily as grain prices rose; in the last fifteen years of the century, despite the impact of yet another war in the 1790s, wheat prices and industrial output once again fluctuated inversely as they had done in the early part of the century.

Thus, the evidence is consistent with the view that, in peace-time at least, the state of the harvest continued to be the major determinant of short-term fluctuations in industrial demand. Nevertheless, it must be emphasised that in terms of long-term trends the experience of the second half of the century was quite different from the first. Whereas in the period before 1750 the trend of grain prices was steadily downwards, in the latter part of the century it was just as clearly upwards – yet industrial output per head probably continued to expand in the third quarter of the century as fast as it had done earlier, and by the last two decades of the century it was evidently growing at an unprecedented rate. There is nothing surprising about the fact that food prices rose in the later period, since population was increasing more, and agricultural productivity was probably growing less rapidly than it had done earlier. To be sure, it was not long before output per head in agriculture was again displaying a strong upward tendency, and, if the national income estimates are to be believed, it is possible that, in the middle decades of the nineteenth century, real product per head of the occupied population rose faster in agriculture than in other sectors of the national economy (Deane and Cole 1967: 172), just as it seems to have done in the first half of the eighteenth. But whereas the earlier advances in labour productivity were apparently the outcome of relatively inexpensive technical improvements which made it possible to produce larger supplies of food at lower unit costs, so those of later periods seem to have been the product of costly schemes of Parliamentary enclosure, land reclamation and drainage, and the introduction of labour-saving machinery and chemical fertilisers, all of which demanded relatively high capital outlays. In other words, agriculture's role in the process of economic growth had become passive, not active; improvements in farming were not so much a force propelling the economy upwards as a response to the pressures of demand generated by population growth and developments in other sectors of the economy. If this was so, what was it that gave the British economy its upward thrust in the decades after 1750? Why was it that, in the third quarter of the century, total output and incomes expanded more rapidly, and average real incomes and industrial output per head continued to grow at roughly the same rate, when agriculture had ceased to perform the dynamic role it had played earlier?

The growth of the home market 1750–80

In the present state of our knowledge, our answers to these questions must necessarily be somewhat speculative and imprecise. There is no mystery about the fact that, as the estimates in table 3.2 (p. 57) suggest, industrial output which, in the early part of the century, had increased at roughly the same rate as the output of agriculture, now grew distinctly faster. For just as in the earlier period the movement of relative prices had tended to stimulate a relative increase in food consumption, so now it had the reverse effect; if we make the plausible assumption that the average income elasticity of demand for manufactured goods was slightly higher than that for food, then the estimated trends are roughly what we might expect. On the other hand, whereas in the early part of the century the burden of government on the economy had tended to decline, it now began to rise again as a result of the increasing frequency of wars in the middle decades of the century. These countervailing pressures meant, of course, that industrial output per head of the population could hardly have continued to expand as it had done previously unless average incomes were also growing.

Now, curiously enough, despite the evidence of the national product estimates, the available data on the movement of real wages give no indication that the real incomes of the labouring population were increasing during this period. In the first half of the century, as can be seen from figure 3.2, the long-term trends

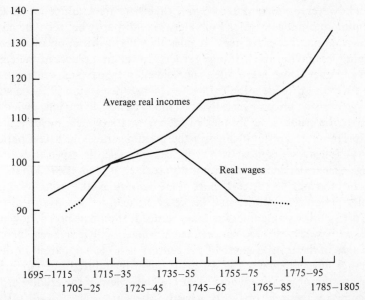

Figure 3.2 Trends in real wages, average real output and incomes 1695–1805 (log vertical scale: 1715–35 = 100). Sources: Average real output and incomes from table 3.2 (p. 64); real wages from the general index of money wages in table 5 of Deane and Cole (1967: 19) deflated by the cost-of-living index in Gilboy (1936).

in real wages and average real output and incomes were roughly similar, with the former tending to grow more rapidly than the latter until the 1730s and more slowly thereafter. In the second half of the century, on the other hand, average real output and incomes continued to increase, while real wages apparently fell.

Since the estimates of average product in fact relate to real output rather than incomes, it is likely that part of this disparity was due to the unfavourable movement of the terms of trade in the 1740s and 1750s, although the gap showed little sign of narrowing in the 1760s when the terms of trade again swung sharply in Britain's favour. It has been suggested that the growth of industrial demand in the third quarter of the century was to a large extent due to the increase in 'middle-class' incomes; this could have come about either as a result of a redistribution of incomes, or because a general growth in incomes brought an increasing proportion of the population into the 'spending' category (Eversley 1967). At first sight, the evidence on real wages would appear to suggest that the former explanation was the more likely and we certainly cannot rule out the possibility that there was some change in the distribution of income, for as was suggested in chapter 2 we might expect a rapidly growing population to push up land rents in relation to wages, while the spread of industrialisation may have led to some increase in the share of capital in the national product.

It is, however, important to recognise that there are a number of reasons why we cannot automatically infer from a growing disparity between the movement of real wages and average real incomes that the distribution of incomes was becoming less favourable to wage earners. In the first place, in the eighteenth century, money wages were often supplemented by payments in kind, and the latter tended to provide a limited hedge against the erosion of living standards in an age of rising prices. Secondly, the Gilboy cost-of-living index which is used to deflate the crude general index of money wages (which, incidentally, refers only to labourers and craftsmen in the building trades in a few parts of the country), is heavily weighted with the prices of foodstuffs, especially cereals; just as wage-earners tended to benefit most in real terms from the fall in the relative prices of foodstuffs in the early part of the century, so the rising food prices of the later period would have had the reverse effect, irrespective of any change in the distribution of incomes in money terms. It should be noted, however, that the disparity we have noted between the movement of average real incomes and real wages in the third quarter of the century is no less apparent in the trends of average *money* incomes and wages. It might be inferred, therefore, that this factor was not of great significance, although in view of the crudity of the data on incomes, wages and prices, it is hard to be sure.

Perhaps more important than either of these considerations is the fact that figures of average wages are not synonymous with actual earnings. Deane and Cole argued that in the early part of the century, wage-earners might have been inclined to take out part of the benefit of rising real wages in the form of increased leisure rather than higher earnings. In the same way, they suggested that, in the second half of the century, labourers may have been willing to work harder and longer to maintain their incomes in the face of rising prices, and it is also possible that earlier marriage and increasing dependency ratios could have had a similar effect. The emphasis in Deane and Cole's analysis was on the desire of workers to maintain a traditional standard of life, but the argument could be extended to cover a wish to preserve the gains made in the earlier period, or even to realise the rising expectations which may have been engendered by the increasing real wages of the first few decades of the century. It would clearly be unwise to make too much of this point, but in view of the contemporary evidence, referred to by Deane and Cole, of changing attitudes to labour about the middle of the century, of the well-attested propensity of the lower orders to 'ape their betters', and of the tendency for comparative luxuries, such as tea, to become in course of time, 'artificial necessaries', it would be equally rash to dismiss it entirely.

Moreover, there is also some evidence, though it is not easily quantifiable, that a somewhat larger proportion of the population may have begun to participate in productive activities about this time. It is well known that women and children had long been employed in domestic industries and on the farms. But it has also been suggested that, from about the 1760s onwards, more women and children began to be drawn into employment in the potteries and textile mills. How important the tendency was in this period we do not know. When it did occur, the result might be that, even though women and children earned much less than men, each family's income would be increased without any change in the wage-rates involved. This would not only tend to boost per capita incomes, but would also produce for employers the pleasant experience of rising demand for the products of their industries, coupled with falling unit labour costs (McKendrick 1974).

Both these considerations would suggest that increasing labour inputs may have helped to push up per capita incomes despite static or even falling wages. But we cannot ignore the possibility that there may also have been some gains in the output per unit of labour employed which were stimulated by the same forces which tended to encourage higher labour inputs. We saw in the first chapter that whereas a simple Malthusian model might lead us to expect that a rising population would tend to depress average incomes, it is also possible that, by stimulating investment and innovation (and labour inputs), it could actually have the opposite effect. At first sight, these models, based as they are on different assumptions, appear to be irreconcilable. But it is well known that the effect of an increase in population on real output and incomes depends on the balance between population and other factors of production, notably land and capital, and the rate of technical progress. Thus, if an economy is under-populated and relatively well endowed with land and capital, an increase in its population, and hence in its labour force, will lead, not only to an increase in total output, but also – as a result of increased opportunities for the more efficient utilisation of resources, specialisation and division of labour, and lower transaction costs in the commercial sector – to an increase in average output and for incomes as well. Moreover, in such an economy, characterised by increasing returns to labour, the marginal product of labour, and hence real wages, are likely to rise even more than average output and incomes.

But as population approaches its 'optimum' level, these gains will begin to be exhausted and diminishing returns will set in. Since the supply of land is fixed, at least in a closed economy, diminishing returns to labour are likely to become apparent first in the agricultural sector. Hence it is not surprising to find that if we disaggregate the figures for England in the late eighteenth century, real wages were still rising in the industrial districts of Lancashire when they were apparently falling quite fast in the rural areas of the south. At this stage we may also find that even though average real wages are falling, average output and incomes continue to rise: indeed, they will continue to do so as long as the output of each additional unit of labour is higher than the average of those already employed. But eventually a point is reached at which the marginal product of labour falls below its average product and then, of course, average output and incomes must also begin to fall.

60

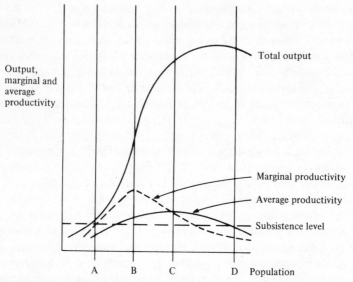

Figure 3.3 The link between population and output. A. Physiological minimum population. B. Population level where the marginal productivity of labour is at a peak, i.e. total output grows at its fastest rate. C. Population level consonant with the highest per capita income level. D. Physiological maximum population. Source: Derived from De Vries (1974: 78).

So far we have been dealing with a static portrayal of the model, as illustrated in figure 3.3, in which it is assumed that the state of technology is fixed. But, in practice, new techiques may well be introduced, and in that case the economy's position on the economic curves marked in the diagram will be pushed back to the left. Now Malthusian versions of the model do not assert that increases in real incomes never occur or that no new techniques are ever introduced, but only that in the long run the tendency towards diminishing returns engendered by a steadily rising population is likely to outweigh the influence of these countervailing tendencies. If, however, the flow of new technology is great enough then the economy will be able to achieve sustained growth and so escape the Malthusian trap. What the alternative version of the model referred to above suggests is that this outcome may be made more likely if the increase in aggregate demand engendered by an increasing population stimulates investment and innovation and an intensified search for new techniques. Whether this favourable outcome actually materialises depends not only on the rate of population growth and the economic opportunities available in any particular situation, but also on the response of the human beings involved.

What insights does this version of the model offer us for illuminating the economic experience of England in the third quarter of the eighteeenth century during the run up to the 'industrial revolution'? No-one would claim that there were no innovations in agriculture or industry at the time, but even a nodding acquaintance with the economic history of the period would suggest that among the more important developments must be numbered the improvements in inland transport, notably the extension of turnpike roads and the construction of the first proper canals. These advances did not, of course, take place suddenly in the second half of the century: there had been significant improvements in river navigation well before 1750, and the turnpiking of the major routes radiating from London was, for the most part, carried out in the 1730s and 1740s. Nevertheless, the second half of the century did witness a quickening of the tempo of investment in the transport sector which is of particular significance from our present point of view. For investments of this kind are likely to be particularly sensitive to changes in aggregate demand, since the capital outlays involved are both 'lumpy' and relatively large, and the prospects of an adequate return for the private investor depend heavily on the actual or potential volume of goods and passengers to be carried. Hence if the slow expansion of the economy had already begun to generate expenditure on transport improvements before 1750, we might well expect that the faster growth of population and total output after that date would encourage a corresponding increase of activity in this field. Unfortunately the precise effects of these developments on per capita incomes in the third quarter of the century is at present unknown. It has, however, been estimated that as a result of the coming of the railways in the nineteenth century the national income in 1865 was perhaps ten per cent higher than it otherwise would have been; the rough estimate in chapter 12 suggests that the social savings achieved by the canals of the eighteenth century were probably of the same order of magnitude. If we suppose that the effects of improvements in the roads and the construction of canals combined meant that in, say, 1780, the national income of England and Wales was ten per cent greater than it would have been in their absence, this would imply in the relatively slow moving economy of that period that most of the improvement in average incomes during the previous thirty or forty years could be attributed to these developments alone.

But if advances in transport during this period did have a significant impact on the economy as a whole, we may well ask why the gains achieved are not reflected in the movement of real wages. The answer is not far to seek. For the apparent decline in real wages in the period 1750–80 (and, indeed the increase in the early part of the century) is largely due to the movement of Mrs Gilboy's cost-of-living index which has been used to deflate the index of money wages. The prices used in the construction of this index were those paid by institutions in southern England; all of them were for goods bought on contract for periods of varying length, some approximated to wholesale rather than retail prices, and several of the series were for unprocessed foods and raw materials, which would be unlikely to reflect any fall in cash terms as a result of economies in transport and distribution. Given the movement of agricultural prices, it is not surprising that the index indicates no clear trend in the cost of living between 1730 and 1755 and a fairly steady increase thereafter. An alternative index by Dr Tucker (1936) which is based wholly on the retail prices of finished consumer goods in London, indicates that the cost of living was rising in the 1730s and 1740s and was more stable between 1753 and 1793. As it happens, Tucker's index has not always been favoured by historians, and it was not used here, partly because it only starts in 1729, and partly because its construction involved a good deal of interpolation for the part of the eighteenth century which it does cover. But it certainly provides an important corrective to the Gilboy index, and may well indicate more accurately what was happening to the cost of living during the third quarter of the century.

In short the argument so far suggests that per capita incomes continued to increase after 1750, partly because the pressure of a more rapidly increasing population on living standards may have encouraged more people to seek employment and those who were already employed to work harder and longer hours, and partly because the increase in aggregate incomes and demand may have prompted businessmen and others to invest resources in more efficient methods of production, particularly, but by no means exclusively, in the field of transport. But in the tug of war which was generated by a rising population, between diminishing returns in agriculture and harder and more productive effort by enterprising people in other sectors of the economy, living standards might well not have survived long if the farming community had remained inert. In fact, however, we know that it did not. It seems possible that in the long period of slow but steady agricultural advance in the century before 1750 most of the productivity gains which could easily be won from the light soils of eastern England had already been achieved, and, in the third quarter of the century, agricultural improvement in this area seems to have been somewhat muted. But the upward movement of agricultural prices which characterised the late eighteenth century was also accompanied by successive waves of Parliamentary enclosure which helped to facilitate the extention of improved techniques into the heavier, wetter soils of midland England. The first of these waves reached its peak around 1770 when the real price of wheat was back to the high level of 1710, and, as we have seen, farm prices dropped sharply in the years which followed. During the period of the American War, the income released by this relatively cheap food, coupled with the high level of government spending referred to in the first chapter may have helped to sustain economic activity at home in the face of the collapse of exports, albeit at the expense of a sharp, if temporary, deterioration in the country's trade balance. When peace returned, exports revived and food prices remained low, conditions were unusually favourable for the surge of innovation in the cotton and iron industries which has traditionally been regarded as marking the onset of the industrial revolution. And when that happened, of course, the demand for manufactured goods was no longer primarily dependent on overseas markets, or on modest productivity gains in other sectors of the domestic economy, but could begin to expand at an unprecedented rate as a result of much more rapid advances in productivity in the industrial sector itself.

Concluding remarks

The discussion in this chapter has been far from exhaustive; but enough has been said to indicate that changes in the composition and level of demand have a part to play in explaining how and why England became the world's first industrial nation. We saw in the first chapter that while some economists accord considerable importance to the role of demand in the process of economic growth, others deny that at the level of the economy as a whole it has any independent significance. The issues in dispute will recur later in this book, but in the light of the discussion here it may perhaps be suggested that it is ultimately impossible to accommodate the complexity of historical experience within the straightjacket of any single economic model. Supply may create its own demand, but only if there are customers both able and willing to buy; and no amount of demand will generate an increase in supply unless producers are both able and willing to respond. On both sides of the equation economic constraints are involved, but on both sides, too, there are human beings whose behaviour helps to determine whether opportunities for the creation and consumption of wealth are seized or go by default. The long swings in the growth of population and changing conditions in international markets, for example, which helped to shape the economic opportunities open to successive generations of eighteenth-century Englishmen, were not without parallel in earlier periods of history. But part at least of the explanation of how and why Britain experienced both growth and a unique and remarkable transformation of her economy during that period must surely be that the economic expectations of her people were rising and that enough of them, both as producers and consumers, were willing and able to take the steps necessary to satisfy them.

Appendix
Estimates of English national product in the eighteenth century

The estimates in table 3.2 are based on revised versions of the index numbers of real output in Deane & Cole (1967: 78). Deane and Cole's index for Government services and defence was used unchanged. So, too, was their index of the output of industry and commerce, except that minor corrections were made to the figures for 1780–1800, since in constructing their sub-index of the output of export industries they apparently omitted to make the necessary adjustment to allow for the fact that the trade figures for the later years of the century refer to Great Britain, and not England and Wales. The index

Table 3.2. *The national product of England and Wales in the eighteenth century*

	Agriculture		Agriculture and commerce		All other		Total	Average
	(£m.)	(%)	(£m.)	(%)	(£m.)	(%)	(£m.)	(%)
			A. At 1700 prices					
1700	20.0	40	16.5	33	13.5	27	50.0	9.45
1710	20.6	38	17.2	32	16.2	30	53.9	9.79
1720	24.1	42	19.6	34	13.9	24	57.5	10.16
1730	23.6	40	21.1	36	14.0	24	58.7	10.50
1740	26.1	41	21.6	34	16.4	26	64.1	10.80
1750	28.1	40	24.6	35	17.7	25	70.4	11.35
1760	28.9	35	29.6	36	23.4	29	81.9	12.37
1770	29.0	36	33.0	41	18.3	23	80.3	11.52
1780	31.5	34	32.2	35	28.3	31	92.0	12.16
1790	33.4	32	46.2	44	24.4	23	104.1	12.67
1800	36.2	27	61.0	45	38.6	28	135.8	14.83
			B. At current prices					
1700	20.0	40	16.5	33	13.5	27	50.0	9.45
1710	20.4	39	16.2	31	15.3	29	51.9	9.41
1720	18.2	38	17.1	36	12.2	26	47.4	8.38
1730	18.2	38	18.0	37	12.0	25	48.2	8.63
1740	18.4	37	18.1	36	13.8	27	50.3	8.46
1750	20.7	37	20.6	37	14.9	26	56.2	9.06
1760	25.1	34	27.1	37	21.4	29	73.6	11.11
1770	33.5	41	30.5	38	16.9	21	80.9	11.60
1780	34.1	35	33.1	34	29.1	30	96.4	12.73
1790	40.6	35	49.8	43	26.2	22	116.6	14.20
1800	74.3	35	84.8	40	53.6	25	212.7	23.22

numbers for agriculture and rents and services (other than government and defence) were re-computed on the basis of the new population estimates in chapter 2 above, and the agricultural index for 1700–40 was also revised in accordance with the method proposed by Crafts (1976).

The index numbers of real output were then converted into estimates of the value of national product at the prices of *c*. 1700 on the arbitrary assumption that the national income in 1700 was £50 million and its industrial distribution the same as that suggested by Gregory King's estimates for 1688. Rough estimates of national product at current prices were obtained by multiplying the figures for the real product of agriculture by Deane and Cole's index of wheat prices and for all other sectors by their index of other prices (Deane and Cole 1967: 91).

It should be emphasised that these revised estimates are still very crude, and the figures for individual decades are subject to the same qualifications as Deane and Cole's original series. But the revised figures should indicate more accurately the pattern of change in the course of the century; and it is interesting to note that the estimate of the national product at current prices *c*. 1800 is broadly consistent with Deane and Cole's estimate of £232 million in 1801 for Great Britain (or about £200 million for England and Wales alone), and that the industrial distribution is also very similar. The new estimates also suggest similar proportions for the major sectors to those implied in Arthur Young's estimate for 1770, although the absolute levels of the new figures are, of course, much lower than his.

4

Agriculture, 1700–80

E. L. JONES

Agricultural output

In terms of the efficiency of resource use and the absolute increase of output the achievement of British agriculture during the eighteenth century was a considerable one. It was not, however, dramatic or dramatically brought about. The methods used and the institutional forms were in neither case new and no convincing starting date can be found during the century for any process that might be labelled an 'agricultural revolution'. The agricultural growth of the eighteenth century was, as it were, a part of the history of an expanding universe, not something that began with a 'big bang'.

Although total output rose markedly the increase can be measured only imperfectly, while assessments of the changes in factor inputs and the shifts in technologies employed are more imperfect still. The difficulties stem from an almost total absence of aggregate data – no national production figures were collected – or of data which may be summed into aggregates. There was of course a large number of landed estates and a very large number of farms, indeed more business units than in any other sector of the economy, and documentary evidence survives for a large absolute number of these, though it is hard to be sure how reliably any sample of this evidence represents the universe from which it was drawn. Certainly the evidence, supplemented by contemporary publications of a descriptive or expository kind which became numerous towards the end of the century, conveys the impression of intense managerial and technically innovative activity. This does not demonstrate indisputably that aggregate output went up, but no-one who has worked through any substantial fraction of the evidence would suppose anything else.

Material of this type does permit some understanding of the technological and organisational machinery that ground out a bigger output. In the absence of aggregate data, and with a proper concern for 'how' as well as precisely 'how much', the specialist literature of agricultural history has concentrated on describing this machinery, in its infinite local adaptations, in an effort to replace the 'stylised facts' that make up, or until recently made up, accounts of an 'agricultural revolution' in textbooks of economic history. Much of this work has been inspired by an intuition that because changes in agriculture were

66

obviously important to the industrial changes of the late eighteenth century the changes in the two sectors were essentially contemporaneous. Studies have accordingly not probed as far back before that century as the nature of agricultural growth seems to warrant.

There are, then, virtually no direct figures on aggregate agricultural supply. Some aggregate trade data do exist, but by themselves they are not very informative. They show that the net export of wheat and wheaten flour, which was rising in the late seventeenth and early eighteenth centuries until it reached a peak in 1750, turned into a net import in the years 1757 and 1758 and regularly from 1767. The last thirty years of the century also experienced a steep fall in the export of malt. Further, the abolition of the protective Cattle Acts (dating from the 1660s) permitted livestock products to come in from Ireland after 1758. Data on the Irish trade are more than usually insecure because large differences exist between the series for Irish despatches and British receipts, but apparently between 1760 and 1790 beef exports from Ireland to Great Britain rose by 297 per cent, butter by 494 per cent, and pork by 247 per cent (Cullen 1968: table 17, p. 70). It is impossible to say with any accuracy what proportion of the British population was fed by these imports without assuming the answer to a question which exercises scholars, that is, what was the average annual consumption of various foods per capita. Nevertheless it is possible, on flimsily validated assumptions about average per capita consumption, to multiply such figures by population totals and obtain some notion not only of the proportion of the population fed by imports (as well as the additional population which early eighteenth-century grain exports might have fed) but also of hypothetical domestic output totals. This may be done for 1700 and 1800, for which dates we have both trade and population estimates, the comparison of which gives us a measure of eighteenth-century agricultural performance. The results are of course purely illustrative and are not intended to masquerade as historical data.

Concerning the proportion of the British population that may have been fed from the export or import of all foods that were traded on any scale (Deane & Cole 1967; Mitchell & Deane 1962; Cullen 1968): 444 590 cwt of meat (beef and port) imported from Ireland in 1800 at a 1940s British ration allowance of 8 ounces per week, a figure chosen to provide a low standard of consumption, would have given 1 915 156 annual rations, or enough to have fed 18 per cent of the (1801) population of 10 686 000; 208 686 cwt of Irish butter, at a 1940s ration of a total of 6 ounces of butter and margarine per week, would have supplied 1 198 589 annual rations, or enough to have fed 11 per cent of the population; 1 243 000 qtrs of wheat and wheaten flour imported net in 1800, at an annual consumption of one quarter per head as suggested by contemporary assertions, would have supplied the equivalent of 12 per cent of the population; an export of 98 000 qtrs in 1700 (the figure is actually that for 1701, which is much more representative of the decade 1700–09) could have fed the equivalent

Table 4.1 *English population and agricultural output* 1500–1800

1500	3 000 000 population = output
1600	Between 3 750 000 and 4 100 000 population = output
1700/01	5 070 000 population + 1 % = output
1800/01	9 170 000 population − 10 % = output
1600/1500	Output gain of between 25 % and 37 %
1700/1600	Output gain of between 25 % and 36 %
1800/1700	Output gain of 61 %

Sources: (Clapham 1949: 186; see table chapter 2.1, p. 21 above; Clarkson 1971: 26 and passim).
Note: = in this table means that the population was fed by the agricultural output of the time, plus or minus exports and imports

of 1.4 per cent of the population (6 866 000). Since wheat did not constitute the sole item of diet we may say for the sake of argument that food production for the equivalent of 1 per cent of the British population was exported in 1700.

The implication of these calculations may be that something of the approximate order of 90 per cent of the population of Great Britain was being fed by domestic agricultural production in 1800 whereas 101 per cent had been in 1700. If the figure for 1800 seems out of line with the calculations about imports this is because an allowance has been made for spoilage during storage and distribution and because the use of 1940s ration allowances as deflators may be severe. This of course fails to take into account trends in the output of a wide range of minor foodstuffs, while any concentration on food alone must slight the role of agriculture as a producer of fibres and other raw materials, of horses for transport and industry, and miscellaneous products.

If the unknowns of real incomes and demand elasticities may be ignored, although doing so actually involves quite strong assumptions, these calculations may be extended to make a comparison – for England and Wales only – of the proportionate increases in domestic farm output during the sixteenth, seventeenth and eighteenth centuries. By equating the supply of all agricultural products with the demand for them as indicated by estimates of the population (see chapter 2 above), adding 1 per cent for net exports in 1700 and subtracting the notional 1 per cent for imports in 1800 (i.e. ignoring pre-eighteenth-century trade in food, which was small, as well as any trade with Scotland, ignoring any change in the share of grain output saved for seed, and ignoring any change in the output of substitutes such as the catch of fish) the range of figures in table 4.1 is generated.

We may conclude that the percentage increase in total output during the eighteenth century – which is what we are asked to explain – was approximately double that of each of the two preceding centuries. In terms of quality of output the performance may have been even better, giving nutritionally superior diets and more choice of products, though associated improvements in communications, handling and distribution made some of them consequent on the concentration of facilities that accompanied greater regional specialisation. Of course, in finer focus the history of eighteenth-century agriculture becomes an account of numerous adjustments in the volume and composition of output to changing price levels and changes in the relative prices of products, an eloquent instance being the rapidity with which sheep breeds were remoulded, and new breeds evolved, in response to alterations in the ratio of mutton and wool prices.

Factor inputs

The output gains of the preceding centuries had probably only been made by devoting very large shares of society's resources to agriculture; the eighteenth century, with smaller reserves of wasteland to start with and a much more marked withdrawal of resources into the urban and industrial sectors, may have achieved what it did with a proportionately smaller increase in inputs. Certainly there is a considerable intrinsic interest in eighteenth-century agriculture since even in 1800 it was a very large sector of the economy, employing almost one-third of the occupied population, accounting for almost two-thirds of the national capital stock, and producing over one-third of national income (Deane & Cole 1967: 142, 161, 271), as well as exerting a strong influence on the forms of urbanisation and industrialisation. At the national aggregate level there are however almost no reliable figures for factor inputs and any discussion of productivity gains involves some element of shadow-boxing. Fortunately there are enough fragments of primary evidence about individual inputs and their combination to throw some light on an achievement that we know was of positive sign and healthy magnitude. An indirect light is also available from the batteries of price, wage and rent data (see chapter 6).

In the long run production alters because of changes in the use of the following factors: land, labour, investment capital, technology and methods of organisa- tion. We will first discuss some major influences on the provision and quality of the three classical factors (land, labour, investment capital), rather briefly given the paucity of aggregate estimates, and devote our main discussion to various improvements in the way the factors were combined and to the socio-political determinants of agricultural growth.

Land

First, land. According to the only available estimate the 'used area' of England and Wales was 29 000 000 acres in 1696, or more probably *c.* 1688 (Williams 1970: 55–69). This figure is obtained by subtracting Gregory King's estimate of the extent of 'wasteland' from the total area of the two countries. *Circa* 1800 the 'used area', obtained by the same method, was 31 810 000 acres, indicating an accession of 'used land' by reclamation from the 'waste' of 7.3 per cent. The problem is to establish what the residual category here called 'used land' may mean. Obviously the bulk, of it was farmland but this does not demonstrate that the addition to it from the 'waste' represented a *net* gain of agricultural land. On the one hand much of this 'waste' was already in agricultural use, mostly as common land used for pastoral purposes, and therefore at a low intensity. The *General Views* of the agriculture of individual counties, from which the estimate for 1800 is derived, variously describe it as common, fen, bog, salt-marsh, marsh, moor, forest, heath and warren. Reclamation of land of these types often meant an increased intensity of occupation rather than totally new additions to the cropped acreage such as assarting (grubbing up woodland) would give. On the other hand in a time of rapid industrialisation and urbanisation there were offsetting transfers of land to non-agricultural uses, which a calculation based on estimates of wasteland cannot allow for. 7.3 per cent must therefore be treated as an upper bound; perhaps 5 per cent would be a reasonable figure for the increase in agricultural land. It is out of the question that the proportionate addition to the area of farmland during the eighteenth century could have matched the estimated increase of 61 per cent in total agricultural output. That came from a greater intensity of land use. Using the estimates of 'used land' and assuming again that 101 per cent of the population of England and Wales was fed from domestic supplies in 1700 and 90 per cent in 1800, one acre would have fed 0.18 persons in 1700 and 0.26 persons in 1800. In other words output per acre had risen 44 per cent.

2. *Labour*

Second, labour. It is possible to make some calculations as to the magnitude of the labour supply at the beginning and end of the eighteenth century, once again with no special confidence. Gregory King's view, according to Kuznets, was that *c.* 1688 some 60 per cent of the population (Kuznets 1963: 143) or according to Deane 68 per cent (Deane 1965: 13–14) of families were occupied wholly in agriculture. The number of mixed occupations was however very large and it is not clear how 'pure' the farmers were. Many farm families, especially on small acreages and particularly in the north and north-west of the country, were heavily involved with rural domestic manufacturing and with distribution and various services. The farmers of some districts were farmers in name only. Daniel Defoe's *A Tour Through England and Wales* (1724), which referred in reality mainly to the reign of Queen Anne (1702–14), provides an illustration from the West Riding, where a dense population was no more engaged in farming than to run a few hens and a horse or two (used to pack cloth to market) behind the cottages in which was carried on the business of weaving. Measuring labour time, not individuals, in agriculture, though impossible in practice, is really what a situation with mixed occupations calls for. It may be acceptable to assign 60 per cent of the population to farming in 1700, i.e. 3042000 in England and Wales. For 1801 we have the census proportion of 36 per cent of the population in agriculture, forestry and fishing, giving the slightly inflated 'agricultural' figure of 3301000 or an increase of 8.5 per cent over the century. (Compare chapter 1 above. The 60 per cent proportion in agriculture in 1700 is readily acceptable for a country which had relatively high per capita real incomes.) The proportionate rise is more significant than the absolute figures, which are fractions of the whole population and not of the occupied portion. As with land, the increase in the input of labour is far below the figure of 61 per cent for the increase in total output. Measured in terms of labour productivity, agriculture had made big strides. One way of assessing this, using the figures for labour force and output advanced, is to say that one person engaged in farming in 1700 fed 1.7 persons, whereas in 1800 one person fed 2.5 persons, an increase of 47 per cent.

The so-called New Husbandry of the eighteenth century demanded a larger absolute workforce (for some calculations for notional farms, see Timmer 1969). The farm workforce, however, grew by only some 8.5 per cent compared with a rise of 81 per cent in the total population of England and Wales. There was sufficient demand for labour outside agriculture in a period of urbanisation and industrialisation to hold the growth of the sector's labour force to this lower rate. Its recruitment was from a fraction of the natural increase in the rural population, coupled with the extension of wage labour among that self-employed cottager class which decreased sharply after the time of Gregory King, who put it at 25 per cent of the population. This potential source of labour included many who did not strictly farm, for they had no rights to cultivate land (or enough land), only rights to gather the natural products of the soil and to run a few stock. As new areas were brought under cultivation and the commons abridged, this peripheral population was provided with new, on-the-spot opportunities of wage-earning to offer the reduced opportunities to pick up a thin, independent, living. The enclosure movement, by overriding mere hearsay and customary rights, regularised the employment of these people.

As to changes in the quality of the labour supply, few useful aggregative statements may be made. Some remarks may however be passed about 'qualitative' improvements in the sense of a more flexible supply. As the relaxation of settlement laws (part of the poor laws which had restricted migration within the country) permitted permanent movements into areas with a rising demand for labour, such as newly-cultivated districts, it may be said that the available labour force was deployed more efficiently. Agricultural labourers 'ranged from parish to parish and from county to county unthinking of and undeterred by the law of settlement' (John Howlett 1978; quoted by Holderness 1976: 193). In addition there was no check to the continued elaboration of a network of seasonal flows towards districts with heavy demands for labour at certain times of the year, such as turnip-hoeing (sometimes carried out by specialist gangs even at the beginning of the eighteenth century), hay-making and the harvests of fruit, hops, and grain. There were already in 1700 established annual migrations of harvesters and hop-pickers deep into England from Wales and Scotland and these grew over time. Within England areas where the usual time of harvest differed by a few weeks effectively exchanged harvest labour. There was a holiday atmosphere about harvesting as well as bonus rates of pay which continued to draw out urban labour into the fields in late summer, to the dismay of manufacturers whose demands for labour were also likely to be at a peak at that season as they tried to stock up for post-harvest sales. Since some manufacturing work was still performed by the farm sector at the end of the century, perhaps the intersectoral exchanges of labour cancel out. At any rate it may be observed that farmers enjoyed a more sensitively responsive labour market than was once thought.

3. Capital

Third, capital. Estimates of total capital in the agricultural sector are still more precarious than those available for land and labour and are sometimes unusable because they lump together land and capital or are even obtained by grossing up parliamentary enclosure costs alone. While it would be possible to construct series on capital formation from samples of estate and farm accounts the enormous labour involved has not yet been undertaken. We do have the estimates by Feinstein (see chapter 7 below) of fixed capital formation and working capital in agriculture, though unfortunately only for the period from 1760 (table 4.2).

Fixed capital was built up by the construction of new farmhouses and steadings, accommodation roads, fences and ditches. Many of these items represented some net addition to the stock of farm capital, though the gain was not as substantial as appears at first sight. For example, the farmsteads erected in the centre of new, ring-fenced holdings after enclosure or reclamation were not necessarily completely new units. They were typically superior replacements for farms originally in the village street, the original farmhouses being retained and subdivided into workers' cottages. Much of the actual land remodelling consequent on reclamation of the 'waste' or enclosure involved of course an addition pure and simple to the stock of physical assets; but much of the investment in it may not have involved the investment of savings or the borrowing of capital, but rather may have been created by the redeployment of the existing farm workforce in slack seasons. The evidence of activity in these respects during the first sixty years of the century does suggest that there was a sizeable net addition to fixed capital in agriculture over the century as a whole.

Similarly, growth in farm operators' working capital over the entire century

Table 4.2. *Capital and capital formation in agriculture* 1760–1810

(a) Fixed capital formation in agriculture (at 1851–60 prices)		
1761–70	£2.18m. p.a.	
1801–10	£4.06m. p.a.	

(b) Working capital in agriculture (at 1851–60 prices)		
	1760	1800
Harvested and standing crops £56m.	£69m.	
Livestock	£66m.	£89m.
Farm horses	£16m.	£27m.
Total	£138m.	£185m.

Source: Feinstein 1978.

is not to be doubted. Until the founding of the country banks towards the end of the century there was no normal, impersonal market on which farmers could borrow to augment their working capital. But there were extensive chains of credit within the rural community, often pieced together by attorneys who as a profession had apparently been drawn to this activity by the volume of business involved in land sales soon after the Civil War and the emergence at that period of an active mortgage market.

The one systematic, though local and cautious, study (Holderness 1975: 94–115) surveys the evidence of 'credits' listed in the probate inventories for part of Lincolnshire and describes some interesting features, though the area was one in which the role of big landowners may have been less than would have been the case over much of the country. Conclusions of general applicability, since they accord with scattered evidence from elsewhere, are that there was no real class of usurers; loans from kinsfolk (which were treated in a businesslike manner) and from landowners and (at times when farmers had cash-flow difficulties) from shopkeepers provided the flow of credit. All available local funds were seemingly out at interest, at rates comparable with those in London. The flow of credit did fluctuate with major swings in farm product prices, suggesting a tightening in working capital available for big projects during price depressions, though the diffusion of 'new' crops was not interrupted and the suggestion is that expenditures on household goods and farm equipment were maintained at such times out of reserves. The overall impression is that expenditures on items of working capital, including the comparatively cheap requirements for extending mixed farming on established farms, were not much curtailed by spells of low product prices, although there were complaints by farmers at times of general money shortage that they had inadequate funds for restocking; an example is for instance William Marshall's comments on 1782 (Marshall 1795: vol. II, 102–7). As to the security of capital investment, this was strengthened during the century by the spread of fire insurance cover and by government compensation for animals slaughtered during cattle plagues. Working capital was informally but perhaps decisively free from some of the short-term risk caused by price falls by the periodic, even rhythmic, acceptance of part of the loss by landowners who remitted a portion of the rent or absolved tenants from some rent arrears.

Social and political context

The various increases in factor inputs worked themselves out within a particular structure of society and polity which had attained a distinct new flexibility during the previous century, notably in the period after the Restoration. A very large fraction of all farm output was now intended for the market. Within agriculture, several technological and organisational developments popularly associated with the eighteenth century had been pioneered, even established quite firmly, at that time (Thirsk 1970; Jones 1970). The political circumstances of the seventeenth century had enabled diverse groups of Englishmen of the landed class to obtain experience of the intensive farming of the Low Countries and to adapt methods and crops from there to the circumstances of many parts of Britain long before the century was out. Trade involving the export of malting barley to the Low Countries and the import of clover seed thence was developed. Most significant of all, parliaments after the Restoration of 1660 and *a fortiori* after the Glorious Revolution of 1688 entrenched their own landowner interests so deeply that government became thoroughly responsive to the interests of the farm producers rather than the interests of the crown's subjects as consumers, hitherto afforded the supposed protection of Acts restricting enclosure, trade in grain, and the like. Adam Smith, who was much impressed by the notion that welfare increases not only as income rises but as it is spread evenly over time, and by the regulating function of the corn merchant in bringing this about, thought that an Act for the encouragement of trade (1663) (Statutes of the realm, vol. 5, pp. 449–52) 'has perhaps contributed more to the plentiful supply of the home market and to the increase of tillage, than any other law in the statute book'. This was an Act which permitted the buying of grain to sell it again as long as prices did not rise above certain rather high levels (Smith 1776: vol. II, 34). As further examples, general tax revenues were employed to pay bounties on the export of grain, until the burden on the exchequer became insupportable in 1750; compensation was offered for cattle slaughtered in the epizoötics (animal plagues) of 1714 and the mid-eighteeenth century, while impediments to enclosure and investment in agricultural land in general were removed in the 1660s (Jones 1970: 65–6). With these and other instances of tenderness towards production – such as an unprecedented tendency to favour enclosure – the environment of risk for farming was rendered a little less rocky.

There were favourable changes in the infrastructure as well as in the institutional rules governing agriculture. Regional specialisation, begun much earlier under the sway of the London market, was accelerated by transport improvements, notably the canalisation of rivers during the seventeenth century – again especially after the Restoration. Of the mileage of navigable waterway at 1800, about one-third was naturally navigable, and another third was river canalised between 1600 and 1760, and the remaining third consisted of canals built from 1760 to 1800. Although, by 1750, 55 turnpike acts had already been passed, it was the extension of navigable waterway that was important for the movement of agricultural commodities, chiefly grain, since livestock continued to travel to market 'on the hoof' until the railway age.

The hardening three-way socioeconomic division into landowners, tenant farmers, and hired labourers touched production more directly. These categories gained ground at the expense of the smaller owner-occupiers and the class of independent cottagers with enough miscellaneous common rights, real or assumed, to have kept them largely out of the wage labour market hitherto. The landed estate system, with capital, enterprise and management supplied jointly by the landowner (increasingly supported by an army of professional stewards, land agents, surveyors and so forth) and the tenant may be conceptualised as a device for sharing risk. The manner in which landowners characteristically came to remit a proportion of the rent or wrote off arrears in years of very low prices, although they doubtless set the nominal level of rent high enough to recoup on an average of years, indicates a stabilising function.

The security of the estate system had been heightened by a device of Restoration conveyancers, strict settlement, which broke through the common law's stern time limits on restrictions over powers of ownership. Strict settlement made the eldest son of a landed family the life tenant of an estate instead of an absolute owner who could sell the land to pay his personal debts. As life tenant, however, he was able to obtain large mortgages against the estate's rental income, a practice that reached its extreme in the system of 'post-obiting' whereby a son took loans from London money-lenders, to be repaid, at frightful rates of interest, on coming into the estate at his father's death. Such a situation gave the landowner or prospective landowner, as life tenant, an inducement to seek out efficient stewards and tenants who would keep up or advance the level of rent payments, as well as some incentive, strongly abetted by fashion, to take a personal interest in farming methods. The central puzzle is the emergence of a British taste for hobby farming and agricultural improvement; across the Channel landowner interest in rents was often more parasitic. The estate system may or may not have been the optimal means of combining land, capital, enterprise and management, but it was effective in terms of the historically relevant criterion, that is it brought more of these inputs into fruitful combination than ever before. Subsequent institutional changes in this system were refinements: the system was well established when the eighteenth century opened.

Within these political and socioeconomic structures there seems little reason to suppose that market-responsive agriculture as it had been constituted by the late seventeenth century would fail to become progressively more efficient in the absence of major negative shocks. The agricultural sector contained no major discernible impediments to its own growth. There seem to have been no crippling supply constraints on land, labour or capital, or on the supply of simple, suitable technologies, and the institutional context in which agriculture found itself had become propitious. The better documentation of the eighteenth century as compared with the seventeenth century, together with the importance of agriculture for industrialisation in the eighteenth century may mislead us into supposing that the fundamental sources of agricultural growth are to be sought in the eighteenth century. They are not. They largely date from the seventeenth century. Given the rearrangements of that period it is difficult to think why agriculture should not already have been experiencing cumulative growth when the eighteenth century began, and have gone on experiencing it. Indeed, just as French scholars use a 'long sixteenth century' as a unit of historical study, so it may be for purposes of British agricultural history that a proper chronological unit would be a 'long eighteenth century' from somewhere in the middle of the seventeenth century to near the end of the Napoleonic wars.

Quality of the human agent

The entrepreneurial, innovating landowner, personally knowledgeable about and concerned with methods of husbandry and farm business management, had become a common type before the end of the seventeenth century – in wool growing long before. The coming into being of a distinct body of landowners who engaged vigorously in farming or overseeing their estates represented a parameter shift induced, no doubt, partly by prior growth, but to which the whole economic system had to make a radical adjustment. Perhaps the essential quality of these men was their detached concern for farming, their ability to view it as a series of rather abstract problems while engaging in it from day to day. They were scarcely scientists but they were often 'experimentalists' in the sense then used. By the standards of many European landed proprietors they were a down-to-earth class, their interests being still rural, especially in sports involving the use or abuse of animals, yet sharing in some degree in the cultural and intellectual expansion of the day. Because they were interested in farming for its own sake and had access to information at a national level, rather more than their tenant farmers, as well as being subject to the pressures and rewards of active, non-local, markets, they were well placed to seek better combinations of factors of production via technological and organisational change. They were commonly good observers and read the agricultural treatises of classical authors and those of their own time. The 'experiments' they performed may often have lacked controls, their scientific reasoning may often have been naive, yet they were vastly different beings from most of their predecessors in earlier periods. Some of them joined the emergent scientific bodies, which always cast half an eye over agriculture, and in the eighteenth century they swelled the membership of the new, specialist, national and regional agricultural societies. They were the type of people who, as was said of Wordsworth, had one eye on a daffodil and the other on a canal share.

The chief spin-off from this involvement of landowners was more mundane than the advance of science or even the transmission to the land of high science. It was the greater exchange of practical knowledge and materials. As men declared their interests in husbandry matters and met together to confer about them, there developed a constant exchange of seeds and stud animals about the country. Landowners had plenty of reasons to visit London and it was there that a traffic involving widely separated localities was centred. This seems to have overcome local pride and conservatism, for although strains of crops and breeds of livestock continued to bear regional names and associations a constant remaking with the aid of non-local materials was beginning to take place underneath this antique patina. As importantly, all the activity helped to increase managerial alertness. The involvement of large numbers of people helped to make self-perpetuating an interest in matters technological and commercial. This very condition can be treated as a proximate cause of the better factor combinations and rising agricultural productivity. The ultimate cause must presumably be sought in general politics and culture, whereby landowners increasingly found it possible and pleasant as well as profitable to turn their attentions from the grosser forms of bucolic indulgence to a businesslike hobby interest in farming. This deeper shift is elusive but none the less powerful. Obviously there were laggard individuals and groups and regions, but similar impulses affected the upper layers of farmers, particularly as landowners selected richer and more alert tenants.

The society that was evolving in Britain was increasingly urban and this affected agriculture in ways other than the mere expansion of the market. First, as has been mentioned, London and its institutions in which the landowner class was involved, and with its dominating social season, afforded a centre in which new farming inputs, whether material or conceptual, could be discussed, sold, exchanged, and re-transmitted to the ends of the country. English landowners came to occupy a peculiar double niche in town and country. Secondly, the close-spaced cathedral cities and market towns with their society of apothecaries and physicians and lawyers and eventually newspaper editors, a steadily-growing division of professional labour, provided an atmosphere, outwardly relaxed though it was, conducive to serious interest in the field science and all aspects of the management of land. Towns acted as nodes for the further diffusion of new ideas. The services available to agriculture became more specialised and professional and the social atmosphere became tolerant, even encouraging, of scientific enquiry. Despite the classicial orientation of the grammar schools there was a commercial strand in many of them which catered to farmers' sons who were to follow the plough. Educational, cultural and intellectual life was conducive to agricultural improvement.

Technological change

There was a high degree of innovative activity in the broad area of technology. As has been described for rural America in the nineteenth century (Parker 1965) there was non-pecuniary competition in agricultural improvement, though it tended to occur among higher classes in Britain. There was a social yield from this process in the constant diffusion of better farm layouts, and superior tillage and other practices. However the show nature of the competitive thrust, the intensely fashionable element, also encouraged the 'prize marrow' fallacy whereby livestock, say, were bred for physical 'points' instead of better feed conversion ratios and higher profits. This was an incidental drawback arising from the involvement of rich men with technical farming matters. In contrast, the commercial success of the Hereford breed of cattle was attributed to the fact that it was developed not by men of fashion and deep pockets who made a sport of production and carried zeal to excess, but by dirty-boot tenant farmers.

The central improvements of the period related to the intensity and ecological sensitivity of land usage. From remote times the farming of individual communities had been nicely adapted to local environments, but while markets remained fairly local each district tended to grow some crops that could have been grown better elsewhere. It is evident that there had been regular countrywide competition in livestock production (as well as extensive competition in cereals) long before, but specialisation at the regional level was still far from complete. With the transport advances and consolidation of a national market in the seventeenth and eighteenth centuries the comparative advantage of different regions became more marked and regional specialisation grew. (For further discussion of comparative advantage see chapter 5.) Additionally, regional specialisation offered the possibility of economies of scale in handling, storing and processing.

Regional specialisation was founded not only on superior means of exchanging the products of various parts of the country but on the shift in comparative advantage induced by different technical possibilities, on different soils, of developing new farming systems based on the 'new' fodder crops. Sown grasses, legumes and roots eaten off *in situ* facilitated the return of dung to the fields on which they were grown. On the heaviest, worst-drained clays, where roots could not be lifted in winter and livestock became bogged down, these new fodder crops were not grown much until the tile-draining of the nineteenth century (chapter 10). But in many areas the manure produced from the 'new' crops progressively removed the need for resting the land under fallows. They were important land-saving innovations. On thin, light soils that had previously been unable to sustain permanent cropping they were especially potent, once they were integrated into mixed farming systems.

By the industrial and mechanical textbook standards of invention the 'new husbandry' that had been devised in the seventeenth century and continued to be developed and extended throughout the eighteenth century was a diffuse affair. It was a series of farming operations conflated to form a novel system of untidy and constantly changing variety. The only new components, the 'new' fodder crops, had usually been available in England since the sixteenth century; the novelty lay in the sequences of cropping and their integration with stock husbandry. Sheep flocks and to a lesser, or at any rate more localised, extent yarded cattle were fed on these crops of roots, legumes and 'seeds'. The dung of the fat stock or store (growing) stock and the meat, tallow and hides were all outputs of the system, though the dung was recycled to compensate for soil nutrients that the intervening 'white straw' (cereal) crops took out. This system of mixed farming producing livestock products and grain from the same permanently-tilled, non-fallowed, fields represented a solution to the most severe technical problem of pre-modern European agriculture: maintaining soil fertility.

Cultivation could now be extended onto once-permanent sheep pastures in districts of light soil, a process often involving the enclosure by agreement of common grazings. These areas had incidental benefits for the arable producer, such as lower traction costs than the clays and freer drainage which meant that the land could be worked through more months of the year. As the light soils were converted to ploughland, so the clay vales were converted in the opposite direction, from arable to permanent pasture. This regional re-sorting of farming systems was the chief among a number of intensified regional specialisations. Apparently it originated as a creative response to the relative prices of the late seventeenth century, either because the national average price of grain fell relative to livestock products (partly through demand-side changes, partly through technical improvement) or because transport improvements integrated the national market more closely, permitting regions to specialise, or one suspects through their joint action. During the prolonged series of readjustments at all levels that came about, cereal production for the market did continue on heavy as well as light soils. Product specialisation by regions was a tendency; it never reached a clear-cut conclusion. The spread of cereal production onto light land at the expense of a proportion of heavy land production did however have some stabilising effect on the national harvest and therefore on the fluctuations which variations in the harvest could set up in the economy at large.

As corn grows equally upon high and low lands, upon grounds that are disposed to be too wet, and upon those that are disposed to be too dry, either the drought or the rain which is hurtful to one part of the country is favourable to another; and though both in the wet and in the dry season the crop is a good deal less than in one more properly tempered, yet in both what is lost in one part of the country is in some measure compensated by what is gained in the other [Smith 1776, vol. II: 26].

The elementary principle underlying mixed farming should not lead one to overlook the fact that it comprised a wide and adaptable range of rotations and feeding arrangements. The variants were required to fit the continuum of change in conditions of soil, slope, aspect and market demand. A prolonged, in fact an endless, process of trial-and-error was needed to get an ecological fit in each and every locality, and to take advantage of new ways of combining the elements of the system. The spread of mixed farming was an interacting series of diffusions of crops, lifestock, and the practices needed to work them in together. Thus the output of the land was raised; changes in regional specialisation and the intensity of land use seem to have been more responsible for this than the comparatively slight increase in new land available for farming.

Some yield increases also resulted from responses to problems caused by ecological disharmonies brought about by excessive or uneven change in the component parts of the technical farming system. There was a similar response to the minor negative shocks received by the agricultural system during the century, shocks such as the cattle plagues which were temporarily serious for one enterprise but not critical for the whole sector. The tendency to respond positively to such problems meant that they acted as 'focusing devices' for inventive and innovative effort (Rosenberg 1960: 11–12, n. 24). Three instances of scientific or managerial responses must suffice. First, there were scientific publications elicited by the urgency of disease and pest problems, such as those on cattle diseases from Thomas Bate's paper in the *Philosophical Transactions of the Royal Society* for 1718 through to Erasmus Darwin's note on the subject in 1783. Darwin subsequently published his *Phytologia* (1800) in which he recommended a good insecticide and proposed that insect pests be biologically controlled by introducing parasites on their larvae, for which he has been called the forerunner of modern economic entomology (Schofield 1963: 397, 400–1). Second, there were the sponsored diffusions of superior crops in response to particular ecological problems as in the case of the swede or swedish turnip. The large and growing national flock of sheep had come to depend for winter feed on the common turnip, which had a tendency to freeze in cold snaps and rot in thaws and was therefore a somewhat unreliable resource. The hard winters of 1794–95 and 1798–99 gave a real impetus to the adoption of the hardier, less watery, more frost-resistant swede. 'Swedish turnip', wrote Arthur Young in 1799, 'very fortunately for the agricultural interest of the Kingdom, Lord Romney last winter presented the Board of Agriculture with four sacks of the seed of this invaluable root, which was distributed in parcels of four or five pounds to a great number of gentlemen, and to all the provincial societies in the Kingdom.' Third, there were responses from within the farming community to specific ecological problems, an instance of which was the development by a Hampshire farmer of a drench which would supposedly cure liver rot in sheep. Thomas Fleet, from near Basingstoke, advertised his drench in a printed circular listing sixteen other farmers who attested that they had seen sheep originally delivered to Fleet in June 1793 in the 'last stage of Rot' back in a thriving condition by November. Fleet volunteered a trial with any given number of sheep, one-third of which were to be secured by his medicine against contracting the rot, the remainder to be put into 'the most rotting Ground possible' and half of them to be left to die and the others to be cured his way. 'All the Sheep shall be together during the Experiment, and live in the same Manner, the *Drenching* only accepted' (Copy in Willoughby Coll., Oxfordshire Record Office Wi IX/Ic, reprinted in *Annals of Agriculture* XXII (1794) 19–23). This example catches the style of the better contemporary experiments. Presumably Fleet's drench proved unsatisfactory, for it passed out of sight, but he had at least reached the degree of sophistication necessary to suggest a controlled experiment. Before the formal emergence in the nineteenth century of the sciences on which agriculture is based it is not perhaps to be expected that there would be very much success in controlling pests and diseases, but there was bound to be some pay-off, in terms of adjusting crops and stock to natural conditions, from the vigorous empirical activity in which contemporaries engaged.

Ecological disharmonies in farming systems obtruded on the notice and acted as catalysts. Problems of this type are endemic to agriculture because by their nature they represent environmental disturbance. The question is why had the farm community, and landowners, and proto-scientists, become so responsive? Direct financial inducements are hardly a sufficient answer since although the rewards for solving problems would have been great, it was extraordinarily difficult, and remained so, to patent the rather elementary biological-cum-managerial solutions that the age could devise. The South Sea Bubble-ish desperation of the advertiser in 1788 of 'an entirely new mode of Winter Feeding Sheep', which he claimed would increase the farmer's profit by fifty to one hundred per cent, but which he offered to disclose only for one thousand subscriptions at twenty guineas apiece, suggests that it was difficult to capture the gains of innovation (*The County Magazine* Salisbury, ii, 1788, 15/12/1788). The roots of the persistent concern with solving agricultural problems go deeper than the market place, though they undoubtedly run through it, down into the

'Scientific Revolution' of the seventeenth century and its footing in the first organised natural history, as well as into an agrarian social structure that could make 'research' a consumption good and throw up a royal hobby farmer in George III. If research were not whole-heartedly motivated by profit, it may be plausibly argued that development was. Yet the social forms of British agriculture meant that research often merely meant a landowner or farmer finding better ways to arrange farming routines and development meant his putting them into practice. The landed estate system was nicely adapted to ensure the diffusion of new ideas along these lines.

Organisational change

Not only was the estate system an essential part of the way new crops, livestock breeds and farm practices were diffused in England but it was the means of their translocation to Scotland and Wales. As the Earl of Haddington (1680–1735) wrote about his East Lothian estate, 'I got a farmer and his family from Dorsetshire in hopes that he would instruct my people in the right way of inclosing, and teach them to manage grass seeds...This improvement was new in this country till I got the people from Dorsetshire' (Handley 1953: 146). In Wales, right from the 1660s, there had been a diffusion of clover from centres in Herefordshire and of sainfoin from Oxfordshire, *via* landowners and their stewards who busily scanned printed sources, sowed trial plots, wrote round to English and other Welsh agriculturists for advice, and encouraged their tenants to take up the crops. A secondary diffusion followed as tenants on neighbouring estates imitated the practice (Emery 1976: 35–48).

From the Royal Society in the 1660s to the Lunar Society of Birmingham in the late eighteenth century groups of men with status and power engaged personally in experiments in agricultural science, or at least in recording their agricultural observations, just as those of them who had made their money from trade had almost automatically bought themselves estates. The government did not fund agricultural research. The societies were private, voluntary associations. They played a real part in disseminating useful knowledge, although as the historians of the Royal Society of Arts observe, individual improvers have tended to get the credit (Hudson & Luckhurst 1954: 57). And as the London-based societies gave, so the regional societies reached out and took. The Gordon's Mill Farming Club, to name one, introduced the Tullian system of perpetually cropping wheat from England to the Aberdeen area, and later, in the 1760s, brought in the Norfolk four-course rotation (Smith 1962). Not all such transfers were appropriate and successful but there was sufficient activity for a few failures to be swamped in the general progress.

Technological progress and organisational forms cannot be decisively separated, as the function of the landed estate in promoting innovation shows. Indeed some recent treatments equate new institutions with technologies in the sense that they too can be devised and disseminated in order to capture externalities or raise productivity. In this regard the eighteenth century saw comparatively little true novelty. The organisational framework had been to all intents and purposes built up before or during the second half of the seventeenth century. Farm book-keeping, prescriptive texts, land surveying methods, the specialisation of professional functions concerning land law and estate management, societies with an interest in scientific agriculture, even much of the legal apparatus relating to land tenure and to transactions in landed produce, all were in being before 1700. There was elaboration during the eighteenth century, but mostly on unsurprising lines. Even the looming change of enclosure was not new. Only about half of the area of England remained unenclosed in 1700, while of enclosure procedures the Act of parliament itself had been employed as long before as 1607–8 to bring about the enclosure of Marden and Bodenham in Herefordshire. The appropriate questions might be why before 1760 did enclosure tend to proceed by agreement (enrolled in the Court of Chancery) and why were enclosures by parliamentary Act only common afterwards? A supplementary question, giving the first its point, is what contribution did enclosure make to improved productivity?

Views differ as to whether or not parliamentary enclosure as a device for consolidating land holdings and property rights in land was resorted to because it became cheaper than enclosure by agreement or because, though dearer in terms of initial outlay, no less coercive method could achieve the result in resistant, laggard parishes. The hold of big landowners on parliament was surely tight enough for the method to have been used extensively from at least the Restoration and the sudden increase in parliamentary enclosure in the mid-eighteenth century (36 bills in the 1740s, 137 in the 1750s) does not at first sight seem explicable in terms of a new cheapness of the form. A possible proximate explanation for the fervour with which the parliamentary form was embraced in the second half of the eighteenth century lies in the gains accruing to one category of the owners of rights, the tithe owners, about one-third of whom were lay impropriators, i.e. not clergy at all (Evans 1976). Collecting tithes, especially tithes in kind, was costly. By receiving land in lieu of them the tithe owners could escape the chore and the odium of collecting them while sharing the profit and status that in a time of rising product prices seemed certain to derive from the ownership of farmland. Tithe owners were asked to bear no part of the costs of enclosure by Act and were entitled to nominate one of the commissioners (usually of three) solely to look after their interests. They tended to receive first pick of the land at allotment. Sixty to seventy per cent of all Acts exonerated tithes (i.e. exchanged land for them) and in open-field villages the bulk did so. Whereas tithe owners had often accepted less than one-tenth of the produce because collection costs were so high, on enclosure by Act between the 1750s and the mid-1770s they received one-eighth or one-seventh of the whole of the land in lieu, and by the 1790s allotments in lieu of arable tithes were as high as one-fifth or even two-ninths of the land. Since tithe owners were well represented in parliament at earlier dates, it is not clear why the legislators, notably the House of Lords, should have coddled them as much as they did from the middle of the eighteenth century. Tithe payers had a more obvious incentive to aquiesce to enclosure in that with rising product prices more vigorous collection threatened, and the arrangements were less generous to the tithe owners than they appear; one-tenth of all the produce was more than the tithe owners would receive as the landlord's share (let us say one-third) of the proceeds from coming to own even as much as two-ninths of the land.

The main incentive to enclose was perhaps external – the fairly rapid rise in farm product prices after mid-century. Some improvements in efficiency on enclosure were likely, from consolidating holdings and thus reducing the ratio of perimeter to area and the encroachment of weeds and spillover of drainage water, as well as saving on the 'journey to work' around scattered strips. But the efficiency gains are easily exaggerated. One of the most cited sources of gain from enclosure, the suppression of indiscriminate breeding among farm animals on the commons – the mating of everybody's son with nobody's daughter – had long since been rendered virtually unnecessary by the presence of enough closes almost everywhere to allow control over livestock breeding. It did not take many closes even in open-field areas, or many communal regulations to enforce the castration of scrub bulls, to gain effective control over animal breeding. There was even an old Act empowering constables to seize under-sized stone horses (stallions) running on the commons (The Bill for the breed of horses (1540) Statutes of the Realm, vol. 3, pp. 758–60). Further, the 'new' forage crops that were absolutely central to raising productivity were neither dependent on prior enclosure nor did they automatically follow it. In the anciently-enclosed areas of the Weald of Sussex and Kent crops like clover and turnips were adopted very late (Kenyon 1955: 78–156; Chalklin 1962: 29–45). In many areas of the country the lag in adopting the 'new' crops after eighteenth-century enclosures was quite long. In Oxfordshire there is the clearest evidence that these crops came in first on light soils even in the open fields, rather than on heavy clays whether enclosed or not (Havinden 1961: 73–83). Nevertheless it would be astonishing if reducing day-to-day running costs and cutting down the negative externalities of other men's negligent husbandry did not follow the consolidation of intermingled strips, and if private and social costs were not brought more into line (or if the transactions costs of equating them were not lowered) where the commons and open fields were enclosed. The best indicator of a rise in output as a result of enclosure is the subsequent rise in rents, which has been preliminarily calculated at 13 per cent on the enclosure of open-field villages (McCloskey 1975: 155–60).

Conclusions

During the eighteenth century, supply and price fluctuations for farm products were evident, though at the national level they were not abnormally damaging. By modern standards government policy and private business instruments to dampen down these fluctuations were few and weak, but by earlier norms they had become remarkably deliberate. They included the bounties on exported grain, government compensation for cattle slaughtered during epizoötics, and the extension of business by the fire offices. While the role of government was mostly the creation of a stable framework within which producers could pursue their own interests, these measures and some others seemed positively helpful to them. They may be viewed as the use or innovation of pieces of institutional technology.

In the main the productivity gains of eighteenth-century agriculture were made by extending techniques pioneered, and more than merely pioneered, before 1700, within a set of institutions also brought into being then. There were innumerable small changes in the way farming was carried on, many shifts in the location of production, and substantial fluctuations in prices. The concept of an 'agricultural revolution' is not appropriate for such a set of changes. They were more like a tide, its turn only just discernible, submerging under its waves a group of islands one by one. If there was a revolutionary phase it was the start of such a process and had come during the Commonwealth and Restoration periods. The fundamental change depended on society's ability to devise and go on spreading mixed farming routines of high productivity, routines which permitted soil fertility to be upgraded and held at high levels.

Why did the essentially simple diffusion of integrated grain and livestock farming take from well before the eighteenth century to the middle of the nineteenth century to be completed? (chapter 10). Part of the answer seems to be that even with market incentives and a responsive set of producers, the technical or ecological problems were too various to be overcome in a hurry. Farms in Britain are immensely diverse. Numberless trials were needed to fit mixed farming to each individual assemblage of fields with different slopes, shapes, sizes, aspects, accessibility, soil types, drainage, and buildings. Mixed farming itself, and other more specialised farming systems, never ceased to evolve. Eighteenth-century agriculture was obliged to absorb and re-absorb changes that were like a series of slow waves breaking on shifting sand. The changes were a succession of best-practice diffusions repeatedly bringing each district up towards the level of the most advanced district or bringing the productivity of the majority of farmers up towards the level of the leaders.

Conceivably the pace of change in cropping systems, though not in livestock breeding or parliamentary enclosure, slowed down after about 1760, indicating limitations on agriculture's earlier display of considerable price responsiveness.

Much of the activity between the mid-seventeeth century and the mid-eighteenth century may have been in response to a price–cost squeeze on the cereal enterprises, inducing their close linkage with the livestock enterprises. When cereal prices began to rise steeply, agriculturists may have begun to reap an economic rent. Arthur Young, who constantly reported the wide dispersion in technological level among regions and farms, wrote of Norfolk farmers that 'for 30 years from 1730 to 1760, the great improvements of the north western part of the county took place... For the next 30 years to about 1790 they nearly stood still; they *reposed upon their laurels*' (Young 1804: 31). Incentive to adopt further novelties was reduced when rising prices tumbled extra profits into the laps of farmers whose mixed farming systems were established. What followed tended to be capital-consuming improvements like enclosure, to ease the transition of laggard areas into the world of mixed farming. The central productivity gains of the century still relied of course on introducing and improving and operating systems of mixed farming. By the end of the century they had only the very heavy clays to colonise.

5

Overseas trade and empire 1700–1860

R. P. THOMAS & D. N. McCLOSKEY

In attempting to explain the upturn in the rate of growth of the British economy in the middle of the eighteenth century economic historians have often searched for a pre-eminent factor, a determining cause – one factor that caused all the others. Overseas trade has received more than its proper share of attention for several reasons. Foreign trade during the century expanded more rapidly than did the economy as a whole; export industries in particular grew more rapidly than the industrial sector; the statistics of the growth are relatively easy to collect; and many of the external signs of economic growth during the century were closely associated with the expansion of foreign commerce. H. J. Habakkuk and Phyllis Deane (1963) and Ralph Davis (1954, 1962a) have investigated the role played by the growth of foreign trade and given it pre-eminence as the cause of the growth of the British economy. The assertion of pre-eminence is disputed by Deane and Cole (1967), Hartwell (1965), and Thompson (1973). There is, however, no dispute among historians over the importance of foreign trade to the growth of certain industries, textiles for instance. And there is little doubt that the expansion of foreign trade was to some extent important for rapid economic growth in the eighteenth and early nineteenth centuries (Thompson 1973: 94). Deane and Cole, for example, state, 'There can, of course, be no doubt of the central importance of overseas trade in the expansion of the economy during this period' (1967: 83). We shall see.

The expansion of British overseas trade during the eighteenth century did not take place within a free trade world, but within an imperial system designed to direct trade to the benefit of the mother country. There are two important questions to be asked about overseas trade during this century: (1) did the elaborate and complex regulations that governed trade actually contribute to the wealth of the mother country, and (2) how and by how much did the expansion of trade contribute to the growth of the British economy during the eighteenth century? It is best to begin by considering the overall evidence.

The evidence: statistics of trade

One of the reasons that the growth of the foreign trade sector has been accorded a leading role in explanations of the English industrial revolution is that

87

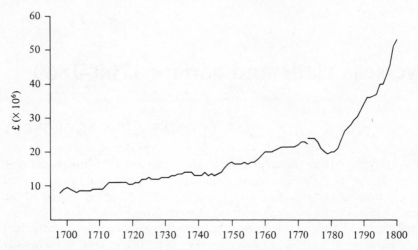

Figure 5.1 English foreign trade in the eighteenth century (net imports plus domestic exports; official values). Notes: (1) The statistics on which this figure is based are taken from Deane and Cole (1967: 48 and appendix 1). (2) The statistics are for official values of imports and exports, as explained in the text. They are therefore a rough approximation to a series of the volume of trade. (3) The statistics are for England, 1697–1774, and for Great Britain, 1772–1800. A three-year moving average has been computed from the original series.

reasonably reliable statistics of foreign trade are available annually for the eighteenth century. Indeed, the foreign trade statistics are the only annual series available for the entire century. These statistics show dramatic increases, especially for the last half of the century. The temptation is great to attribute to so well-documented a sector a causal rather than a dependent role.

Records of English overseas trade from 1696 onwards (of Scotland from 1755) give an annual record of English imports, exports and re-exports (re-exports are goods first imported into England and then exported to be consumed elsewhere). These statistics are not the usual modern foreign trade statistics recording the annual value of trade. The quantities traded were entered annually, but the entries were valued at fixed prices selected at the beginning of the century . Such statistics therefore approximate a quantity index of the physical volume of foreign trade rather than a value index. The existing foreign trade statistics depict fairly accurately the course of the foreign trade of England (and after 1772 of Great Britain: Shumpeter 1960; Davis 1954, 1962a; Deane and Cole 1967; Minchinton 1969); the detailed statistics have recently been reworked by Davis, who also provides a detailed guide to this complicated subject and a valuable discussion of trends in trade (Davis 1979).

The statistics show that between 1700 and 1800 imports expanded 523 per cent

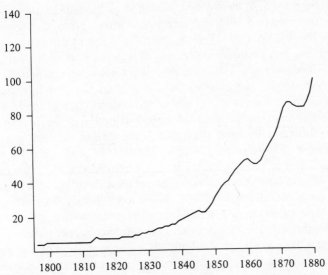

Figure 5.2 English foreign trade 1800–60 (domestic exports; index of trade volume, 1880 = 100). Notes: (1) The statistics on which this figure is based are taken from Mitchell and Deane (1962: 328) and are themselves based on a series given in Imlah (1958: 94–8 and 205–7). (2) The statistics are an index, with base of 100 in 1880, of the volume of exports of the United Kingdom. A three-year moving average has been computed from the original series.

and the exports and re-exports used to pay for the imports 568 per cent and 906 per cent (Deane and Cole 1967: 46). Since the population of England increased by only 257 per cent, it is clear that foreign trade became increasingly important on a per capita basis. There is little doubt that foreign commerce over the century became a more important component of national income.

The growth of English foreign trade is shown in figures 5.1 and 5.2. Although these statistics have not been rigorously analysed, Deane and Cole have discerned that the century can be divided, like Gaul, into three parts. In terms of exports and imports the period 1700 to 1740 reflected relatively slow growth. The pace of expansion picked up between 1740 and 1770 and between 1770 and 1800 rapidly expanded. Summing exports and imports (see figure 5.1) in order to look at the rate of expansion of the foreign trade sector as a whole shows that the rate of growth between 1700 and 1740 was 0.8 per cent annually, that between 1740 and 1770 it was almost twice as great (1.7 per cent annually, and that for the years between 1770 and 1800 it was over three times the rate of the earliest period, or 2.6 per cent annually).

The foreign trade of England during the eighteenth century did not however, accelerate in a smoothly continuous manner. The major interruptions were foreign wars (John 1955; Wilson 1965), over half of the century being years of war. Foreign trade was particularly susceptible to interruption: the dips in trade for the years 1702–13, 1739–48, 1756–63 and 1775–83 and from 1793 to the end of the century can be explained in this way. Likewise, part of the subsequent expansion in foreign trade following the wars may be accounted for by catching-up. Yet despite the interruptions it is clear that foreign trade was expanding much more rapidly at the end of the century than at the beginning.

The growth of foreign trade reinforced the redistribution of the English labour force. In 1700 substantially more than half of the English labour force was in agriculture (68 per cent according to one estimate); by 1800 only 36 per cent were. The expansion of the foreign trade sector coincided with this transition. Deane and Cole calculate that export industries grew from 100 to 544 over the century while the home industries grew from 100 to 152 (1967: 78). Furthermore, in calculating the total expansion of industry and commerce they give the export industries a weight of 60, suggesting that they felt that export industries, even in the base year 1700, were most of all industry. The expansion of foreign trade during the century induced the English economy to become more specialised in manufacturing and less dependent upon agriculture, beginning a process that was to continue until the late nineteenth century.

The geographical distribution of foreign trade

English foreign trade at the beginning of the eighteenth century was heavily concentrated on the European continent. England imported £3.9 million worth of goods from Europe or about £0.67 for each man, woman, and child on the island, two-thirds of all imports (Schumpeter 1960: 11), including linen, wine, timber, naval stores, and bar iron. Most of these came from areas north of the Netherlands. There was little legal trade with the French because of the high duties levied on goods from France and the intermittent wars. English imports were then paid for by exports of £3.8 million and re-exports of £1.8 million, both to Europe (especially Northern Europe). The English exported mostly woollens, the staple for centuries, but also a miscellany of processed and manufactured goods. The English re-exported tropical produce, such as tobacco, sugar, and dyes, imported from her colonial possessions. Europe at the beginning of the century received 85 per cent of both English exports and re-exports.

A notable fact about England's trade in the eighteenth century is that Europe's relative importance as a source of imports to England or as markets for its exports declined (see table 5.1). By the end of the century, although most re-exports still went to Europe, only 29 per cent of English imports still came from Europe and only 21 per cent of English exports went there. The relative decline was due arithmetically speaking to the rapid growth of the colonial markets, particularly those bordering on the Atlantic Ocean. In 1700, English

Table 5.1. *The geography of British commodity trade* 1700–97 (*per cent distributions*)

	1700–01 England	1797–98 Britain
Retained imports from:		
Ireland	5	13
Europe	62	29
North America	6	7
West Indies	14	25
East Indies and other	14	26
Total	100	100
	[£5820000]	[£23900000]
Domestic exports to:		
Ireland	3	9
Europe	82	21
North America	6	32
West Indies	5	25
East Indies and other	4	12
Total	100	100
	[£4460000]	[£18300000]
Re-exports to:		
Ireland	7	11
Europe	77	78
North America	5	3
West Indies	6	4
East Indies and other	4	4
Total	100	100
	[£2140000]	[£11800000]

Source: Deane and Cole 1967: 87; official values.

possessions in North America and the West Indies accounted for only 20 per cent of English imports, 11 per cent of re-exports, and 11 per cent of domestic exports. After a century of expansion (increasing by a factor of 6.5) they were the source of 32 per cent of English imports. English combined exports to the North American colonies and the West Indies expanded by an astounding 2300 per cent over the century. The Atlantic colonies at the end of the century took over half of all the goods exported from the mother country.

The rapid growth of its non-European markets allowed England to continue to import large quantities of European goods and to pay for them using re-exports of tropical produce, such as tobacco from Virginia and spices from Java, to cancel a substantial deficit. England throughout the century continued to import textile materials in large quantities from northern Europe. Linen yarn was the most important single commodity but substantial amounts of both flax and hemp and finished linens were imported from Holland as well as Ireland; timber and naval stores came throughout the century from the Baltic, wines (and gold) mostly from Portugal, and some brandy from France. The items imported remained remarkably similar throughout the century, as did the exported: England imported raw materials and semi-finished goods and exported in turn finished goods.

The presence of protective (often prohibitive) duties on many English manufactured goods in European markets severely limited the abilities of English merchants to export to the continent. The same was true for European goods in English markets. It was the growth of colonial possessions – North American and West Indian – that accounts for much of the growth in English exports. England was blessed with prosperous colonies, required by law to buy their hats and iron and the like from the mother country.

A significant detail in the picture was the change in England's position from an exporter of grains to a net importer. In 1772 only 0.7 per cent of imports (according to the official values) were grains, but by 1790 this figure had increased to 4.4 per cent and by 1800 to 8.7 per cent. The availability of colonial goods to re-export to Europe allowed English imports from Europe to continue at a high-level despite the difficulties of exporting directly to that region: again, England became over the century increasingly specialised in producing and trading manufactured goods, depending on foreigners for some of its food supply (though not much by the standard of the late nineteenth century).

The growing volume of overseas trade and its shifting geographical pattern affected the relative importance of English ports. London at the beginning of the century accounted for 80 per cent of England's imports; 69 per cent of England's exports left from there as did 86 per cent of all re-exports. The absolute expansion in overseas trade coupled with the relative decline of Europe as England's trading partner and the relative rise of the colonies coincided with the rise to prominence of the outports: Whitehaven, Liverpool, Newcastle, and Bristol as a group expanded more rapidly than London (Schumpeter 1960: 9–10), with the result that by the end of the eighteenth century London's dominance was somewhat reduced.

The growth in foreign trade shown by the trade statistics measures directly the rapid expansion in goods exchanged overseas, but they also measure indirectly the services that someone must have been providing in connection with the exchange of goods. Shipping and the requisite merchant services (together called 'invisibles') must have grown at least as rapidly as did the exchange of goods ('visibles'). The issue of the seventeenth century – whether foreigners or Englishmen were to provide these services – was settled by the early eighteenth century. Encouraged by edict (the Navigation Acts) and by force of arms (the Dutch Wars), the English merchant fleet had become in the eighteenth century the most efficient in the world (Davis 1962b: 13). With the Dutch interlopers ruined, the English merchant fleet grew hand-in-hand with English trade. The size of the fleet measured in tons increased over 326 per cent between 1702 and 1788 (Davis 1962b: 27).

Along with the expansion of the merchant marine went the growth in numbers and size of the merchant houses that owned and managed them. The earnings in the invisibles trade were not trivial. In the tobacco trade, for instance, it was customary early in the century to estimate one penny for each pound weight for purchase, transport and petty charges (Gray 1933: 224). It was estimated in 1737 by a merchant in the Virginia trade that the normal purchase price of tobacco in Virginia was one and three-quarters pence per pound and the re-export price four pence (not including the duties). The difference between the two prices represents the payments for mercantile services including shipping. These charges, then, could easily be twice the amount received by the tobacco planter. Later in the century it was reported that the mercantile charges on sugar were only 38 per cent of the gross receipts on sales (Sheridan 1968: 51), indicating, perhaps, that markets were becoming more efficient as the volume of colonial commerce grew.

Government policy towards trade

Although it could hardly be called a nation of free trade, England in 1689 was not wedded to protection of interests at home. The importation of a few things, most notably wool cloth, was prohibited, but the prohibitions were minor compared with later practice. The tax on most goods was five per cent on the value of both exports and imports (compared with 30 per cent in 1840, at the end of the protectionist period). The value was calculated not on the true cost but on a book of official and unalterable rates, so that what appeared to be an 'ad valorem' duty (i.e. in proportion to value) was in fact a 'specific' duty (i.e. so many shillings per ounce or yard, regardless of its shifting value). Exceptions were wine and spirits and tobacco, which paid higher duties as luxury goods that could easily bear the weight. The colonial goods among these, such as sugar and tobacco, were in exchange given a monopoly of the home market assured by prohibitive duties on foreign sugar and tobacco, but such duties obviously aided colonials not Englishmen: there was little protection for English industry in the tariff structure inherited by William and Mary.

In short order, however, the new unity of purpose between monarch and Parliament led to a search for new revenue and to a jump in duties on foreign trade. Between 1690 and 1704 the average level on imports roughly quadrupled (Davis 1966: 306). These higher duties of the 1690s, designed merely to enrich the exchequer, exposed a number of specific trades to severe hardship and the government to vehement protests by the merchants involved. The protests were met by a series of modifications and exemptions, setting a disastrous precedent for future manipulation of the tariff in aid of special interests. The result during the course of the century was a list fascinating in its complexity of special prohibitions, duties, exemptions, drawbacks and bounties. The rise of protection, in short, was the accidental consequence of taxation for revenue.

94

So too was the other half of policy towards trade an accident – the tying by the 'Navigation Acts' of an enormous empire to the economy of England. The first British empire reached its height in 1763, the spoils of victory in the Seven Years' War. The empire included the kingdom of Great Britain and Ireland and the outlying islands, scattered trading forts around the world, and three major overseas regions: North America, the West Indies, and Bengal in India. The British North American colonies included the thirteen American colonies, the Eastern shores of the present day Canada, Florida, and the lands West of the American colonies to the Mississippi River. The possessions in the West Indies consisted of Antigua, Barbados, Dominica, Grenada, Montserrat, Nevis, St Kitts, St Lucia, St Vincent, Tobago, Tortola and, above all, Jamaica.

The Navigation Acts, dating from a century before, although repeatedly revised, consisted of four types of regulations, governing: first, the nationality of the crews and the ownership of vessels in which foreign trade could be carried; second, the destinations to which certain colonial goods could be shipped; third, an elaborate system of rebates, drawbacks, import and export bounties and export taxes in aid of particular industries at home; and, fourth, the manufactures in which the colonies were allowed to engage.

The laws regulating the nationality of crews and ownership of vessels were as mentioned earlier designed initially to exclude the more efficient Dutch from the colonial carrying trade. Colonial (e.g. North American) ships were considered to be English under these laws. By the eighteenth century, English shipping had become as efficient as the Dutch and would have won a large share of the carrying trade even in the absence of the laws. The laws, however, ensured that Englishmen as a whole held an unbreakable monopoly of the carrying trade and that the other more restrictive Navigation Acts could be more easily enforced.

The most restrictive laws from the colonial point of view, and the most valuable from the English, were those controlling the destinations of colonial goods. Specified ('enumerated') colonial goods could only be exported to the mother country. This list originally contained only tobacco, sugar, indigo, cotton, ginger, fustic and other dyewoods; later naval stores, hemp, rice, molasses, beaver skins, furs and copper were added; and still later, by the Sugar Act of 1764, coffee, pimento, coconuts, whale fins, raw silk, hides and skins, potash and pearl ash. The laws made England the first market of the colonies, and only if the goods could stand the costs involved would English merchants re-export them to other European countries or back to other colonies. Since the importation of non-British goods also had to come from England, they were more expensive for colonials to buy than if they had been imported directly. Furthermore, bounties were granted to English manufacturers of linen, gunpowder, silks and many non-woollen textiles to allow them to compete with foreign manufacturers in the colonial markets. In line with the desire to protect home industries, the colonials were prohibited from the manufacture of certain goods, such as wool, hats, and iron.

The Atlantic empire thus centred in the mother country. The Atlantic colonies produced food and raw materials that did not compete with domestic English agriculture and shipped them to England. Some of these imports were subsequently re-exported. England in turn provided manufactures and goods of foreign (i.e. neither British nor colonial) origin to the colonies, such as slaves to augment the colonial labour force. The first British empire, bound by the laws of trade, was a self-sufficient and expanding economy enriching its centre, surely, but also its periphery.

but at the same time it was enriching itself and underdeveloping its periphery - such as the systematic exploitation

The economic effects of British trade policy — *and underdevelopment of Bengal - built the destructive of the developed ? Silk Inddstry*

The question of whether or not trade policy actually contributed to the economic growth of Britain has received much attention from economic historians, most of it from Americans concerned with the causes of their Revolution. The Navigation Acts placed a burden on the thirteen North American colonies, and the task has been to measure it. A related task has been measuring the benefits and costs of the colonies to Britain, especially the West Indian possessions, which in the eighteenth century were viewed as the chief jewels of the empire.

American historians had long debated without conclusion the effects of the Navigation Acts on the North American colonies before Lawrence Harper in 1939 attempted to measure their effects quantitatively. Harper found that the Acts 'placed a heavy burden upon the colonies' (1942: 3); but nearly a quarter of a century later a similar but more sophisticated attempt to apply the tools of economic analysis to the problem came to the opposite conclusion (Thomas 1965). Subsequent contributions (Ransom 1968; Thomas 1968; McClelland 1969; Reid 1970; and Walton 1971) refined the techniques of measurement without substantially changing the conclusion. *? - Taxes ?*

The conclusion was that membership in the British empire did not impose a significant hardship on the American colonies, at any rate not from the strictly economic consequences of the Navigation Acts. Because of the doubtful quality of eighteenth-century statistics no attempt was made to estimate the actual costs or benefits to the last shilling. The strategy, a common one in the new economic history, was instead to obtain estimates admittedly crude but biassed against the conclusion. The costs imposed by the Acts, in other words, were deliberately overestimated and the benefits to the colonies from their colonial status (such as protection from Indians) deliberately underestimated. If the burden by this estimate was small, then one could state with some confidence that the true burden was smaller still. *Native American people, - they needed Protection not the colonialists.*

All attempts at explanation or measurement require a standard of comparison. The comparative, or alternative arrangement – a world without British colonies in North America, say – is called a 'hypothetical alternative'or a 'counter-factual'. The very meaning of measuring the importance of colonial rule entails imagining the world without it: the tasks remaining are to select the most convincing counterfactual and to find some way of measuring its dimentions. Harper, Thomas, and others chose to compare what actually happened to what would have happened had the thirteen colonies in 1763–72 been outside the British or French or Spanish empires but still within an otherwise mercantilistic world. The Americans were in fact outside the empire after the War of Independence, making it possible to use facts from after the War to represent a world without British colonies in North America before.

The major burden of the Navigation Act, as Harper discovered, fell upon colonial exports of enumerated goods, such as tobacco, forced to travel through Britain on their way to their final destination rather than directly to the final market in, say, Holland. The increased costs involved in these trans-shipments had the effect of increasing the price of tobacco in Holland, reducing the quantity consumed, and reducing the price received for exports by its colonial producers. The question is, what would have been the price of tobacco in Virginia without the burdensome extra transportation imposed by the Navigation Acts? The answer is that the price can be inferred from prices in circumstances similar to the counterfactual; namely, the ratio of Dutch to Virginia prices after the Revolution can be imagined to apply before the Revolution. If one knows the Dutch price before (one does), then one can infer what the Virginia price would have been had the after-Revolution ratio – free of the Navigation Acts – applied in 1763–72. The result is that without the Navigation Acts tobacco prices would have been about a third higher in Virginia than they actually were. It is then a simple matter to calculate the total cost to Virginians. Roughly speaking, a planter earning £100 within the British Empire would have earned £133 outside, presuming (no obvious presumption) that the alternative to British rule in 1770 was independence, not Dutch or French rule. Enumerated commodities like tobacco were about half of commodity exports from the colonies, for the reach of mercantilism was limited; commodities were about three-quarters of all exports, for the colonists exported shipping services as well; and exports were about one-seventh of colonial income, for the colonists mainly ate what they produced. A gain of one-third on enumerated commodities, then, would have raised colonial income by only $(\frac{1}{3})(\frac{1}{2})(\frac{3}{4})(\frac{1}{7}) = 1.8$ per cent. Such were the burdens of empire.

The other aspects of the Navigation Acts – the burden upon colonial imports and the benefits of bounties granted to produce certain colonial goods – can be estimated in a similar fashion and a total burden calculated. The benefits derived by the colonies from membership in the British empire must be subtracted from the burden to arrive at the net effect. The final estimates suggest that once the benefits of protection and government are subtracted from the burdens the net cost to the colonies was very small, perhaps as little as one quarter of a per cent of income in 1770 and certainly not more than one per cent. And, to repeat, the conclusions can be stated with some confidence because the estimates were purposely biased against the hypothesis (the burdens overstated, the benefits underestimated).

The benefit to the home country corresponding to the burden on the North American colonies was still smaller. In fact, it was itself probably a burden, not a benefit. Requiring certain colonial exports and imports to pass through Britain had the beneficial effect of reducing the prices of such goods to British consumers. If, at the extreme, British consumers were enabled to pay as low a price for tobacco and so forth as did American consumers – namely, the one-third lower price assumed above – the gain would be at most a third of the value of the enumerated goods consumed in Britain. But Britain retained only about 15 per cent of the £1.5 million of enumerated goods imported in 1770 from North America (most was re-exported to Europe). The gain, then, was at most ($\frac{1}{3}$) (0.15) (£1.5 million) or about £75,000 annually. The cost to British taxpayers of defending and administering the North American colonies was, by contrast, some £400,000 annually, five times the maximum benefit. The net burden was no great cost to Britain relative to British income (roughly £130 million in 1770) – although defending it against first the French and then the colonists themselves in the Seven Years War and the War of Independence was in fact a very great if non-routine cost. But the North American colonies were, it is plain, no way to wealth for the home country.

What then, of the other and apparently more valuable component of the Old Empire, the West Indies? Did they contribute to the growth of the wealth of England? The question is as old as the colonies themselves. Adam Smith thought all the Atlantic colonies were 'mere loss instead of profit' (1776: 900), but his opinion has not been adopted widely. The more extreme view maintains in Leninist fashion that British prosperity depended entirely on her empire; R. B. Sheridan can stand as the representative of a more moderate view. He maintains that the British West Indies made a substantial contribution to the economic development of the mother country before 1800 (Sheridan 1965), contending that Jamaica in particular 'yielded an economic surplus which contributed in no small way to the growth of the metropolitan economy' (1965: 311). Sheridan estimated that eight to ten per cent of the income of the mother country came from the West Indies in the closing years of the eighteeenth century and probably a larger percentage before the War of Independence.

Sheridan's views have been strongly contested by new economic historians. Thomas (1965) used the data presented by Sheridan to test the proposition put forward by Adam Smith that colonies in practice were an economic drain on the mother country. The propostion was tested by constructing estimates of the income earned in the West Indies and of the capital investment required to earn

you don't agree they!

Toff pot

the income. The estimates were biased against the proposition – the income account purposely overstated and the capital account underestimated – giving a high estimate of the rate of return on the capital invested. The resulting rate of return was compared with a hypothetical alternative: had the money instead been invested in the home country, what rate of return would it have earned? The rate of return on British government bonds at the time was 3.5 per cent. The overestimated social return on the British investment in the West Indies was a mere 2 per cent: in other words instead of being a source of profit for the mother country the West Indies generated a loss, in money terms a loss of over £600000 a year. Such were the rewards of empire.

Philip R. P. Coelho has investigated the same problem from a slightly different angle (1969, 1973). He asked, would British income have been higher or lower than it in fact was during 1768–72 had the West Indian colonies belonged to some other European power? Britain could have benefited from the possession of colonies if the colonial arrangements imposed by the mother country had allowed the importation of colonial goods at lower than the world market prices. Now the main commodities imported from the British West Indies were sugar, cocoa, coffee, cotton, ginger, indigo, molasses, pimento and rum, with sugar the most important, accounting for over two-thirds of the total. But the preferences accorded to sugar imported from the West Indies meant that the price of sugar in the mother country was higher, not lower than the world market price. Preferential duties were awarded other imports from the West Indies with much the same effect: West Indian landlords benefited at the expense of British consumers. Coelho was able to find only one West Indian import, ginger, for which Englishmen paid less than the world price. The result was that instead of providing a benefit in the form of lower import prices, imports from the West Indies cost the English consumer over £1.5 million a year.

Imports from the West Indies, then, were no bargain. Likewise Coelho could find no evidence that Britain benefited from a monopoly of exports to the West Indies, since the export industries were sufficiently competitive within Great Britain that only competitive returns could be earned in the trade. The British government was required to pay significant amounts for protecting and governing the colonies, only a part of which was offset by a $4\frac{1}{2}$ per cent tax levied on exports. The net result was that the possession of West Indian colonies cost England over £1 million annually, over ten per cent of the total revenues of the British government. Sheridan had found the colonies to have been marginally profitable and Thomas had found that they were marginally unprofitable; Coelho found that British national income would have been considerably higher 'if the West Indian colonies had been given away' (1973: 254).

If the West Indian colonies, not to speak of the colonies of the mainland, were a net economic drain on the economy of the mother country, why were they retained? The answer is that the estimates measure the social not the private profitability. It is obvious that the colonial plantations and farms were privately profitable to their owners. The costs of the sugar preferences were borne by the British consumer and the costs of administration and protection by the British tax payer. The costs were widely diffused, but the benefits accrued to a small group of owners who happened to be well represented in Parliament. British mercantilism during the eighteenth century was not a consistent national policy designed to maximise the wealth of Britain; nor was it a preview of the alleged enrichment of capitalist nations by nineteenth-century empires. It was instead, as Ralph Davis suggests, a means to provide revenue to the government (1966: 313) and a device to enrich special interest groups. The truth of the matter is that what was in the interest of the Manchester textile manufacturer or the Bristol slave trader or the West Indian planter was usually not in the interest of the British economy as a whole. As Adam Smith remarked at the time:

> To found a great empire for the sole purpose of raising up a people of customers, may at first sight appear a project fit only for a nation of shopkeepers. It is, however, a project altogether unfit for a nation of shopkeepers; but extremely fit for a nation whose government is influenced by shopkeepers [1776: bk. IV, ch. VII, pt III].

Overseas trade and British economic growth

If public policy towards overseas trade and the empire had few effects on income, and those negative, perhaps the trade itself stimulated economic growth. England's treasure by foreign trade has long seemed a likely cause of enrichment, because England has long been unusually deeply involved with the rest of the world. In the late eighteenth century, especially, the parallel expansion of industry at home and trade abroad has lent credence to the view that trade was an engine of growth. The engine has been said to work in two ways: the first by way of providing markets for the products of industry.

Consider the first view, then, that certain of the overseas trades provided profits for the feeding of British industry. We have seen already that the colonies themselves are doubtful as a source of profit. An alternative, put foward by Eric Williams (1944) long ago but still persuasive to many minds, is the slave trade: it is said that the 'fabled' profits earned in the slave trade and in employing slaves in the plantation colonies provided the original accumulation of capital for the industrial revolution. The interpretation appears plausible enough on the surface, for a slave produced more than he ate and there were many slaves. The question is, however, who earned the profits? The Jamaican planter bought the slave from a Jamaican dealer, who in turn bought the slave from a shipper, who in his turn bought the slave from an African dealer. At each stage the competition of eager buyers would drive the price up to the point at which buying the slave earned only normal profits: if the profit were in excess of normal the competition to buy would intensify and the price paid would rise to capture the excess. The surplus of a slave's production over his consumption, then, was passed back along the line of dealers in men and reached the original source – the enslaver. Enslavement in African was a consequence of war or kidnapping among Africans themselves, that is, it was a fishing for men. And in the analogy with fishing lies the answer to the question: as in fishing in the sea, the profits were wasted encouraging too many Africans to do too much slave hunting. No one owned the right to hunt for slaves, as no one owns the sea fisheries, and therefore the resource (the populated regions of Africa; the sea) was overused. So long as the transatlantic slave trade was open – effectively until the 1830s and beyond, when the British themselves closed it by interposing their navy between Africa and the New World – the economic profits of the trade were merely wasted in Africa, not funnelled into industry in Britain (cf. LeVeen 1971 and 1975).

In like manner no single trade was crucial to the nation's prosperity. If imports of grain from Prussia were cut off by the fortunes of the war against Napoleon then the United States could supply much of the deficit. If France at long last, after many years of war, cut itself off from British exports of cotton textiles, no matter: other countries stood ready to buy a good that Britain made so well and, especially, so cheaply. Notice the bellicose nature of these examples. During the long eighteenth century, beginning in 1688 and ending in 1815, the shocks of war were occasions for frequent if unintended economic experiments in the essentiality of particular trading partners or particular trades. The experiments do exhibit the agility of the economy, but are otherwise misleading. One must not use the disruptive effects of a sudden closing of a market to demonstrate the long-term importance of the product marketed, because over the long-term one demander of cotton cloth or supplier of sugar is as good as another.

The same argument applies to foreign trade as a whole. Domestic demand or supply within limits, could replace foreign demand or supply. The case of exports of manufactures has been the most important. At first it seems odd to argue that without foreign markets for its output of cotton textiles – exports were a sixth of output in the mid 1780s, and in the nineteenth century were never below a half (Deane and Cole 1967: 185–7) – Britain would have been able to find markets at home. The result, it seems, would have been a land choked with cotton, from cotton nappies to cotton shrouds. In the long run, however, the men and money used to make the excess cotton could have been turned towards making beer, roads, houses, and other domestic things. As the demand shifted home (it did in the early nineteenth century, as we shall see in the next chapter) so too would the supply. The reasoning used here is characteristic of economics, and therefore of applications of economics to history: because all things are substitutes the actual division of British exports between (say) Europe and the New World, and even the division of British output between exports and domestic use, is an interesting fact but not one obviously significant for British economic growth.

It is possible that the significance of foreign trade, especially foreign demand (exports) can be rescued by asserting that exports were a net addition to the demand facing Britain, that the nation of shopkeepers opened a new branch abroad. But many economists would be inclined to suppose, counter to much of the literature on trade as an engine of growth, that the possibility was remote. Two points are worth emphasising here. First, an export is not of itself a good thing. The end of economic activity is not production but consumption; exporting therefore is merely a lamentable sacrifice of resources consumable at home that is made worthwhile only by the importing it allows. More exports, in other words, are not to be identified with more income. Contrary to the hardy mercantilism of politicians and professors, exports are not economic growth.

Second, exports do not appear in the British case to have had even an initiating role in growth. The point is a factual not a logical one, and is controversial. It rests on evidence of the price of exports and imports, particularly their quotient, 'the terms of trade', which measures the amount of imports gained by each amount of exports shipped abroad. To take the most controversial example, if in the explosion of exports in the two decades after the end of the American War of Independence the price of exports had risen sharply relative to imports one would be justified in attributing the growth of exports to foreign demand. Simply put, the new eagerness of foreigners to buy British would reveal itself in a favourable move in the terms of trade (a rise in the price of exports divided by the price of imports). Less simply but more exactly put, the demand curve of exports would be moving out faster than the supply curve, and the price, therefore, would rise. But in fact – and here is the matter of controversy, for the statistics are uncertain – the terms of trade during the 1780s and early 1790s shows a tendency, if anything, to fall (Deane and Cole 1967: 85). The pattern is clearer in the nineteenth century, although the pattern must be seen against powerful trends that increased exports ten times over from 1800 to 1860 and cut the terms of trade in half (Imlah 1958: 94–8). Decades with the fastest growth in exports – the 1830s and the 1850s, for example – are also those with the fastest, not slowest, deterioration in the terms of trade. In the long and medium term, to put it another way, the British supply of exports from its more efficient factories and mines was more expansive than the foreign demand.

All this is not to say that foreign demand was bad for Britain. A nation, like a person, is made better off by greater demand, and if greater demand abroad was not a leading sector in British growth it is not on that account to be scorned. Like the dog that did not bark in *The Hound of the Baskervilles*, the demand that did not stagnate or decline can be considered significant. The extent to which Britain was made better off depends on how much the terms of trade improved (or how much they failed to deteriorate) and on the importance of foreign trade. An analogy is useful. Just as the output of steel requires a sacrifice of inputs of iron ore, coal and so forth, likewise an output from the foreign trade 'industry' of imports requires a sacrifice of inputs into it of exports. The efficiency with which exports of woollens, cottons, and coal were transformed into sugar, timber, and wheat is the terms of trade, the price of exports divided by the price of imports. The national importance of, say, the building industry is clearly the value of its output divided by national output. Likewise, the national importance of the foreign trade industry is the value of imports divided by national output, or in the decades around 1800 about 0.10 to 0.15. The terms of trade, recall, fell by some 50 per cent from 1800 to 1860. Had they fallen because of sluggish foreign demand as much as an additional 10 per cent, say, national income would have fallen on this account by 10 (0.10) or 10 (0.15), that is, only 1.0 or 1.5 per cent. The horsepower of trade as an engine of growth seems low.

The method is symmetrical for improvements in the terms of trade. Between the five years around 1780 and around 1785, moving from years of war to years of peace, the money price of Jamaican sugar fell 20 per cent, that of English broadcloth rose 4 per cent (Deane & Cole 1967: 84). If these two goods were representative of English imports and exports, then the terms of trade improved about 24 per cent (i.e. the price of exports rose 24 per cent relative to the falling price of imports) at a time during which imports were some 5 or 7 per cent of English national income, yielding a rise in income of 24 (0.05) or 24 (0.07), that is, a 1.2 or 1.7 per cent increase from the great boom in foreign trade after the Treaty of Paris. The moral of the arithmetic is plain: gains there were from increased demand abroad, but relative to the great increase in national income per head that began to accumulate in the nineteenth century – doubling in six decades – they were small. At no time did the gains from trade revolutionise the economic strength of the nation.

Britain experienced a commercial revolution before an industrial revolution. The inconsiderable little island of the sixteenth century, a mere dwarf beside the Spanish and Portuguese giants, had become by the last third of the eighteenth century the most powerful empire in the world. The loss of British North America gave in the end no lasting hurt to this power, for trade with the United States continued to grow. And in the century after the American War of Independence the trade of Britain reached a volume relative to all economic activity that would have startled an observer transported from 1700. By nineteenth-century standards the trade of the eighteenth century was no great matter. Britain's full involvement in foreign commerce – her unprecedented specialisation in manufacturing, her astonishing foreign investment and emigration – waited on the industrial revolution. The commercial revolution had some small role in industrialisation, very small if the calculations in this chapter are to be believed. As began to be apparent in the late eighteenth century, the strongest effect between commerce abroad and industry at home was from industrialisation to commerce, not the reverse. Trade was the child of industry.

6

The industrial revolution 1780–1860: a survey

D. N. McCLOSKEY

The quiet revolution and its historians

In the eighty years or so after 1780 the population of Britain nearly tripled, the towns of Liverpool and Manchester became gigantic cities, the average income of the population more than doubled, the share of farming fell from just under half to just under one-fifth of the nation's output, and the making of textiles and iron moved into the steam-driven factories. So strange were these events that before they happened they were not anticipated, and while they were happening they were not comprehended. In 1700 a percipient observer of Britain looking towards 1780 might have anticipated its enlarged foreign trade and more active workshops (as, in fact, Daniel Defoe had); in 1860 he might have anticipated the competition of new industrial nations or the application of science to factory and farm during the half-century to come, and by 1900 he would at least have comprehended these events happening (as, in fact, the economist Alfred Marshall and others did). Yet in 1776 Adam Smith predicted a Britain of merchants, farmers, and artificers increasing their incomes at a moderate pace through specialisation and trade (after which national income increased in eight decades by a factor of nearly seven); in 1817 David Ricardo predicted that landlords would swallow whatever the increase would bring (after which rents as a share of national income fell, 1801 to 1861, from about 17 per cent to about $8\frac{1}{2}$ per cent); and in 1848 Karl Marx, in the midst of economic events belying his prediction, predicted that monopoly capital would swallow all (after which the share of labour in income rose, and the real wages of the exploited classes increased in ten or fifteen years by some fifteen per cent and in fifty years by eighty per cent). The British economy from 1780 to 1860 was unpredictable because it was novel, not to say bizarre.

By analogy with the political revolution in France in the 1790s the transformation of economic life in Britain was called, after it had happened, an 'industrial revolution', although its impact on the way people lived was greater, if slower, than most political revolutions. True, its immediate impact on culture or politics was slight. Although some novelists – sociologists before sociology – depicted industrial characters, poets and painters locked their gaze on mountains and marigolds, the odd satanic mill aside. A contemporaneous but otherwise unrelated rationalisation of methods of government had perhaps as much impact on the Reform Bill of 1832 or the crumbling of mercantilist restrictions culminating in the repeal of the Corn Laws in 1846 as did the new economic power of Manchester. Landed wealth bought members and membership of Parliament and staffed its governments until well after commercial and manufacturing wealth had come to exceed land in economic weight. From the introduction of a liberal dole for agricultural workers in the revolutionary year of 1795 to the panic of the 'last labourers' revolt' in 1830 the agricultural poor and their revolutionary potential exercised the thoughts of ministers and militia officers well after factory hands had outnumbered farm hands.

Yet, for all that, the industrial revolution was the central event of modern history, British or other, more in memory than in happening. The British example of the early nineteenth century inspired frantic emulation in the late nineteenth century, and myths of how Britain did it influence economic policy to this day. The fascination in poor countries now with industrialisation on the British pattern, complete with exports of manufactures (in an age of ubiquitous skill in making them), puffing railways (in an age of cheap road transport), and centralised factories (in an age of electric power) would seem odd without the historical example in mind. The ghosts of grasping capitalists, expropriated small farmers, and exploited factory workers still haunt economics and politics.

The economic transformation of Britain from 1780 to 1860, then, is strange and important. Although explaining it has been the preoccupation of a battalion of scholars for a century or more, they have so far had only partial success. The history was not a simple experiment. The growth of cities, the increase in population, the rise in national income per head, and the shift from farm to factory happened together, were in some ways connected, but were not connected by mutual necessity. Britain could have industrialised without expanding her population or urbanised without enriching herself. Yet in fact she did all these things at once, confounding the effects of one with the effects of the other. Nor was the experiment controlled. Britain fought, for example, an expensive war against Napoleon in the middle of the period, and her governments, reacting to this and other vicissitudes, repeatedly altered the import duties, monetary arrangements, taxes, and regulations of economic life. The evidence of the experiment is elusive. The evidence is there, waiting to be mined from archives in large quantities, but the proportion of miners to consumers of this intellectual ore has been low. Oddly, much of the quantitative evidence of Britain's industrialisation has been uncovered by foreign scholars. Until Deane and Cole produced their pathbreaking estimates of national income for the period (Deane 1955, 1957a, 1961; Deane and Cole 1967), the statistics of industrial output (Hoffmann 1955), the balance of payments (Imlah 1958), foreign trade (Schlöte 1952), prices (Rousseaux 1938), and the business cycle

(Gayer, Rostow, and Schwartz 1953a), were imports to Britain. The evidence has sometimes been mishandled by accumulating data in favour of an interpretation rather than searching for data that might put the interpretation in jeopardy, a choice of method to be expected in the history of a period so charged with political passion. Finally, and most important, the interpretations of the evidence have been armoured against testing by clothing them in metaphors and abstraction, conveying the impression of understanding without its substance. Some of these metaphorical abstractions are merely vacuous, such as 'the process of industrialisation' or 'primary growth sector'; some are short-cuts to unwarranted conclusions, such as the assertion that the British people 'depended' on foreign trade or that foreign trade was 'an engine of growth'; and some, such as W. W. Rostow's famous assertion (1960) that Britain in this period experienced a 'take-off into self-sustained growth' summarise a grand if empty theory with the merit, at least, of stimulating controversy but the demerit of turning the controversy off the trail.

More and richer people

The cure for excess in metaphor is counting:

Boswell: Sir Alexander Dick tells me, that he remembers having a thousand people in
    a year to dine at his house...
Johnson: That, Sir, is about three a day.
Boswell: How your statement lessens the idea.
Johnson: That, Sir, is the good of counting. It brings everything to a certainty, which
    before floated in the mind indefinitely.
(Boswell's *Life of Johnson* (Everyman edition, London, 1949), vol. II, p. 456)

The most important count, made difficult by the absence of a census until 1801, is of heads. For all the difficulty it is plain that from 1780 to 1860 the population increased to an astonishing and unprecedented degree, increasing in England and Wales by about $1\frac{1}{4}$ per cent per year, with a rising rate in the first half of the period and a falling rate in the second. One and a quarter per cent per year does not sound large, but it was in fact near the highest in Europe at the time and among the highest rates of growth observed in settled communities before the twentieth century. Like Johnson's calculation, the percentage lessens the idea: the result was that for each Englishman in 1780 there were in 1860 2.7; for each in 1760 there were 3.0.

The histories surrounding this statistic are rich. Population grows when births exceed the total of deaths and emigrations, posing the question of which one changed and why. From what statistics have been gathered so far it would appear that from 1780 to 1860 the main change in the nation as a whole was a fall in the death rate (but see chapter 2 above). Whether and why this was so is still uncertain, because the work of recording births and deaths was not taken over by the state from the Church of England until 1838, well after nonconformity and a deterioration in the quality of parish registers had introduced biases into the figures. In any case, as T. H. Marshall remarked fifty years ago, 'a horizontal line on a graph may be as dynamic as a diagonal; the forces that prevent a birth-rate from falling may be as significant as those that make it rise' (1929: 107). What one believes must be explained depends on what one expects, a point that recurs many times in this book. What one expects is altered if British population is viewed from other countries at the time rather than from Britain earlier, for the growth of population was great elsewhere in Europe as well. Until the famine of the 1840s, for example, it was great in Ireland: in 1801 a hostile Catholic island off the coast of Britain had a population over a third of the new United Kingdom; in 1861 it was just over a fifth and, as O'Briens and O'Connors had fewer children and sent large numbers of them to New York, Liverpool and Glasgow, the proportion was falling rapidly.

The cities grew faster than other places, the choice of explanation for this depending once again on what one has come to expect. The arithmetical reasons for the relative growth of cities were, of course, continued migration from the countryside and, less obviously, a fall in the urban death rate that by around 1800 (judging from the statistics for London) allowed cities for the first time to grow more people then they killed. London was by far the largest city, as always, but grew slower than the rest. In 1801 one in seven Englishmen lived in cities larger than 50000 people, and three-quarters of these were Londoners: in 1860 over one in four did, and less than half were Londoners. The list of cities growing fastest – Liverpool, Manchester, Birmingham, Leeds, and Sheffield among the largest ones in 1861; Bradford, Salford, Oldham, Preston and Wolverhampton among the second rank – tells its own story, of the population in the four most industrial counties (the West Riding of Yorkshire, Staffordshire, Warwickshire, and – above all – Lancashire) increasing from 17 per cent of the population in 1781 to 26 per cent in 1861 (Deane and Cole 1967: 103, column for 1781; Mitchell and Deane 1962: 22).

The increase and redistribution of the population was accompanied by its enrichment, contrary to all reasonable expectations: this is the conclusion of the second piece of counting, the counting of national income. The work of Deane and Cole and others implies that the amounts of bread, beer, trousers, shoes, trips to London, warmth in winter, and protection against conquest increased from £11 per head in 1780 to £28 in 1860 (Feinstein 1978: 84, col. 5; Deane and Cole 1967: 78, last column). This is a real increase, no monetary trick: the money income is measured in the prices of one time (the decade of the 1850s here). Because he produced two and a half times more than his great grandfather produced in 1780, the average person in 1860 could buy and use two and a half times more goods and services. If the wheat grown per farm hand or houses cleaned per maid did not increase by two and a half times (they did not) the output of cotton yarn per spinner or tons of freight shipped per sailor would increase by more than two and a half times (they did). The average worker was a great deal more productive than he had been before.

The halving of the population in fourteenth-century England had increased income per worker by a third; in the other direction the doubling of the population in sixteenth-century England had halved income per worker. The expectation warranted by the experience of earlier centuries, then, would have been a fall, not a rise, in income per head after 1780 as the number of heads increased, an expectation confirmed by economic reasoning. The reasoning is not that a fixed income of the nation was in 1860 to be divided among nearly three times more people than it had been in 1780. Pleasing as such arithmetic may seem, it is incorrect, for it involves the elementary (if common) fallacy of supposing that a nation's output is unrelated to the number of people producing it. The correct reasoning, embodied in the dismal predictions by Ricardo and Malthus of the immiseration to come, is that more people produce more (not the same amount, as in the arithmetical reasoning), but less in proportion to their increase if the tools and land they work with do not increase as well. This proposition is known as the law of diminishing returns: growth bumps against inputs that are not reproducible.

Land, in particular, was not reproducible. True, landlords could and did increase the effective amount of land by fertilising and hedging it, and freeing it of ancient customs – or, for that matter, by creating new land from swamps or the sea, as on the Somerset Levels and the Fens. But the source of much of the value of the land was irreproducible and unaugmentable. An owner of the 'original and indestructible powers of the soil', as Ricardo (who first made the point) described them, earned from them 'pure rents', and the very fact that the owner's tenant farmers were willing to pay him the rents indicate that these powers of the soil were useful in production. How useful is measured by the share of pure rents in national income – before 1815 some 17 per cent. Unlike ploughs and engines, the 'free gifts of nature' could not grow in proportion to population: strictly speaking they could not grow at all. In other words, Britain was agricultural (albeit less so at the time than any other country except perhaps Holland), pure rent was a large part of agricultural income (albeit diminishing), and, therefore, a large share of national output depended on a factor that could not grow.

In the eighty years after 1780 the tools with which Englishmen worked did, in fact, grow. By setting aside each year a portion of the nation's resources to invest in repairing old shovels, ships, roads, spindles, and docks and in making new ones Britain increased her panoply from 1780 to 1860 by about 1.6 per cent per year. The number of workers using these tools increased somewhat slower (at 1.3 per cent per year), which is to say that Britain somewhat increased the value of tools per worker. On this count she offset diminishing returns a little.

She offset them much more by using inputs better. What was extraordinary about the industrial revolution is that better land, better machines and better people so decisively overcame diminishing returns. Had the machines and men of 1860 embodied the same knowledge of how to spin cotton or move cargo that they had in 1780 the large number of spindles and ships would have barely offset the fixity of land. Income per head would have remained at its level in 1780, about £11, instead of rising to £28 by 1860 (see the final table in appendix 6.1 below). The larger quantities of capital did make a difference. Had the effort of investment in new capital from 1780 to 1860 not been made – that is, if the Englishman's tools in 1860 had been the same in quantity as well as quality as they had been in 1780 – income per head would have fallen to £6.4. The possibility was remote, for the rate of savings to be used for new capital changed little in the period, and there is no reason to suppose that it would have fallen to zero. The larger part of the difference between this dismal possibility and the £28 per head actually achieved by 1860 was attributable to better technology. In short – and this is the main point – ingenuity rather than abstention governed the industrial revolution.

The location of ingenuity

Great Inventions have usually symbolised this ingenuity. In textiles, first in cotton and with a lag of one or two decades in linen and wool, the inventions harnessed non-human power, initially the power of falling water and later steam, as a team of horses is harnessed to a plough. In the 1770s and 1780s water-driven spindles allowing one factory worker to produce rapidly and simultaneously many strands of cotton yarn initiated the obsolescence of the root meaning of the word 'spinster'. Steam power applied to the weaving of the yarn into cotton cloth began in the early years of the new century (although its massive application awaited the 1820s and later). If cotton cloth is the symbolic consumers' good of the industrial revolution, iron is the symbolic producers' good, and was similarly transformed: in the last two decades of the eighteenth century steam and water power were applied to the bellows in the furnace that melted ore into iron and to mills that rolled out useful shapes as a cook rolls out a pie-crust. The culinary metaphor applies also to the premier innovation in iron, 'puddling', in which, from the 1780s on, a hand process of stirring a soup of iron and boiling off carbon (which weakens the metal) replaced the smith's way of making 'wrought' iron, i.e. hammering it in little pieces (or large pieces: power had been applied to the hammering as well). With the introduction in the 1830s of preheating the air from the bellows the iron industry took the technical form it retained until the introduction of cheap steel (steel is purified and lower-carbon iron) in the 1860s. Cheap iron gradually replaced wood in the construction of bridges, ships, and, eventually, buildings; with the adaptation of wood drills and lathes to iron – no easy task – it replaced wood in machinery as well, allowing machines to run faster and with more precision. The steam engine, of course, was the characteristic iron machine: the steam pump, the steam locomotive, the steam factory, the steam ship, the steam tractor, the steam this and that made it possible for Britain to substitute her large endowment of coal for men, horses, wind and water.

The list of inventions could be extended without limit; clay drainage pipes made by machine and chemical fertiliser in farming from the 1840s on; lathes for making metal bolts and screws from the 1800s; the safety lamp in mining from the 1810s and the wire rope (permitting very deep working) from the 1840s; and scores of others. Few of these ideas were entirely novel, for scientific history is not the same as technological history. Steam engines had existed as toys in classical times, and 'atmospheric engines' (in which condensing steam created a vacuum against which atmospheric pressure pushed) were raising water from mines from the early eighteenth century. Agricultural crops that came to prominence in the industrial revolution, most notably the potato, were novelties only in their new extent. Rails carried coal from the face to the ship long before they carried passengers behind a locomotive.

A list of inventions, furthermore, is not a list of adoptions, for technological history is not the same as economic history. The contrary view was expressed to the historian of the industrial revolution, T. S. Ashton, with unconscious brilliance by a student: 'About 1760 a wave of gadgets swept over England' (Ashton, 1948: 59). The gadgets came more like a gentle (though unprecedented) rain, gathering here and there in puddles. By 1860 the ground was wet, but by no means soaked, even at the wetter spots. Looms run by hand and factories run by water survived in the cotton textile industry in 1860, as in wool, linen and silk. Around 1860 more shipping capacity was built of wood than of iron, and new sailing ship capacity was two and a half times larger than new steamship capacity, not to speak of existing ships – overwhelmingly wood under sail.

The rain left much of the ground untouched. Down to 1860 the places in the economy that the new techniques could touch were manufacturing, mining, and building – what usually spring to mind when one thinks of 'industry' – and trade and transport. From 1801 to 1861 about half of the economy's resources were allocated to these sectors, but within them many of the old ways persisted. The allocation of one resource, labour, is known from the decennial census in greater detail and permits a more illuminating calculation. In 1861, at the end of the customary dating of the industrial revolution, only about 30 per cent of the labour force was employed in activities that had been radically transformed in technique since 1780, railways, ships, mining, metal and machines, chemicals and textiles, and a handful of smaller industries (such as pottery). Britain was not in 1861 a cotton mill. By 1911, by contrast, it is easier to list the classes of employment that had not been transformed: public administration, the professions, commerce (but consider the typewriter), roads, fishing, and (the largest of these) domestic service, taking together the same percentage of the labour force as had in 1861 been taken by partially modernised industries – namely, 30 per cent (Mitchell and Deane 1962: 60) removing from the denominator the unclassified 'All others occupied'. Agriculture acquired its reapers, clothing its sewing machines, food its steam flour mills and refrigerators, building its steam shovels well after the novelty of an accelerated pace of economic life had worn off.

If so much remained to be done in 1860 the great rise in productivity during the 80 preceding years would seem to be a puzzle. The puzzle is merely superficial, however, because the history of the adoption of new techniques is not the history of their economic impact. A steam locomotive pulling coal trucks over rails is from the technological point of view radically different from a horse pulling a coal barge in a canal. The adoption of the new technique, however, may or may not have had a large impact in reducing the cost of transporting coal: that the new technology was revolutionary in form and was adopted is consistent with both a trivial and a significant advantage over the old technology. The advantage must be measured directly, not inferred from the outlandishness of new machines or the rapidity with which they superseded old machines.

And, in fact, many of the few novelties adopted between 1780 and 1860 had great advantages. The most spectacular case is cotton cloth. A piece of cloth that sold in the 1780s for 70 or 80 shillings was selling in the 1850s for around 5 shillings. Some of this decline was attributable to declines in the prices of the inputs to cloths, especially raw cotton after the introduction of the cotton gin (picking out the seeds in the raw cotton) and the consequent extension of cotton growing in the United States. But most of the decline was attributable to innovations in preparing, spinning, and weaving the cotton which enormously decreased the cost of the resources to produce a piece of cloth. From 1780 to 1860 on average these technological changes appear to have reduced the materials, labour, and capital per piece by over 2.5 per cent each year, or, to put it in alternative but equivalent words, they raised by over 2.5 per cent per year the amount of cloth producible from a given bundle of resources. A number rising at over 2.5 per cent a year reaches nearly eight times its initial level in eighty years. By 1860 the new techniques permitted cloth to be produced at a cost about one eighth what it would have cost in 1780: that is, a given bundle of cotton, labour, and machines in 1860 produced eight times more cotton cloth than it did in 1780.

Most of this accomplishment (and all of it before 1812–15) can be attributed to the mechanisation of combing out (carding) the raw cotton and twisting (spinning) it into yarn rather than to the mechanisation of weaving. By 1860, as table 6.1 indicates, the price of cloth would have fallen to a quarter of its

Table 6.1. *The fall in the real cost of cotton cloth* 1780–1860

	Real cost Index	Percentage rate of growth of productivity
c. 1780	100	
		3.4 (3.4)
c. 1812–15	32 (32)	
		2.0 (0.65)
c. 1860	13 (24)	

( ) = without weaving productivity growth
Source: See table 6.2

level in 1780 even had weaving not moved out of the weavers cottages and into factories. Although the power loom was invented in the 1780s, its application awaited later improvements in design and materials, and only after the Napoleonic War did it contribute to productivity change (albeit for a decade or two massively: nearly all the 50 per cent decline in real costs 1815–40 is accounted for by innovations in weaving, concentrated in the late 1820s and 1830s). The same point applies to carding and spinning machinery, and, indeed, to innovations in most industries. The heroic age of invention in cotton had ended by the late 1780s, yet the bulk of the resource savings promised by the inventions of Hargreaves, Arkwright, Kay, Crompton, and Cartwright required the ingenuity of later, lesser men – lesser, at least, in glory. By 1799, which may be taken as the end of the first harvest of inventions, the real price of cloth compared to its level in 1780 had halved; but it was to halve twice more by 1860.

Other industries, such as other textiles, had a similar experience of slow perfection of bright ideas. The devices applied to cotton were applicable to any fibre, but between this obvious conception and the actual creation fell a long shadow of adaptation, adapting machinery to silk, flax, and, most important, wool. Wool weavers in Scotland with their hand looms could still sing in the 1840s:

There's folk independent of other trademen's wark,
For women need no barbers and the dyker's need no clerk;
But none of them can do without a coat or a sark...
So the weaving's a trade that never can fail,
While we aye need a clout to hold another hale.

Though they would very soon join their Lancashire colleagues:

Come all you cotton weavers, your looms you may pull down,
You must get employed in factories, in country or in town,
For our cotton masters have found out a wonderful scheme,

112

These calico goods now wove by hand they're going to weave by steam.
(Dallas 1974: 97, 119)

The railway is another case among many. The dates of opening of the first railway, the Stockton and Darlington (1825) and of the Liverpool and Manchester (1830) stick in the mind as emblems of the dawn, but in the perspective of what followed the charming little engines and trucks were mere experiments. Further developments reduced the resource cost of railways by at least half by 1860.

The impact of the novelties, then, was spread through many years. Their significance depended on the sizes of the industries they transformed. If cotton was used only for kerchiefs and iron only for nails the speed with which their productivity grew would perhaps be interesting in itself (as is the cheapening of clay cups and plates in this period) but not vital to the history of the nation. The appropriate measure of size must be a money measure, for the brute fact that in 1800 Britain produced about 50 million pounds of cotton yarn to be woven into cloth and about 200000 tons of pig iron to be made into castings and wrought iron is uninterpretable. The cloth and the iron must be brought into a unit of account – pounds sterling – that allows them to be compared. And the money measure must be compared with national income as a whole. That the cloth sold for about £17 million and the products of iron for about £2.7 million makes the important point that the characteristic consumers' good of the industrial revolution in fact dwarfed the characteristic producers' good, but beyond this the figures are by themselves unintelligible. The ratio of cotton output to national income in 1800 was about 0.07, the ratio of iron about 0.01. In other words, even very great changes in the productivity of ironmaking would have had little effect on national productivity in 1800 (although more by 1860, when the ratio for iron reached about 0.03).

Cotton is quite another story. The 2.6 per cent of the resources it (had) used that were freed by technical change each year for alternative uses in the economy amounted nationally to (0.07) (2.6 per cent) = 0.18 per cent per year. The calculation can stand for the whole period, because the size of the industry was smaller when (1780 to 1800) its rate of productivity growth was larger and its size larger when (1800 to 1860) its growth was smaller. Now the rate of growth of productivity in the economy as a whole 1780 to 1860 was about 1.2 per cent per year. Cotton alone, therefore, accounted each year on average for 0.18/1.2 per cent or 15 per cent of the total. Five or six more such industries as Lancashire cotton would have made Britain's fortune.

The location of ingenuity was not in fact so concentrated as this. Nonetheless, a relative handful of other industries with large and easily measurable changes in 'productivity' account for a good deal of the fortune's history. Productivity, recall, means the efficiency with which inputs of *all* kinds, not only the labour, are used. Statistics of the prices of products and of the human inputs and materials used to make them can be employed to measure productivity in this sense. The reasoning involved, which has already been used in describing the innovations in cotton, is simple and is at this point worth making explicit. To put it in a sentence, the reasoning is that better ways of making things will result in those things becoming cheaper. To put it more fully, in the absence of changes in productivity the price of, say, cotton cloth will move with the prices of raw cotton, labour and capital employed, with each input carrying a fixed weight in the total change equal to its share in the costs of cloth. If we calculate a weighted average in this way of the prices for the inputs to the manufacture of cloth, we then have a measure of changes in the price of the output, cotton cloth, which would have occurred in the absence of productivity change. Such a measure of the productivity-absent price of cloth might rise or fall; to be concrete, the prices of inputs, and thus of this 'productivity-absent' price, were falling rapidly, for example, in most of the twenty years after the Napoleonic wars. If the actual price of cloth was falling even faster, as it was, then the relative fall is evidence that savings in the costs of inputs were being achieved over and above those from the fall in their prices. That is, cloth was being made with fewer and fewer inputs: productivity was increasing. The difference between the rate of fall in the cloth price and the rate of fall in the input prices is the measure of the increase of productivity.

For the history of national income the industry's productivity change measured in this way is to be multiplied (and was above) by the value of the industry's output divided by national income: 0.07 in the case of cotton. This measure of the importance of cotton (and of other industries) to the nation can be understood as follows. In the four years from 1826 to 1830, at the height of the introduction of power looms, the industry saved through productivity change 13 per cent of its costs. If all its costs (equal, of course, to the value of its output) were, in 1828, $£V$, then it released over the next four years $£0.13V$ worth of resources to serve other demands in the economy. The value of its output in 1828 expressed as a ratio to national income (called $£I$) is $£V/£I$, and multiplying this ratio by the percentage productivity change in the industry (i.e. $£0.13V/£V$) will give $£0.13V/£I$, that is, the resources saved in cotton as a percentage of all resources in the economy. In other words, applying the ratio to the industry's rate of productivity change will give the contribution of that productivity change to national productivity change. And this is what is wanted: a way of gauging the significance of power looms, potteries, and puddling to British economic growth.

The measure here of an industry's importance is not the usual one, although it is the correct one. Happily, the correct measure is typically easy to calculate. National income is here divided into the whole value of the industry's output (output multiplied by its price), not merely (to give the more usual measure of

Table 6.2. *Crude approximations to annual productivity change by sector* 1780–1860

		(1) Rates of growth of productivity (per cent per year)	(2) Value of output divided by national income (1780– 1860 on average)	(3) Contribution to the national growth of pro- ductivity = (1) × (2) (per cent per year)
1	Cotton	2.6	0.07	0.18
2	Worsteds	1.8	0.035	0.06
3	Woollens	0.9	0.035	0.03
4	Iron	0.9	0.02	0.018
5	Canals and railways	1.3	0.07	0.09
6	Coastal and foreign shipping	2.3	0.06	0.14
	Sum of these modernised sectors	1.8 (Average weighted by share in Col. 2)	0.29	0.52
7	Agriculture	0.45	0.27	0.12
8	All other sectors	0.65	0.85	0.55
	Total		1.41	1.19

Sources: For sources and methods of calculation see Appendix 6.1.

importance) into its value *added*. Value added is the portion of the whole value paid directly to labour and capital in the industry, as distinct from payments for material or services from other sectors of the economy (for example, the importing of raw cotton for the material or the mining of coal for the powered machines). It is customary to think of the size of incomes earned *directly* in an industry such as cotton as the appropriate measure of the 'contribution' of the industry to national income, and therefore as the appropriate measure of its importance. The arithmetic of this custom seems plausible, for the sum of all direct earnings (values added) is indeed national income. But for present and most other purposes the raw materials cannot be left out: for measuring productivity change it matters that prices of raw materials are often known with fair precision when prices of value added (labour, capital, and land) are not; for understanding and assessing the productivity change it matters that an industry's innovations often save materials and thereby save the nation's labour and machinery and land indirectly: and for applying the understanding to the history of the industry itself it matters that the cost of materials as well as of labour and the rest determine the supply price of its product.

Applying such thoughts to what is now known of the prices and outputs of Britain's economy during the industrial revolution yields a table (table 6.2) of 'contributions' of each of eight parts of the economy to national productivity change. The figures are very crude approximations, and are to be viewed as first attempts. Nonetheless, they provide a useful framework for the narrative.

The statistics of 'All other sectors' (Row 8) are calculated from what is left over from the whole (1.41) ratio value of output to value added and from the whole (1.19%) national growth in productivity per year. The other seven parts of the whole are based on evidence about the part in question, though it should be emphasised again that the evidence is sparse. The best way to appreciate the sparseness is to read the footnotes to the table. Differences in detail between estimates here and estimates in other chapters result from different choices of how to leap over gaps in the data. The leaps are necessary, but each student of the subject makes them in a personal style: the statistical and the literary approaches to history are not so very far apart.

The result can be looked at in two ways, depending on whether one sees the glass as half full or half empty. The half full way of looking at it is to note with wonderment how very rapid productivity change was in the six 'modernised sectors' distinguished in the table, and how large a share of national productivity change these sectors can explain – 0.52 per cent per year for them alone out of a total of 1.19 per cent per year for the nation. The half empty way of looking at it is to note with equal or greater wonderment how much was left over for sectors unaffected by steam and iron before 1860 to contribute. Their productivity change was slower but their importance was larger, with the result that their contribution to the explanation of national productivity change was larger than that of the modernised sectors. Ingenuity in the industrial revolution was either wonderfully concentrated or wonderfully dispersed, depending on what excites one's sense of wonder.

The wonder of cotton textiles (row 1) has been discussed in detail already. The industry of row 2, worsteds – long-staple wool spun into thin, compact yarn and woven flat, with no nap to the cloth – was similar to cotton in technique, and was quick to adopt the advantageous novelties invented in cotton. The productivity change given in row 3 for the other wool product, woollens, is a mere guess, but probably of the right order of magnitude. Its relative lowness fits at any rate the narrative evidence. That iron's productivity (row 4) grew at about the same rate, high nationally but low by comparison with the other modernised sectors, does not fit the narrative evidence. So much the worse for the narrative evidence. Spectacular though they were in a technical sense, puddling and the hot blast were able to cut the price of bar iron (and its raw material, pig iron) only in half from the 1780s to the 1850s, in the face of little change in the prices of raw materials, especially coal. Coal itself is not included in the table because it is difficult at present to know even the few facts the method requires: the pithead price of coal, wages, owner's royalties, and their shares in costs at the beginning and end of the period. In view of the stable price of coal shipped to London it would be surprising if its productivity change were great, though apparently sufficient to offset the higher costs of deeper mines. The large factor of multiplication from the 1780s to 1860 in the output of coal – 11, when national income was increased by a factor of seven (Clapham 1926–38: vol. 1, 431; Mitchell and Deane 1962: 115) – and the truly stupendous one for iron – 56 (Mitchell and Deane 1972: 131) – were achieved not by producing a great deal more output from the same inputs but by drawing inputs from other industries and setting them to work in mine and furnace.

Transport, on the other hand (rows 5 and 6), had rapid productivity change. Transport rates fell to a third of their former levels on the routes of canals, and if the railway had a less spectacular immediate effect it was less confined by the need for water in its choice of routes and continued to cheapen down to 1860 and beyond. Productivity change in ocean transport was still more rapid. Especially on long hauls the improvement is attributable not to the application of iron and steam to shipping (which came on a large scale later) but to bigger sailing ships with smaller crews per ton of cargo (North 1968). Textiles and transport figure heavily in the explanation of national productivity change, 1780 to 1860; together they account for over two-fifths of it.

Agriculture is more typical of the other sectors of the economy. Productivity change did occur, but at a modest 0.45 per cent per year instead of the 1.8 per cent per year average in cotton and the rest. All the other sectors – commerce as distinct from transportation, the making of clothes as distinct from the making of cloth, food processing (bread-making, beer, canning and so forth) as distinct from food growing, machinery and implements as distinct from the iron raw material, together with domestic service, building and the professsions (having little or no technical change) and chemicals, pottery, glass, gasworks, tanning, furniture (having a good deal of technical change) – experienced productivity change at 0.65 per cent per year on average.

Small though it is by comparison with textiles or transport, 0.65 per cent per year is no trivial achievement. Had agricultural productivity grown as it did (i.e. at 0.45 per cent per year) and had all other sectors grown at this 0.65 per cent per year (instead of some at 1.8 per cent per year), national income per head would still have grown substantially: it would have doubled from 1780 to 1860, rising from £11 to £22 per head (rather than from £11 to £28). The Great Inventions – mule spinning, power weaving, steam traction, and behind these the steam engine – deserve special attention, for their effects were indeed out of proportion to the sizes of the industries in which they flourished. But the doubling of income that would have occurred even had they been Ordinary Inventions serves as a warning: ordinary inventiveness was widespread in the British economy 1780 to 1860.

Explanations: supply

The chronology of growth so far established sets limits on explanations of it. There is something to be explained, something unexpected, namely substantial growth of income per head in the face of a sharp rise in the number of heads. British growth from 1780 to 1860 was not uniquely fast. The rate of growth of income per head was equal or greater in later periods of comparable length. And by comparison with countries industrialising after Britain and having therefore the benefit of techniques perfected in Britain the rate was not spectacular. Yet these very facts are notable. That Britain's experience from 1780 to 1860 was the prelude to modern economic growth at home and abroad, with real incomes per head routinely doubling every half century, demands explanation.

The explanation cannot, it would appear, rely on the accumulation of capital. True, there was a new enthusiasm for projects such as canals and enclosures involving large investments and large but distant returns, whether from a fall in the interest rate (Ashton 1948) or, more fundamentally, from a rise in the national propensity to save (Rostow 1960). As was shown above, however, rises in income that are not explicable as more machines per man dominate the story. This is a bitter disappointment to economists. The scientists of scarcity delight in the thought that more consumption later can come only from abstinence now. As it is put in the mildly comical jargon of the discipline, there is no such thing as a free lunch. Yet indubitably Britain from 1780 to 1860 ate a massive free lunch. The normal return on investment was 10 or 15 per cent per year, the return that would bring the benefits from investment into that equality with costs so pleasing to economists. Yet in fact the nation was earning 12 per cent or so in addition to this on the investments with no corresponding costs, if one attributes all a year's productivity gain to capital. The story that might be called vulgar capitalism – more savings produces more capital which produces more income which produces savings and so again in a 'self-sustained virtuous spiral' (the usual tired witticism) – lacks force for this reason, among others. The higher income was attributable largely to something outside the spiral, namely, technological change.

The significance of capital accumulation for British economic growth can be rescued in various ways, none wholly persuasive. It can be argued that better technology was embodied in new capital equipment, and therefore that the nation could not have had the advantage of the better technology without the new investment. Old spindles and ships, it is said, could not simply be sped up or enlarged or redesigned as the knowledge of how to do so became available.

The persuasive sound of the argument, however, springs from the element of tautology embedded (not to say embodied) in it rather than from any great logical or empirical power. Of course better weaving technology, say, required new looms. But this does not imply that productivity change in weaving required a rise in the nation's savings. Replacement investment provided an occasion, a frequent one, for introducing the better technique. And were this not fast enough to suit businessmen they could divert saving from sectors with low rates of embodied technical change (building and agriculture, for example) to those with high rates (textiles and transport), as did early cotton manufacturers who set up business in disused warehouses rather than spend on buildings money better spent on primitive machines (Crouzet 1972: 38), or as did landlords investing agricultural incomes in canals.

A deeper argument is that investment is under-measured. Knowledge is not free, as Faust could testify, and apprenticeship, schooling, and inventive effort might be viewed as payments to the devil of scarcity. The educational portion of the argument, the only portion that is easily measurable, is not strong on the face of it: although literacy at marriage did increase from 1780 to 1860, especially women's literacy (from an appalling 38 per cent to 65 per cent), the increase was no revolution and the low (and sometimes falling) rates that persisted in industrial areas down to the end of the period confirm the natural supposition that the ability to read was unimportant to a factory hand (Schofield 1973). Still, it has been estimated tentatively that the cost of maintaining the literacy there was – literacy, alas, is not inherited – was as high as 1 per cent of national income in the 1830s (West 1970, but see Hurt 1971a and West 1971), or 7 per cent of total investment in more conventional forms of capital. Admitting the desirability of counting all the costs of achieving higher income, however, the size, and what is more to the point the rate of increase, of non-measured capital would have to have been impossibly large from 1780 to 1860 to account fully for the change in productivity (Deane 1973).

The rejection of capital accumulation makes it necessary to search the menu of the free lunch. If great inventions were most of the story the search could narrow to great inventors, proceeding by a reduction to individual biography. This is the style of much industrial history, still more of business history, and for the task of explaining a handful of definite innovations it has merit. But it was shown earlier that contrary to much thinking on the matter innovation was widespread. The industrial revolution was not the Age of Cotton or of Railways or even of Steam entirely; it was an age of improvement.

Although widespread consequences do not invariably have widespread causes, the betting would have to be on that side. Resources were being allocated better in many places. A favourite locus of improved allocation, for example, is the capital market, for the notion that accumulation governed the industrial revolution dies hard. In the simplest form it is believed that if merchants or landlords can be shown to have invested heavily in railways or coal mines (as they can be), then the original accumulation of industrial capital, in Marx's phrase, will have been identified. Reallocations of capital, however, are ill-matched to the task of explaining a doubling of income per head. The reasoning is simple and distressingly decisive, applying with equal force to reallocations of labour: it can be shown that the potential gains from eliminating misallocation were small. Too much capital is applied to, say, agriculture if capital earns less in agriculture than elsewhere, perhaps 5 per cent a year rather than (to take a generously high figure) the 15 per cent to be earned in manufacturing or transport or other projects. The net gain to the nation of moving £1-worth of agricultural capital into the other projects is clearly $(0.15-0.05)(£1) = £0.1$ per year. As more £1-worths are so moved, however, the differential return narrows (capital become relatively less abundant and therefore more valuable in agriculture and more abundant and less valuable elsewhere), being zero when capital is allocated correctly. The total gain to national income is the area, as it were, of a triangle with a height equal to the amount of capital (in pounds) to be reallocated, a base of 0.15–0.05, and an apex at the point of zero differential. If the percentage allocation of the nation's capital to agriculture in 1860 (25 per cent) is taken as the correct allocation in 1780 (when it was in fact 50 per cent), the correct allocation would require the movement of a quarter of the nation's total capital stock of £670 million. The height of the triangle of gain to reallocation is therefore $(\frac{1}{4}) \times (£670) = £168$ m. and the area of gain is $(\frac{1}{2}) \times (£168m)(0.10) = £8.4$ million. This is only $8\frac{1}{2}$ per cent of British national income in 1780, as against an increase to be explained of 150 per cent per capita down to 1860. No doubt this argument and its conclusion will appear strange at first, but on second thought they can be seen to be in accord with common sense: were differentials in returns to labour or capital very large the labourers or capitalists could be expected in so developed an economy as Britain in 1780 to have exploited them already; and the reallocations that in fact took place between 1780 and 1860 involved no very large portion of the nation's labour and capital. The upshot is a moderate gain on a moderate portion of the nation's resources, not the stuff of revolutions in economic life.

The explanation of the revolution must be sought in less definite reallocations, of human effort and spirit, and in the luck of invention. These are old and obvious notions, although they have not been tested persuasively. Studies of individual enterprise and invention are less conclusive than they are numerous, for what is wanted is general evidence rather than doubtfully representative cases in point. A much-travelled path to general evidence is by way of comparisons, most fruitfully between successful and unsuccessful parts of the country (for example, the vigorous industrial North *versus* the sleepy agricultural South), although more usually between Britain and France. There is growing evidence that the contrast with France has been overdrawn, that if France was for much of the period a country with less freedom for enterprise and more rigid social stratification, this did not long retard the development of new techniques in industry and agriculture (O'Brien and Keyder 1978; Roehl 1976). The industrialization of northern England was merely a little earlier and a little faster than the industrialisation of northern France, Belgium, and the Prussian Rhineland.

Whatever the seed, the ground in these places was fertile. Farmers do not debate whether it is the seed or the soil that causes their crops, nor perhaps should historians, though recognising that both were present. Nothing very definite can be said about the 'preconditions' for British growth, which leaves room for unrestrained speculation on what they were. Security of property, peace, an acquisitive and inquisitive mentality among the people, a hostility to monopolies propped up by government, the ability of the occasional ploughboy to rise to a seat in Parliament are all candidates, and for each an opposing candidate can be found: as to peace, the first half of the period consisted largely of French wars, albeit not on British soil; as to laissez faire and security of property against government, the new interventionism of factory acts replaced the old interventionism of wage regulation (though both were at this time ineffective), and the same French wars left taxes high (though smaller than they were to become in the twentieth century). Fixed backgrounds, by definition, do not move, making it difficult to detect their contribution to the play. Moving them in the imagination is delicate work. One is free to imagine a Britain of lazy businessmen, say, but it is hazardous to infer from the mental comparisons that vigorous businessmen were a prerequisite for British growth. The most that economic reasoning can offer at present is the valuable thought that one condition for growth can substitute for the lack of another. To return to the comical jargon of the field, there is more than one way to skin a cat, and more than one way to grow in wealth (Gerschenkron 1962). How exactly the cat was skinned in Britain from 1780 to 1860 remains uncertain: we know less what it was than what it was not.

Explanations: demand

One thing it probably was not was a response to demand. It is proper to treat demand symmetrically with supply in explaining the growth of iron output or wheat output, but for the nation as a whole it is improper. The demand for things-in-general is income itself, which is determined by the resources and technology supplied to the nation. In the aggregate (with some exceptions to be mentioned below) demand is not an independent factor causing income to grow (Mokyr 1977).

Judging from the frequency with which it has eluded writers on the industrial revolution the point is an elusive one. The simplest way to grasp it is to think of Britain as that favourite of economic exposition, Robinson Crusoe (before

Friday). Obviously, if Crusoe decides to demand more wheat – from himself – his total product, taking wheat and fish together, does not *ipso facto* grow, for he must give up fish to acquire the time to grow more wheat. Still more obviously, if he decides to eat more with his left hand than with his right his total product does not grow, for what goes into one hand must come from the other. Britain, likewise, could (and did) demand more iron for itself, but only at the expense of other things, the factors of supply being given. An expansion of the iron industry caused by a rise in the demand for iron did not 'generate' income, either in the iron industry itself or, though what are wisely known as 'backward linkages' and 'multipliers', in the mines and factories that supplied inputs to the iron industry: it merely redistributed the income. Similarly, like left and right hands, an enrichment of one group (say producers of grain during the Napoleonic Wars) and the consequent increase in their demands for manufactured goods comes at the expense of impoverishment of another (consumers of grain) and a decrease in their demands (Hueckel 1973).

There are two conditions under which demand in the aggregate can nonetheless have an effect on the size of national income. Neither was important. The first is foreign trade, which can again be made clear by reference to Crusoe. If Crusoe trades with someone, say Friday, demand – Friday's demand, not his own – does affect his income. The increase in population and wealth abroad undoubtedly did increase British national income, but the increase attributable to this cause was small. The second condition under which aggregate demand would have a role of its own is mass unemployment. If Crusoe behaved like another shipwrecked sailor

...my grandfather knew
Who had so many things which he wanted to do
That, whenever he thought it was time to begin,
He couldn't because of the state he was in.

(Milne 1927: 36)

he would be behaving like a modern economy in depression. For reasons that are still unclear, the business cycle in virulent form appears to have begun during the industrial revolution (Gayer, Rostow, and Schwartz 1953a). Crop failures in an agricultural economy evoked prayerful resignation: business failures in an industrial economy, man-made as they were, evoked social criticism. The social disease at which the diagnoses and cures were directed, however, was an episodic one, not chronic. This is the critical and frequently overlooked point for the role of aggregate demand in British economic growth. Crusoe can overcome his indecision and end his involuntary idleness, raising his income by the amount of the increase in demand, but from one episode of full employment to another his income is constrained by supply, not demand. And at the peaks of the business cycles Britain was near full employment. The force of the argument can be made plain in a simple calculation. The increase in income to be explained is an increase from £11 per head in 1780 to £28 in 1860. Suppose, to take the most favourable case, that 1780 to 1860 was one long secular boom, with previously unemployed resources set to work by a rise in aggregate demand – it does not matter whether the rise was itself a consequence of external demand (more foreign trade) or internal demand (less hoarding of money or more creation of money by the government). To sustain the interpretation, unemployment in 1780 would have to have been at least $(28-11)/28 = 61$ per cent. The figure is absurd – the most enthusiastic believer in open or disguised unemployment as a factor in economic life would not advance a figure above, say, 20 per cent at this time – and therefore the premise that aggregate demand dominated the industrial revolution is absurd as well.

Demand is a more plausible cause of growth if its effects are constrained to work through the composition of output. Here, again, the verdict is not decided, but possibilities may be offered. The oldest argument, a neglected fruit of Adam Smith's thinking, is that the division of labour is limited by the extent of the market. Put in more general language, it could well be that a rise in the demand for, say, cotton allowed the industry to exploit economies of scale, to train a highly differentiated and specialised work-force, for example, or to support specialised sub-industries, such as cotton marketing or machinery-making.

There is a version of this thought with a special air of economic precision that must be rejected at once. It is commonly said that the expansion of the textile or iron industry led to larger firms which could, as it is put, spread fixed costs over a larger output, and therefore produce textiles or iron at lower total cost. But if the size of firms did increase during the industrial revolution (frequently, in fact, the size decreased, by the very specialisation being discussed) it is not because the industries in which they were worked were larger. The size of a single small firm is determined by the size best suited to the money-making purposes of the firm, not by the size of the industry. To suppose otherwise is to suppose that market demand is shared out to firms in a centralised and egalitarian fashion, one Nth share to each of N firms. The truth is the opposite: each of the N firms decides what it will supply independently, adjusting its independent decision to the prevailing price. A larger total demand for cotton or iron will encourage more firms of the optimal size to enter these industries, not increase the size of existing firms, and certainly not induce the existing firms to move down along their separate cost curves: each firm will already have exploited economies of scale within its walls, for each wishes, naturally, to produce for sale at the lowest possible cost.

Any economies of scale initiated by increases in demand, therefore, would have been economies of a whole industry's scale. In this form the argument is cogent. But whether it is true and significant in the industrial revolution remains to be seen. The increase in one demand, to repeat, must be achieved at the expense of a decrease in another. If potential economies of scale were scattered about the economy at random then what was gained on the swings might be lost on the roundabouts. If they were located in the sectors made relatively larger by demand then there may have been a net gain to the nation. We do not know.

Nor do we know the significance of another and related argument from demand, that disproportionate rises in the demand for one or another product induced technological change, although ignorance has not forestalled confident assertions that it was or was not significant. To return to an earlier line of argument, if technological change is costly then one can expect technological change to occur in those industries in which demand is rising rather than falling, just as any costly factor of production is allocated to expanding industries. Like economies of scale, however, the effect must be asymmetrical to lend significance to demand. It is entirely plausible that the textile industries were ripe for technological revolution from the middle of the eighteenth century on, but it must be shown that some other industry – furniture, say – whose demand languished because textiles grew (a foolish premise, but adequate for the point) was not thereby robbed of its own technological revolution. In any case, the notion of technological ripeness turns attention back to supply, to the initial supply of technological knowledge and the supply of vigour to exploit it.

A more mechanical argument capturing the effects of demand is available, and has the great merit of being testable. Suppose that technological change descended on industries for reasons unconnected with their sizes. In that case the national rate of technological change would depend on the importance of the various industries, that is, on the composition of demand. A smaller cotton industry would have the same rate of technological change but would contribute less to national growth than a larger one. The argument has in fact already been tested: it was found earlier that had the modernised industries mentioned in table 6.2 experienced productivity growth at 0.65 rather than 1.8 per cent per year (which is equivalent to reducing their size to about 40 per cent of their actual size), income per head would nonetheless have doubled between 1780 and 1860, not far short of its actual increase. And so the circle is complete. The pursuit of effects on income related to demand has come back to supply, that extraordinary flowering of ingenuity in many sectors of the British economy known as the industrial revolution.

The causes of the industrial revolution are uncertain, to be sure, but not therefore mysteries beyond knowledge. If many of the explanations proposed can be shown to fail the tests of economic fact, the failures themselves are increments to knowledge. Later chapters examine the intellectual successes and failures in more detail. Chapters 7, 8 and 11 describe the histories of the two major resources of the nation, accumulated capital and human effort, showing how

124

exactly machines and men were brought to the factory. Chapters 10 and 12 describe two great sectors, agriculture and transport, each of whose links with the industrial revolution have been considered vital. Chapters 9 and 14 describe the consequence of the revolution for the distribution of income and for the social and political life of the nation. As will become clear, the explanation and evaluation of the industrial revolution is not the only task of British economic history for the period 1780–1860. To repeat an earlier theme, much of Britain's economic life was only lightly touched by it. But it was, in more ways than one, the primary event.

Appendix 6.1
Sources and methods of calculation for table 6.2

Except for row 8 (which is discussed below), the sources are arranged by rows. Column 1 is the estimate of productivity, usually estimated by subtracting the rate of growth of output price (e.g. cotton cloth) from the rate of growth of input price (e.g. spinning labour and raw cotton). Column 2 is the ratio of the industry's value of output to national income averaged over 1780–1860.

As explained in the text, column 3 is the product of these two, i.e. the industry's productivity growth per year weighted by the industry's importance in national product.

Row 1 (cotton): column 1
Because raw cotton is an import its price is well known (Mitchell and Deane 1962: 490–1). As such things go, the wage of labour in cotton is also well known (Wood 1910 can be extrapolated back to 1780 by Gilboy's Lancashire wages in Gilboy 1934: 282). The crucial and difficult statistic is the price of the output, i.e. yarn and cloth of average quality. The sources were Sandberg 1974: 239–48; Edwards 1967: 240–2; Ellison 1886: 55, 61. The calculations in the text of productivity change in spinning and weaving separately use cost shares of the two processes in the final product.

Row 1 (cotton): column 2
Deane and Cole (1967: 185, 187) estimate the gross value of cottons produced; and on p. 166 estimate British national income from 1801 on by decades. The estimate of 0.07 is if anything an understatement of the ratio of the two 1780–1860 (making due allowance for the low ratio likely before 1800).

Rows 2 and 3 (worsted and woollens): column 1
The best estimates, so to speak, are the worsteds. The essential fact is that, around 1805, a worsted piece cost four times the value of the raw wool, around 1857 only two times (Deane and Cole 1967: 198). In the meantime the price of raw wool had fallen at 0.7 per cent per year (Deane and Cole 1967: 196, column 2 divided by column 1). These two facts together imply that the price of a worsted piece fell 1805–57 at 2.0 per cent per year. Labour's wage did not change much (Mitchell and Deane 1962: 348, note 3 to table). The fall in the output price minus the fall in the price of raw wool weighted by its share in costs (the latter being the average of 0.25 and 0.50) yields 1.77 per cent per year, or about 1.8. The woollens productivity is a mere guess – half the worsted, on the grounds that the mechanisation begun in cotton came next to worsteds and only tardily to woollens.

Rows 2 and 3 (worsteds and woollens): column 2
Deane and Cole (1967: 196, 198) estimate woollens and worsted as roughly equal in size, and some 7 per cent of national income together (e.g. p. 196, col 4 for 1805 divided by p. 166, last column, for 1801–11 averaged equals 8.4 per cent; likewise for 1855–64 and 1861 equals 6.4 per cent).

Row 4 (iron): column 1
Pig iron prices (coke made) for 1780 are from Charles K. Hyde 1973: 401–14. For 1860 they are from Mitchell and Deane 1962: 493. Prices for wrought iron are from Ashton (1924: 101), which is a mere remark on the fall in price from £20 to £12 down to 1812. Birch (1967: 42) reports a price of £16 a ton in 1787, which lends credence to the estimate of £20 in 1780. The price for 1860 is taken to be the £8 a ton figure for the 1850s given in Mitchell and Deane (1962: 493). With equal weights on cast and wrought iron the price falls at about 1.0 per cent per year 1780–1860. Coal prices fell somewhat in the period, making 1.0 per cent an overestimate. The estimate of 0.9 per cent allows for a modest fall in the prices of inputs into iron.

Row 4 (iron): column 2
Average of 1 per cent around 1800 and 3 per cent around 1860. Numerators are tons of pig iron (Mitchell and Deane 1962: 131), in the two years multiplied by its price (ibid: 492f) multiplied by 2 to allow for fabrication into wrought (much fabrication) and cast (little fabrication) products.

Row 5 (canals and railways): column 1
The railway estimate of 2.2 per cent per year is Hawke's (1970: 302, col. 10), assumed to apply back to 1830. Before 1830 the source of productivity change is assumed to be canals, cutting overland transport costs by perhaps two-thirds on the perhaps half of the transport experiencing improvement down to 1860. The implication of these guesses is a rate of 0.8 per cent per year from 1780 to 1830, the end of substantial canal building. The entire productivity-experiencing sector, then, had productivity growth at $(50/80)$ $(0.8) + (30/80)$ $(2.2) = 1.3$ per cent per year over the entire period 1780 to 1860.

Row 5 (canals and railways): column 2
Railway receipts were only about 4 per cent of British national income in 1861 (Mitchell and Deane 1962: 225; Deane and Cole 1967: 166). The rest of the productivity-experiencing portion of transport might add another 3 per cent for 7 in all.

Row 5 (coastal and foreign shipping): column 1
D. C. North (1968) estimates productivity change in Atlantic ocean shipping 1814 to 1860 at 3.30 per cent per year. He estimates it at 0.45 per cent per year from 1600 to 1784: a guess of 1.0 per cent per year 1780–1814 is perhaps reasonable. The resulting average for the entire period would be $(35/80)$ $(1.0) + (45/80)$ $(3.3) = 2.3$ per cent per year.

Row 6 (coastal and foreign shipping): column 2
Imlah's estimates for the balance of international payments of Net Credits from Shipping (1958: 70–2, col. F) divided by British national income (Mitchell and Deane 1962: 366) give 3.2 per cent for 1820 and 4.5 for 1860. Foreign earnings, which these are, were probably growing faster than coastal shipping. The figure of 6.0 per cent for both makes a crude allowance for this fact.

Row 7 (agriculture): column 1
The rate of change of labour and land prices (weighted 0.75 for labour, 0.25 for land) minus the rate of change of output prices. Labour's wage (England and Wales) from Mitchell and Deane (1962: 348f); land's rent from Norton, Trist and Gilbert, 'A Century of Land Values: England and Wales' (1891), reprinted in E. M. Carus-Wilson, ed. (1962: vol. III, 128f). Output price is the Gayer, Rostow and Schwartz index of 'Domestic Commodities' (largely agricultural) in Mitchell and Deane (1962: 470), extrapolated to 1860 by relation to Rousseaux's index of total agricultural products (Mitchell and Deane 1962: 471f) 1840–50. The resulting productivity change was assumed to apply to the 1780–95 period as well.

Row 7 (agriculture): column 2
Deane and Cole (1967: 166), average share 1780–1861 of agriculture in national income (agriculture has very few purchased inputs), with 1780 and 1790 assumed to be the same as 1801.

Row 9 (total)
The total requires estimates of national productivity, which in turn requires estimates of national outputs and inputs. The basic source is Feinstein (1978). The initial date used here is 1780 instead of 1760, which necessitates some interpolation. The principle in the interpolation is that 1760–80 was a time of war, in which income and capital per man could be expected to remain constant. Therefore, Feinstein's estimate (based on those in Deane and Cole) of gross British domestic product per head of population in 1760 (i.e. £11 – Feinstein's table 25, col. 5) is used for 1780 as well; so too is his 1760 estimate in constant prices of domestic reproducible capital (place cited, col. 1, 1760 level blown up by change in number of workers 1760–80). The number of workers in 1780 is derived by applying the 1801 participation rate (0.44) to the 1780 population of Britain (as Feinstein did for 1760). The 1780 population is derived by calculating the Scotland/England and Wales ratio for 1761 and 1791 (Deane and Cole, 1967: 6) using Feinstein's implied figure for Scotland in 1761 of 1.3 million; then interpolating this ratio by a straight line to 1780; then applying the interpolated rate to the (allegedly known) population of England and Wales in 1781 to get Scottish population. Interpolating the Scottish growth rate 1761–91 gives very similar results.

Basic statistics of income, labour and capital

	Income per head	Labour	Capital	Capital labourer
1780	£11	3.93m.	£670	£170
1860	£28	10.8m.	£2770	£256

To do productivity calculations one needs shares.
Land's share: This is meant to comprise pure rents alone, not returns on capital. Feinstein gives (1978: part V, section 5, p. 72, 'Farm land') estimates of the unimproved value of farm land at his four benchmark dates and also the year's purchase applied to all rents (not only pure rents). Dividing the years' purchase into the unimproved value should give

annual pure rent; 1760 = £15.2 m., 1800 = £22.5 m., 1830 = £29.3 m., 1860 = £45.0 m. These appear to be reasonable in relation to agricultural income. Feinstein uses 20 years' purchase to capitalise urban rents (p. 73). Applying this, as with farm land, to his estimates of the capital value of urban land rent (1978: table 15, p. 68, line 6) and then removing his deflation to 1851–60 prices (table 5, p. 38, col. 1) yields annual urban rents of $1760 = (15.2 + 0.9)/90 = 0.18$; $1800 = (22.5 + 1.0)/140 = 0.17$; $1830 = (29.3 + 1.9)/310 = 0.10$: $1860 = (34.0 = 21)/650 = 0.085$. The arithmetic average, presumably typical of 1780–1860, is 0.13.

Labour's share: The estimate by Deane and Cole of wages and salaries in 1801, 1831 and 1861 (1967: 152) was divided by their estimate of gross national income minus income from abroad (p. 166):

	1801	1831	1861
Wages and salaries	104	148	315
GNI	232	336	648
Share	0.45	0.44	0.49

The 1780 share was supposed to be equal to the 1801 share. The average is $[2(0.45) + 0.44 + 0.49]/4 = 0.46$.

Capital's share: As usual, a residual. The simplest calculation is: $1.00 - 0.46 - 0.13 = 0.41$. The result is:

	Growth rate (per cent per year)	Share	Contribution to 'Explaining' change in income per head (per cent per year)
Income/head	1.17	—	—
Capital/labour	0.35	0.41	+0.14
Land/labour	−1.26	0.13	−0.16
Residual	1.19	—	+1.19

The assertions earlier in the text about diminishing returns derive from recombinations of these facts.

7

Capital accumulation and the industrial revolution

C. H. FEINSTEIN

Introduction

One characteristic that distinguishes the century 1760 to 1860 from all preceding economic change is the great increase in the range and quantity of durable assets (other than land) used in the production of goods and services. In 1760, on the eve of the industrial revolution, these assets accounted for less than a third of the national capital of Great Britain; a century later, when the total capital had risen almost sixfold in value, their share had increased to one half. Over the same period there was a corresponding decline in the relative importance of unimproved land, the oldest asset and the only one not made by man. If we focus our attention on the sectors of the economy most closely associated with industrialisation, the rise in the importance of these durable assets is even more marked: the share of the national capital invested in them in industry, trade and transport increased dramatically from a negligible 5 per cent to a substantial 26 per cent.

The form and the effect of the accumulation of 'fixed' capital – including factories and farmsteads, mines and machines, private houses and public halls, irrigation and drainage works, roads and sewers, canals, ships and railways – is the main theme here. 'Human' capital is the subject of chapter 11. There are two other types of non-human capital accumulation: additions to the crops and livestock on farms, to the stocks of raw materials, semi-manufactured products and finished goods held by manufacturers and traders, and to work in progress (all subsequently referred to for brevity as 'stocks'); and the net acquisition of foreign capital, both physical and financial. These are also covered, but more briefly than fixed capital. The concept of capital here (durable capital in the form of fixed capital and stocks) differs substantially from the concept of capital as generally understood by businessmen and shown in ordinary business accounts. The latter would usually include not only physical assets but also non-tangible assets (good will) and the financial capital required to cover trade debts, payment of wages, and so fourth; and they might also make a provision for the depreciation of fixed assets, whereas the present estimates do not do so. They measure the value of capital by adding up its original costs with no deduction for subsequent wear and tear or for obsolescence.

128

Table 7.1. *National capital by sector and type of asset, Great Britain* 1760 *and* 1860 (£ *million at current prices, and as a percentage*)

	1760 (£m.)	1760 (%)	1860 (£m.)	1860 (%)
I. By sector				
1. Residential and social capital	130	16	860	18
2. Agriculture	600	74	1710	36
3. Industry and commerce	60	7	1120	24
4. Transport	20	3	590	12
5. Overseas assets	—	—	470	10
Total	810	100	4750	100
II. By type of asset				
6a. Land – Farm	380	47	1020	21
b. non-farm	30	4	420	9
7a. Domestic fixed capital – farm	110	14	440	9
b. non-farm	150	18	1930	41
8a. Stocks – farm	110	13	250	5
b. non-farm	30	4	220	5
9. Total domestic capital	810	100	4280	90
10. Overseas assets	—	—	470	10
Total	810	100	4750	100

Source: Feinstein (1978: tables 8 and 15), adjusted to current prices. All estimates are rounded to nearest £10m.

Note: This table does not cover the total national wealth since it excludes (a) naval vessels, barracks and other military assets and (b) furniture, works of art, plate, etc. At a very rough guess these assets would add about £100m. in 1760 and about £600m. in 1860. See Feinstein (1978: 82).

If the concepts behind the measurements are sophisticated, the measures themselves are nonetheless crude. The margins of error of the estimates of the national capital and of the flows of capital formation are large, usually between 10 and 25 per cent, and more in a few cases. (For a detailed account of the sources and methods of estimation see Feinstein (1978: 35–82)). With few exceptions the estimates cannot be based on yearly statistics of the number and prices of assets produced or of actual expenditures for capital each year. Especially before 1800, it is necessary to rely on fragments of evidence glued together with rough guesses and more or less arbitrary assumptions. The results indicate broad orders of magnitude, but that is the most that can be claimed for them, and accordingly they must be used with due care. Similar reservations apply to the estimates of output, population and labour supply which are used later in this chapter and elsewhere in this book. The point is by now a familiar one: economic statistics past or present are not literally 'data' or 'given', to be believed in every digit and manipulated without care.

The changing pattern of national capital

A broad picture of the changes in the national capital over the century from 1760 is given by table 7.1. The transformation reflected in this table is quite striking. In total, the *value* of the national capital increased almost sixfold over the period. The greater part of this expansion (roughtly 60 per cent) was the outcome of a real increase in the quantity of capital; the balance results from the fact that prices roughly doubled over the century. At the same time there were sweeping changes in the composition of the total. At the beginning of the period the capital engaged in agriculture accounted for 74 per cent of the total; at the end its share had fallen to 36 per cent (row 2). Within this sector the contribution of unimproved farm land fell from 47 per cent to 21 per cent (row 6a) and the farm crops and livestock declined in relative importance from 15 per cent to 6 per cent (row 8a). A corresponding gain occurred in capital invested in industry, commerce and transport from 10 per cent to 36 per cent (rows 3 and 4), with the greater part of this increase in the form of fixed capital. Note especially the large rise in the importance of fixed capital relative to stocks: from 1:1 in 1760 to almost 6:1 in 1860. This change in turn led to major alterations in both the organisation of industrial production and in the methods by which finance was raised. Note, finally, the one exception to the picture of large shifts in the composition of the national capital by sector and by type of asset: the relative importance of the stocks of dwellings, inns, public buildings and other social capital remained broadly unchanged over the century (row 1).

Annual capital formation

In order to examine more closely the factors lying behind the increase in quantity and change in the composition of the stock of capital we turn next to the annual flows of capital expenditure. The basic relationship of the stocks to the flows of reproducible capital (assuming no change in prices) is simplicity itself: the new stock is the old stock plus the inflow of new capital (births, so to speak) minus the outflow of old capital (deaths or retirements). In 1800, for example

$$G_{1800} = G_{1799} + I_{1800} - R_{1800}$$

where G_{1800} or G_{1799} = Gross stock at the end of the year, 1800 or 1799
I_{1800} = Investment in new capital during 1800
R_{1800} = Retirement (scrapping or sales) of capital assets during 1800.

We generally assume, for want of better information on how it dies, that all capital was automatically retired at the end of its working life of a certain number

Table 7.2. *Total investment, Great Britain* 1760–1860 (£ *million p.a., decade average, at* 1851–60 *prices*)

	Fixed capital formation (1)	Stock-building (2)	Foriegn investment (3)	Total investment (4)	Total as % of GNP (5)
1761–70	6.5	1.0	0.5	8.0	8
1771–80	7.0	2.0	1.0	10.0	10
1781–90	11.0	2.0	1.5	14.5	13
1791–1800	14.5	3.0	1.5	19.0	14
1801–10	16.5	1.0	−2.0	15.5	10
1811–20	20.5	2.0	5.0	27.5	14
1821–30	28.5	4.0	7.5	40.0	14
1831–40	38.5	3.5	4.5	46.5	13
1841–50	49.5	5.0	6.5	61.0	13
1851–60	58.0	3.5	20.0	81.5	13

Source: Feinstein (1978: tables 6, 16 and 28); all estimates are rounded to the nearest £0.5m.

of years. If barns and bridges built in 1770 were worn out in thirty years, for example, the investments of 1770 in those assets would become the retirements of 1800. Clearly, then, the barns and bridges still standing in 1800 will be all those built since 1770 because all those built before 1770 would in 1800 long since have been retired (in 1799, 1798 and so forth), and all those built since 1770 would still be standing in 1800. The upshot is that the capital stock in 1800, for example, can be estimated by adding up the annual flows back to the years of birth of the capital assets:

$$G_{1800} = I_{1799} + I_{1798} + I_{1797} + \ldots + I_{1771} + I_{1770}$$

This equation permits one to move freely between evidence on stocks (from, for example, a census of bridges in a particular year) and evidence on flows (from, for example, annual orders of iron by bridge-builders). The logic is exactly analogous to that applied in earlier chapters to the human population. The stock of equipment, as of people, is the result of past births and deaths.

There are three forms of the annual flow of investment: gross domestic fixed capital investment (for brevity, fixed capital investment), additions to stocks and work in progress (stockbuilding), and foreign investment. The last two can of course be negative, but they were probably usually positive in this period. The three series are set out in table 7.2. All the series are measured at the prices of one date (the decade 1851–60), so as to provide a comparison of changes over time in the volume of investment (and savings) which is not affected by the very large price movements that occurred during the century, in particular the steep rise from about 1793 to 1813 and the equally steep fall in the next two decades.

The increase in the volume of total investment was very marked: from about £8m. p.a. in the 1760s to about £80m. p.a. in the 1850s (col. 4). The dominant element in this expansion was domestic fixed capital formation, but in the final decade it was supported by the beginning of the upsurge in foreign investment which was to be such a prominent feature of the late nineteenth century. By contrast, the expenditure on stockbuilding fell sharply in relative importance: in the first two decades covered by table 7.2 it amounted to almost 20 per cent of investment at home but by the last two decades its share had dropped to 7 per cent (cols. 1 and 2).

The most interesting conclusion to be drawn from col. 5 of table 7.2 however, is that for most of the hundred-year period the rising level of national investment did no more than keep pace with the growth of national income. The ratio of investment to income appears on the basis of these estimates to have changed significantly only between the 1760s and the 1790s, when it rose from 8 per cent to 14 per cent: Thereafter it was broadly stable at between 13 and 14 per cent, except for 1801–10 when it shows – as might be expected in a decade of feverish borrowing by the government to fight the French – a sharp fall.

The composition of fixed capital formation

Further consideration of the rising levels of investment requires breaking down the series for fixed capital formation into its parts, as is done in table 7.3, for averages over periods of two or three decades. The volume of fixed investment in agriculture, that is the capital outlays by landowners (and, to a much smaller extent, by tenant farmers) on such items as enclosures, drainage and the construction of farm buildings, nearly trebled yet its importance in the overall picture declined sharply (col. 1). The estimates for agriculture are based on crude guesses about the ratio of capital outlays to gross rental income, that is about what share of their income landlords put back into the land (Feinstein 1978: 48–9). The ratio appears to have been about 6 per cent in the 1760s, rising rapidly to a peak of around 16 per cent during the years 1795–1815 when enclosure and improvement in response to the war boom in agriculture was at its maximum. With the onset of falling prices and agricultural depression after the war the rate of capital spending dropped back again, leaving the absolute volume roughly stable down to 1840. In the last two decades the ratio rose again as new techniques and improved markets initiated the 'golden age' of British farming, with landlords spending liberally on drainage, covered yards, steam engines, modern iron implements and other improvements (see ch. 10 and vol. 2, ch. 8). Above all, however, the century was one of industrial revolution: at the beginning, agriculture was the largest of the five sectors chronicled in the table, accounting for 33 per cent of total investment; by the end it was the smallest, accounting for only 12 per cent.

Table 7.3. *Gross domestic fixed capital formation by sector 1761–1860. (£ million p.a. at 1851–60 prices and as a percentage)*

	Agriculture (1)	Industry and trade (2)	Railways (3)	Other transport (4)	Residential and social (5)	Total (6)
			(£ millions)			
1761–90	2.5	2.0	—	2.0	2.0	8.0
1791–1820	4.0	4.5	—	3.5	5.0	17.0
1821–40	4.5	11.5	2.0	4.5	11.0	33.5
1841–60	6.5	17.5	11.5	7.5	11.0	54.0
			(percentage)			
1761–90	33	22	—	23	22	100
1791–1820	25	26	—	20	29	100
1821–40	13	35	6	14	32	100
1841–60	12	33	21	14	20	100

Source: Feinstein (1978: table 6); all estimates are rounded to the nearest £0.5m. Components may not add to total because of rounding.

In sharp contrast to the position in agriculture there was a rapid expansion of fixed capital in the industrial and commercial sector (col. 2). The annual capital spending leapt from about £2 million per annum in the late eighteenth century to about £17 million in the mid-nineteenth century, accounting for one third of the total. Outlays on machines grew most rapidly, and these machines – especially such schoolboy favourites as Boulton and Watt's steam engine, Crompton's mule, Cort's puddling furnace, and Maudslay's machine tools – symbolise the industrial revolution. It is important to note, however, that the outlays involved were quite small relative to national investment as a whole and even relative to the sums expended within the industrial and trade sector on mills, factories, shops, inns and other buildings. The division of the totals early and late in the century was (in £ million):

	Machinery and equipment	Industrial and commercial buildings	Mines, gas and water works
1761–90	0.5	1.5	—
1841–60	5.0	9.5	3.0

The machines embodying novel techniques were cheap relative to their housing.

The outlays for transport (cols. 3 and 4) accounted for a steady one fifth of the total until 1840; then in the next two decades the massive investment in railways (col. 3) raised the share to just over one third. Other transport (which is also discussed in chapter 12) includes, first, canals and inland waterways, investment in which reached a peak of some £1 million per annum in the canal mania of the 1790s and then fell away. It includes, second, the roads and the carriages and coaches which travelled upon them. Increasing production and trade called for better roads and these in turn encouraged greater use of road transport. Outlays on the steady extension and improvement of turnpike and parish roads averaged about £0.5 m. p.a. from 1760 to 1810 and doubled to about £1.0 m. p.a. in the remaining decades as the willingness to pay for easier and more rapid transport increased, and the road-building techniques of McAdam and others were more widely adopted. Finally, other transport includes the merchant navy and the associated docks and harbours. The capital spending on new ships rose rapidly from around £1 m. p.a. in the decades to 1820, to almost £4 m. p.a. on average in the years 1841–60, reflecting the application of iron and steam to ships and the expansion of Britain's overseas trade.

These sums however, are dwarfed by the capital absorbed by the railways (col. 3). The annual outlays soared from around £4 m. in the 1830s to an average of £15m. in the 1840s, and then fell back to about £9 m. in the closing decade. At its peak in the 1840s this capital expenditure accounted for some 28 per cent of total fixed capital formation and provided for an increase in track from 1500 to 6000 miles. The ability of the country to finance this vast programme is considered below, but we may note here that the rise in the share of the total fixed investment taken by the railways from 1841 to 1860 is almost entirely offset by a decline in the proportion used for residential and social capital (col. 5). Considering that expenditure on social capital (basically public health and sanitation) was rising in relative importance in these decades, the fall was borne entirely by the expenditure on new housing. It remains to be seen whether a financial mechanism can be traced whereby capital was diverted from house building to railway construction. In any event, the sudden diversion of the nation's savings to the railway justifies a long-standing description of the middle decades of the nineteenth century: The Railway Age.

The investment ratio and the standard of living

The facts of investment shed light on two interrelated issues which have been the subject of historical debate, the share of the national product allocated to investment (with its implied consequences for the rate of growth of the economy) and the share available for consumption (with its implications for the standard of living of the community, given the rate of growth of population).

A fundamental proposition about the role of capital accumulation in economic growth was advanced by W. A. Lewis (1954: 155): 'The central problem in the theory of economic development is to understand the process by which a community which was previously saving and investing 4 or 5 per cent of its national income or less, converts itself into an economy where voluntary saving is running at about 12 to 15 per cent of national income or more. This is the central problem because the central fact of economic development is rapid capital accumulation.' A similar view was advanced by W. W. Rostow (1956, 1960), but was challenged on empirical grounds by Habakkuk and Deane (1963: 63–82). (For a more extended survey of this debate see Crouzet, 1972: 8–39.)

The ratio of investment (or savings) to national income given in col. 5 of table 7.2 clearly supports Lewis' view that the ratio increases at the beginning of modern economic growth. It also appears to confirm the customary location of the critical turning point, that it came in the late eighteenth century, though it does not support the Rostovian compression of this period into as short a span as two decades. The view that the initial process of industrialisation is character- ised by an increase in the rate of investment would probably be clearer still if we could carry the comparison back to include the decades immediately before 1760: it seems likely that the savings ratio was even lower than 8 per cent in the first half of the eighteenth century and that it did not begin to change until the 1740s or 1750s (Deane 1961: 367–8). The estimates also suggest that the upward movement in the ratio had come to a halt by the end of the eighteenth century. Thereafter, ignoring the temporary fall during the wartime decade 1801–10, the ratio was broadly stable, even with the development of the capital–hungry railways in the 1840s and 1850s. It was very early industrialisa- tion, not the railway, that accompanied the rise in thrift.

The exact significance of this reinstatement of the older view (of Lewis and Rostow) that the savings ratio rose sharply in the early part of the industrial revolution will become clear later. For the present we can consider the implications of the observed trend in the ratio for the second controversy, that about the effects of the industrial revolution on the living standards of the working classes. (For another discussion of this topic, using different approaches, see chapter 9.) One argument, as advanced for example by Pollard (1958: 215–26) is that the need for 'massive simultaneous investment' imposed by the initial process of industrialisation proved an exceptionally heavy burden, and depressed the consumption of most of the people. Pollard also suggested that, in the case of Britain, the real costs of industrialisation were 'greatly increased by the... misapplication of resources, false starts, errors and rapid obsolescence inevitable in a pioneer economy' (1958: 219).

We can best examine this argument by looking at the four components of the nation's expenditure (or equivalently, of the nation's income or output): private consumption, government consumption, investment at home, and investment abroad: decade average estimates are set out in table 7.4, all measured at constant prices, with the column for 'private consumption' put late in the table to indicate that it is calculated as a residual from total expenditure (col. 1) and the other items of expenditure (cols. 2, 3 and 4). Private consumption is then

Table 7.4. *Real consumption per head, Great Britain 1760–1860* (decade averages, at 1851–60 prices)

	(£ million p.a.)						Consumption per head (£ p.a.) (7)
	Gross national product (1)	Government expenditure (2)	Gross domestic investment (3)	Foreign investment (4)	Private consumption (5)	Population (6)	
1761–70	93	7	7.5	0.5	78	8.1	9.6
1771–80	98	7	9	1.0	81	8.7	9.3
1781–90	111	8	13	1.5	88	9.3	9.5
1791–1800	134	15	17.5	1.5	100	10.2	9.8
1801–10	161	25	17.5	−2.0	120	11.4	10.5
1811–20	203	26	22.5	5.0	149	13.2	11.3
1821–30	278	14	32.5	7.5	224	15.3	14.6
1831–40	372	12	42.0	4.5	313	17.5	17.9
1841–50	460	16	54.5	6.5	383	19.7	19.4
1851–60	610	25	61.5	20.0	503	22.0	22.9

Source:
(1) Based on estimated by Deane (1968) and Deane and Cole (1967); see, further, Feinstein (1978: table 28).
(2) Current expenditure on the army and navy from Mitchell and Deane (1962: 390–7) deflated by an index of wholesale prices, see Feinstein (1978: table 5).
(3) and (4) see table 7.3 above. Col. (4) equals the balance of payments on current account, and covers the net acquisition of foreign assets and of gold and silver bullion and specie.
(5) $(1)-(2+3+4)$.
(6) Deane and Cole (1967: 6–8), averages of estimates for the beginning and end of each decade.
(7) $(5) \div (6)$.

divided by the total population to get real consumption per head (col. 7), a measure of the trends in one of the major aspects of the 'standard of living'. There are of course, other non-material aspects (such as the hours and conditions of work or the impact on the environment of rapid urbanisation) which would have to be brought into the reckoning in any overall assessment of the effect of industrialisation on living standards and the 'quality of life' (for which see again chapter 9).

The underlying estimates are all too uncertain to attach significance to small changes in the series for per capita consumption, but it is possible to draw four broad conclusions from table 7.4. First, it seems clear from this evidence that there was no worthwhile improvement in real consumption of goods and services per head during the first six decades of industrialisation. It was not until the 1820s that the average level of consumption rose appreciably above the level of the 1760s, and so far as the mass of the population was concerned the benefits of industrialisation were delayed for a very long time. Second, however, it cannot be argued that average consumption was actually reduced during the initial stage of industrialisation: it did not rise, but neither did it fall. Third, the rise in domestic investment was *not* a major factor in holding back the improvement of the standard of consumption. If domestic investment had stayed the same proportion of national expenditure in 1791–1800 as it was in 1761–70 (about 8 per cent) the level of per capita consumption (at 1851–60 prices) would have been about £10.5 instead of £9.8, i.e. only about 7 per cent higher than it actually was. In subsequent decades the effect of maintaining the investment ratio steady at the 1761–70 proportion would have raised consumption per head by no more than 4 or 5 per cent. The increased government spending on the army and navy during the Napoleonic Wars (col. 2) had an effect on living standards about equal to that of the rise in the investment ratio; and the rapid growth of population (col. 6) was a far more important factor than either (at least in an arithmetic sense) in holding back any improvement in average per capita consumption.

The fourth and final conclusion which may be drawn from table 7.4 is that the 1820s and beyond did see a quite substantial improvement in the standard of per capita consumption. After the Napoleonic War, the domestic investment ratio and the percentage of national income absorbed by military expenditure both fell; and the total national income was growing almost twice as fast as it had done in the earlier decades. The balance available for consumption thus increased at a quite satisfactory rate (just over 3 per cent p.a.). With population growing at only 1.3 per cent p.a., this permitted real per capita consumption to rise at just under 2 per cent p.a., to a level in 1851–60 of around £20, or roughly double that of 1811–20.

These broad conclusions – the absence of any marked improvement or deterioration before the 1820s, the relatively small influence of increased domestic investment, and the substantial measure of progress after the 1820s – must be qualified in various ways. The basic estimates are far from reliable and the movements of output, prices and population over the period 1760–1810 are particularly uncertain. By looking at the trend in decade averages we are taking a long view and ignoring the effects on employment and income of short-term booms and busts. The changes in per capita consumption capture only one aspect of the effect of industrialisation on living standards and the other less tangible but equally important aspects must also be considered. The last and perhaps the most crucial qualification is that the series for per capita consumption derived in col. (7) of table 7.4 relates only to the average over the population as a whole. It is almost certain, for example, that there was a shift in the distribution of income in favour of the recipients of profits and rents during the Napoleonic Wars. This could have meant that the apparent stability of average consumption per head was consistent with a significant fall in the consumption standards of other sections of the population, with industrial workers particularly vulnerable to the steeply rising food prices associated with the increase in land rents. Similarly it is known that not all groups of workers and all regions enjoyed the improvement shown by the average for the decades from 1821–60. It would have been no comfort to the handloom weavers or the framework knitters or to agricultural labourers in the south and south-west to be told that their distressed condition in the 1820s to 1840s was statistically more than offset by the growing prosperity of the skilled artisans and others who worked with and benefited from the new machines. Such is the way of averages.

Capital, labour and output

We turn back now to the average growth of all output (not merely consumption), and its relation to the stock of capital, the supply of labour, and the level of technique.

As a first step we consider the main trends in three series. As our measure of capital we take the stock of domestic reproducible capital, including improvements to land but not unimproved land, which corresponds to rows 7 and 8 of table 7.1, but is measured at 1851–60 prices). This is given in table 7.5 for four specimen years, together with estimates for the labour supply and real output. From these series three further series are derived (cols. 5 to 7): the ratio of capital to labour, of capital to output and of output to labour. The estimates of the rate of growth of the labour supply are almost identical to those for the rate of growth of the total population, and so series for output or capital per head would show essentially the same rates of growth as those for output or capital per worker.

The main results may be summarised as follows:

(i) From 1760 to 1830 the growth of capital and of labour kept broadly in step, meaning that there was effectively no change in capital per worker. From 1831 to 1860 the rate of growth of capital accelerated to about 2 per cent p.a. while the labour supply continued to increase at the previous rate of about 1.4 per cent p.a. It was thus possible for the capital–labour ratio to rise by about one fifth (col. 4). In considering the significance of this initial stability and subsequent rise in capital per worker it is, of course, necessary to bear in mind that the stock of capital in question includes not only directly productive buildings and equipment but also dwellings, shops, transport facilities, and other capital of a less spectacularly industrial sort.

(ii) Output and capital stock grew at broadly the same rate over the decades 1760–1800, but real output accelerated later much more strongly, and the capital–output ratio dropped sharply from around 7:1 in 1800 to about 5:1 in 1830. It continued to fall, though less swiftly, down to 1860 (col. 5).

(iii) The rate of growth of real output exceeded that of the labour supply throughout the period: by a modest margin in the first four decades and by over 1 per cent p.a. in the remaining period. The level of output per worker (labour productivity) in 1860 was thus double that of 1800 (col. 6).

Table 7.5. *Levels and rates of growth of domestic reproducible capital, labour supply and real output, Great Britain 1760–1860*

	Domestic reproducible capital (£m.) (1)	Labour supply (m.) (2)	Real output (GDP) (£m.) (3)	Capital per worker (£) (4)	Capital– output ratio (5)	Output per worker (£) (6)
			A. End-year levels			
1760	670	3.5	90	191	7.4	26
1800	990	4.8	140	206	7.1	29
1830	1510	7.2	310	210	4.9	43
1860	2760	10.8	650	256	4.3	60
			B. Growth rates (% p.a.)			
1761–1800	1.0	0.8	1.1	0.2	−0.1	0.3
1801–30	1.4	1.4	2.7	.	−1.2	1.3
1831–60	2.0	1.4	2.5	0.7	−0.4	1.1
1761–1860	1.4	1.1	2.0	0.3	−0.6	0.9

Source: Feinstein (1978: tables 25 and 26).
Note: Cols. (1), (3), (4) and (6) are measured at 1851–60 prices.

Output and productivity

From table 7.5 we have two measures of 'partial productivity': output per worker (col. 6) and output per unit of capital (the reciprocal of the capital–output ratio in col. 5). Another way to think of the notion of 'total factor productivity' introduced and used in earlier chapters is that total factor productivity is an average of the partial productivities, yielding measures of total input relative to output. Estimates of total factor productivity in this period, derived from table 7.5 are set out in table 7.6. Taking the period as a whole we can calculate from table 7.6 that approximately 65 per cent (i.e. $(1.3/2.0) \times 100$) of the growth of real output was accounted for by the increased inputs of labour and capital and approximately 35 per cent $((0.7/2.0) \times 100)$ by the rise in total factor productivity. Another way to express the same facts is to put them in terms of output per worker. If we take output per worker as the series whose growth is to be explained, that is by eliminating directly that part of the increased output due solely to the increased labour input, then we find that approximately 22 per cent $((0.2/0.9) \times 100)$ of the rise in labour productivity can be accounted for by the increased supply of capital per worker and about 78 per cent by total factor productivity (table 7.7). Three quarters of the enrichment came, therefore, from *better* techniques, and not from a more intense application of existing techniques.

As chapters 1 and 6 argued, this last finding is most important for understanding the industrial revolution. But what exactly does it mean? In chapter 1 it was said that total factor productivity, or as it is often called, the 'residual',

Table 7.6. *Output, inputs and total factor productivity, Great Britain 1760–1860*

	Real output (GDP) (1)	Total inputs (2)	Total factor productivity (3)
A. End-year levels (Index number, 1860 = 100)			
1760	14	28	49
1800	21	40	53
1830	48	61	79
1860	100	100	100
B. Growth-rates (% p.a.)			
1761–1800	1.1	0.9	0.2
1801–30	2.7	1.4	1.3
1831–60	2.5	1.7	0.8
1761–1860	2.0	1.3	0.7

Source:
(1) Table 7.5, col. (3).
(2) Table 7.5, cols. (1) and (2) weighted according to respective factor shares in 1860, taken (as a rough approximation) as 0.5 each; see Feinstein (1978: table 26).
(3) (1) ÷ (2).
Note: Col. (3) and the growth rates for all series calculated before rounding.

was a difficult measure to interpret. It hides, in fact, a multitude of sins, which we can consider under three headings:

(i) *Errors*. Under this heading we have:

a. Conceptual errors. Even if we can in principle specify the measures of output or inputs that would be conceptually most appropriate (and sometimes we cannot), in practice we may not be able to obtain estimates for the ideal measures, and must rely instead on approximations. For example it would be appropriate to measure real output net of depreciation (i.e. deducting the costs of making up for wear and tear in already existing capital) rather than gross; or to measure the flow of services rendered by capital rather than the stock of capital. The evidence for the better measures does not exist. These errors are probably not very significant, but they will have some effect on the estimate of productivity.

b. Errors of measurement. Once we have decided on the most appropriate available series we have to recognise that inevitably there will be errors in the estimation of that series, and any such errors will be reflected automatically in the derived index of productivity. Foreign investment, for example, is estimated here from statistics on exports and imports: having accepted the potential error in using this concept rather than, say, direct estimates of loans to foreigners, one is still faced with the likelihood of errors of measurement in the statistics of exports and imports. The inadequacy of the basic statistics for the period covered in this chapter is such that errors of this type could be substantial.

Table 7.7. *Output per worker, capital per worker and total factor productivity, Great Britain 1760–1860. (Rates of growth, per cent p.a.)*

	Output per worker (1)	Share of capital in GNP × capital per worker (2)	Total factor productivity (3)
1761–1800	0.3	0.1	0.2
1801–30	1.3	—	1.3
1831–60	1.1	0.3	0.8
1761–1860	0.9	0.2	0.7

Source: See text and tables 7. 5 and 7.6.

c. Errors of specification. In order to derive the estimate of total factor productivity it is necessary to make certain assumptions about the nature of the aggregate production function and the economy surrounding it, i.e. about the particular way in which different combinations of labour and capital combine to produce varying levels of output. To the extent that the economy behaves in a different fashion from that assumed – as inevitably it must to some extent – the estimate of productivity will be affected. If, for example, there are economies of scale (so that adding say 1 per cent to all inputs raises output by more than 1 per cent), whereas the function we used assumed constant returns to scale, then the gain from the economies of scale will be captured by the index. It is difficult to assess the extent of these errors of specification but at best the results can give only a broad approximation, and the effect of economies of scale, in particular, could be quite important.

(ii) *Sources of growth not separately specified.* For the present exercise we have distinguished between total factor productivity and that part of the growth of output due to increased inputs of labour and capital. In principle, however, it is possible to identify and estimate a number of other sources of growth (apart from technical progress, which we consider separately below). The basic data are too weak to warrant such estimation for the period covered here (for an outstanding illustration of this approach applied to more modern periods see Denison (1967)); but we can briefly list some of the main factors which should be borne in mind as possible sources of part of the observed increase:

a. Changes in the quantity of labour input arising from changes in either the number of hours worked per year or the effort and intensity of work (see chapter 11).

b. Improvements in the quality of labour as a result of increased experience, training, formal education, improved health, etc. (see chapters 1 and 6).

c. Changes in the structure of the economy from sectors of relatively low productivity to sectors of higher productivity. This would raise output per worker even if there were no rise in productivity within each sector (see chapter 6).

d. Changes in the rate of utilisation of capital as a result of cyclical factors or variations in the extent of shift work and of hours of work more generally.

(iii) *Technical progress.* The final element reflected in the series is technical progress. This covers the application to the process of production of all advances in knowledge, both technological and managerial. This cannot be measured directly but could be estimated indirectly if we could make quantitative allowance for the errors and for the other factors specified above and so deduct the effect on growth attributable to these factors from the estimate. In the absence of such calculations – and it must be clear by now that they are impossible – it would be wrong to take the estimates in table 7.7 as an approximate indicator of the contribution of technical progress to the growth of output per head, but it might be reasonable to conclude from the estimates that it must have played a significant part. The origins and character of this element are the subject of the following chapter.

It might appear from all this that capital played a relatively small role in bringing about the expansion of output per worker, but (as earlier chapters have noted) such an inference would not be correct. Capital contributes to the growth of output partly by providing additional assets to keep pace with the growth of the labour supply (capital widening), partly by substituting for labour so that more capital and less labour is required for a given unit of output (capital deepening), and partly by acting as the carrier for technical progress. Even if we discount the first two aspects it would still be essential to pay regard to the third. It is clearly not necessary for all forms of technical progress to find expression in physical capital. For example, improvements in the organisation of production (such as plant lay-out) or in industrial relations might make a significant contribution to higher output without needing any additional capital. There will, however, be many forms of technological advance which can only take effect when 'embodied' in new capital goods. The spinning jennies, steam engines, and blast furnaces were the embodiment of the industrial revolution. As pointed out above the value of such capital was quite small. It is, however, essential that a society should be able both to organise the process of production so as to incorporate the new techniques in appropriate assets, and to save a sufficient sum to provide the finance for those acquiring the capital goods. Without this it would not be possible to benefit from technical progress however readily the knowledge might be available. In this sense at least, the process of capital accumulation must still occupy a central role in any explanation of the growth of output and productivity.

8

Technical progress during the industrial revolution

G. N. VON TUNZELMANN

For the legions of schoolchildren accustomed to envisaging the industrial revolution in terms of waves of gadgets, the conclusions of chapter 6 with their emphatic support for the role of ingenuity may have come as a welcome respite amidst all the iconoclasm. To a degree, such confidence in the traditional values might be undermined by the present chapter, for it will be shown that the usual stress on a handful of dramatic breakthroughs is seriously open to question. Yet the points of view expressed here can be fully reconciled with the judgements of chapter 6. It is the variety and pervasiveness of innovation during British industrialisation – concentrated in some sectors more than others it is true – which will be argued as having been the key to the growth process.

The springs of invention

In table 6.2 it was found that as much as 52 per cent of the achieved technical progress between 1780 and 1860, measured according to the contribution to aggregate economic growth, arose in a few development-oriented sectors. What caused those sectors to be the lucky ones, and what was the nature of their development or modernisation? The view that we can take of the role of innovation in British industrialisation as a whole depends on the answer to this question. Yet the explanation of technological change and of its effects has stretched the intellectual capacity of a whole panoply of disciplines. In the social sciences alone, economic, sociological and even psychological theories of invention have been advanced, and no theory commands general acceptance. All that we can do, therefore, is to try to isolate the factors within the economy and society which, during the industrial revolution, conditioned the search for innovation. Some attempts at innovation were successful, some unsuccessful, and some successful only to be rendered obsolete very swiftly; some were the product of change, others were sought deliberately for many years.

The particular circumstances, as distinct from the general economic and social climate, which give rise to technical change – to the invention of new techniques and their innovation into production – are sometimes known as 'inducement

143

mechanisms'. Conventionally, these are divided into demand factors, outward shifts of the demand curve for a given industry or industries, and supply factors, upward shifts of the short period supply curve. Neither demand nor supply factors are likely to have been stagnant before the industrial revolution, and we must therefore look for factors which might have produced an acceleration in the growth of demand or of the ability to supply. With this in mind, we shall begin with demand. This section, though written independently, generally follows the cautious line toed by Mokyr (1977).

Demand

Population growth. It is commonplace to link technical changes to the rise of a mass market and hence to the growth of population. However, if national income grows only about as fast as population, so that average incomes do not change, industrialisation may not be greatly assisted. In such circumstances, and with the low income levels which obtained in the eighteenth century, increased numbers will exert most of their effect on the demand for basic necessities, not on the demand for the more highly industrial goods with which we are concerned here. Increased demand for food might retard, or even reverse, a shift of labour towards industry. Unless, therefore, average incomes grew, increasing population can only have affected methods of production by making it possible for entrepreneurs to realise economies of scale, in which production costs per unit of output are reduced because of mass production. But it is doubtful whether there was much scope for such economies, since the output of the typical unit of production – the individual worker in his cottage – was so small, and remained so during the early industrial revolution. While there may well have been economies of scale, created by a rising population, in the transport and marketing of goods, and possibly within the 'putting-out' or domestic system of production, because of the need for more efficient organisation to deal with a larger number of domestic workers, such economies were organisational rather than technological.

Rising incomes. If average incomes rose, however, this would reinforce the effect of rising population and lead to radical changes in methods of production. It used to be thought that incomes per capita stagnated during the early years of the eighteenth century, but Crafts has shown that a substantial improvement in incomes and incomes per head probably occurred between 1700 and 1740 (Crafts 1976; ch. 1). In the middle years of the century, by contrast, the growth rate of incomes was reduced (Crafts 1976; Little 1976). On this basis, incomes grew before the classic years of industrialisation and technical change in the mid to late eighteenth century, and grew less during those classic years when most writers presume that industrialisation took hold. If rising incomes did exert an effect on industrialisation and technology, therefore, the effect must have been complex and lagged.

Income redistribution. Shifts in the distribution of income towards middle or higher income groups could in principle have favoured industrialisation by concentrating demand on goods ripe for technological advance, focusing for example on what Eversley (1967) described as 'decencies' as opposed to bare necessities: pottery 'seconds', better clothing (like muslins and good calicoes), stoves, and so forth. However, the evidence for income redistribution of this kind in the mid-eighteenth century is almost purely circumstantial. Some writers have reasoned from changes in relative prices, but the patterns here are inconclusive to say the least (see e.g. Felix 1956) and more importantly the link between rising prices and rising real incomes can be upheld only with the support of much more evidence than is yet available. Second, it is possible that *falling* prices of consumption goods – middle-class consumption goods – could have given rise to the redistribution towards middle incomes, if there was any. If so, we again need to know the cause and effect. It may just be that the cheapening of those 'decencies' came from the very innovation for which we are trying to find a cause. It remains only to repeat how much of the information on this topic is conjectural (though see Soltow 1968, and Schwarz 1979). Williamson's recent reinvestigation indicates if anything a squeeze on middle incomes in the middle years of the eighteenth century (Williamson 1979).

Foreign demand. There are a number of difficulties with accepting this popular causal factor. Few British industries began to grow by exporting – generally they had to build up something of a home market and cheapen their production costs before they could compete internationally and attract foreign custom. But if this is so, then some of the major technical advances which lowered costs must presumably have already taken place before the British industrialist was able to capture sizeable overseas markets. The influence of foreign trade could also of course, be felt the other way round, via imports and the home market. In cotton, the mule of Samuel Crompton (invented 1799) allowed Britons to spin the fine yarns for muslins and the like by mechanical means, whereas previously such qualities had had to be imported from the hand-spinners of India.

Changes in consumer tastes. Once again, one must beware: most of the examples of changes in tastes toward industrial goods to be found in the secondary literature are in fact responses to relative price falls for those items; and these in turn must therefore be due either to demand factors of the kind noted above, or else to changes from the supply side. Yet some genuine changes in taste do appear to have occurred. In clothing, the impact of Beau Brummell and others of his ilk has been claimed as significant in shifting the emphasis in fashion from the *nature* of the cloth (whether velvet, silk, etc.) to its *cut*, thereby opening the floodgates of demand for well-cut and well-laundered cotton clothes (e.g. Edwards 1967: chapter 3). In a similar way, imitations of the dazzling and continually altering French fashions gave scope for British textile manufacturers to undertake import-substituting innovation of the type referred to in the previous paragraph. In hosiery, lace, etc., year-to-year changes necessitated frequent mechanical advance to permit the varying patterns and fabrics to be produced in Britain.

For all these reasons, the *a priori* case that technical change stemmed from changes in demand is disquietingly slim, and this negative conclusion remains even when we examine particular instances of change. Such examination has often been cast in terms of challenge and response, as a set of changes in one sector of an industry causes demand pressures on another sector. Landes (1969: 92; cf. Hyde 1977: 75) drew attention to the interaction between the various branches of the iron industry; innovations in the furnace were, for example, matched by innovations in the forge. An even more famous example is that of cotton. Cotton weaving is said to have been already more productive than spinning at the outset of the eighteenth century – it took about three spinners to supply each weaver with yarn. Improvements in weaving, especially Kay's flying shuttle of 1737, increased the alleged degree of imbalance. Thus the pressure of demand for improvement came to fall on the spinning branch, and gave rise to Hargreaves' jenny and Arkwright's water frame in the 1760s. In fact, with these machines and Crompton's mule (an ingenious combination of the two) the challenge was reversed and came to fall back upon the weavers. The steam-powered loom for weaving was the eventual response (though note that it was not until the 1820s at the earliest that an efficient power-loom was widely disseminated in even the coarse sector of the cotton industry).

The traditional argument in this guise is unobjectionable but unsatisfying. Why, after (say) Kay's flying shuttle, could not a producer simply bring more and more spinners into action to supply the quicker weavers? Transport charges would certainly rise as he sought further afield for the extra spinners; but cotton was not a bulky material, and transport costs were only a small portion of its final costs of production. It has been argued, however (e.g. Smelser 1959), that textiles were at this stage a domestic industry, organised in the home on a family basis or in the village on a small-community basis. Father did the weaving and mother the spinning, with their children aiding them both. The speed-up of weaving thus exhausted local supplies of women and girls. Adult males could have been drafted in to spin alongside the females, but such male labour was about three times as expensive as female labour, and unquestionably this solution would have pushed up the supply price of yarn. Thus the imbalance resulting from the flying shuttle lay as much in the structure of the family and the community as in the structure of production. In that manner, supply-side considerations emerged in a supposedly demand-side model, as the long-run supply curve turned more steeply upwards.

The difficulty of distinguishing between demand-side and supply-side effects emerges again when we examine scarcities of resources. If demand were to grow at no more than pre-industrial rates, but in doing so were to produce increasing scarcity of one or more of the resources required, then it might seem that this would be an obvious case of difficulties of supply likely to produce resource-saving innovation. It has been conjectured by many authors that this was true for wood in eighteenth-century Britain – there was insufficient to meet the needs for timber or charcoal except at sharply rising costs, hence dictating a shift towards coke fuel for iron-smelting, etc. A similar argument has been made for water power, giving way to steam power near the end of the century (see Deane 1965: 129–30).

In the example of charcoal vs. coke smelting of iron, Hyde (1973) established that, given that coke pig iron was inferior to the pig iron smelted using charcoal, the shift from the latter to the former was justifiable on cost grounds only after the 1760s in most products, and that fuel price changes were indeed the main cause of the shift. But what in turn caused the changes in relative fuel prices? Here, Hammersley (1973) has argued that *demand* factors rather than those of supply were responsible. It was not a case of running down the most accessible supplies of wood in order to meet *existing* demands, but rather one of an increase in the scale of operations to meet newly extended demands that raised charcoal prices. After all, charcoal-fired blast furnaces and forges had no need of huge areas of woodland while they were at work – Hammersley suggests that 7000 acres of woodland could supply a seventeenth-century blast furnace *in perpetuity*, and 6000 acres a forge; altogether he estimates an annual consumption of 22000 acres of coppice to supply the whole of the British iron industry in the early eighteenth century. Moreover, ironmasters took great care over replanting and timber conservation. Thus, if he is right, the well-known innovation of iron-smelting by coke is also a consequence rather than a cause of economic and population growth at this early stage. Hyde's subsequent work (1977: 57–8) reaffirms the importance of demand conditions flowing from industrialisation elsewhere in the economy as underlying the relative rise of charcoal prices. However, a supply-side explanation flowing from differentially rapid productivity growth in coke as opposed to charcoal smelting is equally consistent with his results (e.g. pp. 59, 62 of his book).

Supply

Even at the level of individual innovations, therefore, demand determinants *and* supply determinants interact like Alfred Marshall's blades of the scissors, with both doing the cutting (Rosenberg 1972: 51). There is, however, one further possible source of change. If it could be demonstrated that the supply of inventions increased through the application of scientific research, conducted merely for its own intellectual sake and applied only later to industrial production, then we would have a clear supply-side explanation.

148

The thesis that the supply of inventions increased through scientific research has proved especially attractive to historians concerned with the global question of why Britain, of all the possible industrialising countries, should have acted as the birthplace of industrialisation. The celebrated theory of a 'take-off into self-sustained growth', put forward by Rostow, is a good example. In asking *How It All Began*, Rostow implies:

It is the central thesis of this book that the scientific revolution, in all its consequences, is the element in the equation of history that distinguishes early modern Europe from all previous periods of economic expansion...We know or sense that the scientific revolution irreversibly changed the way man thought and felt about himself and society, about the physical world, and about religion.The scientific revolution also related, somehow, to the coming of the first industrial revolution at the end of the eighteenth century [Rostow 1975: 133].

While it is arguable that religious upheaval, and in particular the rise of Protestantism, was a cause rather than a consequence of changing attitudes to science (Merton 1970; Mathias 1972: chs. 1–2), there is no doubt of the importance of the tentative steps which were taken in the seventeenth century towards seeing man's future as in some degree determinable or predictable, for example by scientific experimentation. There is also no doubt that the scientific revolution, dated either at the foundation of the Royal Society in 1662 or earlier in the century (Webster 1975) preceded the financial revolution, the commercial revolution, the transport revolution and the industrial revolution as these overlappping changes are conventionally dated.

But to what extent was scientific progress a precondition, or even the fundamental precondition, for economic and industrial growth?

Historians of science have traditionally repudiated the argument that science, rather than necessity, may have been the mother of invention at this time. There were dramatic advances in pure science, to be sure, but for the most part this science bred only more science instead of being applied to the needs of industry. In discussing the years between 1760 and 1860 Lord Ashby stated that 'There was practically no exchange of ideas between the scientists and the designers of industrial processes', and he has been echoed by the majority of economic historians (e.g. Mathias 1972: ch. 3). One school of economic historians has, however, vigorously dissented. On the basis of a very detailed consideration of James Watt and similar men, the Manchester historians, A. E. Musson and E. Robinson, conclude that it is misreading the historical evidence to claim that there were no links between scientists and industrialists; on the contrary, they claim the opportunities for mutual discussion were extensive and persistent (Musson and Robinson 1969).

There are, however, good reasons to retain the traditional view:

(a) At the broadest level, contemporary science could scarcely be described as a goldmine for those fossicking from industry. First, in most areas science was disarticulated; the illuminating insights obtained by the members of the Royal Society had not been brought together into a consistent overall framework. Second, much of the so-called science was frankly wrong-headed. The caloric theory of heat – which envisaged heat as a substance – positively obstructed study of the theory of the steam engine. Admittedly, useful discoveries followed on occasions from this bogus science; Jethro Tull, for example, believed that air was the best of all possible manures and developed his famous and useful seed drill on that fallacious precept – but this was exceptional. Normally, bogus theories like perpetual motion wasted inordinate amounts of the brain-power of well-intentioned people. Third, and even more important, scientific study was rarely directed near the most vital needs of industry. The great achievements of science lay in fields such as astronomy, analytical mechanics, crystallography, magnetism etc. – miles away from the domain of the major industrial advances. Industry could have benefited, for example, from a workable theory of heat, a knowledge of the chemistry of the blast furnace for the iron industry or of fermentation for brewing – all discoveries not forthcoming until well into the nineteenth century (C. C. Gillispie, in Mathias 1972).

(b) Even where overlap between science and industry was conceivable in the eighteenth century, the practical significance of the new horizons that the new scientific methods opened up is in doubt. The idea that James Watt's greatest inventions (especially the separate condenser) were logically derived from the theory of latent heat is nowadays dismissed by historians of science as a myth, as indeed it was by Watt himself (Cardwell 1971). Two advances in chemicals are emphasised by the 'Manchester school': Berthollet's use of chlorine for bleaching, breaking a bottleneck that could have critically hampered the continued expansion of the textile industries at the end of the eighteenth century; and Leblanc's process for making soda. The latter was, however, another example of bogus science that paid off against all odds (Leblanc drew a quite spurious analogy with iron-smelting); while the former, though less of a fluke, owed nothing to the revolutionary reorganisation of chemistry in the eighteenth century formulated by men such as Lavoisier, but instead derived from certain knowledge about chemical properties that had been widespread for over a century.

(c) Science was in vastly better shape on Continental Europe, and especially in France, than in Britain; this was a state of affairs that was to continue well beyond the industrial revolution. Practical English mechanics scoffed at French theorists for their lack of acquaintance with the industrial world and the absurdity of their theoretical constructs. Certainly the French were pioneers in a wide range of theoretical fields – not just the parade of French chemists such as Lavoisier, Leblanc, and Berthollet, since they were equally far advanced in such as civil engineering, power engineering and thermodynamics. All these are areas that one would expect to have outstanding practical application. In response to the founding of the Royal Society, the French set up their even more impressive rival, the Académie, four years later. The Académie was to pump funds directly and indirectly into industry on a scale quite unknown in Britain before the present century, while the early interest of the Royal Society in utilitarian ends had lapsed by the end of the seventeenth century.

(d) The line of causation in Britain was probably far more often in the reverse direction, i.e. from technological advance back to science. The scientist, L. J. Henderson, alluded to this many years ago, in stating that 'science owed vastly more to the steam engine than the steam engine ever owed to science' (quoted in Mathias 1972: 123). It was discovered in the second decade of the nineteenth century that the type of steam engine being used to drain mines in Cornwall was performing much more efficiently than contemporary physics said was theoretically possible. But there the engines stood, pumping away, and in due course even the sceptics had to accept the evidence of the productivity statistics. The seeming ingratitude of the Cornish steam engine to physicists before long paved the way for the laws of thermodynamics.

In sum, although one would expect that, almost randomly, science and industry would pursue paths that would intersect from time to time, the instances of intersection are unexpectedly few. Nevertheless, the research of Musson and Robinson had produced many insights. They draw particular attention to institutions that brought together scientists and businessmen, including the celebrated Lunar Society in Birmingham. It is debatable, however, whether this led to direct flows of substantive information – one study of another such body, the Manchester Literary and Philosophical Society showed that during the many years of its vigorous activity through the classic period of the industrial revolution in 'Coketown' only one industrialist ever came to display a formal interest in science, and he became a world expert on spiders (but see Kargon 1977). But at least the contacts existed.

But what of generalised knowledge? It has sometimes been said that the characteristic of American industry that brought it to world dominance by the end of the nineteenth century was 'inventing a method of inventing'. So it might be that the scientific revolution induced certain intellectual or educational standards or approaches, without necessarily communicating its precise findings to the artisans. The experimental method was soon translated to mechanical and related problems, there to replace the Aristotelian method of logic and argument. The experiments carried out by eighteenth-century engineers were no doubt crude, but they were replicated to exhaustion and were arguably decisive in wide areas of engineering practice. The findings of John Smeaton, the great British civil engineer of the eighteenth century, concerning windmills, water-wheels, and atmospheric steam engines, were quickly digested and never forgotten.

Thus the quest for factors provoking the search for innovation has rejected the implementation of major scientific discoveries but accepted practical experimentation and on-the-job tinkering. If the example of the steam engine is any guide, much of the technological advance came, not from a few big inventions connoting major discontinuities, but from a mass of small-scale improvements, frequently conducted. Landes, in *The Unbound Prometheus* (1969), emphasises what he describes as 'anonymous technical change', i.e. small refinements to existing plant or equipment each by themselves so insignificant that their inventors have often gone unrecorded, but cumulatively of such importance as to be, in his opinion, at least on a par with the great leaps forwards. Mathias too (1972), speaks of a continuum of improvement; of a kind of technological Darwinism sustained over a long period of time. Much of this anonymous technical change was product innovation rather than process innovation, or when it was process innovation it could be accommodating a standard process to a new range of uses. As a result, substantial changes in processing costs tended to occur discontinuously, e.g. when patent right expired. Nevertheless the underlying 'technological Darwinism' was an important reason for the English mechanic feeling able – almost justifiably – to scoff at French theorists. As one example, the productivity of the steam engine was increased almost fourfold in the first half of the nineteenth century in Cornwall; this was done largely by men on the job learning how to run their engines at higher pressures with safety, how to avoid heat losses by lagging the steam pipes, etc. By contrast, James Watt, whose engine was being bettered in these respects, had managed to increase the productivity of the engine by about $2\frac{1}{2}$ times at most.

The diffusion of innovations

The above discussion has considered invention and innovation interchangeably; inventions which failed to be adopted are not our concern. It is often permissible to blur the edges between invention and innovation in successful cases because frequently the inventors and the innovators were one and the same person. In several instances, however – including several of the most famous – there was a notable gap before the innovation was adopted more widely, while there are many cases in which there were long delays before an innovation was adopted throughout an industry.

It is normally argued that the first type of delay, which Hyde has named the 'gestation lag', progressively shortened during the eighteenth and nineteenth centuries. Hyde argued this in particular for the iron industry (Hyde 1977: 195) but von Tunzelmann (1978: 297) found contradictory evidence for the cotton industry. It is possible that the difference between these two crucial industries sprang from two factors. First, cotton was, in the eighteenth century, a much more competitive industry than iron, where regional differences were important; the market pressures to rapid imitation were therefore weaker in iron (Hyde 1977: 202–3). Second, it is likely that both industries are special cases of the

152

general point that the speed of imitation and diffusion was a function of the cost advantage of the newer technique; it so happened that the earlier developments in iron (like Darby's coke-smelting) took a long time to emerge as superior on cost grounds, whereas in cotton the reverse was true (nineteenth-century advances like the self-acting mule and power-loom took longer to assert cost superiority, cf. von Tunzelmann, 1978: 187–202).

Following the 'gestation lag' the innovations would diffuse, at first with increasing rapidity, then tapering off, to most other firms. Hyde (1977: 195–6) spoke of this as the 'supersession period' which lasted until 90 per cent or so of output was being produced by the newer method. Apart from the relative profitability of new versus old methods – almost certainly the most important cause – several kinds of factors seem to have influenced the rate of diffusion or supersession. For one thing, it could depend on the ratio of fixed costs to working costs. An entrepreneur already using the existing technique ought to switch to a new one only when the total (i.e. fixed plus working) costs of the new plant are lower than the working costs alone of the existing plant. Consequently, whenever fixed costs are important to a productive process there will always be a 'bias' towards retaining the older process; this bias, it must be emphasised, reflects rational economic behaviour by the entrepreneur, and *not* irrational conservatism. Such factors seem to have been involved in technical diffusion in the iron industry (Hyde 1977: 29–30), the cotton industry (von Tunzelmann, 1978: 191–2), and probably many others. Obviously the impact of this influence would be reduced (a) if demand were growing rapidly, since for newly-established firms the relevant consideration would be the comparative *total* costs of the two different methods, or (b) if the existing fixed installations of plant and equipment required little or no change in order to incorporate the new concepts, so that existing entrepreneurs needed to take relative working costs alone into account. Important instances of the latter occurred in cotton and steam power (von Tunzelmann 1978: 191, 258–61).

A second possible determinant of the rate of diffusion was the general state of economic prosperity. There is however no general agreement about the way in which this may have worked. Some claim that booms encourage adventurousness, risk-taking, and thus high innovation; others see booms as encouraging entrepreneurial complacency, with the result that slumps were needed to stimulate more innovation. Twentieth-century findings point to a compromise (Mansfield 1968: 117). A generalisation that is more helpful and appears to be as true of the eighteenth and nineteenth as of the twentieth centuries is that the response to boom or slump depends on whether the innovation requires large or small additional outlays on fixed capital:

The conversion of low pressure [steam] engines to high-pressure action would qualify as an example of cheap or largely disembodied innovation (with some reservations about boilers); so would much of the power-driven machinery [so that these would be more rapidly diffused in periods of economic adversity]. But the diffusion of the engines themselves (i.e the cylinder, boilers, pumps, and works) might be better favoured by the easier credit conditions and higher profit expectations of the upswing [von Tunzelmann 1978: 296].

In the same fashion Matthews (1954: 131) spoke of 'semi-reserve capacity', by which he meant that entrepreneurs in cotton invested 'excessively' in mills and power in booms and filled them up with machinery such as power-looms in the ensuing slump. Hyde (1977: 199–200), having noted that, 'The diffusion of new techniques like coke-smelting or puddling required substantial capital invest-ments in new sites and equipment', therefore came to the conclusion that in iron, 'The eighteenth-century entrepreneur often made innovations in order to increase output and to earn windfall profits. His nineteenth-century counterpart was *forced* to adopt new methods in order to maintain profits threatened by falling price levels and by increased competition.' However, his own earlier analysis showed even eighteenth-century ironmasters facing external competitive pressures, e.g. from Swedish bar iron.

Of the other 'inducement mechanisms' towards technical change, two merit special attention. The role of wars has been an especially controversial one. In the twentieth century wartime has typically witnessed a flood of new products and processes. In similar fashion the French wars (1793–1815) and even some of those earlier in the eighteenth century have been regarded as a stimulus to metallurgical and other industries. Certainly iron output rose rapidly (Riden 1977; Hyde 1977: 112–16), but as Hyde shows this was mainly through the diffusion of already existing techniques (particularly Cort's puddling and rolling process, which was perfected at the Cyfarthfa ironworks in the early 1790s.) Whether this speed-up of diffusion could have obtained in industrial fields apart from metallurgy is however in some doubt. So far as growth of output is concerned, Mokyr and Savin (1976) were able to show that peacetime rates of growth of most industrial indices were faster than wartime rates. Deane and Cole's estimates (1967: 166) indicate that the share of manufacturing, mining and building in national income *fell* from 23.4 per cent in 1801 to 20.8 per cent in 1811; similarly that of trade and transport fell from 17.4 per cent to 16.6 per cent (agriculture was the main relative beneficiary). But much research still needs to be done on the wartime patterns of innovation.

The second possibility has been well described by Rosenberg (1976: 117–20):

The view was widely expressed in nineteenth-century England, especially in the period 1820–60, that strikes were a major reason for innovation. Contemporary observers who agreed on little else, who were as far apart in their ideological biases and commitments as, say, Karl Marx and Samuel Smiles, were in complete accord on this point. We have, moreover, the evidence of numerous inventors themselves, who testified that they undertook the search process which led to a particular invention as the result of a strike or the threat of a strike [ibid., pp 117–18].

Rosenberg goes on to cite Roberts' self-acting mule as a case in point. There is no doubt that strikes conditioned Roberts' search process: as Rosenberg implies, we have the inventor's word for it. The gestation and supersession lags do not, however, seem to have been much affected by this factor over the years which Rosenberg discusses (1820–60). A possible reason is that most of the strikes in the cotton industry between 1825 and 1850 were rearguard operations, fighting against wage cuts rather than conspiring to raise them, and were generally short-lived (von Tunzelmann 1978: 194; but see Turner 1962). The available evidence suggests that long-term considerations of profitability rather than short-term obsessions with labour disputes were the chief determinant of the diffusion of the self-acting mule.

The impact of technical change on British industrialisation

The transference of labour from non-industrial uses including agriculture to industry, which measures the change in the centre of gravity of the economy towards industrialisation, will be governed by the supply of labour from non-industrial uses and the demand for it from industry. As was demonstrated in chapter 1, the supply depends on population growth and on agricultural improvement. If these are both running at fairly high levels, then the supply curve of labour to industry will be relatively elastic (i.e. flat), with the result that the speed at which the industrial demand curve for labour shifts outwards will become the primary constraint on industrialisation. This demand curve in turn may be taken to be generated by capital formation and by technical progress. For the time being these are regarded as independent to simplify the exposition. We should note, however, the possibility of extensive 'embodiment' of innovation in capital investment referred to in chapter 7, as well as the reservations expressed in the section on capital below.

Leaving capital formation aside, we can assess the influence of industrial innovation on shifts in the demand curve for labour under two headings. First, there is the 'intensity' of the innovations – their shock effect in expanding production possibilities. For example, we may contrast big but sporadic break-throughs with the small but frequent 'anonymous' changes. Secondly, the innovations may have a particular 'factor-bias'. A labour-saving change will twist the new demand curve such that less labour will be called for at the new level of wages. Note carefully that 'labour-saving' is here used in the sense attributed by Hicks (1932) rather than that of Harrod, more familiar to growth theorists. In Hicks' definition a 'labour-saving' technical change is one in which the innovation causes the rate of profit to rise faster than the wage rate, for any given capital–labour ratio. It may be noted that, if the transference of labour into industry is in fact the key to industrialisation, then a labour-intensive technical change may be more advantageous than a labour-saving one (the comparatively elastic supply of labour available to industry is important in obtaining this result). On the other hand, the 'intensity' of labour-saving changes may be greater than that of labour-intensive ones; and, moreover, profits are likely to be especially boosted by labour-saving changes, so stimulating investment in later periods.

A guide to the overall 'intensity' is provided by the growth rate of the 'residual', as was set out in tables 7.6 and 7.7. It appears that capital was growing more than twice as fast as total factor productivity, the 'residual', in the late eighteenth century and again between 1831 and 1860; only in the period comprising the years 1801–30 did the growth rate of the 'residual' approach that of capital formation. Even so, total productivity was growing at rates comparable with those achieved in the late nineteenth century (cf. vol. 2, chapter 1) and again in the middle quarters of the twentieth century in Britain. However, to compare productivity growth with that of the factor inputs is to assume that what matters is the aggregate size of the economy. In its stead, the growth of output *per head* is usually taken to be a more worthy indicator of economic advance. The data in table 7.7 show that it was apparently not until the second quarter of the nineteenth century that capital grew much faster than labour. From about 1760 to 1830, increases in output per capita rested on providing the worker with 'better equipment' rather than with 'more equipment' (this result has been attained by a similar route in chapter 7).

While these results would seem to demonstrate the importance of technological change ('better equipment') to the British economy, the method by which they have been achieved is fraught with difficulties. Many things other than technological change in the strict sense are included within the residual. Moreover, the results are very general, and it may be better to proceed by studying the impact of individual innovations rather than drawing dubious conclusions from aggregate data. Chapter 12 discusses one instance, the impact of railways and canals; here we shall consider another, the impact of the steam engine.

The economic contribution of the steam engine

Partly for technical, and partly for historical, reasons, the stationary steam engine has frequently been regarded as one of the most important single inventions underlying British industrialisation – several highly-respected authors have gone so far as to believe it to be the most important of all (Kuznets 1966: 10; Mathias 1969: 134). The technical reasons at issue are generally thought of as having to do with the role of the steam engine as 'prime mover'; that is, it supplied the energy to work the machinery which in turn produced the consumer goods. In this manner, improved techniques of energy supply could affect a very wide range of industrial activities; conversely, an antiquated or exhaustible energy resourse could be envisaged as hampering industrialisation across many sectors. Historically, the steam engine has been singled out for attention because of its development in the years of 'warm-up to take-off'. This combination of technical and historical factors has been re-emphasised by Rostow, in stating that, by 1800:

modern industry had acquired its most essential long-term foundation. The short-run effects of this radical reduction in the cost of power and its almost complete locational mobility had revolutionary consequences over a wide range of industrial processes [Rostow 1975: 166–7].

In practice, the concentration by historians like Rostow on the late eighteenth century for evidence of British industrialisation has implied a concentration on the steam engine as developed by James Watt in a series of patents from 1769. Watt improved on the engines of his predecessors – the Savery engine of 1695, the Newcomen engine, first erected in 1712, and the various modifications wrought to both of those types later in the eighteenth century – in two main ways. In the first place, he reduced the fuel consumption of the engine, principally by his invention of the 'separate condenser'. Secondly, he designed the first effective *rotative* engine, in which the motion of the engine could be communicated directly to turning the mill machinery, instead of having to be transmitted by interposing a water wheel between the (pumping) engine and the machinery (the bulk of the subsequent material is drawn from von Tunzelmann 1978: chapter 6).

Compared, first, to the best 'atmospheric' engines (especially the Newcomen engine as improved by Smeaton in and after the late 1750s), a Watt engine in similarly good working order reduced fuel requirements by more than two-fifths in the case of the Watt rotative engine and by three-fifths for the Watt reciprocating (i.e. pumping) engine. The economic benefit to the country will therefore hinge on the rate of diffusion of the Watt engines, and on the cost of fuel. A recent calculation (ibid.: chapter 2) indicates that a much larger total of horsepower was installed as Watt engines by the time Watt's patents expired in 1800 than was previously thought: around 12 500 horsepower altogether. The price of fuel for these engines varied enormously across the country, but these variations can largely be taken into account by individual computations for each county of the British Isles. The result is an estimated fuel saving of about £185 000 in 1800; in other words, if 'atmospheric' engines had been required to do the same job in 1800 as the Watt type were then doing, the country's fuel bill for power supplies would have been £185 000 higher.

Second, the 'atmospheric' engine of Savery and Newcomen worked too jerkily to drive flimsy machinery or to spin delicate fibres. The solution that had been adopted since the early 1750s had been to use the 'atmospheric' engine purely to pump water to the top of a water wheel; the wheel could then be relied on for a very regular drive. This added to capital costs, not just because of the installation of a supplementary water wheel, but because an engine one-third larger was needed to make up for the loss in efficiency arising out of the use of a water wheel. Moreover, efficient 'atmospheric' engines could not be built in sizes as large as the largest Watt engines; for example, at coal mines it was usually cheaper to continue to erect Newcomen engines, even after 1769, because of their lower purchase price, yet nevertheless Watt engines were often introduced when the pits were sunk much deeper because one Watt engine was cheaper than two Newcomens (Mott 1962–63). The total addition to capital costs that would have been required had 'atmospheric' engines been called upon to carry out the functions of all the Watt type erected to 1800 would have been about £140000; or £8400 per annum if industrialists had been obliged to meet interest rates of 6 per cent annually. Finally, one ought to add to Watt's credit engines not built by his firm but which pirated his inventions, especially the separate condenser. The aggregate 'social savings', to use a concept which is fully explained in chapter 12, attributable to James Watt, when all these factors have been taken into account, comes to about £230000. Is this figure large or small? It is equivalent to just over one thousandth of the probable level of national income in 1800. If the economy had been forced to do without the Watt engines, and therefore use atmospheric engines to do the same work, the additional cost of £230000 could have been borne by diverting only one-month's economic growth to that purpose.

It is possible, though with more dubious data, to calculate the 'social savings' of all steam engines, i.e. Watt and 'atmospheric' alike. Had steam power not been used at all in 1800, then power supplies of a more medieval nature would have had to be used instead. As Rostow observed, one benefit of the steam engine was that it gave 'locational mobility' in comparison with previous forms of power such as windmills or waterwheels. Nevertheless, if we make a number of reasonable assumptions about this and other matters which affect the comparison, we can calcuate that a combination of water wheels, windmills, and animal 'gins' could have been employed in lieu of all the steam engines of 1800 (estimated at 29000 horsepower) at an additional cost of about £2¼ millions. Of this, some £1¾ millions represent rising rents hypothetically payable to owners of water rights because those rights would have become more valuable had steam power not been used (note that in many cases the mill owners also owned the water rights, so that they would be paying these hypothetical rents to themselves). The remainder, £½ million, can be taken as the saving in resources for the nation arising from the use of steam rather than earlier forms of power. In terms of the comparison made above, £½ million was only two-months' growth in the national output around 1800.

Apart from the application of the steam engine to locomotive and shipping purposes (for which see ch. 12 and vol. 2, ch. 3), the most important 'spin-off' of the steam engine so far as manufacturing industry was concerned did not come until forty to sixty years into the nineteenth century. Those mid-century years saw the diffusion of the *high*-pressure stationary engine in manufacturing industry. This resulted in the first substantial decline of power costs since the 1790s (other than reductions caused by falling coal prices in some parts of the country). Lower costs of power encouraged textile manufacturers, for instance, to run their machinery at considerably higher speeds (rather than directly reducing their expenditures on power, because higher speeds involved more power per spindle as a quid pro quo – see von Tunzelmann 1978: chs. 7–8) and in so doing helped pave the way for the faster-running equipment increasingly resorted to in the later years of the nineteenth century (cf. vol. 2, ch. 5 for ring-spinning).

Ultimately, therefore, the impact of the stationary steam engine became massive, and technical advances in the engine promulgated technical advances in other machinery. But this happened much later than the classic period of 'take-off' or of the industrial revolution as generally understood. During the 'take-off' years the social-saving calculations contradict the belief that the engine overcame a particularly constrictive bottleneck.

Whether the same is true of the other great gadgets before the railway age remains an open question. Rough estimates suggest the traditional emphasis on the early textile innovations to be better placed. In the woollen industry, the jenny must have saved about 2 per cent of national income by 1800, not counting its contribution in cottons. Data currently available point to especially notable cost reductions *before* the factory age proper. Mechanisation barely allowed the rapidly expanding worsted industry to compete in cost terms with the older woollen products, so long produced by a simpler technology.

The 'factor-bias' of innovation

It was suggested in the previous section that, until about 1830, capital and labour grew at roughly similar rates. If the productivity figures that lead to this initially surprising result are to be believed, there was no pronounced tendency towards saving labour. Labour-intensive technical changes must have been about as powerful as labour-saving ones in their effects, so that up to about 1830 the direction of technical change was neutral as between capital and labour.

These results may seem surprising, in that they contradict normal views of the industrial revolution as the period in which growth was achieved by substituting machines for men. One explanation may be the imperfections which are inherent in measuring the 'residual' and which are fully discussed above and in chapter 7. However, there are good reasons for believing in the results, and for accepting that labour-intensive technical change can be advantageous, particularly in shifting labour from one sector to another within the economy. That such shifts

Table 8.1. *Real consumption per head and real wages in Great Britain 1761–1860* (*decade averages*)

Years	Consumption per head (£)	Real wages (1788–92 = 100)
1761–70	9.6	100
1771–80	9.3	100
1781–90	9.5	99
1791–1800	9.8	96
1801–10	10.5	96
1811–20	11.3	104
1821–30	14.6	128
1831–40	17.9	132
1841–50	19.4	144
1851–60	22.9	n.c.

Sources: Consumption per head from table 7.4. All figures expressed at 1851–60 prices. Real wages calculated from first and second principal components of money wages and prices given in von Tunzelmann (1979) (n.c. = not computed).

were taking place is indicated by the urbanisation of Britain in this period, but its impact on productivity change can be seen by disaggregating the figures for the growth of the economy between 1800 and 1830. Overall, wealth, capital and labour grew at identical rates (Feinstein 1978; Deane and Cole 1967: 143). However, within the 'agricultural sector' the growth-rates differed widely; wealth grew by 1.1 per cent per annum, reproducible capital by 0.7 per cent and labour by 0.2 per cent. When one turns to the rest of the economy, the 'non-agricultural' sector, the growth rates also differ, but again show relatively slow growth of the labour force. The labour force grows at 1.4 per cent, and wealth and reproducible capital both by 2.0 per cent. This apparently curious result contradicting the aggregate trend comes about because agriculture is more capital intensive than the rest of the economy, both between 1800 and 1830 and between 1761 and 1800, for which the same result appears; but capital and labour are both growing more rapidly in the non-agricultural sector, as labour moves from agriculture to the towns. Within manufacturing industry alone, very sketchy evidence suggests that capital and labour grew at identical rates of about $2\frac{1}{2}$ per cent during the early part of the nineteenth century.

These findings are consistent with data on consumption and real wages. This is suggested by table 8.1, where real consumption and real wages are seen to rise only modestly before 1820, before rising more rapidly thereafter, at 1.1 per cent per annum for real wages and 1.8 per cent for real consumption.

If, therefore, we can conclude that the evidence is consistent with an approximately equal growth of capital and labour, we would expect this equality to be reflected in the type of technical change and innovation which can be observed in Britain. (It should, however, be noted that the concept of 'real wages' that is relevant for inducing labour-saving technical change differs from the measure of real wages used as an indicator of standard of living in table 8.1). One might also expect to find a contrast between the British experience and that of the United States, where it is generally agreed that technological change was distinctly capital-intensive and labour saving; it was this possibility that led Habakkuk to formulate, without the benefit of productivity calculations, his much-debated 'labour-saving' hypothesis (Habakkuk, 1962: vol. 2, chapters 1 and 5). What then was the experience of technological change in Britain?

Capital

Before the coming of the railways, investment in transportation formed a declining proportion of gross domestic investment (table 7.3). Although much of this investment in transport took place in activities that were innovative (canals, turnpikes, etc.), the sums involved were quite small. Crouzet (1972: 40–1) estimated that the construction of all new canals between 1700 and 1815 called for outlays of no more than £20 millions, by comparison with government loans totalling £440 millions floated in the much shorter period from 1793 to 1815. In the same vein, the capital stock embodied in turnpikes in the late 1830s was around £35 millions (from figures in Feinstein 1978).

Similarly, industrial machinery was generally inexpensive and until late in the day was often put together by the firm which was to employ it. The same goes for industrial plant – the factory, or blast furnace, or forge, or coalpit, or whatever, was commonly constructed by the firm's own labour force using cheap, readily available raw materials (local building stone and timber, etc.). Professor Pollard considered the purchase of a steam engine one of the few exceptions to this rule (Crouzet 1972: 151), and the capital stock embodied in steam engines in 1830 would have been less than £10 millions.

Moreover, too much attention can be lavished on the most eye-catching advances. Only a tiny fraction of the country's labour force worked in mills and factories in 1830. Samuel (1977) has shown that pockets of extraordinarily labour-intensive operation continued in almost every industry throughout the nineteenth century. Even where technical change did smite, its normally small-scale character meant that there was little demand for large capital expenditures. This was true *a fortiori* of changes that were merely reorganisational, or financial – falling in the realm of 'disembodied' technical change. Innovations, in T. S. Ashton's phrase, had the power to 'liberate capital'; steam engines, big and bulky as they were, nevertheless allowed the entrepreneur to avoid the even larger capital cost of, say, a team of horses (Ashton 1955: 110–11). More broadly, the whole transition from a domestic, putting-out industrial system to organised factory production helped to 'liberate capital'. The large amount of capital tied up as work in progress in the traditional putting-out structure (i.e. the cloth, etc., at each stage of production) could be economised upon by the quick, on-the-spot processing involved in a textile mill – recall the relative shift from working to fixed capital between 1760 and 1860 (tables 7.1 and 7.2). So there is no great difficulty in accounting at the historical and technical levels for the lack of 'capital deepening' for the bulk of the industrial revolution.

Labour

If innovation was thus not especially labour saving, why did labourers appear to greet mechanisation with such hostility? The years 1811–13 in particular gave the word Luddism to the English language. Why should Luddites have deliberately wrecked machinery and risked death by hanging when machinery was, on balance, growing no faster then employment?

In the first place, the overall tendency clearly masks individual cases of technological unemployment. The French Wars of the late eighteenth and early nineteenth centuries, especially, were an important period for the diffusion of manpower-saving equipment (nearly half a million men were at one time or another on active service against Napoleon). The problem for the craftsmen who had not volunteered for, or been press-ganged into, the Wars was not, therefore, an inadequate demand for labour; it was 'labour dilution', i.e. the use of machinery to replace craft labour with that of unskilled workers, women, or apprenticed youths.

For example, 'General Ludd's' well-organised centre of operations lay in the hosiery trade of Nottingham. It was the stocking frame of the hosiers that was at the receiving end of Luddite hatchets. But the stocking frame was neither especially labour-saving nor new; its use had been spreading in the Midlands since its invention in the reign of Elizabeth I. It was the use of the frame for the manufacture of low-quality goods (described as 'cut-ups') which aroused fear and hatred, since for these cheap items the skills of the craftsmen stockingers were unnecessary. Attacks were selectively directed against employers who transgressed by lowering their standards – employers sympathetic to traditional craftsmanship protected themselves by hanging notices in their windows like, 'This frame is making full fashioned work at the Full Price' (E. P. Thompson, 1963: 607). Thomis (1970) concludes, 'The depressed stocking knitters were not the victims of the Industrial Revolution; their problem was that it was passing them by, that their industry was becoming obsolete in technology.'

This was not true for all Luddites, e.g. the Yorkshire cloth-dressers were thrown out of work by machinery that substituted directly for their labour; but it was true of the majority.

This discussion is not intended to be an apologia for machinery. Labour dilution could give rise to social evils at least as great as unemployment. The exploitation of unprotected female and especially child labour has always been counted amongst the most vicious and immoral effects of the industrial revolution. Karl Marx, in volume I of *Capital*, classified the effects of British mechanisation under three headings.

(i) He spoke of the increased exploitation of women and children of the kind just instanced.

(ii) He considered that the working day had been prolonged in the remorseless hunt for profits. A detailed study of working hours (Bienefeld 1972) indeed showed the preindustrial daily norm of ten hours being stretched to thirteen or even more hours in textile mills in the heyday of the industrial revolution (less so in other fields). Similarly the working week filled up as the casual attitude to work discipline characteristic of an underemployed preindustrial economy was eroded (e.g. the disappearance of 'Saint Monday').

(iii) He spelled out the paradoxical tendency for machinery that was introduced to dispense with hand labour actually having the effect of intensifying that labour. An example he gave was the introduction of the high-pressure steam engines causing a rise in operation speeds of the machinery it drove, an example encountered above. 'High-pressure engines had their counterpart in high-pressure work' (Samuel 1977: 8).

Raw materials

Explanations of industrialisation which rest upon the idea that particular raw materials were being depleted have been enountered several times in the preceding discussion. Wilkinson (1973) has made use of the theories of Thomas Malthus to argue for the existence of an acute shortage of land in the face of population pressure. One victim was the supply of wood. Just as coal replaced wood in iron-smelting as a result of economic growth, so the output – iron – replaced timber as well. The first iron-framed buildings date from the last few years of the eighteenth century; similarly, early machinery such as that for textiles was largely constructed of wood in both stationary and moving parts. As the highly competent French observer, Baron Dupin, summed it up in 1817, 'This continuous substitution of wood by iron is not at all the result of a craze or a passing fancy; it stems from a comparison of the low price of this metal with the dearness of timber which is excessive throughout Britain.'

In the case of the other industry often viewed as heralding the industrial revolution, namely cotton textiles, Britain was able to evade the limitations imposed by its own fixed and confined supply of land by tapping the land and slave labour resources of the southern states of the USA. In general, then, the inventions of the industrial revolution allowed British manufacturers to replace materials in inelastic supply (such that, had development gone on without technical change, costs would have risen markedly) with goods like iron or cotton whose supply was comparatively elastic. In some cases, like cotton, the multiplier effects of industrialisation were transmitted abroad (Habakkuk & Deane 1963), though they may have come back to Britain, scarcely diminished, in later rounds.

Innovation thus conquered the diminishing returns that lay in store for an economy dependent for its growth on capital formation alone. Output per head rose more through a host of small-scale changes stemming from practical experimentation at every level than through a handful of big breakthroughs.

9

Changes in income and its distribution during the industrial revolution

P. K. O'BRIEN & S. L. ENGERMAN

The discussion of the impact upon the labouring classes of the economic changes in the late eighteenth and the first half of the nineteenth century has had a long and vigorous historiography (Taylor 1975; Deane 1965). As the 'standard of living' controversy it is certainly the most debated issue in British economic history. As in most such controversies there is both a narrow technical debate about the 'facts' of what happened to the course of 'real wages' over a period running roughly from about the 1780s to the 1840s (the choice of years to be studied is itself an issue of contention) and a broader discussion of what all the changes in the period meant for the 'quality of life'. Even more broadly the debate is an attempt to evaluate the costs and benefits of the onset of industrial capitalism. On the one hand there is the argument that the costs of growth were paid for by the lower classes, whose benefits, at least initially, were trivial. On the other hand there is the argument that industrialisation provided benefits to a broad spectrum of the population (if not during the period of industrialisation itself, at least in the next generation), and that conditions would have been even worse if there had been no industrialisation.

Economic change, particularly when as sharp and as profound as in the industrial revolution, involves substantial adjustments in the ways of living and working of the population. There were shifts in the location of the population. The proportion residing in urban areas, with worse health and mortality conditions than those in the countryside, rose from about 15 per cent in 1750 to 25 per cent in 1801, and to about 60 per cent of the British population in the mid-nineteenth century. The location of the workplace and the nature of work performed also changed with the rise of the factory system and machine production. These and other changes not only influenced the economic rewards of the population, but had quite marked impacts on the entire social and political life of Great Britain. Discontent periodically erupted into riots, disturbances, and protest and at times, such as the 'Peterloo Massacre' of 1819, these were met with government force. The Luddites smashed machines, there was agrarian violence in 1816 and in several other years, and Chartism became a major political movement in the 1840s. This period also saw the emergence of state

164

legislation to restrict the actions of employers in the labour market, beginning with the control of daily hours of pauper children in the cotton-textile industry in Peel's Factory Act of 1802, and including the 1833 Factory Act regulating hours of all children in textiles, the Ten Hours Act of 1847, and the 1850 Factory Act which included restrictions on the hours of female mill hands. It is no easy task to sort out these disparate reactions and arrive at a judgment on the effects of economic change in this period on the living conditions of the labouring classes and upon the distribution of the benefits of economic growth.

The substantive questions are difficult enough by themselves; they are made more difficult by questions of method. The usefulness of quantitative methods has been questioned – to what extent can real wages be measured and what would such measures show? Would these measures capture some relevant changes or are they merely artificial figments abstracted from reality? Not accidentally, perhaps, the dispute on method has become mixed with the debate on substance. The so-called optimists (those who argue for improvements in the standard of living) seem disposed to accept quantitative measures, while the pessimists (who argue for a worsening of the standard of living) stress their limitations. This, however, is not an inevitable pairing. Indeed, the 'modern' debate on the 'standard of living' (or Hobsbawm vs. Hartwell) (Taylor 1975) was given a quantitative thrust by the pessimist, Eric Hobsbawm. More usually the pessimists have emphasised the quality of life – either in terms of a sombre picture of changes in the basket of goods consumed (with bleak portrayals of slums and food adulteration) or of broader changes in the pattern of work and living, with apparent impacts in changing the nature of the family, attitudes to status, and the mechanisms of political and social control. More recently, however, the optimists have also pointed to aspects of these qualitative factors which they argue changed for the 'better', and have made clear that linking of methods and conclusion is not inevitable.

Another difficulty is that while both sides seem to be arguing about the course of 'real wages', embedded in the dispute are a number of counterfactual comparisons and assumptions as to what could or should have happened. The optimists attempt to isolate and explain away those changes which they argue were not attributable to the industrial capitalism of the period. Thus they would exclude years of harvest crises and the period of the Napoleonic Wars and its inflationary financing (as events unrelated to the rise of industry). The pessimists, however, would include these events since they did form an important part of the actual historical experience.

Also at issue are the extent to which population movements, and changes in birth and death rates, were related to the course of economic change. To what extent did economic change affect the decision to have more children (thus allowing part of the increased potential consumption to be taken out in the form of more children, leading to a lower measured per capita income); and to what extent did the changing productivity of agriculture and industry affect mortality and morbidity? The optimists often postulate a counterfactual which compares England and Ireland, and ask what would have been the impact upon living standards in England of the large increase in population which occurred in the absence of industrial development. For, as shown in chapters 2 and 11, population began growing at a relatively high rate some time after the middle of the eighteenth century, and this was apparently the consequence of both higher fertility and lowered mortality. While mortality probably declined in rural and in urban areas, the shift of the population to the higher mortality urban areas means a lesser, if any, decline in the national mortality rate. This population increase was accomplished without the very extensive out-migration which accompanied the higher rates of population growth in much of Europe in the middle of the nineteenth century. Presumably even if 'real wages' were to be found falling, the optimists would argue that the same population change in the absence of industrial growth would have meant an even sharper reduction in labour incomes.

The pessimists accept what tables 7.4 and 7.5 indicate, that the period of the industrial revolution was one of relatively rapid growth in per capita income, even with the large growth in population. Their major concern, however, is the distribution of this increase in average income. They raise the possibility that the increase went mainly (or exclusively) to those already in the higher income groups, so that the lower income groups did not benefit, or at least did not do so to the same extent. More specifically, no matter whether real wages increased or not, the pessimists seem to be considering a counterfactual in which the rates of growth would not have been lowered by changes in the distribution of income, tax burdens, and living conditions, and in which economic growth could have been achieved in the long run with an income distribution more favourable to the lower income groups. This counterfactual contains, of course, significant implicit hypotheses about the determinants of labour supply and of savings behaviour.

For these several reasons it is probably fruitless to expect agreement about the evaluation of changes in living standards during the industrial revolution. But that does not mean that agreement is not in principle possible concerning some of the specific questions to be asked. For that reason several issues will be discussed, and relevant empirical evidence presented. As will be made clear the data themselves are frequently the subject of controversy, and various biases and inadequacies have been pointed out. Yet that does not mean that these data cannot be useful in narrowing the range of disagreement or that further data collection is not important to the study of this set of questions. It is sometimes possible to estimate the direction and magnitude of biases. and the effects of revisions to the data. There seems no need to accept the nihilistic counsel of despair and reject outright any such calculations; indeed the importance of new data collection and analysis is to be emphasised.

Measuring real wages and its difficulties

A central question has been the trend in the real wages paid to the labouring classes. This involves measuring both the money wages paid to workers and the cost of the goods and services they consumed. To do this, data are needed on the money wages paid to various categories of workers, on the composition of their expenditures, and on the changing prices paid for goods and services over time. Clearly there is a need for more and better data on wages and prices, since much of the present debate is based on reworking a very small number of available statistical series (which are subject to reservations) with only limited effort given to the derivation of better statistical data.

The reason for the use of 'real wages' – money wages adjusted for changes in the price of goods and services purchased – is that prices and money wages can move independently and even in different directions. To look only at changes in money wages will not measure the changes in the quantity of goods and services to be consumed. Money wages are used to purchase goods and services, and changes in consumption due to changes in the prices paid for specific commodities (arising from harvest fluctuations, changes in import tariffs, and money supply variations) would be ignored if money wages alone were examined. As shown by the data in table 9.1 real wages often moved in the opposite direction to money wages. The inflation of the 1790s raised money wages at an annual rate of 3.1 per cent. This was, however, a rate of increase less than that of consumer prices, so real wages fell. In the deflation after the end of the Napoleonic Wars, money wages fell but consumer prices fell even more sharply, and the real wages of those employed rose.

There are serious problems of interpretation which arise because of substantial differences in wages by occupation and by region (Neale 1966; Gourvish 1972). There is also an issue of appropriate geographic coverage. Should Ireland be included, and what should be the treatment of the wages of the Irish migrants to England when comparing movements in English wages over time? The Deane and Cole (1967: 23) estimates of money wages for Ireland show a substantial decline in the early nineteenth century, and combined with British price indices these would show a smaller rise in Irish than in British real wages. As noted before, some point to Ireland as a relevant comparison to make with England to show what might have happened in England when its population grew, if there had been no industrialisation (although others point to the Irish pattern as indicating the impact of imperialism).

Even if one focuses on England, according to Gilboy (1934), in 1770, London and Kent craftsmen received money wages about fifty per cent greater than did labourers in those regions, while the wage rate in London was one-third above that of Kent. Since wages by occupations and wages and prices in various regions not only differ at a moment of time, but change by different amounts

168

(and, at times, in different directions), it is difficult to say what happened to the 'typical worker', even later in the nineteenth century (Hunt 1973). There are two approaches generally used to attempt to determine the fortunes of this 'typical workers'. First, by using the wage pattern for one occupational class or one region to represent the total population, and, second, by combining the information for various groups so as to present an average for all classes in the population (Wood 1899; Deane and Cole 1967). Both methods have their pitfalls, given the absence of complete information for all groups, and the range of differentials observed in those for which data survive. Moreover, to say average real wages have risen does not mean that all groups have benefited, or to the same extent, but rather that overall there were probably more workers who gained than lost over this period. The hardships of certain groups, e.g. the handloom weavers, are obvious, and it is quite clear that these and other groups suffered during the process of industrialisation. Yet it is often overlooked that this worsening could have meant that other workers benefited, directly due to increased employment as well as indirectly in the form of lower prices of goods consumed. The use of aggregate data does not deny the specific cases of decline, but rather measures the impact upon a larger, more inclusive, group of workers (Gilboy 1936; Flinn 1974).

The composite real wage index may increase due to an increase in the wages in each sector, but an increase in the average wage rate can also occur even with constant wage rates within each occupation or within each region. Skilled wages exceed those of the unskilled, and as more workers enter into skilled categories this means an increase in the average wage since more workers how have higher incomes. Similarly when there are regional differences, and there is a movement from lower to higher wage regions, constant wages in each region are consistent with improvements in average wages per worker. Since there were both increases in skill levels and movements to higher income regions in the period of the industrial revolution there could have been a sharper increase in the average wage than there was in many skill-specific and region-specific wage rates (Deane and Cole 1967).

Similarly the preparation of the relevant consumer price index poses problems of aggregating both at a moment of time as well as in making comparisons over time. Expenditure patterns differ among individuals and income levels at a point in time, while over time the relative importance of expenditures upon different items may change and new goods (or different qualities of the same goods) are frequently introduced. Thus if consumers spend less on a commodity whose price has risen relatively more than that of other commodities, failure to allow for the reduced importance of this commodity in the consumers' budget will lead to an overstatement of the actual increase in the consumers' cost of living. Estimates of per capita consumption of, e.g., meat, fish, sugar, tea, tobacco, and wine, have often figured in the debate on the 'standard of living', with rather mixed results, since the changes differ from commodity to commodity. Although existing

Table 9.1. '*Real wages*', *Great Britain 1790–1850*

	(1) Money wages	(2) Index of British commodity prices	(3) 'Real wages'
1790	70	87	80
1795	82	112	73
1800	95	147	65
1805	109	133	82
1810	124	150	83
1816	117	116	101
1820	110	113	97
1824	105	99	106
1831	101	93	109
1840	100	100	100
1845	98	81	121
1850	100	72	139

(1840 = 100)

Sources:

(1) Deane and Cole (1967: 23) (derived from Bowley and Wood). There remain major difficulties in the underlying series of money wages, both as to weighting and representativeness, and their implications must be regarded with great caution.

(2) Mitchell and Deane (1962: 470) (Gayer–Rostow–Schwartz index of British commodity prices; domestic and imported commodities).

(3) $\frac{(1)}{(2)} \times 100$.

consumer price indices have been justly criticised for being based on unrepresentative expenditure patterns, it should be possible to provide adjusted estimates. For example, the budget underlying the frequently used Silberling index excludes certain items of consumption, but a critique should indicate the relationship between the prices of the goods excluded and those included, not merely dismiss the index completely.

There are major problems in the use of the price index presented in table 9.1, since it measures changes in wholesale, not retail, prices, and is based upon a set of commodities weighted quite differently than they would be if based on consumer expenditure patterns. In general wholesale price indexes tend to fluctuate more widely than do consumer price indexes, and thus their use accentuates movements in real wages. Nevertheless, the Gayer–Rostow–Schwartz index of wholesale commodity prices is generally regarded as a reasonable substitute for a consumer price index (Flinn 1974). It is, of course, possible that some future direct estimate of a more properly constructed consumer price index might revise the pattern presented.

The most reasonable series of money wage and price level changes (with the Gayer–Rostow–Schwartz wholesale commodity price index used as a proxy for a consumer price index) covering the period 1790–1850 are shown in table 9.1. Real wages rose at a rate of 0.9 per cent per annum between 1790 and 1850, with rather marked differences among subperiods. From 1790 to 1800, real wages declined by almost 2.1 per cent per annum while from 1800 to 1850, real wages rose at a rate of 1.5 per cent per annum (in contrast with a 1.2 per cent per annum increase in per capita income). The growth shown in the 1840s, however, was unusually rapid, and from 1800 to 1840 the increase was at a rate of about 1.1 per cent per annum (with per capita income increasing at a rate of 1.3 per cent). Whatever may be the historical justification, table 9.1 indicates that the use of 1800 as a starting year in these measures does provide the most favourable year for optimistic conclusions on real wage changes. While subject to numerous caveats, it seems that (with the exception of the 1790s) there was an increase in real wages in the early nineteenth century, and the largest increases occurred at the end of the Napoleonic Wars (when price reductions were crucial), and in the 1840s. The increase in real wages shown by the series used in table 9.1 is among the largest indicated by available wage series, and must be regarded cautiously. The money wage series estimated by Deane and Cole does have some advantage over the others, however, in that it allows for the shifting composition of the labour force. There are enough difficulties, however, to raise great scepticism about these measures, although it should be pointed out that the direction of bias is not obvious.

A recent article by Flinn (1974) demonstrates the importance of avoiding certain pitfalls in discussing measured changes in real wages. Care must be taken to avoid comparing years of different phases in the business cycle (some form of averaging over the entire cycle would be preferable). The measures presented by Flinn show the sensitivity to the specific years examined, but the conclusions he draws from examining the available wage and price series are consistent with those inferred from table 9.1. Flinn's broad conclusion is that there was no marked trend in real wages between 1750 and the Napoleonic Wars, at the start of which there was a relatively sharp decline. This decline occurred with heavy taxation and a large increase in the government share of national expenditure, so that the fall in real wages may have reflected a shift in the distribution of income to the government, not necessarily the upper income groups. The immediate postwar increase in real wages was dramatic, and there was then no marked upsurge in the level of real wages until the 1840s.

One frequent reservation to the drawing of inferences from the observed wage rates is that they are relevant only to those who are employed. To the extent that the rate of unemployment increased, the wage data must be adjusted to reflect this fact. If, however, unemployment rates did not rise secularly (i.e. in the long term rather than simply in slumps or depressions) then the comparison of wage rates over time can provide a valid measure. This does not, of course, mean that the level of unemployment did not represent a social and economic problem. For this reason evidence on unemployment, as well as estimates of changes in the amount of unemployment suggested by changes in the number on poor relief, would form an important contribution to the debate. At present the answers to this issue are somewhat inconclusive due to lack of evidence (Gayer, Rostow, and Schwartz 1953a). There are no clearcut theoretical presumptions. Industrialisation made for greater variations in the level of unemployment attributable to changes in business demand conditions, and there were cyclical peaks in industrial unemployment every four or five years. There were, however, no apparent trends in the level of unemployment in this period. There was, moreover, a lessened dependence on the harvest with its own independent variation, which had also led to changes in the effective employment of labour.

Another drawback to the use of daily wage rates is the difficulty of adjusting for variations in the number of hours worked. If the wage per day increased less than hours worked, this would mean that the payment per unit of time worked fell. Leisure has value, and recent estimates suggest that an increase in the time spent away from work (fewer hours per day, fewer days per year) has been a major 'expenditure' of the increased potential income derived from economic growth. Little is certain about the trends in hours worked in the nineteenth century, particularly the first half, and what is required are comparisons not only of changes within a given industry, but also comparisons between hours of work in agriculture and those in manufacturing (Bienefeld 1972). Such comparisons are not conclusive, since there were, no doubt, differences in the intensity of labour input per hour as well as in the working conditions at the place of employment. It is possible that agricultural employment was considered more desirable by workers, necessitating a high, equalising wage differential to be paid to attract workers into factories. Moreover, the discussion of working conditions in the factories, the horrors of which figure so heavily in the Parliamentary Blue Books, must be considered in the debate on real wages, since the analysis should be based on not just the consumption permitted by the wages received by workers, but also on the psychological and physical costs of the work effort needed to acquire that income (see chapter 13; Thompson 1967).

Did the distribution of income change?

The extent and magnitude of increases in the average of real wages during the period of the industrial revolution has remained under dispute. It has been argued, however, that even though some increases in the level of real wages occurred, the distribution of income shifted so that the relative income of the lower income groups fell compared to those at the upper end of the income scale. An important part of the pessimists' contention is that whatever were the changes in the absolute standard of living, the benefits of British growth went, to a great extent, to the rich, and their share in total income increased. Unfortunately, however, there are available no reliable data to test statements about income distribution in this period, while attempts to draw inferences concerning income distribution from comparisons of changes in real wages and in per capita income provide somewhat ambiguous results.

It is useful to consider those arguments which draw inferences about trends in inequality from changes in the rate of capital formation. Generally most of the measured savings in a society are done by individuals with high incomes and some optimists and pessimists argue that increased income inequality made an important contribution in providing the necessary investment to promote growth. Hartwell, for example, has suggested that the increased rate of capital formation in the period of the industrial revolution justified any worsening of the distribution of income that might have occurred, since it led to higher wage income in future years. Recent estimates by Feinstein (1978: 82–94) and others show that the rates of capital formation in England were relatively low compared to those of the later developing countries, and much industrial capital was generated by the reinvestment of profits. Feinstein estimates (see chapter 7) that the share of national income invested rose from 8 per cent in the 1760s to 13 per cent in the 1840s. This relatively small increase means that most of the increased output which the economy produced over this period went for consumption not investment, and that the rate of increase of per capita consumption was nearly the same as that of per capita income. Yet the fact that the capital requirements for growth were not large does not provide any indication of actual changes in income distribution. Rather it means only that a frequent justification for any worsening of the income distribution has been shown to be inappropriate.

There is only very limited evidence available on the distribution of income and wealth in England prior to the twentieth century. Several earlier estimates which have been used to examine this issue have been collected and re-analysed by Lee Soltow (1968). The 'Lorenz curves' which he has derived for the years 1688, 1801, 1867 and several subsequent years are presented in figure 9.1. Incomes per person are arrayed from lowest to highest, and the Lorenz curves compare cumulative percentiles of the population with cumulative proportions of income earned. In 1801–3, for example, it is estimated that the 60 per cent of the population with lowest incomes received only 20 per cent of British income, while the 20 per cent with the highest incomes received about 60 per cent. The diagonal line represents the line of perfect equality. A reduction in inequality is indicated by the shift leftward of the curves measuring inequality in each year, a movement closer to the line of perfect equality.

There is little, if any, apparent increase in income inequality from 1688 to 1801, and some narrowing in the nineteenth century. These measures are, however, based upon not very reliable data and the intertemporal comparisons, given

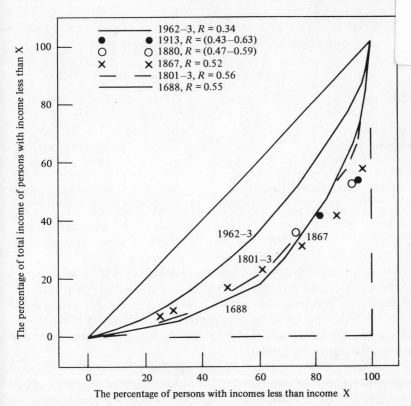

Figure 9.1 Lorenz curves of frequency distributions of income of persons in Great Britain in selected years from 1688 to 1963. Source: Soltow (1968: 20). Note: R is the Gini coefficient of concentration, a measure of inequality.

shifts in concepts of income and coverage of individuals, are somewhat uncertain. A related measure of income inequality drawn from tax data which provides information on the distribution among the relatively high income groups suggests that there was no worsening in the income distribution over the period from 1688 to 1867 (Soltow 1968).

Yet what is most striking in Soltow's presentation is the magnitude of the degree of inequality which existed in England in each time period. For those making an implicit comparison with an equal income distribution, these differences seem large. And if one makes comparisons of the shares of income going to the upper income groups in the United Kingdom and elsewhere in the late nineteenth and twentieth centuries, the United Kingdom income distribution was considerably more unequal than those in the European nations for which data are available, as well as for the United States (see table 9.2). A similar

174

Table 9.2. *Shares in national income of top 5 per cent of tax units or consuming units, various countries, late nineteenth and early twentieth centuries*

	1870s and 1880s	1890s and 1900s	1910s
United Kingdom	48	—	43
Prussia	26	27	30
Saxony	34	36	33
Denmark	36.5	28	—
Norway: country districts	—	—	27
United States before tax	—	—	24

Source: Kuznets (1966: 208–11). These data are to be regarded as suggestive, since they are based on somewhat different concepts and prepared by different statisticians for each country. The results are quite sensitive to the age distribution of the population (since incomes vary with age) and the size of families. For a discussion, see Kuznets (1976). It is most doubtful, however, that these factors would be sufficient to modify the broad implications of these comparisons.

conclusion as to relative British inequality is suggested by a comparison of the relative shares of income going to labour and to capital in the nineteenth century. The British share of income going to capital was probably the highest in western Europe and North America in the nineteenth century (Kuznets 1966: 168–9). Together these estimates suggest that inequality in Britain was large relative to that in other developed economies.

In general developed nations have a more equal distribution of income than, do the underdeveloped. At some state in the process of economic development equality increases. Clearly this is true of the British case, as was seen in the sharp reduction of inequality in the twentieth century. There is generally, however, a widening in the equality of income in the early stages of economic development, although this need not have occurred in the British case. Nevertheless, even if inequality widened in the period of the industrial revolution this does not necessarily mean a decline in the absolute incomes of most of the lower income groups.

The probability that growth in per capita income was sufficient for the absolute living standards of the broadly defined lower income groups to have increased, even if there had been a worsening of the income distribution, is suggested by two crude, but illustrative calculations, with available data. Arthur Bowley (1938: 16) has estimated that wage-earners in 1880 represented about 83 per cent of all income earners, and that they received 41.3 per cent of national income. Given that per capita income increased at a rate of about 1.2 per cent per annum from 1800 to 1850 and assuming that the distribution of income was as unequal in 1850 as Bowley estimates it was in 1880, for there to have been no increase in income per wage-earner the wage share of income in 1800 would have needed to be 76 per cent. This is inconceivable: Deane and Cole (1967:

301) estimate the share of employment incomes in British national income in 1801 as 44 per cent. Therefore some part of the increased per capita income over these years must have gone to the lower income, wage-earning group. Similarly Harold Perkin (1969: 135–6) has used income tax data to argue for an increased share of income going to the top group of income recipients in the first half of the nineteenth century. He argues that those highest income tax payers who represented 1.14 per cent of the population had 25.4 per cent of national income in 1801, while the highest income 1.18 per cent in 1848 had a share of 34.9 per cent. Yet even if we were to accept the income tax data as being comparable over this half century, these estimates indicate that the per capita income of the lower income groups would have risen in absolute terms, at a rate of about 1 per cent per annum, even with the relative decline argued for by Perkin. While in both of these calculations the lower income category is overly inclusive, and specific individuals and groups suffered absolute declines in living standards, they do serve to illustrate the distinction between changes in the distribution of income and changes in the level of per capita income. It can be argued whether changes in the absolute level of income or in the relative distribution of income should be accorded more attention in evaluating the outcome of economic change, but clearly an increase in inequality need not mean that the lower income groups were left with fewer goods to consume.

Changes in 'income' not measured by real wages and distribution

There has been difficulty in reaching judgements about the movements in real wages and in the distribution of income during the industrial revolution. This has been due mainly to the lack of adequate statistical evidence to answer questions which can be quite specifically posed. For other questions, however, the lack of agreement reflects not merely problems of evidence but also the importance to interpretation of broader social and political concerns. While these are clearly important issues, our present focus means that less attention will be given them than may be customary. Nevertheless, it will be useful to discuss them briefly.

'The quality of life'. The discussion of the 'quality of life' (presumably in contrast to the 'quantity of goods') has both a narrow and a broad focus. The narrower focus, within the context of the standard of living debate, evaluates the changes in the quality of the goods available to consumers. The discussion of food, for example, details the changes in impurities and the extent of adulteration. The descriptions of housing conditions range from quantitative indications of the extent of crowding to the lurid depictions of living conditions in the cities that featured so heavily in Engels' *The Condition of the Working Class in England* (1845), as well as in the Parliamentary Blue Books, the writings of

Tory critics of the rising industrialists, and the descriptions of European travellers (chapter 11). Here, again, we must be aware of the implicit counterfactuals involved. The optimists will respond that things would have been even worse, either then or in future years without industrialisation, a rather coldblooded, if (some may think) plausible, response to the conditions of urban life in nineteenth-century Britain. This discussion of urban food and housing conditions does however raise to the fore an important question underlying the debate about the standard of living. To what extent can movement to urban areas be regarded as voluntary in response to the higher urban than rural wages? If this urban migration were considered voluntary, it could be regarded as an indication of individual expectations of improvement in the standard of living, given the available opportunities. The question of migration options has political as well as economic aspects, and, e.g., the attention paid to the enclosure movement partly reflects its possible importance as a factor which forced movement to the city. The recent view, stated most forcibly by Chambers (1953), that enclosure was not directly responsible for forcing large numbers to leave the land for urban areas, would seem to buttress the optimists' position. Nevertheless, the examination of the impact of the shift from predominantly rural to urban residence, with its implications for the intensity and nature of work, for the role of women and children, and for the nature of family relations, remains a highly charged and controversial area (chapter 11).

Another significant question in analysing the impact of the industrial revolution concerns its impact upon the labour force participation rates of family members other than the primary male wage-earners. In examining the relationship of wage rates to family income, the earnings of women and children must be considered. Yet to do so often entails comparisons for which the data are not fully available. In addition to the need for detailed estimates of the labour force by age and sex, the interpretation of any trend will depend upon the causes of change. The proportion of women recorded as occupied increased in the mid-nineteenth century (Mitchell and Deane 1962: 60). This could be attributed to a reduction in the income of the head of household (as the pessimists argue) or to the liberation of females and their greater ease in finding a job (as the optimists argue).

One of the leading indictments of industrialisation is the use of child labour in factories. It led to major governmental interferences with the labour market to offset the costs of industrialisation, starting with Peel's Act in 1802. The horrors of long hours of work and difficult working conditions have frequently been described, but less attention has been paid to determining the magnitude of child labour and its long-range consequence. For example, while it has been argued that those children working in factories suffered stunted physical development, data on the height of British marines in the eighteenth and nineteenth centuries indicate that, in general, adults were growing taller during the period of industrial revolution. And the recent work on literacy indicates that education was not ignored and that children were being schooled prior to the passage of compulsory education acts in the last half of the nineteenth century. This is not to deny the horrors – but to point out that the Blue Books were a guide to social reform, not descriptions of the relative importance of different patterns of work. And, of course, it was the industrial revolution which, for the first time, improved productivity sufficiently for the economy to dispense with child labour.

The causes and consequences of population growth and movement. As shown in chapter 2, the industrial revolution was marked, if not inaugurated, by a sharp increase in the rate of growth of population. The causes of population growth are still debated, but it is doubtful that these changes were unrelated to movements in potential living standards. To the extent that the increase reflected a higher birth rate, this might plausibly be explained as a result of earlier marriage permitted by economic improvement. The fact that people may have chosen to have more children may indicate a faith in economic improvement, although in the short term the choice of children rather than goods cuts income per head as normally measured. To the extent that the key factor was a decline in death rates, and this occurred in the period before major developments in medicine or large-scale measures to improve public health, the role of improvements in material standards of living has been stressed (chapter 11). While demographic studies remain controversial, both in the discussion of the links between diet, nutrition, and mortality, and in regard to the explanation of mortality decline, increased life expectation in both urban and rural areas occurred in this period. Urban death rates did remain considerably above those in rural areas, particularly before the development of better methods of sanitation, due to higher population density and greater spread of infectious diseases. Since in Britain, as elsewhere, the urban populations were expanding relative to those in rural areas, primarily due to internal migration, the increase in life expectation shown by national figures understates the improvement in the urban and in the rural areas.

Intra- and intergenerational mobility. Studies of the changing patterns of income and wealth distribution are based on the shares of top percentiles. While these indicate the extent of inequality at a point in time, they are inadequate as measures of the returns to specific individuals and families over time. Our interpretation of the meaning of inequality will differ if the upper income groups remain unchanged over time, or if there is turnover within that group with new individuals rising to the top. Situations such as the latter, with opportunities for upwards social and economic mobility, may provide incentives to the lower classes and may co-opt people into accepting social systems in which inequality persists. It is here – intragenerational and intergenerational mobility – that much more work is necessary before we can understand the changes wrought by the industrial revolution. The available evidence indicates that most of the emerging entrepreneurs, while not from the poorest segment, were not from the most wealthy. There was upward mobility near the top, and indeed the analysis of changes in the structure of political power in the nineteenth century, which culminated with the Reform Act of 1832 and the highly symbolic Corn Laws of 1846, suggests the rise of a 'new class' to economic and political power. Nevertheless, W. D. Rubinstein's (1974) study of top wealthholders in the mid-nineteenth century shows that these still were mainly landowners and middlemen, although there was a greater share of 'self-made' millionaires in the nineteenth than in the first half of the twentieth century (ch. 13 and vol. 2 ch. 9). Even less is known about social and economic mobility in the middle of the income and social scale and among the lower classes. While it is probable that social mobility in Britain was less than in the United States, studies of the opportunities opened up by industrialisation and economic growth should help clarify this aspect of economic change.

Implications

The measures of changes in real wages and the distribution of income have broad implications for the study of British economic, political and social history. This section will discuss two issues for which the findings about changes in the standard of living provide necessary background.

The causes of growth in demand for output. The debates on the standard of living and on the causes of the industrial revolution have been intertwined. A pessimistic position on the former, since it presumes inadequate domestic demand, is consistent with an emphasis placed upon the role of foreign markets in generating growth during the industrial revolution. Recent work on foreign trade patterns and upon the sources of demand, demonstrates, however, that the home market was a major factor in the demand for increased production, and that the home market must have accounted for much of the increase in output demand in this period (Bairoch 1976). Accounting for this increased demand is important, since an increased demand for goods rather than leisure, or for market output rather than home production, could have had a significant impact on the available labour supply by increasing labour force participation rates and hours worked. What Gilboy (1932) somewhat misleadingly calls the 'demand factor in economic growth' is more reasonably seen as an increased labour input in the market sector. Why workers responded to the opportunities for higher potential incomes by increasing their labour force participation, rather than increasing their leisure, is a problem that demands broader social explanation. One possibility is that an increased desire for goods was related to the pattern of income distribution. The lower income groups presumably found it desirable, as well as possible, to emulate the wealthy. The pattern of income distribution may thus have generated patterns of labour supply conducive to higher measured output, and analysis of consumption and labour force participation rates in the transitional period is important.

The response to the consequences of economic change. An argument that the growth must have led to immiseration is based upon the movements for reform which industrialisation generated. Clearly Parliament felt a need to restrict somewhat the freedom of entrepreneurs in the labour market, and introduced such constraints as the series of Factory Acts starting in the early nineteenth century to control the employment of child, then female, labour. The first of these Acts applied to hours of work by children, which may have influenced the hours of workers not covered in the Acts. Nevertheless both the impact and the extent of enforcement of these acts remain uncertain, although enforcement was apparently minimal. The debates over poor relief were extensive, leading to the introduction of various schemes such as the Speenhamland system in 1795, and ultimately the broad revision of the relief system provided by the New Poor Law in 1834 (Marshall 1968; Rose 1972; Blaug 1963; McCloskey 1973). Urbanisation led to the drive for improved sanitation, and various public health measures were undertaken with respect to purification of the water supply and improved sewerage. Popular protest was present – in the form of food riots, strikes, and Luddite actions – although it is not clear to what extent this represented a change from earlier, 'preindustrial' times. Trade unions, initially organisations primarily of artisan and skilled workers, developed both as a forum for confrontation with employers and in order to attempt to exert political influence, such as the Chartist movement of the 1840s. There was frequent private and public action in reaction to developments in the period of industrialisation, which has implications for the interpretation of changes in absolute levels of income. Yet there are certain qualifications before we can be certain exactly what has been shown in regard to the standard of living debate by arguments from these reform measures. For they may not represent a reaction to deterioration relative to the past, but rather a major change in perceptions, with a heightened concern about, and more confidence in, the ability to handle problems which were not considered to be soluble at earlier stages. The emergence of new attitudes to social problems remains an interesting study for intellectual and social history, and reforms which seem impossible at low levels of income may become possible at higher income levels (and, also, with higher population densities). Although the legal changes may reflect the success of this reform movement, further analysis may demonstrate that important contributions to improving living standards were the outcome of other factors. West, for example, has argued that legislation regarding education in the 1870s did not have as large an effect as had been earlier argued (West 1970 and 1975; Hurt 1976; Blaug 1975; Webster 1976), while the impact of trade unions on wage levels remains an issue of great controversy. To point out that the evidence of reform cannot be used to argue for deterioration is not to deny the importance of the issues being dealt with or to argue against the need for or desirability to reform. Rather it is an attempt to place these in appropriate perspective for the specific questions being asked.

Conclusions

This chapter has concentrated on relatively narrow aspects of the discussion of the standard of living, and has dealt with these at a level removed from detailed depiction of actual conditions and discussion of changes in a chronological framework. We have attempted to answer some of the specific questions which have been asked, and tried to indicate the comparisons which have been most often suggested. Answers to even these questions are by no means easy. In terms of the central debate – about the impact of industrialisation – episodes such as the resource drain and inflation of the Napoleonic Wars pose a major problem. Since real wages fell, a decline in living standards is clear. Yet, given the heavy government demands on the economy, it is not clear whether this decline is to be regarded as part of the costs of industrialisation or as an exogenous influence which has no bearing on measuring the costs of industrialisation. Further issues arise in examining and evaluating the causes of labourers' decisions about how much and where to work. Were these due to a change in their tastes for income or were they forced from above? However antithetical to the later observer, voluntary migration to cities and decisions to increase labour input may have reflected individual preferences at the time. Of course this is somewhat simplistic, since the creation of a factory labour force requires the enhanced desire for goods and a certain set of work characteristics, and these may be imposed upon the workers, thus making interpretation of their desire for enhanced monetary rewards more debatable. The mix of voluntary acceptance and compulsion in the creation of a work discipline remains among the many important questions requiring further study.

But clearly one of the major difficulties is that the industrial revolution generated such a sweeping transformation of ways of living that these seem to swamp the importance of measured changes in the basket of goods consumed. To evaluate the industrial revolution is to raise questions about the desirability of those social transformations which have led to the rise of modern society. The movement of the population from rural to urban areas, increased work for owners in large-scale industrial establishments, widespread geographic mobility, changes in the numbers of births per family and in familial arrangements, a shift from a society with some degree of paternalistic concern and customary rights within settled areas to one with the chaos, and freedom, of the new social and political order – all are so profound that judgement of each, let alone a summary balance sheet, is impossible. To say this does not mean that issues of real wages, or of income per capita, are to be considered unimportant. While they should not be asked to prove more than they can, the evidence they bring to bear should not be ignored.

10

Agriculture during industrialisation

G. HUECKEL

Introduction

The first two-thirds of the nineteenth century was a turbulent period for British agriculture. The century opened in the midst of a major and prolonged war against France, lasting with minor interruptions from 1793 to 1815. The disruptions to food imports caused by the war placed an added burden on the domestic agricultural sector to feed a rapidly growing population at home (see chapter 2) as well as to provide occasional exports to hard-pressed allies, while the country's civilian labour supply was reduced some 6 per cent to meet the needs of the growing military force (John 1966: 28; Deane and Cole 1967: 143; Schwarz 1976: 97). The impact of the war-induced pressures was aggravated by repeated poor seasons from 1795 to 1800 and again between 1808 and 1812, reducing the carry-over stocks of grain and animals and contributing to the pronounced increases in prices in those years (Jones 1964b: 153–6, 158–9; Chambers and Mingay 1966: 109). Conditions changed dramatically with the end of the war, however, and the 1820s and 1840s were a period of adjustment to the lower peacetime prices. Finally, the decade of the 1840s introduced a new era for British agriculture. With the repeal of the Corn Laws (tariffs on imported grain) in 1846, the agricultural sector stood unprotected against foreign competition. The costs of ocean transport prevented an absolute fall in British grain prices until the 1870s, but grain imports increased immediately. Indeed, if the per capita annual consumption of wheat at mid-century was unchanged from the level of 8 bushels normally assumed by writers fifty years earlier, then the share of the British population fed on foreign wheat and wheat flour rose from one-eighth in 1840 to over one-quarter in 1860. Thus, for the first time, British farmers faced the loss of a significant share of their domestic markets to imports, forcing a gradual reduction in total acreage in production and in the share devoted to grain – a trend which accelerated after 1870 (see vol. 2, ch. 8).

The changing demand and supply conditions were revealed to British farmers by movements in the prices they received. Those price movements were highly variable, especially during the war period, when peaks were reached in 1800–1 and again in 1812–13 of over 100 per cent above the prewar base and over 50 per cent above the trough of the intervening years. However, their long-run

182

Table 10.1. *Trends in agricultural prices 1790–1870 (average annual percentage rates of change)*

	1790–1815	1812–22	1822–45	1846–70
Grain prices	+2.5	−6.6	−0.1	+0.2
Animal product prices	+2.7	−4.5	+0.2	+0.7

Source: Calculated from trend lines fitted to price indexes with 1790–92 as the base period. Prices for the period before 1850 were obtained from Gayer, et al. (1953b: beef, 603–4; butter, 605–6; mutton, 623; oats, 625–6; pork, 633; wheat, 1270–2) and from Mitchell and Deane (1972: barley, 488–9). For the period after 1850, animal product prices were taken from Sauerbeck (1886: 637); and grain prices were taken from Mitchell & Deane (1972: 488–9). Weights were calculated from McCulloch (1839: 532–2). The animal product index is composed of beef (0.39), butter (0.31), mutton (0.27), and pork (0.03); and the grain index is composed of wheat (0.58), oats (0.32), and barley (0.1).

Table 10.2. *Meat/wheat price relatives 1790–1815 (average 1790–92 = 100)*

	1790–94	1795–99	1800–4	1805–9	1810–15
Beef/wheat	108	120	115	99	117
Mutton/wheat	99	93	106	90	96
Pork/wheat	99	78	80	66	74

Source: See table 10.1.

trends can be discerned by determining the slope of a line which when plotted on a graph of the observed prices yields the minimum deviation between the observations and that 'trend line'. The results of such an exercise are displayed in table 10.1, where the changing market conditions are clearly evident in the relative inflation of the war period, the rapid fall in prices between 1812 and 1822, the nearly horizontal course of grain prices thereafter, and the gradual recovery of animal product prices, especially after 1845.

More important for an analysis of British agriculture itself during this period is the relative movement in the prices of the two general classes of agricultural products. After the war there is a clear shift in relative prices in favour of animal products: while all prices fall after 1812 and rise after 1845, the prices of animal products fall more slowly and rise more rapidly than do those of grain. The situation during the war is less clear. The apparent differential in favour of animal product prices is too small to be accepted as representing anything more than simply random error in the data. However, the trends in average price for product groups shown in table 10.1 conceal important changes in the relative prices of individual commodity-pairs. Table 10.2 displays indexes formed from the price ratios of the three chief meat products to wheat – the primary bread grain. An entry over 100 indicates that the increase in the meat price since the 1790–2 base period was greater than the increase in the wheat price and vice versa for a number less than 100. Table 10.2 indicates that the price of beef rose relative to that of wheat over most of the war period while the relative prices of the other two meats fell. Movements in relative prices are the signals on which production decisions are based, and the trends illustrated here were reflected in the changes which occurred during the nineteenth century in the quantity and composition of agricultural output and in the techniques by which that output was obtained.

Agricultural prices and production during wartime

In spite of the pressures imposed on the agricultural sector by weather and war in the opening decade of the century, the needs of the British population for food were met, though not without scattered bread riots in the worst years (Stern 1964). Moreover, those needs were filled primarily by an increasing output from domestic farmers. Even at their wartime peak, in 1810, imports of wheat and wheat flour probably fed no larger a share of the population than the 12 per cent estimated for the previous peak years of 1800–1 (chapter 4). Since the population rose some 14 per cent between those dates, domestic production of grain probably rose at about the same rate.

The increased output was obtained from larger quantities of inputs devoted to agricultural production (especially land and capital) and from changes in techniques designed to increase the productivity of those inputs. Indeed, the two forces were inextricably intertwined as much of the new land brought into production was in the regions of thin, light soils of chalk, limestone, or sand, which could not yield repeated crops of grain without the new techniques (see chapter 4).

The supply of land

The war years witnessed an extension of the area under cultivation to a point reached neither before nor since. Much of the new land was obtained through the process of Parliamentary enclosure discussed in chapter 4. The number of acres enclosed by Act of Parliament during the war period reached a peak of over 3 million acres, about 10 per cent of the entire cultivated area and a half-million acres more than the total enclosed in the sixty years before the war (Slater 1906: 37–40). That peak is probably exaggerated by the omission from the acreage figures of the area enclosed privately, an activity which left no documentary evidence for the historian. Because private enclosure was not so difficult as to require the expense of a private act of Parliament and government enclosure commissioners, it probably occurred to a greater degree in the earlier period. Thus, combining the acreage so enclosed with the figures for Parliamentary enclosure would flatten somewhat the wartime peak (Jones 1967: 13–14).

About one third of the acres enclosed by wartime acts of Parliament represented previously untilled land. The prewar share was about 20 per cent, a shift which illustrates the war time preoccupation with efforts to expand the cultivated area. Indeed, with the addition of privately enclosed land to the 1 million previously untilled acres enclosed by act, perhaps 5 per cent of the wartime cultivated area represented a recent, net gain to the stock of land in production.

New farming practices and relative prices

The practices of the most successful nineteenth-century farmers were those described in chapter 4. Innovation in agricultural technology during this period was biological rather than mechanical – that is, the increased agricultural output was not obtained through the introduction of new machines but through the use of new crops and new breeds of livestock. Arable and livestock production were linked by the cultivation of a wide variety of fodder crops, which allowed the farmer to maintain larger quantities of livestock than had previously been possible. Besides increasing the output of animal products, the larger herds provided the farmer with increased quantities of manure which could be applied to the land, increasing the yields of the arable crops. While the details of the rotations were altered by region to suit local conditions, all of those local variants emphasised livestock production as an important source of fertiliser. Consequently, the diffusion of such techniques would have been facilitated by shifts in relative prices which offered increased profits on animal products.

Relative price shifts can result from a variety of causes. A rise in the relative price of a commodity can signify either a relative increase in the demand for that commodity or a relative decrease in its supply. In the former case, if nothing else changes, the quantity supplied by producers would rise as they seek to gain the higher profits offered by the higher price; but in the latter case the quantity supplied would clearly fall. It is possible that a commodity would have its supply increased relative to another by the introduction of some cost-reducing technological change. In that case, the relative price of the commodity benefiting from the new technology would fall (in the absence of countervailing demand movements), but the quantity supplied would rise as producers seek to obtain the higher profits made possible by the lower production costs.

British farmers in the nineteenth century seem to have been very sensitive to such price movements and quickly altered their crop rotations to take advantage of changes in market conditions. Many farmers were able quickly to alter their rotations to take advantage of both the temporary price shifts and the long-run trends. With the high grain prices of 1800 fresh in their memories, farmers in the parish of Cowfold, Sussex, were reported to 'have been induced to sow a larger quantity of wheat for the last two years in consequence of the high price it has been sold for at the Horsham Market' (Henderson 1951–2: 58). The response could occur just as quickly in the other direction when price movements warranted, as indicated by the incumbent at Egton in the North Riding who reported that because 'the blessing of heaven' had reduced the price of grain after the harvest of 1801, 'farmers intended to avoid toil' by converting some of their arable to pasture (Churley 1953: 184).

While the short-run response of farmers took the form of temporary alterations in their grain acreage, their long-run response was a sustained effort to obtain a relative increase in the output of animal products. The nature of that effort varied considerably according to local conditions. Those farmers who, like J. Badcock of Radley, Berkshire, were favourably situated on land well-suited to both arable and pasture could achieve considerable increases in their output of both grain and livestock. In Badcock's case, grain production rose some 30 per cent over the war period while beef animals and pigs were increased 70 per cent and 25 per cent. Other farmers, located on the heavier clay lands, ill-suited to low-cost arable cultivation, allocated the bulk of their attention to grazing and to the dairy at the expense of their grain output. Thus, a Wiltshire farm whose records have survived saw its grain production fall nearly 20 per cent over the period while that of livestock and dairy products rose 20–25 per cent (Hueckel 1976).

The intimate production relationships of the new practices, which 'mixed' arable and livestock production, were not limited to those between livestock and grain yields. Farmers who increased the output of their dairy found that that made possible an increase in pork production as well because 'pigs [were] looked upon to be a necessary appendage to every dairy farm; a great number [were] bred with the whey and offal of the dairy' (Davis 1794: 122). The ability to make profitable use of waste products was not a monopoly of farmers. London distillers had learned early in the eighteenth century to turn their waste to account as feed for cattle and pigs, a practice which appears to have increased during the war period under the combined spurs of a malt tax (which encouraged the use of unmalted grain in the distilling process, providing a more effective feed) and the rising meat prices (Mathias 1952: 249–57).

Changing livestock breeds

The efforts of farmers to increase their meat output were aided by the introduction of new breeds of livestock designed to produce more meat and less bone in a shorter time. Although the new breeds provided little increase in carcass weights over the period, the age at slaughter declined steadily. While it was common to work oxen at the plough for ten years in the eighteenth century, by the early nineteenth century cattle of the Hereford breed, mentioned in chapter 4, were sold fat in their fifth or sixth year; and that age continued to fall, to two years at mid-century. Similar declines were obtained with other breeds (Jones 1974: 146–8; Davis 1794: 204–5). Similarly the old sheep breeds underwent considerable transformation in the late eighteenth century. The new breeds were characterised by a higher ratio of meat to bone and were ready for the butcher in two years rather than the four required earlier (Ernle 1912: 186; Watson 1928: 23).

The effect of these changes – reducing the time an animal had to be fed before it was ready for market and increasing the amount of saleable meat obtained from each animal – was to reduce the costs of meat production. Unless the period witnessed a greater fall in demand for meat, these breed changes should have offered farmers the opportunity of higher profits from their livestock and should have resulted in an increased output of animal products. However, the absence of data on the composition of agricultural output in the early nineteenth century makes impossible a measurement of any such increase. The wartime extension of the arable certainly reduced the acreage devoted to pasture and possibly reduced the numbers of animals kept in certain regions (Jones 1974: 32). Nineteenth-century writers were aware of these forces, but they were convinced that an increase in the nation's meat supply had been achieved. For one writer, 'the decrease in the number of sheep [raised] in many parts of the kingdom, and the vast increase in the consumption of mutton, seems a paradox'. However, the paradox was resolved by noting 'what is certainly the fact, that the animal is now killed at an earlier age than it was formerly'. The increase in the supply of meat resulting from the earlier maturity and from 'the vast increase in the number of livestock kept on arable land' and the observation that 'the markets, except at some particular periods, rarely experience an over-supply', led contemporaries to the conclusion suggested in 1805 by *The Farmer's Magazine*, 'namely, that the demand...is of late materially increased' (Hueckel 1976: 407 and 414; John 1967b: 42). Thus, the testimony of contemporaries and the technical literature suggest that at least part of the fall in the relative price of mutton and pork relative to wheat illustrated in table 10.2 should be viewed as the result of relative increases in the supply of those meats made possible by technological advance in the form of improvements in breeds and in rearing and fattening practices.

Barriers to adoption of the new practices

Land type and input costs. Although there is ample evidence of a shift in techniques on many farms giving greater emphasis to livestock fattening on roots and cultivated grasses, it would be incorrect to conclude that such practices were easily adopted by all farmers. Some of the more improvident farmers were induced by the very high grain prices to 'mine' the land with successive crops of wheat. Those individuals were condemned by contemporary writers as 'bad farmers for present profit' who left their fields in 'a wretched state'. While most farmers ran their businesses with an eye to the future productivity of their land as well as to present profit, some, probably near the end of their leases with no intention of renewal, were tempted to maximise short-run gains at the expense of their landlord, who received a legacy of exhausted fields (Jones 1974: 31; Thirsk 1957: 262).

For some farmers the barrier to adoption of the new practices was a technical one. As noted in chapter 4, those practices were not suited to the heavy, clay lands such as those of the vales and Midlands. These lands, which for centuries had been the traditional grain areas of the country, were poorly drained and expensive to work, requiring several ploughings with three or four horses to the plough instead of the one or two used on the lighter lands of the east and south. Turnips and other root crops so important to mixed farming did poorly on the clays; and even if a good crop was obtained, sheep could not be successfully 'folded' (i.e. put out to graze in a temporary enclosure) as the wet land increased the likelihood of disease. It was possible to lift and cart the roots to the farmyard in some areas, but that was expensive and the land did not get the benefit of the manure. On these undrained lands, fertilisers simply washed away in the winter rains. The high cultivation costs and the difficulty of improving yields through the application of natural or artificial fertilisers left these farmers little choice but to shift their efforts to dairying and stock rearing. To do so, however, required a knowledge of dairy and rearing practices which were unfamiliar to many farmers. Consequently, because the high grain prices of the war period permitted high-cost production techniques, many of these lands witnessed the persistence of the old wheat–bean–fallow rotation throughout the war period, preparing the way for the severe depression of agricultural income in these regions after the war.

Even on the lighter soils, however, where the larger flocks fattened on roots and cultivated grasses provided the manure for greatly increased arable yields, many wartime farmers were prevented by the high cost of the new practices from gaining their full technical benefit. The profit to be gained from a new technique depends upon the cost of its adoption as well as upon the degree to which it increases technical productivity. If the costs of the necessary inputs are rising faster than the price of the product, even the most productive of techniques may be shunned by producers. Thus, while a hallmark of the most technically sophisticated farming systems was the use of phosphates in the form of crushed bones as artificial fertiliser, the rise in the price of such preparations limited their adoption. Similarly, in the south, where in the late eighteenth century it was common to apply such dressings as lime or ashes to the land, it was reported in the early 1800s that such 'artificial manures [were] very rarely made use of' because 'the present price is too high to allow the continuation of it' (Board of Agriculture 1806: 39).

Wartime labour supplies and technological change. The input which bulked largest in the farmer's costs was labour, and the wartime rise in wage costs created the most serious barrier to the adoption of the new techniques. The impact of the war on the labour market was not limited to the 6 per cent of the labour force drawn into the military. Perhaps another 5 per cent took up part-time military duties in the local militia, and an unknown number was supplied to the war industries. Though complaints of labour shortage were heard in all parts of the country, it was most severely felt near the industrial centres and in areas where the extension of the arable was proceeding most rapidly. An inquiry by the Board of Agriculture in 1804 showed the greatest increases in wages since 1790 to have occurred in the industrial counties of Derbyshire, Lancashire, Yorkshire, Northumberland and Nottinghamshire (all of which experienced wage increases of over 65 per cent) and in Cambridgeshire and Lincolnshire, where the rapid expansion of the grain area caused wage increases of over 70 per cent. The effect of such wage movements on the farmer's profits was considerable since, with the exception of the two poor seasons of 1800 and 1801, agricultural prices had not risen more than 45 per cent above their 1790 level. Indeed, their rise did not surpass such wage increases until the next series of poor harvests began in 1809 (Collins 1969b: 68; John 1967b: 32–4; Jones 1974: 34–5. 212–14).

The difficulty these labour conditions created for the new farming techniques arose from the highly labour-intensive nature of those techniques. The heavy investment in land improvements indicated by the large number of wartime enclosures required large labour inputs. Enclosure itself increased the need for labour to provide the new fences, hedges and internal roads necessary on a newly enclosed farm. When the enclosure created new farms entirely out of previously uncultivated land or on land requiring drainage, the need to provide new buildings or drains further increased the labour requirement. Direct labour charges accounted for 60 per cent of the total cost of drainage at mid-century, and that proportion could rise to 70 per cent if certain additional improvements were performed (David 1975: 267). The spread of these improvements was slowed at times by the relative scarcity of labour. In 1806, a correspondent to *The Farmer's Magazine* reported from Lincolnshire that 'our drainage business goes on successfully, though rather slower than could be wished. The scarcity of workmen is great; indeed a sufficient number cannot be obtained on any account...'

Once enclosed, the land could be made to yield increased quantities of output only with the application of the techniques of mixed farming, and these too required a larger input of labour than did the old, two-crop-and-fallow rotation. The root crop required a finely ploughed field, a heavy dressing of manure, and hand hoeing. The latter activity itself required at least as much labour per acre as did the grain harvest, the most labour-intensive period in the farming calendar. When the roots were lifted and carted to the farmyard, that labour input was doubled (Collins 1976: 39). The introduction of sheep folded on the arable increased shepherding costs because fewer sheep could be tended under such conditions than when allowed to run loose on grassland. Even when the new fodder crops were introduced, the heavy labour requirements could prevent their proper cultivation. In South Lincolnshire, turnips and beans were widely cultivated for fodder, but the potential benefits of those crops were lost. The turnips were seldom properly hoed and the sheep were not allowed to feed in the field, depriving the land of the manure. Similarly, the bean fields were described as 'never hoed and full of weeds' (Grigg 1966: 55).

The heavy labour requirements of the new rotations and of enclosure severely limited the degree to which agriculture could supply labour to other sectors of the economy. The rising urban, industrial labour force was not the result of rural enclosure driving labour off the land but of population increase. As chapter 4 noted, some cottagers with a traditional right to keep a cow on the common pasture lost that right through enclosure, and some small-holders may have been forced to sell their land to finance their share of the fencing and administrative costs, but these groups did not leave agriculture altogether. Most of them had earned the bulk of their incomes as wage-earners before enclosure and so they remained, providing the labour required by the new techniques (Chambers 1953; McCloskey 1975).

The higher wage costs resulting from the increased demand for labour in enclosure, drainage, and cultivation led farmers to seek methods to economise on that input. The period of peak labour demand occurred at harvest time, when the crop had to be brought in quickly lest it be lost through shedding or spoiled in wet weather. In response to that demand, there was considerable effort to develop a mechanical reaper, though none of the designs patented was success-fully introduced. Consequently, many areas were forced to rely heavily on temporary inflows of casual workers; indeed, in regions as far apart as Cumberland and Hampshire, those workers were members of the military stationed nearby. Often these labour flows were critical to a successful harvest. In 1808, *The Farmer's Magazine* reported that in Lincolnshire the 'harvest [was] going briskly forward, so far as hands can be procured, though it is to be dreaded that not a little of the grain will be lost for want of reapers,...and should more hands not arrive from Ireland and Scotland the most serious injury will be sustained by many people.'. In a few districts, the harvest difficulties led to some experimentation and adoption of alternative hand tools which allowed the grain to be cut with less labour than was necessary with the sickle (Collins 1969a: 464; 1976; Jones 1974: 35, 213).

Although the wartime efforts to mechanise the haying and harvest operations could not overcome the technical problems involved, farmers were able to adopt devices allowing a reduction in the labour requirements at other times of the year. Thus the thresher (a device to mechanically separate the grain from the straw, a task previously done laboriously with a flail), introduced in the 1780s, was adopted during the war years in the regions experiencing the greatest increases in wages. The widespread appearance of itinerant threshers travelling with their machines among the farms of a region allowed the smallest of farmers the use of a mechanical thresher for a daily rental if local labour costs warranted (John 1967b: 32–5; Jones 1974: 35, 213). Such expedients could not, however, overcome the effects of the rising prices of labour, fertiliser, breed-stock, and seed (the latter leading to a wider use of the drill to permit a more efficient sowing) and the increased requirements for those inputs characteristic of the new practices.

Because agricultural capital-formation (enclosure, drainage, construction of new structures, and other improvements to the land) is a highly labour-intensive process, the rising labour costs raised the capital inputs necessary from British landlords in many areas to allow a shift to the new techniques. Similarly, the tenant faced an increase in his working capital requirements to finance the larger holdings of lifestock and the labour-intensive crops. The tenant's capital requirement has been estimated at 40 per cent greater for the new husbandry than for the old, two-crop-and-fallow rotations (Timmer 1969: 390–1). Contemporary observers suggested that the level of investment necessary for a successful farm doubled over the war period (Parl. Pap. 1813/14: III, 198).

Measures of productivity change

The impact of these changes on agricultural productivity is impossible to measure with precision, but sufficient cost and price data exist to allow the calculation of an estimate using the method described in chapter 6. The major difficulty encountered in such an exercise is the absence of data on the trend in agricultural capital costs. However, because so much of agricultural capital included a very high labour component, it is perhaps not unreasonable to assume that capital costs followed the same trend as wages. The results of the calculation are displayed in table 10.3. They must be viewed as no more than very tentative estimates; there is still much to learn about the precise trends in agricultural costs. Nevertheless, the figures probably represent the correct order of magnitude.

Table 10.3 illustrates a rate of productivity advance in British agriculture considerably below the rates calculated for other industries in chapter 6.

Table 10.3. *Total factor productivity change in agriculture 1790–1870 (average percentage change per year)*

	1790–1815	1816–46	1847–70
	+0.2	+0.3	+0.5

Sources: Output prices were taken from the sources in table 10.1. The wartime rent increase was taken as 85% (Chambers and Mingay 1966: 118; Grigg 1966: 36; Hunt 1959; F. M. L. Thompson 1963: 218–20). Wage data were taken from Mitchell and Deane (1972: 348—9). Postwar rent data obtained from R. J. Thompson (1907: appendix table B). Cost weights used were 0.77 (wages) and 0.23 (rents).

However, the rate calculated for the first half-century matches that obtained in volume 2, chapter 8 for the last quarter-century and the period from Repeal to the onset of falling prices in the 1870s witnessed a slight acceleration in productivity advance. Apparently, the epithet 'Golden Age' applied to the third quarter-century by earlier writers was not entirely undeserved.

In the absence of data on the differentials in cost trends between grain and livestock production it is not possible to disintegrate the productivity estimates shown in table 10.3. There is, however, some evidence that rents on land devoted to the dairy and to stock rearing experienced greater increases during the war and smaller falls afterward (Fussell and Compton 1939; F. M. L. Thompson 1963: 218, 231, 234–5). If that was indeed the case, then the inability of meat prices to rise significantly relative to those of grain during the war, as noted above, suggests that productivity advance in livestock production probably outpaced that for grain at least during the war years. Indeed, the technical literature suggests that such a differential persisted well beyond the war, but verification must await further evidence on relative costs.

The postwar depression in arable and pasture

The dramatic fall in agricultural prices after the war, the demobilisation of a major part of the military and the release of thousands of workers from war industries presented farmers and landlords with a new environment in which the inducement to adopt the practices of mixed farming had changed from the 'carrot' of high incomes to the 'stick' of low prices and threatened bankruptcy. The severity of the distress varied considerably however, being greatest on the clayland arable farms and least in the dairy and stock-rearing districts and in areas like Hereford and Kent where hops and fruit were important crops. The initial response of arable farmers and landlords was to seek legislative relief in the form of protection or reductions in taxes, which tended to remain at high wartime levels. Those agriculturalists provided the bulk of the testimony before the various Parliamentary inquiries into the causes of the 'agricultural distress' which occurred from 1813 to 1837. Hardly a whimper was heard at those hearings from dairy counties like Cheshire and Gloucester, and the only complaints from the rearing counties of Derby and Hereford occurred in the years of very low prices when the demand for livestock to fatten on the eastern, arable farms disappeared. Even on the arable farms, however, costs had adjusted to the lower prices by the 1830s so that, at least on the more advanced of those farms, incomes could begin to climb from the depressed levels of the previous decade (Fussell and Compton 1939: 197–8; Jones 1968: 10–12).

On most farms, some of the burden of adjustment was shouldered by landlords in the form of lower rents and increased outlays for repairs and improvements which previously had been the responsibility of the tenant. Though rents did not always respond immediately to the lower postwar price levels, they had generally begun a decline from their wartime heights by 1820 and continued that trend in many areas into the 1830s (Grigg 1966: 149). The concurrent increase in expenditures by the landlord on improvements was of special importance to the tenant because it allowed him to allocate a larger share of his funds to the working capital requirements of the farm. At the same time, those increased outlays represented little decline in the landlord's net income because they were often offset by reductions in his tax burden (F. M. L. Thompson 1963: 233–7).

In the face of competition from the more advanced farms in the light lands, the clayland farmers experienced the greatest distress. Unable to reduce their cultivation costs, many of these men saw as their only salvation continued agitation for protection, which they carried on with the creation in the early 1840s of various local 'agricultural protection societies' (Mosse 1947). Of course, the highest of tariffs could not protect them from their own countrymen. Consequently, some of this land, especially that near the industrial areas, was laid down to grass to provide the towns with milk, hay for the horses and coal-pit ponies, and some beef. Those clayland farmers who maintained their arable acreage in the persistent hope that the high prices of the war period could somehow be restored were destined to experience continued difficulty until they adjusted their output to the livestock and dairy production for which their land was best suited.

The 'golden age'

Drainage and high farming

The introduction in the 1840s of inexpensive clay pipe and drainage ploughs spurred a renewed interest in land improvement among agricultural writers over the next three decades. The cutting of drains on the clay lands to remove the troublesome excess moisture and permit a shift of techniques to the mixed farming rotations which had proved so beneficial to the light soils was seen as the only salvation for those heavy lands. In the event, however, those hopes were disappointed. By 1880 the most knowledgeable observers estimated that less than one-fifth of the land requiring drainage had received such treatment, and many of the projects completed had been so poorly executed as to have little beneficial effect on costs or yields (Parl. Pap. 1873: XVI, 60–1, 77–8, 285–8). Indeed, even when perfectly executed, drainage could not meet the high hopes of its more optimistic proponents. On the wettest clays, no amount of drainage could make possible the cultivation of turnips or other roots or the folding of sheep in the fields – the practices which were supposed to so improve yields on those lands. In short, in spite of government subsidised loans to encourage drainage, that activity was rarely a profitable investment.

To coat the bitter pill of Repeal, the government offered landlords in 1846 a fund, amounting with later additions to one-sixth of the total estimated expenditure on drainage between 1846 and 1876, to supply loans to finance drainage projects at a rate of 3.5 per cent, about 1.5 percentage points less than the rate charged by private companies providing similar loans. With the relatively low price of wheat at mid-century, the 15 per cent increase in yield suggested by contemporary accounts to have resulted from drainage would have provided an annual return on that investment of about 5.5 per cent (David 1975: 283–5). In fact, however, such a return seems to have been quite rare. The surviving estate accounts illustrate returns on landlord's improvement expenditure of no more than about 3.5 per cent, and in many cases even those returns were ended by the fall in prices in the 1870s before the loans financing the investment had been repaid (F. M. L. Thompson 1963: 250–1; David 1975: 264–5).

If such returns were common, the country would have been better served if the funds used to finance drainage had been allocated to other projects. If the 5 per cent interest on private drainage loans can be taken as a measure of the earnings such funds would have obtained in other uses, the application of those funds to drainage projects earning 3.5 per cent deprived society of the higher product which could have been received from investment in other sectors. Even the 5.5 per cent return estimated for projects providing the rather generous 15 per cent yield increase was below the 8 per cent or 10 per cent considered common on industrial investments carrying similar levels of risk (F. M. L. Thompson 1963: 251–2).

With the low returns earned on drainage projects, it is surprising not that so small an amount of drainage was done but rather that as much was accomplished as contemporary testimony suggests. In an effort to maintain their incomes in an era of static or falling grain prices and rising costs some landlords effectively subsidised their tenants by providing improvements which yielded returns in the form of higher rents of only 3–4 per cent when their funds could have earned 5 per cent or more elsewhere. It did not take many examples of such losses to convince the bulk of British landlords that drainage was not generally a profitable investment. However, there remained some who viewed continued investment in land improvement as the panacea for the low rents received from their clayland arable farms, a misjudgement which volume 2, chapter 8 shows continued into the last quarter of the century.

High farming, prices and Repeal

The limited extent of drainage activity and the low returns earned on such investment make it impossible to attribute much of the accelerating productivity advance after Repeal to land improvement schemes. That productivity gain was obtained through a more intensive application of the techniques of mixed farming on the light lands of eastern and southern England and south-eastern Scotland and a shift on some of the clays, especially those in the north and west of England, to beef and dairy production (Collins and Jones 1967; Sturgess 1967). On the light lands, the objective was an increase in both yields and livestock holdings; and it was approached through a widespread adoption of improved, artificial fertilisers and intensive animal feeding on rich, purchased oilcake. These practices were motivated by the persistent upward trend in the relative prices of animal products noted in table 10.1 resulting from growing domestic incomes and Repeal. The large grain imports following Repeal, noted at the beginning of this chapter, prevented a rising demand from drawing up grain prices as well as those of meat (see vol. 2, ch. 8 for further discussion of this point). Thus, farmers were encouraged to shift more effort to the production of animal products, where prices continued to rise with output.

A limitation of grain price increases was not the only benefit the British consumer received from Repeal. The increasing share of imports drawn from distant sources with climatic conditions very different from those of northern Europe resulted in a reduction in the annual variation in grain prices in addition to that already achieved through the resumption of trade after the war. While nearly three-quarters of Britain's wheat imports were obtained from the Baltic region during the war period, nearly half of the larger imports in the 1850s came from such distant sources as Egypt, Russia, Canada, and the United States. The impact those imports had on the volatility of price movements is illustrated by the fall in the standard deviation of grain prices around their trend (a measure of the average deviation of the observed price in each year from the trend lines in table 10.1). The removal of the wartime disruptions to foreign trade caused that measure to fall from a level of 39 index points during the war period to one of 20 for the postwar years to Repeal, and the new imports after 1846 resulted in a further four-point decline.

The cost and price conditions facing agriculture after Repeal were illustrated in the comments of contemporaries regarding the relative importance to the farmer of the grain and livestock segments of his enterprise. Before the 1850s, the fattening of livestock on arable farms was adopted 'not from a view to profit in the sale of meat, but for the production of dung, and the consequent increase in the corn crop'. Thus, Lincolnshire farmers were willing to keep other men's animals over the winter on straw and the customer's oilcake at no charge simply to obtain the manure. It was a common view in this period that livestock prices did not fully remunerate the high cost of feeding on purchased oilcake, making it necessary to charge off part of that cost to the arable which received the benefit of the increased supplies of dung. However, in the period after Repeal, grain prices were so low in certain years that even wheat was fed to the cattle in the hope of maintaining the farmer's income through the sale of fatstock. Nevertheless, the added dung had a beneficial effect on arable yields. The available evidence suggests an increase in wheat yields of over 50 per cent from the late 1830s to the late 1850s, while the agricultural labour force rose only 5 per cent (Jones 1974: 189, 194–7; Deane and Cole 1967: 143). The increase in yields, which continued throughout the third quarter of the century, and the relatively favourable course of prices from Repeal to the 1870s gave that period an appearance of a 'golden age' for the British farmer.

The dissemination of knowledge

The institutional development to aid the creation of dissemination of agricultural knowledge described in chapter 4 continued apace and facilitated the adoption of the new techniques. The tone of the times was set early in the period at the highest level of society; George III rejoiced in the epithet 'farmer George' and kept a model farm at Windsor where he experimented in stock breeding. The numerous local agricultural societies which emerged in the eighteenth century strove to 'assist in the dissemination of scientific knowledge' among 'gentlemen who are in the habit of agricultural experiment'. The officers of those societies recognised that their membership would be limited to those agriculturalists who could afford the risk of experiment. The majority of farmers were understandably reluctant to accept 'any deviation from the practice of their forefathers and. . . [were] fearful of risquing the moderate certainty they possess for the prospect of greater gains which are yet unknown'. It was the hope of the societies that their efforts would help reduce that risk (Hudson 1972: 2–5).

The commitment to the dissemination of knowledge led many of the local societies (and their national successors, the Highland and Agricultural Society of Scotland and the Royal Agricultural Society of England founded in 1785 and 1838) to publish journals, containing papers by their members on a variety of agricultural subjects, and to hold annual shows where prizes were offered for attempts to improve crops, livestock, implements, and buildings. Some groups maintained fields for experiments and even hired chemists to offer public lectures and perform soil and fertiliser analyses for the members. With the increasing use of artificial fertilisers and oilcake after the 1840s, these chemists helped protect farmers from widespread adulteration of those purchased inputs with sand or sawdust. In 1857, one group noted 'a marked change...in the average value of samples of manure offered for sale...The fraudulent dealer is disappearing or hiding in obscure corners, well knowing that the members of our Society have an infallible test at hand' (Hudson 1972: 35–40; Orwin and Whetham 1964: 30–3).

The efforts of these societies were supplemented after the 1840s by the work of other private institutions. In 1843 J. B. Lawes and G. H. Gilbert began a series of experiments on a farm owned by the former at Rothamsted, Hertfordshire. It was there that Lawes made his discovery of superphosphate, a rich fertiliser obtained from the treatment of bones with sulphuric acid, providing farmers with a valuable supplement to their own farmyard manure. The Rothamsted work was entirely financed by Lawes, who eventually left an endowment to maintain the facility after his death. This pattern of private financing was followed elsewhere with the founding of the Royal College of Veterinary Surgeons in 1844 and the Royal Agricultural College at Cirencester in the next year. Indeed, the sole publically-funded programme in agricultural education during this period was a series of lectures in agricultural chemistry given by Humphry Davy between 1803 and 1813 and sponsored by the Board of Agriculture, the only government agency solely concerned with agricultural matters (Ernle 1912: 216–17). Although Davy published his work on agriculture in the latter year, no further government initiative was taken in the area; and in 1822 even the Board of Agriculture itself was disbanded. It is a mark of the nineteenth-century interest in agricultural improvement that an impressive network of institutions for the dissemination of knowledge was established entirely through private initiative and financing.

Sources of capital

The heavy requirements of mixed farming techniques for both fixed and working capital in the early nineteenth century were met through the same local sources which provided the financing for agricultural investment in the previous century (see chapter 4). Capital exhibited considerable local mobility between sectors. During the war years the high agricultural prices led to an increased demand from local manufacturers and tradesmen for farms. Some of these purchases were small plots used to support a cow and provide some grain for the owner's family, but others represented a more significant investment. In a discussion of the increased demand for farms, *The Farmer's Magazine* reported in 1810 that 'many individuals from other lines have embarked in the business'. Indeed, the increased activity of London distillers in livestock fattening during the war was itself a form of capital inflow to agriculture. Those capital flows could be quickly reversed as well. In 1811, a correspondent reported to *The Farmer's Magazine* from Northumberland that rents were falling in that county as a result of 'a portion of capital employed in farming being withdrawn, and applied to more profitable branches of trade' (Churley 1953: 186; John 1967b: 46). Of course, the gradual, wartime increase in the numbers of small owner-occupiers was reversed in the postwar years, when the burden of falling prices on small owners, many of whom were obligated under debts contracted under high wartime prices, caused the sale of those small farms to the landlords and larger farmers, resuming a slow process of concentration in land ownership which had begun in the early eighteenth century (Chambers and Mingay 1966: 131–2; Hunt 1959: 503–5; F. M. L. Thompson 1963: 233).

The more expensive wartime projects of canal-building and drainage were financed by loans raised locally and repaid out of the canal tolls or a drainage rate levied on the owners. The high prices of the war years provided farmers with high absolute levels of profit which could be made available to finance such schemes either through personal contacts, the purchase of shares for canal-building, or the creation of deposits in country banks. The latter, which increased in number from 230 in 1797 to 721 in 1810, collected the accumulations of local farmers and made them available in loans to landlords for enclosure and drainage, to farmers for working capital, and to drainage and canal companies and enclosure commissioners (Grigg 1966: 40). Those local accumulations could be sizeable. Between 1806 and 1810 John Allright, a Berkshire farmer, had £400 to £1300 (the equivalent of roughly 20–50 per cent of his estimated investment in the farm) distributed among accounts at the Reading Bank, government consols, and personal loans earning from $2\frac{1}{2}$ to 5 per cent; and a Wiltshire farmer included in his accounts receipts of interest of as much as £120 a year on unspecified loans by the end of the war period. If the average interest rate on those loans was 5 per cent, such earnings would represent a total principal of £2400, a figure just over his probable total farm investment.

As the century progressed, the financing of land improvements was increasingly drawn from more distant sources through government loans and private drainage companies, which obtained their funds from the sale of shares throughout the country. The agricultural sector seems to have had little difficulty in obtaining funds to finance its investment. Indeed, in the light of the earlier discussion of the relatively low yields earned on arable drainage projects, it appears that total output of the economy would have been greater had some of the funds which went to agriculture been used elsewhere.

Agricultural labourers during industrialisation

The conditions of the agricultural labourer rose and fell with prices. During the labour shortages and high prices of the Napoleonic period, those who remained in that sector found their earnings rising dramatically. While the wage data for this period are very limited, the information which is available suggests that the trend in wages generally matched that of prices. Indeed, for the relatively skilled and trusted ploughman or shepherd there probably was some gain in real income.

The sharp increase in the private labour supply with postwar demobilisation brought a sudden fall in wages and employment marked by periodic outbreaks of rioting, arson, and machine-breaking, with the severest occurrences in 1816 and 1830 (Jones 1974; 214–17; Kerr 1962: 175). The long-run result of the unemployment was a decline in agricultural wages relative to prices of about 10 per cent between 1820 and 1840 – a decline which slowed, and in some areas reversed, the efforts begun during the war to introduce such labour-saving devices as the scythe (which reduced the numbers required for the harvest) and the thresher (Collins 1969a: 457).

The threat of violence probably induced some farmers to put off the introduction of labour-saving devices, quite apart from the objective forces of relative input prices. It was reported from Kent in the 1830s that the scythe 'on all occasions excited the ill-will of the labourers to a very dangerous extent, for it is a most powerful and efficient implement and it is thought that if brought into use it would extinguish the usual harvest earnings'. Indeed, it was introduced to Lothian farmers with the understanding that it would not displace the local labourers but only the migrants hired as temporary help during the harvest. The problem of rural unemployment was greatest during the winter, however, and many landlords voiced concern over the need to find work for their labourers during that time of the year, recognising that if such employment was not found the workers and their families would have to be supported out of the poor rates. This gave an added dimension to the landlord's expenditures on improvements. In 1833, a Herefordshire landowner wrote, 'I most heartily wish all our improvements were finished, as they are dreadfully Expensive but the labouring Class must be Emp^d. Especially in the winter months or they will poach or go upon the Parish' (Collins 1969a: 464–5; Jones 1974: 216–17).

Such individual efforts could do little for what was in fact a serious long-run problem for which the only lasting solution was a permanent movement of labour out of agriculture. Although the situation improved in some areas around 1845, when in the period of a year some 200000 men (about 4 per cent of the occupied male population, many drawn from agriculture) were recruited for railway construction, lasting change only came a decade later with a persistent upward trend in real wages (Mitchell 1964: 323). In the two decades after 1840, agricultural wages rose some 15 per cent relative to prices as increasing industrial employment and emigration reduced the excess labour supply in the arable districts. The timing of these forces corresponded with a decline in the seasonal flows of migrant labour which throughout the first half of the century had imparted an elasticity to the labour supply at the haying and harvest time. Thus, farmers were faced with a declining and increasingly less elastic labour supply after mid-century. Their response, of course, was to substitute new tools and machines for labour.

From the farmer's viewpoint, the decades after the 1840s witnessed a reversal of the earlier trend in the cost of his labour input. As wage costs rose relative to the prices received for agricultural products, machines and hand tools designed to reduce labour requirements which, because of the costs of introduction, appeared unprofitable in the 1820s or 1830s took on a new aspect after the 1840s. The period was characterised by a rising interest in such devices – an interest which spurred the growth of an industry supplying everything from horse-drawn seed drills to reapers and steam ploughs. However, in spite of the renewed interest, the more costly devices were adopted slowly. Even the mechanical reaper, which was designed to reduce labour requirements in the harvest, did not come into widespread use until late in the century. As the detailed discussion of volume 2, chapter 8 shows, the reaper's rate of adoption was conditioned by cost considerations. Although wage costs were rising from the 1850s, when depreciation, maintenance, and other charges were considered, the investment remained unprofitable for many farmers until at least the 1870s. Rather than adopt the mechanical reaper, most farmers in the 1850s and 1860s chose to introduce the less costly scythe and other hand tools which permitted reductions in their harvest labour requirements of as much as 40 per cent (Collins 1969a: 457–63).

From the viewpoint of the workers who remained in agriculture, the changes in the labour market presented the opportunity for higher real incomes. In addition to the rise in real wages after the 1840s, the introduction of machinery on the larger farms led to new distinctions along skill lines. The need for workers able to tend and maintain the new steam-powered machines encouraged many farmers to provide their labourers with training in the widespread village schools and to pay commensurately higher wages once trained.

Of course, difficulties remained. Inadequate or insufficient cottages and child labour were the most common complaints, the latter giving rise to a government investigation and the passage of regulating acts in 1869 and 1873 (Orwin and Whetham 1964: 79–80, 206–10). However, these problems were gradually diminishing amidst an increasingly tight labour market as farmers sought to maintain their labour supply by providing increased non-pecuniary benefits as well as higher wages. The resulting increase in wages, by diminishing the importance of children's earnings in family income, reduced the incidence of child labour well before the government took an interest in the problem; and new cottages, some with garden land attached, became an important fringe benefit to attract and hold workers. By the 1870s, it was noted that the farmer was 'expected to find the labourer, not only good cottages, allotments, schooling, good wages, but Heaven knows what besides' (Jones 1974: 225).

It was under these conditions that agricultural workers in the 1860s, unlike their predecessors, found themselves able to combine for further improvements in wages. Like the rest of the country, rural society had witnessed attempts at trade union activity as early as the 1830s. Indeed the trial and transportation to Australian penal colonies of six agricultural labourers from Tolpuddle, Dorset in 1837 for the formation of a 'Friendly Society of Agricultural Labourers' became a cause célèbre among the leaders of the Grand National Consolidated Trades Union and their supporters. The trial and severe punishment of these 'Tolpuddle Martyrs' provoked a great outcry and considerable pressure upon the government to grant a pardon, a result which was finally achieved three years later. Those early attempts at combination could not succeed in the face of an abundance of individuals seeking work at the going wage. They achieved little immediate result except the introduction by the authorities of severe measures to seek out and punish the leaders. The idea of a labour organisation was not forgotten, however; and in the 1850s new attempts at combination and short strikes occurred in those regions where a shortage of workers at the prevailing wage gave such attempts the prospect of success. But those and similar events in the early 1860s were still generally confined to a single parish. The first union of more than parish-wide influence in England, the Agricultural Labourers' Protective Association was founded in Kent in 1866 (just a year after the movement began in Scotland) and served as a model for similar organisations founded in Buckinghamshire, Hertfordshire, Lincolnshire, and Norfolk in the next five years. Those organisations and the rioting and strikes which spread with them were indications of the increasingly strong market position held by agricultural workers – a trend which set the stage for the nationwide union activity of the 1870s.

Agriculture and technological response

The combined forces of war and industrialisation presented British agriculture with a rapidly changing environment which required alterations in techniques and factor inputs. During the Napoleonic period, a growing population was fed, though not easily, largely with domestic supplies because British farmers were able to meet the increased demand for their products with new land and new techniques to increase output. While those high wartime prices prolonged the cultivation of lands which would have been better laid down to grass, thus increasing the severity of the postwar depression, those farmers willing and able to adopt the new techniques made the adjustment to peacetime production with considerable speed, rents and incomes in some areas turning upward after the early 1820s.

Of course, those who were unable to shift to the new practices, for reasons of location or lack of capital, had a more difficult passage in spite of a high tariff on foreign grain. For roughly two decades after the Napoleonic period the Corn Laws buoyed up the British price of grain, allowing the adjustments on the clays to take place more slowly than would have been the case under free trade. By the time of Repeal, however, the available supplies of foreign grain were not sufficient in the face of a rising demand to yield a pronounced downtrend in prices. This and the increasingly widespread adoption of the techniques of mixed farming allowed farm incomes to rise through increases in both arable yields and livestock output, the latter being especially important in an era of rising demand for animal products.

Through all these changes agriculture continued to provide industry with an important market. It started the century as the largest single employer, providing income for roughly one-third of the labour force; and some of that income supported a demand for the goods and services of the nonagricultural sector. It was not uncommon for farmers to spend part of their wartime incomes on fabrics, furniture, and tutors and schoolbooks for their children. Of course, those expenditures fell in the postwar depression, but the technological adjustments at mid-century brought rising incomes to both farmers and their labourers. While the share those incomes represented in national output declined over the period to about 15 per cent in 1870, their impact on industry was supplemented by the growing use of agricultural machinery. Increasingly, small, portable steam engines displaced the horse as the power source for machines to thresh and winnow the grain and prepare the fodder. One contemporary estimated that the production of agricultural machinery doubled in only five years after 1851, and such growth was an important element in the mid-Victorian expansion of the iron and machinery industries (Hughes 1960: 221–3).

It is true, of course, that later farmers were to find that the output adjustments which occurred before the 1870s had not gone far enough. The heavy reliance on grain in mixed farming rotations proved a mistake when the fall in prices finally came in the last quarter of the century. However, there were technical barriers to the further expansion of grassland, especially in the cereal area of the east and south; and the flexibility of mixed farming in responding to the variations in the ratio of grain to livestock prices during the 'golden age' stood farmers in good stead in those years (Chambers and Mingay 1966: 185–6; Jones 1968: 23–4).

English agriculture in the age of the industrial revolution, then, far from inhibiting the process of economic growth, advanced that process through its ability to produce the food and raw materials necessary to feed and clothe a growing population without at the same time drawing resources away from manufacturing. Farmers were willing and able to quickly alter their crops and methods in the face of changing market conditions; and when new techniques were resisted it was for good business reasons, not out of respect for irrational traditions. The rate of technological advance, while not up to the pace set in contemporary industry, accelerated over the periods to levels unknown in earlier centuries; and the industry – for that is now what it was – adjusted quickly to the shocks of war and peace, protection and free trade.

11

The labour supply 1780–1860

N. L. TRANTER

The nature of the relationship between the size and character of the labour force and British economic growth in the late eighteenth and first half of the nineteenth centuries has long puzzled economic historians. In the past their attention has focused mainly on the economic consequences of variations in the size of the labour supply or, more specifically, in the relationship between the supply of and demand for labour. On the one hand it has been suggested that a continuing labour shortage, by encouraging entrepreneurs to adopt labour-saving devices, was one of the most important necessary conditions for industrial 'take-off', (Pentland 1968: 183; Habakkuk 1962: 133–5): on the other, that the rate of innovation has normally been greatest in periods of labour abundance rather than scarcity and that an increase in the aggregate stock of labour was crucial in overcoming what had proved a major barrier to development in the first half of the eighteenth century, manpower shortage (Chambers 1957: 37; 1972: 128–49; Deane 1965: 134).

Recently, attention has switched from the economic significance of variations in the quantity of the labour supply to the possible economic consequences of changes in its quality. This change of emphasis stems from recent work by economists showing that in already developed economies, or economies attempting to modernise within the environment of an already advanced world, the quality of human capital and the level of investment in those things which help to determine it – formal education, on the job training, public health and personal medical care and all other items that influence the physical and mental well-being of the individual – have a vital bearing on the productivity of the labour supply and thus on the rate and character of economic development. Expenditure on formal education alone, for example, has been shown to have been responsible for 23 per cent of the increase in national product and 42 per cent of the increase in national product per head in the USA between 1929 and 1958 (Denison 1962: 73). As two distinguished commentators have put it: 'Every effort to promote development...must start from improving the human factor' (Papi 1966: 4). 'Few, if any, countries have achieved sustained economic development without much investment in their labour force' (Becker 1964: 2). Some historians believe this to be as true for the first industrial revolution as for its successors or for the further development of industrial societies (Hartwell 1971: 226–44). Others, however, seem less willing to accept that Britain's industrial 'take-off' owed much to continuous improvements in the quality of its labour inputs, their standards of education, intelligence and aptitude, mobility, emotional and physical health and so on (Deane 1973: 362–3). By itself, of course, the fact that the quality of human capital has been shown to be crucial to the continued development of already industrialised countries or to countries faced with the problem of industrialising in an already advanced world is not sufficient to prove that it must have been equally important in the case of the first industrial revolution. The more advanced the economy and the more sophisticated the technology required for development, the greater the premium attached to the level of skill and adaptability in the workforce and, therefore, to investment in those items which together determine the intellectual and physical quality of human beings. Less sophisticated economies, with small-scale, more rudimentary methods of production, lower productivity levels and less dramatic changes in economic structure are less dependent on variations in the physical, educational and emotional well-being of their labour supply and more dependent on changes in its aggregate size alone.

The conflicting views outlined above are not easily resolved. The absence of reliable data on patterns of fertility, mortality and migration greatly compound the problem of identifying the causes of that massive growth in the size of the labour force which is known to have occurred between the late eighteenth and mid-nineteenth centuries. Reliable, detailed statistics on the size of the labour force, its age and sex composition, its occupational distribution are not available before 1851, and those that are refer only to workers in gainful employment. They tell us nothing about possible variations in the large number of people, mainly women and children, in part-time employment, and therefore grossly understate the true amount of labour available to the economy.

The main features of the labour supply in 1851 may be summarised as follows:

(i) 47 per cent of the population was in full-time employment.

(ii) Employment in the industrial and mining sector of the economy dominated all others, with agriculture, commerce and the personal service sectors taking a roughly equal share of the labour supply (table 11.1).

(iii) Two-thirds of the gainful labour force was male, though the sex ratio of the occupied population varied considerably both by age-group and occupation. The ratio of females to males in full-time work was highest in the age-groups below thirty. After the age of thirty, marriage and child-rearing removed many women from gainful employment and increased the dominance of male over female workers (table 11.2). In most occupations the workforce was predominantly male. Only in domestic service, textiles and clothing was there an excess of females (table 11.3).

(iv) Below the age of fifteen relatively few males were gainfully employed.

Table 11.1. *Size, sectoral distribution of the gainful labour force, and labour participation ratios, Great Britain 1780–1851*

		Sectoral distribution of labour force (%)					
Date	Size of labour force (millions)	Agriculture, forestry and fishing	Manu-facturing, mining and industry	Trade and transport	Domestic and personal	Public, professional and all other	Labour participation ratio (LPR) (%)
1780	4.0	—	—	—	—	—	—
1801	4.8	35.9	29.7	11.1	11.5	11.8	45.7
1811	5.5	33.0	30.2	11.6	11.8	13.3	45.8
1821	6.2	28.4	38.4	12.1	12.7	8.5	44.0
1831	7.2	24.6	40.8	12.4	12.6	9.5	44.2
1841	8.4	22.2	40.5	14.2	14.5	8.5	45.4
1851	9.7	21.7	42.9	15.8	13.0	6.7	46.6

Sources:
   Size of labour force: 1801–51, Deane and Cole (1967: 139, 142–3). The 1780 estimate is based on an assumed population of 8.9 millions (Deane and Cole 1967: 8) and an assumed LPR of around 45%.
   Sectoral distribution: Deane and Cole (1967: 142).
   Labour participation ratios: based on Deane and Cole's estimates of the size of the labour force and the population totals for Great Britain in Mitchell and Deane (1962: 6, 12–13).

Among females the percentage gainfully employed was greatest in the ages 10–29 (table 11.2). On average, the age of the gainful female labour force was lower than that of the male: 60 per cent of all females but only 45 per cent of all males gainfully employed were between 14 and 29 years of age.

(v) Although agriculture and its related activities dominated male employ-ment, men's work spread across the entire spectrum of occupations. Women concentrated on a narrower range of occupations – domestic service, textiles and clothing (together accounting for 80 per cent of the total gainful female labour force) and, to a lesser extent, agriculture (table 11.3).

In the absence of census data of similar quality, it is difficult to say how these characteristics of the gainful labour supply in 1851 compared with those of an earlier period. In some respects there was probably little difference. It is unlikely, for example, that the occupational distribution of the female labour force changed much: women had always made their chief contribution in the domestic service, textile and clothing sectors of the economy. In other respects, however – the size of the gainful labour force, the occupational distribution of adult male workers – there were notable differences. The difficulty lies in quantifying them.

Deane and Cole's estimates of the size and industrial distribution of the labour supply 1801–41 rest on incomplete census data and several highly debatable

Table 11.2. *Age and sex structure of the gainful labour force, Great Britain 1851*

Age group	Male			Female			% of males in total occupied labour force by age group
	(i)	(ii)	(iii)	(iv)	(v)	(vi)	
0–4	1374.4	—	—	1362.5	—	—	—
5–9	1230.6	21.9	0.2	1218.1	15.8	1.3	58.1
10–14	1134.3	401.5	35.4	1111.6	520.6	46.8	43.5
15–19	1025.4	917.2	89.4	1045.3	669.6	64.1	57.8
20–9	1738.8	1691.9	97.3	1934.2	1018.6	52.7	62.4
30–9	1323.3	1298.6	98.1	1418.4	517.6	36.5	71.5
40–9	1001.2	981.7	98.1	1056.7	382.6	36.2	72.0
50–9	695.9	679.1	97.6	749.4	282.3	37.7	70.6
60–9	437.4	419.8	96.0	507.8	182.3	35.9	69.7
70–9	208.7	188.4	90.3	256.1	68.5	26.7	73.3
80 and above	53.6	43.8	81.7	75.9	16.5	21.7	72.6
All ages	10223.6	6643.8	65.0	10735.9	3674.4	34.2	64.4

(i) Total male population (in 000s).   (ii) Total occupied male population (in 000s).   (iii) Male LPR (ii) as % of (1).   (iv) Total female population (in 000s).   (v) Total occupied female population (in 000s).   (vi) Female LPR (v) as % of (iv).

Source: Census of Great Britain, 1851, Population tables II: Ages, Civil condition, Occupations of the People...vol. I, London, 1854, pp. cxxviii–cxlix. All persons described by the census enumerators as children, wives, widows, other relatives, scholars, gentleman or gentlewoman, independent, annuitant, living on income from voluntary sources or rates, prisoners, vagrants, and not given a specified occupation, together with all persons for whom no condition is recorded have been excluded from the gainful labour force. Retired persons, if given an occupation, have been included. For this reason the LPR for the older age groups may slightly overstate the true proportions of those occupied.

assumptions. The 1801–21 estimates, based on calculations of the percentage of men, women, boys and girls in different age-groups and extrapolation from the 1851 census, amount to little more than educated guesses. Those for 1831 and 1841, based on census returns of the number of adult male employees in each occupation and the assumption that the ratio of adult male to total workers was the same as in 1851, appear more secure. But, as Deane and Cole themselves admit, this assumption may not be entirely valid. The proportion of female and child workers in the gainful labour force probably rose in the course of the industrial revolution, although Richards has argued that after 1820 the percentage of women in the labour force declined (Richards 1974: 337–57); his work is marred by an undue concentration on the cotton textile industry and understates the contribution of women in other sectors of the economy. As a result, Deane and Cole's estimates for 1841, and even more so for 1831, exaggerate the size of the labour supply and thus understate its rate of increase. In view of the uncertainties of the data, their implication that the size of the

Table 11.3. *Sex ratio of the gainful labour force by occupational category, Great Britain 1851*

Occupation	Number of males (000s)	% of all males	Number of females (000s)	% of all females	% of males in each occupation	% of females in each occupation
Public administration	64	1.0	3	0.1	95.5	4.5
Armed forces	63	1.0	—	—	100.0	—
Professional and other subordinate services	162	2.5	103	3.6	61.1	38.9
Domestic and personal services	193	2.9	1135	40.1	14.5	85.5
Commerce	91	1.4	—	—	100.0	—
Transport and communications	433	6.6	13	0.5	97.1	2.9
Agriculture, horticulture and forestry	1788	27.3	229	8.1	88.6	11.4
Fishing	36	0.6	1	0	97.3	2.7
Mining and quarrying and workers in products of mines and quarries	383	5.9	11	0.4	97.2	2.8
Metal manufactures, machines, implements, vehicles, precious metals etc.	536	8.2	36	1.3	93.7	6.3
Building and construction	496	7.6	1	0	99.8	0.2
Wood, furniture, fittings and decorations	152	2.3	8	0.3	95.0	5.0
Bricks, cement, pottery and glass	75	1.1	15	0.5	83.3	16.7
Chemicals, oil, soap, resin, etc.	42	0.6	4	0.1	91.3	8.7
Skins, leather, hair and feathers, etc.	55	0.8	5	0.2	91.7	8.3
Paper, printing, books and stationery	62	0.9	16	0.6	79.5	20.5
Textiles	661	10.1	635	22.4	51.0	49.0
Clothing	418	6.4	491	17.3	46.0	54.0
Food, drink and tobacco	348	5.3	53	1.9	86.8	13.2
Gas, water and electricity supply	7	0.1	—	—	100.0	—
All others occupied	438	6.7	75	2.6	85.4	14.6
Total occupied	6545	99.3	2832	100.0	69.8	30.2

Source: Mitchell and Deane (1962: 60).

labour force increased by 143 per cent between 1780 and 1850 should be treated with caution. The estimates of labour participation ratios (i.e. the percentage of the total population in gainful employment) given in table 11.1 depend entirely on the accuracy of those of total manpower, and they too must be regarded as tentative. If the size of the labour force was smaller before 1851 than Deane and Cole suggest, labour participation ratios would have been somewhat lower than those calculated and less stable over time than they appear to have been.

Accompanying the growth in the aggregate size of the labour supply was a dramatic alteration in its sectoral distribution (table 11.1). In the course of the first half of the nineteenth century manufacturing and mining industry overtook agriculture as the dominant employer of labour, a change largely due to alterations in the occupational structure of male employment. During the eighteenth century most gainfully occupied men were concentrated into a relatively narrow band of activities, agriculture, textiles, and clothing, food and drink processing, tobacco and leather manufacturing. By the mid-nineteenth century the range had expanded considerably (table 11.3).

No less deficient than our knowledge of changes in the size and composition of the labour force is our understanding of possible variations in its quality. As yet we know little about its standards of learning and aptitude, emotional and physical health, its attitude to work, its willingness or ability to move between different areas and different occupations, its capacity for organisation, and so on. Until such information becomes available any analysis of the role of labour in the industrial revolution must be tentative.

Even without these factual deficiencies the nature of the link between labour supply and the economy is not easily demonstrated. Economic growth is only one of the factors influencing rates of population growth and, through them, the size and quality of the labour force. In earlier times particularly, population change was also greatly influenced by forces that were independent of the pace and character of economic development – epidemic, disease and climate. And even with the best of data, it is difficult to separate the part played by economic conditions from that of other influences. Labour inputs themselves are but one of many factors which determine the pace of economic advance; here too, in the real world, the problems involved in identifying and quantifying their *relative* contribution are enormous.

The origins of the growth in the labour supply

In aggregate, the needs of the industrial revolution for manpower were far greater than ever the economy had required before. Crucial, therefore, to any analysis of Britain's successful industrialisation is an explanation of the origins of this increase in the total stock of labour.

An increase in the size of a labour force can occur in three ways, (i) through

Table 11.4. *Age structure, England and Wales 1695–1851, Scotland 1755–1851* (*males and females combined*) (%)

	0–9	10–19	20–39	40–59	60 and above
England and Wales					
1695[a]	27.6	20.2	27.2	14.2	10.7
1791[c]	23.8	18.5	26.7	19.1	11.8
1821[a]	27.9	21.1	27.5	15.9	7.3
1831[d]	26.2	22.6	29.0	15.8	7.4
1841	25.2	20.9	30.7	16.0	7.2
1851	24.8	20.5	30.7	16.7	7.3
Scotland					
1755[b]	25.5	18.6	30.5	18.1	7.2
1821[e]	26.6	21.6	27.6	16.0	7.5
1841	25.1	21.7	30.2	15.6	7.4
1851	24.6	21.4	30.1	16.4	7.5

Sources:
[a] P. Laslett, *The world we have lost*, London, 2nd ed., 1971, p. 108.
[b] A. Webster, An account of the number of people in Scotland, 1755, in J. G. Kyd ed., *Scottish population statistics*, Edinburgh, 1952. p. 81. The age groups are 0–10, 11–20, 21–40, 41–60, 61 and above.
[c] W. A. Armstrong, La population de L'Angleterre et du pays de Galles (1789–1815), *Annales de démographie historique*, 2, 1965, p. 140.
[d] J. P. Huzel (1969: 440–1).
[e] T. C. Smout, *A history of the Scottish people, 1560–1830*, London, 1972, p. 244.
All others from Mitchell and Deane (1962: 12–13).

a rise in the labour participation ratio, (ii) by immigration, (iii) through higher rates of natural increase (i.e. the surplus of births over deaths).

Any rise in the labour participation ratio between 1780 and 1860 was probably small and its effect on the size of the gainful labour force modest. In the absence of major changes in the age and sex structure of the population (tables 11.4 and 11.5) rising participation ratios could only have come from increases in the percentage of children, elderly persons or women gainfully employed. Yet in 1851 less than 1 per cent of those whose occupations were given in the census were below the age of fifteen: the percentage of persons aged sixty and above in the total population was always too low for changes in their work habits to have had much influence on the aggregate labour supply: and although variations in the proportion of women fully employed could, theoretically, have had a greater effect on the size of the workforce only about one in three women were gainfully employed in 1851, a ratio that was probably not very much higher than it had been in 1780.

The contribution of immigration to the growth of the labour supply was greater. Throughout the period, Britain gained on balance by migration. The main source of immigration was Ireland. Between 1793 and 1815, when the

Table 11.5. *Sex structure, England and Wales 1574–1851, Scotland 1801–51*

Place	Date	% of males in total population
England and Wales	1690s[a]	49.1
Urban	1690s[a]	44.4–46.5
Rural	1680s–90s[a]	48.0
Urban	18th century[b]	43.5–47.6
Rural	18th century[b]	48.8–49.5
England	1574–1821[c]	47.7
England and Wales	1791[d]	49.6
	1801	47.8
	1811	47.9
	1821	48.8
	1831	48.7
	1841	48.9
	1851	49.0
Scotland	1801	46.0
	1811	45.7
	1821	47.0
	1831	47.1
	1841	47.4
	1851	47.6

Sources:
[a] R. Thompson, Seventeenth century English and colonial sex ratios: a postscript, *Population Studies*, XVIII, 1, 1974, p, 162.
[b] C. M. Law, Local censuses in the eighteenth century, *Population Studies*, XXIII, 1, 1969, p. 89.
[c] P. Laslett, Size and structure of the household in England over three centuries, *Population Studies*, XXIII, 2, 1969, p. 215.
[d] Armstrong, *op. cit.*, p. 140.
All others from Mitchell and Deane (1962: 12–13).

demand for labour was high, an average of 4000 Irish immigrants a year entered the country (Hueckel 1973: 372). The influx remained modest through the 1820s and 1830s. In the 1840s however, when, in the wake of the Famine, Irish immigration reached its peak, around 40000 Irish immigrants a year poured into Britain. The figure excludes the large number of transient Irish immigrants who came over in the summer months to work on the harvest before returning to Ireland. According to a police census taken at Irish ports in the summer of 1841, about 60000 Irish labourers left for Britain between June and August of that year (Parl. Pap., 1843, XXIV, p. xxvi). Between 1841 and 1850 Irish immigration accounted for just under one-fifth of the total increase in Britain's population. But for most of the earlier period of the industrial revolution its contribution to the growth of population and the size of the available labour supply was very much less. As late as 1851 only 4.7 per cent of the population of Great Britain had been born overseas.

By far the greatest part of the growth in the labour force came from the

Table 11.6. *Infants (0–1) deaths per thousand live births*

Clayworth, Notts.[a]	1680–1702	215
Leake, Lincs.[b]	1654–1703	262
	1704–53	233
	1754–1802	189
	1804–43	106
Wrangle, Lincs.[b]	1654–1703	246
	1704–53	226
	1754–1803	215
	1804–43	138
Selected parishes in rural North Shropshire[c]	*1611–60*	*174*
	1661–1710	191
	1711–60	155
	1761–1810	102
Colyton, Devon[d]	1600–49	125–158
	1650–99	118–147
	1700–49	162–203
	1750–1837	122–153
England and Wales[e]	1841–50	154

Sources:
[a] P. Laslett, *The world we have lost*, London, 2nd ed., 1971, p. 132.
[b] F. West, Infant mortality in the East Fen parishes of Leake and Wrangle, *Local Population Studies*, 13, 1974, pp. 43–4.
[c] R. E. Jones, Infant mortality in rural North Shropshire 1561–1810. *Population Studies*, 30, 2, 1976, p. 307.
[d] E. A. Wrigley, Mortality in pre-industrial England: the example of Colyton, Devon, over three centuries, *Daedalus*, 1968, p. 570.
[e] Mitchell and Deane (1962: 36).

increase which occurred in the size of the native-born population. The origin of the dramatic rise in the excess of births over deaths is still in doubt. It has been discussed in chapter 2 above from a preindustrial perspective; here we look at it from an industrial perspective. Without reliable birth and death registration for most of our period we still do not know for certain whether rising fertility or falling mortality was the principal demographic mechanism at work. There is, however, some evidence for assuming a decline in mortality to be the more likely explanation.

(i) An acceleration in the pace of population growth was common to many countries: and in European countries like Norway for which reliable registration data are available falling death-rates were clearly the agency responsible.

(ii) There is a growing body of statistical data to support the view that mortality declined in Britain too (Hollingsworth 1969: 347–51; Lee 1974: 511). Recent work on parish registers points to an unmistakable decline in rates of infant mortality between the late eighteenth and mid-nineteenth centuries (table 11.6). Infant mortality rates derived in this way understate the real level of mortality because unbaptised infants were often not recorded in parish burial registers. Despite this, levels of infant mortality prevailing in rural England during the seventeenth and early eighteenth centuries were well above those for England and Wales as a whole in the 1840s, and these latter include urban communities where infant death rates were relatively high. Whether death rates in other age groups also declined is unclear; infant mortality is usually a good barometer of general standards of health, and it is at least conceivable that they did. In any case, so serious was the loss of life in infancy that any decline in infant death rates was certain to be reflected in the overall level of mortality. In contrast, there is no convincing evidence to suggest a significant increase in fertility in the early nineteenth century (as distinct from the mid-eighteenth century: see chapter 2), and no reason for supposing that any of the factors which determine the levels of fertility (changes in adult mortality rates apart) – levels of fecundity, proportions celibate, ages at marriage, the extent of birth control practices within marriage – altered sufficiently to cause a marked rise in fertility rates.

The fall in death rates 1780–1860 was principally the result of a decline in the fatality of infectious diseases – tuberculosis, typhus, smallpox particularly (McKeown 1976:71–2). There are two possible explanations: either *autonomous* changes in the virulence of infectious diseases themselves or in the resistance of the human host towards them, changes which were totally independent of human agency; or environmental improvements which altered the relationship between parasite and host and, in doing so, reduced the fatality of infective organisms. Among the latter are grouped the following: innovations in medical treatment; advances in public health or personal hygiene which reduced the frequency with which men came into contact with disease organisms; improved standards of nutrition which raised man's resistance to disease.

McKeown has recently dismissed the possibility of an autonomous amelioration in the relationship between parasite and man on the grounds that it is too great a coincidence for such a change to have occurred simultaneously over the wide range of diseases known or suspected to have lessened in severity during the period (McKeown 1976: 73–90, 153). But can the possibility be so readily dismissed? The growth of population was world-wide yet the explanations which are customarily put foward to account for it and which derive from improvement wrought by man to his environment hold true only for some, not all, countries. To talk of health, hygiene, or nutritional advances being common to societies as diverse as China, Russia, India or Latin America is unlikely. Could it be that something other than man's own efforts was responsible? Perhaps the improvement in climatic conditions known to have begun in the later eighteenth century somehow enervated disease organisms or, by leading to better harvests and higher standards of nutrition, raised the level of human resistance to disease (Braudel 1974: 16–20). Until the relationship between the history of climate and disease is more fully explored we cannot hope to know. In the meantime it would be unwise to reject the possibility of a fortuitous diminution in the virulence of disease simply because it cannot be positively documented.

The contribution of medical innovations to falling mortality is more easily determined. Taken together, the impact of the main advances in medical knowledge and practice was very limited. McKeown (1976: 104) reminds us that even in modern times the part played by immunisation and specific medical therapy in reducing mortality has been modest. The limited advances in medical practice during the eighteenth and first half of the nineteenth centuries could hardly have been more significant.

(i) In midwifery, the introduction of lying-in hospitals and the growing use of forceps and other instruments in delivery increased rather than decreased the mortality of mother and child. The trend towards better standards of hygiene in the labour room was more beneficial, but until the significance of environmental conditions for health was realised more clearly by subsequent generations its extent was probably modest (McKeown 1976: 104–6).

(ii) The use of new drugs like mercury and cinchona in the treatment of syphilis and malaria respectively no doubt reduced mortality from these diseases, but since neither ranked high among the causes of death they had little effect on the level of death rates as a whole.

(iii) Smallpox was a far more important killer and the spread of vaccination in the first half of the nineteenth century unquestionably helped lower mortality from it. A similar claim made by Razzell (1965; 312–32) for the earlier, more rudimentary and dangerous technique of inoculation is less acceptable. Inoculation was widely resisted as expensive, unnatural, transitory in its blessings and more likely to spread than contain the disease (Tranter 1973a: 81–4); this is a view shared by modern immunologists (McKeown 1976: 12). If inoculation did contribute to the decline in smallpox mortality its role was a fairly limited one.

(iv) Recent work by Sigsworth (1966) and Cherry (1972) on another of the great eighteenth-century medical innovations, the development of voluntary hospitals and dispensaries, also seems to have claimed too much for their value. The statistical claims for high rates of 'cured and relieved' and low rates of in-patient mortality made in hospital records were chiefly the result of cautious admission policies (which frequently excluded children, infectious and terminal cases), of the restricted range of ailments they were prepared to treat, especially by surgery, and of a tendency to discharge those patients whom they expected to die. As voluntary institutions, relying on charitable bequests for their existence, the new hospitals *had* to appear successful. They rarely tackled the main causes of death. This, and the fact that the ratio of hospital beds and in-patients to total population was low (Woodward 1974: 144), suggests they played little part in the secular decline in death rates. Dispensaries (and hospital out-patient departments) certainly treated many more people (Woodward 1974: 145). But apart from their contribution to a possible rise in standards of personal hygiene (see below), they were only as useful as the treatment and medicines they supplied and, in general, these were of little real value (McKeown 1976: 150).

In the second half of the nineteenth century public health improvements – better housing, purer water supply and more efficient sewage disposal, improved food hygiene, etc. – undoubtedly played a vital role in further reducing mortality from infectious disease. However, before 1860 their influence was negligible. If anything, public health conditions deteriorated rather than improved during the industrial revolution. The number of persons per house hardly altered in the first half of the nineteenth century: the quality of housing itself showed no signs of improving (Chapman 1971: 12): and under the impact of rapid urbanisation sanitary conditions (Flinn 1965: 3–21) and the quality of food supplies (Burnett 1968: 99–118) worsened. Even if enclosures (Philpot 1975) or the migration of people from rural areas to the towns worked to reduce mortality by lessening the prevalence of animal-borne diseases like putrid and intermittent fevers and tuberculosis in the human population, the growing evils of the urban environment probably outweighed any benefits which accrued.

Awareness of the importance of personal cleanliness for health undoubtedly increased in medical circles from the late eighteenth century (Mathias 1975), and the efforts of the medical profession to promote better standards of personal and domestic hygiene met with some success. The per capita production of soap rose in the first half of the nineteenth century: and the appearance of soap in the budgets of Manchester and Duckinfield cotton workers in 1841, together with the proliferation of portable baths, suggests that at least part of this increased output went to domestic consumption rather than industrial purposes. The domestic consumption of cotton goods rose fourfold between 1801 and 1841, while the rising output of soil, linen and woollen goods at least kept pace with the growth of population (Razzell 1974: 16–17). By the middle of the nineteenth century people were washing more frequently and wearing lighter, cleaner clothing than ever before. But the effect of this on the prevalence of infectious disease should not be exaggerated. Except for their contribution to the decline in typhus mortality, improvements in standards of personal hygiene were largely irrelevant to mortality from other infectious diseases since 'it is the condition of the water and food which determines the risks of infection rather than the cleanliness of the hands or utensils on which they are brought to the mouth' (McKeown 1976: 124–7).

The association of falling mortality with rising food production and improvements in nutrition is of long standing. Some historians, Slicher van Bath (1963), Reinhard et al. (1968), McKeown and his associates (1972, 1976) stress the significance of a *general* rise in agricultural production; others the importance of an increase in the output of *particular* products: maize and the potato (Langer 1963, 1975), milk (Beaver 1973). McKeown is impressed by the fact that the 55 per cent increase in the population of Great Britain between 1811 and 1855 was fed without any great increase in the (very small) amounts of food imported (McKeown 1976: 129). If British agriculture was able to achieve this it might be reasonable to suppose that it was capable of providing that little extra per head which for so many people meant the difference between life and death. Admittedly, to date, there is no firm evidence to support the view that per capita food production and nutritional standards rose in the course of the industrial revolution. Indeed, Burnett, the only historian to attempt a general summary of dietary trends, has concluded that the diet of most urban and rural workers was hopelessly deficient in both quantity and quality and showed no indication of improving before 1850 (Burnett 1968: 29, 47, 73). Yet so partial and uncertain are the statistical data upon which this verdict rests that it cannot be regarded as satisfactorily proven. Such evidence as we have on variations in per capita food output is quite inconclusive one way or the other. The per capita output of wheat and beer *may* have fallen, of potatoes, coffee, sugar and milk *may* have risen, of tea *may* have changed little. But we know nothing of the output per head of other important components of diet like meat, vegetables, fruit and dairy products. Until we do so the possibility that rising levels of per capita food output hold the key to the 'population revolution' ought not to be discounted.

In the present state of our knowledge, therefore, there is no convincing evidence to support *any* of the widely-voiced explanations for the decline in mortality which underlay the growth of population and the labour supply in the late eighteenth and nineteenth centuries. However, of all the likely explanations only two, autonomous changes in the relationship betweeen disease parasites and the human host, and improvements in the standard of human nutrition cannot be firmly rejected as of little significance. It is, perhaps, to these two factors that future research on the origins of the growth in population should be directed. Until this research has been carried out it is impossible to say with any certainty whether economic growth before 1860 created its own labour supply or not.

The uses of the available population

We have discussed so far the number of people who were available to work. But the work which was secured from those people depended on their location and their effort.

Labour mobility

Considering its significance to the flexibility of the labour market it is surprising how little we know about the extent and nature of labour mobility in the eighteenth and first half of the nineteenth centuries.

Studies based on taxation lists, muster returns, gild and corporation rolls, parish registers and listings of inhabitants reveal considerable mobility among the populations of preindustrial times (Buckatzsch 1951–52: 62–9; Chambers 1972: 45; Tranter 1967: 276–7). Of the 180 inhabitants of the parish of Cogenhoe in 1628, 52 per cent had moved in during the preceding ten years. Of the 401 residents at Clayworth in 1676, 38 per cent had left the parish by 1688 (Laslett and Harrison 1963: 174, 177). Most migrants, however, moved only very short distances, usually within a radius of fifteen or twenty miles from their place of birth (Chambers 1972: 45).

The volume of net inter-county migration doubled between 1700 and 1800 and rose by a further 40 per cent between 1801–30 and the 1860s (Hunt 1973: 263–4). While this tells only part of the story (it excludes gross migration flows and movement within county boundaries) it does suggest that the extent of migration increased during the period of industrialisation. In view of the many hindrances to mobility and because one of them (the working of the settlement laws and the payment of outdoor relief to able-bodied paupers) *may* have operated more intensely than ever before this is perhaps surprising. On reflection, however, the main barriers to mobility – inadequate transport, poor standards of education and low incomes – were probably less serious during the industrial revolution than in the past. Though they may have tended to reduce the efficiency of the rural workforce (Holderness 1972: 136–8), the belief that the settlement laws seriously limited mobility (Mathias 1969: 261–2) has been judged by the latest authorities to be fallacious (Chambers 1972: 44; Rose 1976: 35–6). Only the payment of outdoor relief, to the extent that it subsidised incomes rather than wages, arguably worked to restrict the amount of labour available (McCloskey 1973: 435) and to discourage migration from overpopulated parishes (Redford 1926: 93–5). But it is doubtful whether even this had much of an impact on the state of the labour market and the extent of labour mobility. Because rural parishes were usually small enough to apply relief payments with care and discretion and because the amounts paid were far too meagre to discourage mobility if there was a chance of employment elsewhere, the allowance system could hardly have acted as a serious disincentive to labour or to migration in search of work (Baugh 1975: 61). In addition, the flexibility inherent in the parochial system of poor relief greatly minimised any tendency it may have had to discourage mobility (Rose 1976: 36).

As in the past, most migrants in the period of the industrial revolution moved only very short distances (Greenwood and Thomas 1973: 90–105). Only 10 per cent of all the heads of cottage households in the Bedfordshire parish of Cardington in 1851 had been born outside the county (Tranter 1973b: 103). Over 40 per cent of all immigrants in Preston in 1851 had come less than ten miles from their place of birth, and 70 per cent less than thirty miles (Anderson 1974: 135). Judging from the evidence for Preston, which may or may not prove typical, most newcomers to the town had come directly from their parish of birth: two-step migration was rare and common only among those relatively few immigrants who had travelled considerable distances from their birthplaces (Anderson 1974: 142). In the Preston area a high percentage of migration occurred between communities of similar economic features – a fact which may have eased the problems of adjustment to the changing environment and resulted in a more settled, less volatile labour force than might otherwise have been the case. Generally, people moved from one manufacturing area to another or between agricultural communities: only a minority transferred directly from agricultural to manufacturing centres (Anderson 1974: 139).

So far as we can tell from such scanty evidence, therefore, no *dramatic* transformation occurred in the character of internal migration in the century or so before 1860. Typically, migrants continued to move only short distances: and although the amount of mobility increased, the extent of geographic migration had always been considerable. The nature of Britain's industrial revolution was not so different from the economic environment it succeeded as to demand radically new patterns of population mobility. Traditional migratory habits and patterns, somethat intensified, were sufficient to provide much of that geographic flexibility of labour required by an emerging industrial economy. Of course, this is not to maintain that the process of migration was capable of ensuring completely adequate flexibility in the labour market. In an economy where the market for labour was highly seasonal this would be expecting too much. Nevertheless, there are signs that the rising volume of migration was sufficient to overcome some of the worst problems of regional and occupational imbalance in labour supplies. Seasonal migrations of agricultural workers, for example, increased sharply during the period 1750–1850 (Collins 1976: 53–9). The difficulties faced by eighteenth-century factory entrepreneurs in attracting workers are well known. Less often stressed is the fact that by the mid-nineteenth century such difficulties had in the main disappeared. And if, as Deane and Cole (1967: 18) suggest, regional wage differentials lessened in the course of the eighteenth century, it is surely a testimony to the success of migration in bringing about a more satisfactory regional distribution of labour.

Hours of work

The notion of regular working hours was alien to preindustrial society. Both in agriculture and in manufacturing, hours of work were highly irregular, with extended bouts of intense labour separated by long periods of inactivity. Partly this was due to the physical frailty of an undernourished, unhealthy population which needed long periods of rest to recover its energies for the next bout of work; partly it was due to the influence of seasonal variations in weather conditions. In manufacturing industry it was also inherent in the methods of production then prevailing. In the putting-out system inadequate transport and fluctuating demand made irregular working habits inevitable; so too did the fact that a large percentage of the manufacturing labour force was part-time, engaged also in agricultural work and switching its attention to industry only when seasonal demands for farm labour were low or weather conditions too severe to permit outdoor work.

Such irregular work habits were not suited to the industrial revolution. The factory, with its minute subdivision of labour and need for close synchronisation between the various productive processes, demanded more consistent hours of work. The introduction of steam power, free from the interruption of season or weather, made them possible (chapter 8). In the handicraft industry, too, though irregular working hours remained the norm through the first half of the nineteenth century, growing competition, more sophisticated methods of production, better transport and speedier, more reliable deliveries of raw materials and finished products intensified the pressure for more regular work patterns. Even in agriculture, enclosures and other improvements encouraged the spread of a more disciplined, less casual approach to labour.

The efforts of early factory entrepreneurs to inculcate the habit of regular working among their employees are adequate testimony to the deficiencies of the traditional labour supply in this respect (Pollard 1968a: 213–31; Chapman 1972: 53–4; McKendrick 1961: 38). By the middle of the nineteenth century however, in the factories anyway, the transition to regular hours of work was well under way. Although problems of irregular attendance continued to bother some factory entrepreneurs, the modern notion of regulating hours of work by the movement of the clock rather than the rhythms of nature had become firmly established (Thompson 1967: 63, 85–6). One of the consequences was surely a general rise in the productivity of the labour force. It is hard to imagine anyone maintaining maximum efficiency through the long bouts of intense labour usual in preindustrial times no matter how prolonged the period of rest in between.

Whether the tendency to work more regular hours during the industrial revolution was accompanied by an increase in the amount of time each individual spent at work is difficult to say. Little statistical data on the number of hours worked per day, week and year has survived for the period before 1800. Most of the data that do exist refer to employees in wage-earning occupations which had fairly regular hours of work. Yet both before and during the industrial revolution a large proportion of the workforce, in agriculture and domestic industry, was part-time and followed the traditional, highly irregular pattern of work. Moreover, such data as we have usually relate to the lengths of time *normally* worked or considered to be normally acceptable. While this may roughly equate with the number of hours *actually* spent at work it is likely that on many occasions actual working time differed substantially from what contemporaries assumed to be the norm. In any case, no brief summary of the kind that follows can hope to do justice to the infinite variety of experience between and within different occupations and periods of time.

It has always been assumed, however, that the length of time the average worker spent at work increased in the period of industrialisation (Deane and Cole 1967: 22; Deane 1965: 137–8; Thomas 1964: 60; Chambers 1972: 149). According to recent estimates by Freudenberger and Cummins, the average working week rose from 30 hours before 1700 to a maximum of 58 hours by 1750 and, for factory workers, to perhaps 72 hours by the early nineteenth century. The number of hours worked per year rose from 3000 in the mid-eighteenth century to 4000 by the early nineteenth. Underlying this trend, they argue, was a marked rise in the standards of nutrition. Until the eighteenth century, low levels of nutrition and thus of health forced the labouring population to spend much of its time 'resting'. As levels of nutrition rose the labour force became capable of sustaining longer hours of work (Freudenberger and Cummins 1976).

It is doubtful, however, whether the increase in working hours was as dramatic as Freudenberger and Cummins claim. They offer relatively little statistical data in support of their conclusions and their explanation possibly exaggerates the rise in nutritional standards during the eighteenth century. Specifically, their estimates of calorie intake at the end of the seventeeth century, based on Gregory King's statistics of grain output, are well below those reckoned from Deane and Cole's higher and more realistic estimates of grain production (Deane and Cole 1967: 62–8). Any rise in standards of nutrition before 1860 probably fell far short of that implied by Freudenberger and Cummins; and its impact on length of time spent at work must, therefore, have been a good deal less than they suggest.

The most extensive collection of data on hours worked has been compiled by Bienefeld. It indicates, contrary to the conclusions of Freudenberger and Cummins, that in the course of the eighteenth century the normal length of the working day both for wage-earners in factories and large workshops and 'self-employed' workers in domestic handicraft industry fell from the twelve hours (exclusive of meal times) common in the sixteenth and seventeenth centuries to ten. A ten hour day remained the norm till the middle of the nineteenth century. Only textile factories and a few 'sweated' trades and domestic industries worked longer days, and in the case of textile factories, where a twelve to fourteen hour day became typical in the early phase of the industrial revolution, the aberration proved temporary (Bienefeld 1972: 11–81).

If the length of the working day was shorter in the eighteenth and early nineteenth centuries than in the sixteenth and seventeenth, the number of days worked each week and year was greater. For most of the eighteenth century, except in factory industries where a six day week was usual, the bulk of the labour force worked an effective five day week. The 'typical' eighteenth-century labourer seems to have worked a ten hour day, five days a week throughout most of the year – a total working year of around 2500 hours. In the late eighteenth and early nineteenth centuries, with the rapid growth of factory and large workshop industry, the proportion of the labour force working a six day week rose. In 1860 a Board of Trade inquiry covering a wide range of industries showed a six day, sixty hour week to be the norm (Bienefeld 1972: 77). In much of domestic industry, where work was irregular and the custom of 'playing' on Mondays or Tuesdays survived, a five day week of nearer fifty than sixty hours, and a working year of about 2500 hours, was more usual. But for most workers in full employment the average working year mid-nineteenth century was probably closer to 3000 hours.

Whenever opportunities for employment existed in preindustrial times, the low adult earnings, poor health and high mortality and the youthful age structure of populations meant that work began early in life. Throughout the eighteenth century, children were regularly employed from the ages of five or six (Pinchbeck 1930: 120, 122, 179, 272). The various Factory and Mine Acts of the first half of the nineteenth century did little to change this, since their effect was limited to a narrow range of industries. Children of eight or nine were not uncommon in the metallurgical industries of South Wales (Pinchbeck 1930: 271); they were employed as scavengers in cotton factories from the age of eight (Smelser 1959: 189); in coal mines from the age of six or seven; in the domestic industries of pillow lace from five, strawplaiting, knitting and embroidering, handloom weaving from six, glove and button making from six to nine; in agriculture from seven or eight and even younger (Pichbeck 1930: 87, 89). Throughout the industrial revolution an early start to working life remained the norm. Indeed, as the scope for child labour widened, the percentage of children in employment probably rose with the result that the *average* age at which work began fell. It is, however, impossible to verify this statistically.

Generalisations about the age at which people normally ceased work are equally difficult. There was no statutory age of retirement. In most cases the end of gainful working life came gradually as physical and mental powers slowly failed. Data on sickness rates in the first half of the nineteenth century show how failing health seriously reduced the capacity for work of persons over the age of fifty (Flinn 165: 290). The varying demands of different occupations led to wide variations in the ages at which individuals ceased to be productive. The more arduous and less healthy the task the more youthful the age-structure of its labour force and the less likely its workers to remain active into mature adulthood (Flinn 1965: 169, 265). As a rough guide only to the usual age of retirement we are forced to rely on evidence collected for members of Friendly Societies in the 1790s (Eden 1797: 702, 775), the 1820s (Parl. Pap., 1825, IV: 27) and 1840s (Flinn 1965: 254). Contributors to Friendly Societies were not entirely typical of the labouring population: the less provident and less well-paid no doubt had to work much later into old age: workers in the most arduous and unhealthy occupations, where aptitudes and strength failed relatively early in life, were often forced to retire much sooner. But for what they are worth the

Friendly Society data suggest that adult males normally expected to retire around the ages of 60 or 65. There is nothing in the evidence from Friendly Societies to indicate that this changed very much between the 1790s and the 1840s, nor that it was any different from that in the period immediately before industrial 'take-off'.

The quality of the labour supply: education, aptitude and skill

That the industrial revolution required a great increase in the quantity of labour is beyond dispute. But was it also necessary that this labour be of higher quality than in the past? In view of the recent emphasis given to the quality of the labour supply in modern economic development and the recent tendency to assume that a rise in the quality of labour was also important in the case of the first industrial revolution, this question is of particular significance.

It has been argued that the industrial revolution came about in spite of, indeed almost because of, a decline in the intellectual and manipulative capacity of its workforce (Mantoux 1964: 454–6; E. P. Thompson 1963: 269–89). The spread of the factory system reduced the working man to 'nothing more than a brute' and the amount of intelligence and skill required in the productive processes to mere supervision of machines 'which a feeble woman or even a child can do quite as well' (Engels 1845: 149–53, 175, 214). In contrast, others have argued that early industrialisation created many more skills than it destroyed, and generally required higher standards of education, intellect and aptitude from its workers than ever before (Ashton 1948: 120–1; Pollard 1968a: 189–212; Mathias 1969: 144; Hartwell 1971: 243).

The controversy is difficult to resolve, partly because we still cannot be sure whether the new processes of production associated with the industrial revolution were more, or less, demanding of skill and intellect than those they superseded, and partly because too many historians in the past have treated standards of formal education, or more specifically an ability to read and write, as the sole criterion of intellectual quality and flexibility. Literacy is certainly one of the essential ingredients for ensuring that a labour force is intellectually capable of adjusting to new techniques and working arrangements. It may indeed be the most important. But it is not the only one. A willingness to adopt novel methods depends also on other factors – the innate intelligence of individuals, the extent to which inherited communal attitudes and organisations are flexible enough to favour the new, the adequacy of the on the job training schemes, the nature of the home environment, and so on. The trouble is that, particularly in societies as barren of the relevant information as pre- and early industrial Britain, these latter determinants of the mental quality and flexibility of labour are difficult to assess precisely: hence the concentration by historians on the one which can be measured, formal education.

It is not easy, however, to chart variations in the level of formal education among the mass of the population. On the contrary, there is considerable disagreement about trends in education standards during the industrial revolution: to some, they declined (Cipolla 1969: 68, 78; Deane 1973: 262–3; Gould 1972: 310–11; Pollard 1968a: 211–12; Hobsbawm 1968: 45); to others, they rose (Hill 1967: 229–30; Hartwell 1971: 241–4; West 1975: 256; 1978). Considering the diversity of the channels through which formal learning was diffused such disagreement is not surprising. But it does not make it any easier to assess the significance of formal education in Britain's early economic development.

Standards of education during the industrial revolution are perhaps best and most directly judged from variations in the rate of literacy. Schofield's work on regional and chronological variations in the proportion of persons signing parish marriage registers, based on a random sample of 274 parishes, provides for the first time a reasonably accurate guide to changes in literacy rates in England between 1754 and 1839 when the Registrar-General's annual statistics take up the story – so long, that is, as we are prepared to make the reasonable assumption that the ability to sign one's name legibly implied a general ability to write; and that the ability to write invariably meant an ability to read as well (Schofield 1973: 441; West 1975: 41; 1978).

Among males, the percentage literate rose from 60 per cent in the period 1754 to the mid-1790s, to 67 per cent in 1840 and 70 per cent in 1850: among females from below 40 per cent in the mid-eighteenth century, to nearly 50 per cent in 1840 and 55 per cent in 1850, with the greatest improvement occurring after 1800 (Schofield 1973: 446). Literacy rates, therefore, improved only slowly during the industrial revolution and chiefly after 1800 when the process of industrialisation was already well under way. If male literacy rates were as low as 30 per cent in 1642 (Stone 1969: 109), the standard of literacy improved more rapidly in the century preceding industrial 'take-off' than it did during the period of early industrialisation itself. Only between 1850 and 1911, by which time 99 per cent of all males were reckoned literate, was there any further dramatic improvement.

A sophisticated analysis of the social rate of return accruing from such investment in formal education as was necessary to produce literacy rates of this level is not possible for eighteenth and early nineteenth century Britain. West's recent attempt to estimate the percentage of national income devoted to elementary education in 1833 is not yet a complete account of its total costs (West 1975). Calculating the economic benefits of expenditures on elementary education is even more difficult. The standard method, which relates earnings to education received, is difficult for Great Britain during the period of industrial 'take-off' in the absence of sufficiently detailed and comparable income and educational statistics. Without a sophisticated analysis of this kind our assessment of the importance of literacy to the industrial revolution can only be impressionistic.

On the eve of industrial 'take-off' a majority of the population was able to read and write. Literacy rates were already comfortably above the minimum, 40 per cent, assumed necessary for the onset of modern economic growth (Anderson 1966: 347). This educational legacy played a significant role in *initiating* the industrial revolution. But the value of formal education for the *continued progress* of the industrial economy during the late eighteenth and first half of the nineteenth centuries is much less obvious. The industrial revolution itself appears to have proceeded quite happily without the need for any further marked rise in literacy standards. Schofield's analysis of regional and occupational differences in literacy rates makes it perfectly clear that in many of the activities most pertinent to the new industrial era standards of literacy were relatively low, sometimes actually declining, and of little practical relevance to the work in hand (Schofield 1973: 452–3). In Lancashire, the very nub of early industrialisation, literacy rates may have declined in the course of the period (Sanderson 1972: 75–86), although there are reasons to doubt this conclusion. Of far greater importance to the continued growth of a suitable labour force was the training in new, practical skills disseminated in the home, the workshop and the factory, a training which developed along with the rise of the industrial economy rather than preceded it, and which was able to make do with a labouring population scarcely more literate than that of the immediate pre-industrial period.

The fact that further dramatic improvements in standards of formal education were unnecessary for successful industrial 'take-off' in Britain reflects the modest nature of the scale and technology of the first industrial revolution itself (Chapter 8). On balance, it is true, the industrial revolution demanded a more intelligent, adaptable and skilled labour force than had ever before been required. Those who see early industrialisation as destructive of the intellect and skills of the workforce are mistaken. First, such writers are prone to overstate the level of intelligence and aptitude required by most preindustrial techniques of production. In truth, many of the occupational skills in preindustrial Britain were of a very low order and easily mastered. A high proportion of the so-called skills destroyed by the progress of technology, handloom weaving for example, were of the simplest kind, no more demanding of intellect and aptitude than the unskilled factory occupations which replaced them. Lengthy periods of apprenticeship in the preindustrial economy were usually less a reflection of the great degree of skill involved than a means of securing cheap labour or of controlling entry into crafts which might otherwise have become impossibly overcrowded. The putting-out system itself was feasible only in an economy where technical processes were simple and able to be performed by unsupervised, generally unskilled labour. The frequency with which many individuals are known to have moved between occupations of apparently very different type (Oosterveen 1974: 38–41) may be taken as yet another indication of the limited demands of most occupations for special skills. Secondly, historians who believe that the industrial revolution turned the working man into 'nothing more than a brute' tend to understate the range of new occupations created in the course of early industrialisation, occupations which required entirely different, often more sophisticated, skills and attitudes from those prevailing among the preindustrial labour force. Pollard has described the burgeoning need for civil engineers, skilled coalcutters, smelters and hammermen, puddlers and rollers, enginemen and engine drivers, navvies, etc. (Pollard 1968a: 197–9, 205–10); McKendrick stresses the crucial role of a new range of highly specialised workers – blockcutters, flat and hollow ware pressers, casters, painters and modellers – in the success of Wedgwood's enterprises (McKendrick 1961: 31–8).

It is nevertheless the case that the needs of the industrial revolution for labour of higher intellectual quality than in the past were moderate. However great the demands of factory work for more intelligent, adaptable and skilled manpower, the fact is that, as late as the mid-nineteenth century, most workers were still to be found employed in the agricultural, domestic industry and personal service sectors of the economy and in other occupations where the basic technology and methods of production had changed relatively little and where, accordingly, demands on the intellect remained much the same as they had always been. The modest additional requirements of early industrialisation for a more intelligent and adaptable labour force could therefore be met, with no great difficulty, simply by capitalising on the legacy of literacy, inherent intelligence and flexibility inherited from the past: they were much too modest to require any great increase in expenditure on items like formal education.

Conclusion

In their search for what has become the modern equivalent of the holy grail, the origins of modern economic growth, economists nowadays stress the relative importance of improvements in the *quality* rather than the *quantity* of the factor inputs of labour and capital. Taking the labour factor, variations in the physical, intellectual and emotional standards of the labour supply are considered to exercise a far greater influence on the pace and character of economic development than variations in its size: and the productivity of labour in workforces similar in size and personal quality is thought to vary greatly according to the manner in which they are organised for production. Recent interpretations of the causes of the British industrial revolution, in emphasising the contribution of education and those other factors which together determined the level and quality of savings and investment, the origins and vitality of entrepreneurship and the suitability of the labour supply, have tended to follow this lead.

Few would dispute that in modern economies or economies seeking to develop in an already advanced world this emphasis on 'residual' explanations of

economic growth is justified. The rapid pace of development and the sophistication of the technology and institutions involved set a high premium on the
intellectual quality of the labour supply and greatly enhance the importance of
those factors which together determine it: and since, in modern economies, the
capacity for labour-saving innovation is relatively great, the mere size of the
human labour force is in any case much less crucial to the process of economic
growth than it once was.

Compared to its successors, however, the British industrial revolution was a
very modest affair which emerged slowly from the past as part of a long
evolutionary process, not as a sharp, instantly recognisable break from traditional
experience; its technology was small-scale and comparatively primitive; it
needed relatively little additional investment capital; its capacity for introducing
labour-saving technology was circumscribed; and its pace was gradual and
uncoordinated (chapter 8).

It is not surprising, then, that such evidence as can be pieced together does
not reveal any *radical* improvement in the quality of the labour supply during
the period of early industrialisation. Of course, there were changes of quality and
quantity of the labour input between 1780 and 1860. Labour was forced to work
longer and more regularly, to be more proficient in a wider range of skills, and
to become differently and more efficiently organised for production than in the
past. It became more mobile between areas and occupations, marginally better
educated and, possibly, physically healthier. It would be wrong to suggest that
such changes were of no value to the process of industrial 'take-off'. Equally,
however, it would be wrong to exaggerate their significance. In some respects
anyway – its standards of education and mobility for example – the labouring
population of the early eighteenth century was already equipped to meet the
needs of industrialisation: and those of its characteristics which were less
well-suited – its irregular work habits, dislike and mistrust of factory work and
lack of particular skills – were not so seriously deficient that they could not be
remedied with little real difficulty during the process of industrialisation itself.

Viewed in this way the role of labour in the British industrial revolution
assumes a rather different character from that in economies which developed at
a later date. The problem most likely to have hindered early British economic
development was not one of inheriting a labour supply unsuitable in quality, but
that it might have been insufficient in quantity. In underdeveloped countries
today the labour problem is the reverse of this, and the solution to it therefore
very different. Manpower is abundant. It is the quality of its work which needs
to be radically altered and upgraded, and this requires massive expenditure on
those items which determine the quality of human capital – education, health
and so on. On this view the lessons afforded by the first industrial revolution
are of only limited value.

12

Transport and social overhead capital

G. R. HAWKE & J. P. P. HIGGINS

The concept of 'social overhead capital'

'Social overhead capital' arose as a concept in development economics and is useful for describing the characteristics of poor countries. It refers to large and bulky items of capital like transport systems, but it is not easy to define in a rigorous way. An early definition in Hirschman (1958: 83–4) is still one of the most acceptable: it is capital formation in an area which is somehow 'basic' to a range of economic activities; it is usually carried out by public authorities or is regulated by government agencies; it is non-importable; and it is associated with technical indivisibilities and high capital–output ratios. Hirschman suggests that a wide notion of social overhead capital is defined by only the first three characteristics and that the addition of the fourth gives a 'narrow' concept, focusing attention on transport facilities and power generation and away from expenditures on things like health and education.

Hirschman was naturally enough concerned with the developing countries of the 1950s. In carrying the concept into historical studies, the requirement that social overhead capital should be formed or at least closely regulated by government agencies is much too restrictive. Such a requirement would make it a nice question whether there was any significant amount in England between 1780 and 1860 and it is more convenient to drop that element of the definition and frame a question as to why England did obtain some without much government involvement (cf. Cootner 1963: 262). In the particular case of Britain between 1780 and 1860, also, the possibility of relying on imports rather than on domestic production is not of great interest. The important notions for our purpose are therefore that it is capital formation of a kind that is important to a number of growing economic activities, and that it is characterised by technically-imposed 'lumpiness', long gestation periods and economies of scale. This is very close to the conclusion reached by Youngson (1967: 68) that 'overhead capital' is a set of properties rather than of things and that the important properties are the extent to which an asset is a source of external economies and the extent to which it has to be provided in large units ahead of demand.

If such definitions seem to have an *ad hoc* nature, they reflect the development of the concept in the literature, e.g. Higgins (1959: 204), Nurkse (1960: 152),

227

Enke (1964: 263–4). The general notions of capital used by society at large rather than particular enterprises and of government involvement are clear enough, but most writers rely eventually on examples to convey the definition. Even Hirschman does so in detailing the difference between his wide and narrow concepts. A theoretical approach would be to link social overhead capital to variables other than those which determine investment in other forms of capital, but this is not easy to do (cf. Cootner 1963: 261–84; Youngson 1959: ch. V.). The concept lives on, and has been taken into the literature of economic history, not because of its analytical attractions but because empirical measurements have suggested that the assets generally understood as belonging within it form substantial fractions of total capital formation as countries industrialise. 'It is population growth and urbanization, social overhead capital and the transport system, which generate the really big demands for capital, and it is necessary to view the relatively modest demands of industrialization proper against this perspective' (Gould 1972: 152). Was this true in Britain from the mid-eighteenth to the mid-nineteenth century?

The forms of social overhead capital between 1780 and 1860

Estimates of capital formation in Britain between 1780 and 1860 have been presented in chapter 7 above. They make it abundantly clear that the major components of capital formation in the period were indeed various forms of buildings and transport systems. Within buildings, the share of the farming sector declined, and although industrial and commercial building increased relative to the total, it was not until the 1840s that it overtook dwellings. While dwellings have an obvious 'social' component, they were mostly built in small units and entirely by private enterprise. The precise level of spending on education is in doubt, but it too was achieved in small units of private activity. Concern with social overhead capital is therefore focused on the development of transport systems, although Gould's linking of it with urbanisation is also compatible with British experience between 1780 and 1860.

Something closer to the contemporary view of expenditures on transport systems than to the modern category of capital formation is shown in fig. 12.1. It is more than usually difficult to separate repairs and maintenance from net capital formation in the case of roads and canals, and eighteenth-century thinking gave little attention to such a distinction. Both activities were included under a heading such as 'improvements', and the diagram follows that practice. It is compiled from the accounting records of bodies such as parish authorities, turnpike trusts and canal companies using a simple 'grossing up' procedure to account for gaps in the accounting material. These gaps are large, but not as large as has usually been assumed, and the figures are more reliable than most economic data of the period. (Their major deficiency is probably the exclusion of road improvements made in the course of enclosures.)

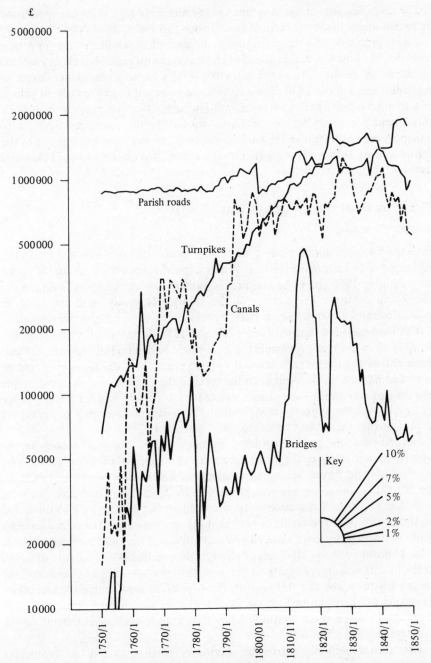

Fig. 12.1 Expenditure on creating, improving and maintaining canals and roads, etc. 1750–1850 (current prices). Source: The immediate source is Higgins (1971). The estimates result from the Sheffield – SSRC project into capital formation and are discussed in Higgins & Pollard (1971) and Feinstein (1978).

The main features of the diagram are the relatively high level of expenditure on parish roads, the fast growth of spending on turnpikes, the eighteenth-century 'booms' in canals and the continued high level of expenditures on 'improvements' in the nineteenth century. Not shown on the diagram, but clearly worthy of attention, is the very rapid growth of railways to even higher levels of expenditures to about 1830. The diagram shows expenditures in current prices, and therefore fluctuations in price levels would affect the pattern; but while adjustment for prices would probably show that the resources devoted to transport improvements in the early nineteenth century were less relative to the period as a whole than is suggested by the graph, it is unlikely to alter the chief features described above.

The growth of transport systems

Roads and canals

Expenditure on maintaining and improving roads was not a new activity in the mid-eighteenth century. Fig. 12.1 shows expenditures on parish roads to be substantial in 1750 and to be maintained rather than markedly increased in the succeeding century. The notion of the 'King's Highway' and the need to maintain travel possibilities go back at least to medieval times. Nevertheless, it is at least possible that between 1750 and 1850 there was an increase in the proportion of road 'improvements' which would be capital formation in modern terms rather than resources devoted only to countering the ravages of winter rains and harvest traffic. And both the total of the expenditure on parish roads and the obvious importance of such roads for local traffic and for feeding other transport systems suggest strongly that the oldest instruments of transport improvements should not be neglected (Chartres 1977).

Nevertheless, the more significant development of the road system in the eighteenth century was the turnpike trust. The inequity of using parish rate assessments and forced labour by residents of a parish to 'improve' roads for the benefit of other people was overcome by forming a trust charged with maintaining a specified section of road and financing its activity by tolls levied on those who used the facilities provided. More precisely, road improvements could be financed by loans secured on future tolls and the loans serviced by those tolls. This did not solve all issues of equity; some residents of a locality objected to the loss of customary rights to use a particular road without charge but the greater inequity was that through traffic subsidised local traffic on turnpikes. Nevertheless, there can be little doubt that the net effect of the development of the turnpike was a more equitable as well as a more efficient allocation of the cost of road-building.

The 'turnpiking' of a particular section of road depended on the private initiative of people concerned with it. There was no central planning of a 'turnpike' system. But the most-used roads were obviously those where the turnpike trust had most to offer both local residents and people engaged in long-distance travel and a mapping of turnpiking suggests more the growth of a road system radiating from London and linking centres of population and economic activity than a random selection of roads (cf. Albert 1972; Pawson 1975; 1977). There were certainly gaps in the system, frequently gaps causing marked inconvenience to travellers and transporters of goods, but then bottle-necks of various kinds are a familiar feature on the centrally-planned motorway systems of the present day.

It was the turnpike trusts which were mainly although not entirely responsible for introducing the technical improvements in road-making associated with names such as Metcalfe, Telford and McAdam. The improvement of road beds to enable the surface to sustain heavier traffic flows whether measured by vehicle numbers or load weights, and the formation of drainage systems to protect roads from water were the main ways in which land transport was facilitated. It was the legislative promise of future toll income that enabled the turnpike trusts to employ engineers to introduce such innovations. The effect is seen most clearly in personal travel; by the 1820s England could be said to have a network of coaching services permitting vastly faster personal travel than had been available in the middle of the eighteenth century. (Hart 1960: 146–50; Pawson 1977: 288–91).

In the transport of goods, the effects of road improvements were outweighed by those of developments in water transport. Like the parish roads, human intervention with natural waterways to make them serviceable transport facili-ties predates the mid-eighteenth century. But from then a number of factors combined to give a new vigour to attempts to improve inland water transport, a vigour that resulted especially in the expenditures on canals shown in fig. 12.1. These factors included: an increased demand for transport, especially for bulky items unsuited to pack-horses and even wagons on improved roads; greater competition for water supplies for industrial and agricultural uses as well as for transport; and an improved technical ability to retain water in a man-made channel and to build locks permitting transport over reasonable gradients (techniques at least in part borrowed from Holland); and after the 1750s, a demonstration that canal building could be a profitable economic activity.

The essence of water transport is that greater weight does no damage to the supporting medium. The essence of a canal is that it provides a water medium more conveniently arranged for transport than is a river in that the water is confined into a channel supplied with a tow path, and free from obstructions such as rapids and the weirs of corn or cotton mills, and substantially free from uncontrolled water currents. The water must still, of course, be obtained from natural sources, and there may still be competition for those supplies, but their seasonality can be better controlled by reservoirs than is possible with a river system. The advantages can be obtained, however, only at the expense of the investment of resources in the canal bed and in facilities such as locks.

Provided it is realised that the line between a canal and a river improvement is far from clear, the first English canal can be recognised as that which linked the Duke of Bridgewater's Worsley coal mines to Manchester in 1761. Its importance is that it showed the profitability of investment in canals. In particular, it revealed the possibility of private profits from building a canal for the use of separate transporters. This was important because Parliament was still suspicious of 'monopolies' and while it was prepared to sanction the building of canals, it insisted on separating their ownership from the carriage of goods along them. The operators of the canal obtained their income from tolls, and with occasional exceptions such as Bridgewater himself, were not permitted to become carriers of goods.

The expectation of profit within this framework was sufficient to stimulate a network of canals. In the eighteenth century, canals linked the major rivers of England – the Trent, Mersey, Severn and Thames – and then added more direct links between major towns and London. From the toll income of early canals, and from new investment, branches were added, extended and 'improved'. It should be noted carefully that a substantial fraction of all canal building took place in the early nineteenth century rather than in the booms of the 1770s and 1790s, which receive disproportionate attention in much of the literature.

Canals were almost entirely built by companies, incorporated with the privileges of limited liability by Act of Parliament along with restrictions imposed in the same way, such as the prohibition of acting as carriers discussed earlier, and often with limitations of permitted tolls or rates of dividend. It is not immediately obvious why canals were organised as private companies while road improvements were entrusted to turnpike trusts, but the main reason was probably that the latter were responsible for part of the 'King's Highway' – public property – while the former were to construct their own thoroughfares more or less *ab initio*. Furthermore, the turnpike trusts evolved from 'justice trusts', essentially the devolution of a local taxing power on the parish apparatus for maintaining roads, and the line from parish to trust to company was one of successive experimentation rather than of logic.

Canal companies were organised in much the same way as modern companies although the unit of investment was larger than is now common and the facilities for exchanging shares very much less developed. Investors in canals were widely spread among the socio-occupational classes as shown in table 12.1. The distribution is not markedly different from that implied by contemporary estimates for the distribution of income among the same groups. The main difference between the two chronological periods is in the share of peers and that is attributable more to the Duke of Bridgewater individually than to any change in the activities of the peerage as a whole. The main investors were the landed

Table 12.1. *Investments in transport systems (percentages of nominal capital invested)*

	Canals 1755–1815 (1)	Railways 1820–44 (2)	Canals 1755–80 (3)	Railways 'early years' (4)	Canals 1780–1815 (5)	Railways 'later years' (6)
1. Peers, gentry, 'gentlemen', etc.	22	28	41	22	22	37
2. Land: farmers, graziers, etc.	2	—	1	—	2	—
3. Commerce: merchants, traders, tradesmen, etc.	39	45	27	52	40	38
4. Manufacturers	15	11	8	15	15	7
5. Professions, including clergymen	16	9	16	8	16	10
6. Women	6	5	8	2	6	8
	100	100	100	100	100	100

Notes and sources: The data are from Ward (1974: 74–5) and Reed (1975: 124, 132, 137, 144, 151, 157, 161, 166, 176, 191).
Row 1: Ward's classes I and II; Reed's class VII.
Row 2: Ward's class II; Reed's class VI.
Row 3: Ward's classes IV and VI; Reed's classes I, III and V.
Row 4: Ward's class V; Reed's class II.
Row 5: Ward's classes VII and VIII; Reed's class IV.
Row 6: Ward's class IC; Reed's class IX.
Reed's class VIII, unspecified, is redistributed proportionately among his other classes. Note that Reed's listing of his classes for individual railways companies differs in order from his description on p. 109. All data are derived from samples. The canal figures use Ward's own summary. The railway figures are derived from Reed's data for 10 companies, weighted by the nominal capital involved in each case. Col. (2) employs all the data cited by Reed. Col. (4) uses the earliest year for which Reed has data for each of the 10 companies. Col. (6) employs the data for the latest year. In the case of the North Midland Railway, the 'latest year' data is estimated from data on the occupational distribution of shareholders (rather than shareholdings) by assuming that the linear relationship between these concepts in 1836 applies also for 1842. The figures would be little affected if the North Midland were excluded altogether.

gentry, merchants, and tradesmen, the first of these being especially prominent in canals with rural hinterlands, the second in other canals, and the tradesmen, consistent with their spread among both larger and smaller urban areas, were about equally prominent in both kinds. Manufacturers are, if anything, less prominent than might be expected, but since their share of investment was much the same as their share of total income, this probably reflects the mistaken nature of our conventional ideas about the size of manufacturing in the eighteenth-century economy. Investors in canals were generally local, except that London investors were to be found in many canals and in the boom or 'stock market mania' of the 1790s investments were more widely spread. It is likely that those who made loans to turnpike trusts were even more localised than was the case with canals and that the landed gentry were more prominent than they are in table 12.1.

Not all the profit expectations of investors in canals were realised. Large profits were made by some of the earlier canals but others received more moderate returns and in the early nineteenth century a substantial fraction of total canal investments were returning no private dividends at all. We cannot determine the average return within a wide margin, but it seems that canal investment was carried to at least the margin of returns available elsewhere in the economy.

The social returns were spread more widely than dividends. Canals cheapened the cost of transporting many commodities, especially those with a high weight:value ratio. All the inputs and outputs of the growing industries of the eighteenth century as well as agricultural products were represented in the freights of canals, but it is likely that coal was by far the largest freight. Bridgewater's reported comment that 'A navigation must have coals at the heels of it' was much more than a comment on his own endeavours; coal was the commodity most in demand in the industrial north, and coal for domestic use and in agriculture was the largest item in the freight of the canals of southern England. This can be inferred from Hadfield (1955) and from some surviving canal records such as those of the Leeds & Liverpool Canal. The limited evidence available suggests that the greatest social gain from canal building was a reduction in the cost of transporting coal, probably by about 50 per cent (Jackman 1916).

We have portrayed the growth of both the road and canal systems between 1750 and c. 1830 as responses to the opportunities for profit created by demand for cheaper transport. In the one case, a semi-public body, the turnpike trust, left the profit to those who benefited from the cheaper transport and those who lent to the trust; in the other, canal companies took some for themselves while making it easier for carriers to earn an income and leaving some of the social gains for consumers of transported goods, especially coal. In neither case is much 'building ahead of demand' apparent; the turnpikes responded to the inadequacies of existing roads and the canals emphasised existing traffic in appealing to investors although their existence may well have stimulated additional traffic. Nor is there much sign that the transport developments were greatly limited by unavailability of investment finance. Although canals and turnpikes obviously depended on the availability of resources for investment, their timing cannot be closely related to national year to year changes in interest rates (cf. Ashton 1959). Rather, each turnpike and canal in the eighteenth century was seen mostly as a regional undertaking, not making an excessive demand on regional sources of investment resources. The eighteenth-century transport developments were in an economy or set of economies in which incomes were not near subsistence.

Railways

Narratives of the development of railways are readily available (e.g. Pollins 1971, Reed 1975) and only the briefest summary will be given here. Railways were essentially a combination of innovations, especially in the successful manufacture of iron rails and in the construction of mobile steam engines, which permitted a marked reduction in the cost of transport. The period of experimentation can be traced back into the eighteenth century (or even earlier in the case of rails alone) and was still going on during the first quarter of the nineteenth century. When the Stockton & Darlington railway was planned in the 1820s, it was not completely fatuous to argue, as some people did, that horse-drawn carts on iron rails were preferable to trains drawn by steam engines.

But that argument was not tenable by the end of the decade. The success of railways like the Stockton & Darlington, and even more of the Liverpool & Manchester railway, the first to be planned and operated as a transport service for people as well as goods, proved that railways offered an improvement over rival transport systems such that the building of railways was a profitable investment opportunity. The profits that could be reasonably be anticipated (even though less than were often in fact anticipated) were large enough to outweigh other economic considerations such as the rate of interest available on government stocks, and the pace of railway building in the 1830s was influenced more by the availability of people like surveyors and by technical considerations of parliamentary procedures than by the variables which are usually prominent in investment decisions. In the course of the 1830s and 1840s most of the trunk lines of the English railway system were built, the exceptions being the Great Northern built in the 1850s and the Great Central built much later in the nineteenth century. In the 1850s and 1860s the trunk system was supplemented by secondary routes, often built by existing railway companies or by contractors intending to sell to an existing company. The British railway system gradually came to resemble a web connecting all significant centres of population.

British railways were built by essentially private companies, although the need for an Act of Parliament to give each company the power to compulsorily acquire land and to provide limited liability meant that the state had a role to play. Railways usually began with local committees formed by people who saw an opportunity for private profits and who were prepared to accept the initial expenses of surveying and obtaining the necessary statutory powers. Once a private Act was obtained the company became a legal entity very much like a modern business corporation, and it was the interval between original formation and statutory incorporation which provided most of the gambling for which railways became renowned. That is, the gambling was in the 'scrip' of unincorporated units rather than in shares, the capital gains coming from selecting those committees which would obtain Parliamentary sanction for their plans.

While railways were often initiated by local interests, companies which had received Parliamentary sanction offered the prospect of good and reliable dividends (although naturally some companies proved to be better than others). Incorporated companies were therefore able to attract investment funds from throughout Britain and most railway companies soon came to have a shareholders' register which was widely distributed geographically. The contemporary view that Liverpool was especially prominent in providing funds for railways has been confirmed by modern research and is presumably to be attributed to the early experience of Lancashire with railways and to the availability of investment funds from the various economic activities epecially prominent in Liverpool. But the railways were soon drawing on something close to a national market for capital.

Similarly, the occupational distribution of shareholders in railways was widely varied. Contemporary sources emphasise the difficulties which some 'hapless widows' and misguided clergymen experienced, but as shown in table 12.1 there can now be no doubt that the most prominent groups among railway shareholders were people whose incomes were derived from trade and commerce. Such people were, of course, those in the best position to judge the likely success of railways schemes. They were even more prominent in the earlier railway schemes: unlike canals, railways needed no aristocratic pioneers.

Most companies were formed to build railways between precisely nominated points, and most began with limited objectives. Some companies then extended their interest, but more prominent in the 1840s was the amalgamation of distinct companies which had some obvious community of interest. Thus the London & Birmingham, Grand Junction, and Liverpool & Manchester Railways came together into the London & North Western Railway in 1846. Even more spectacular was George Hudson's formation of the Midland Railway from a number of railway companies in central England and its gradual evolution into one of the major trunks linking London to the industrial north.

The amalgamation movement was not the only way in which the independent companies were formed into something like a railway 'system' by the middle of the nineteenth century. Perhaps as important was the organisation of the Railway Clearing House whereby passengers (from 1842) and goods (from 1848) could be consigned over the railways of two or more companies in one transaction, the railway companies themselves arranging the appropriate distribution of the receipts. But even more important was the simple geographical extension of railway lines so that there was at least one link between almost any conceivable pair of places.

The role of the state was essentially subsidiary. An Act of Parliament was necessary, and this gave a privileged position to those people represented in the

House of Commons or the House of Lords since they were in a position to obstruct any particular route for a railway line. Agreement was usually reached (although not always) but the need for a parliamentary grant of the power of compulsory acquisition gave a powerful bargaining weapon to such interests as the owners of land. Furthermore, Parliament quickly accepted a responsibility to ensure public safety on railways and so the state became involved in the investigation of accidents and in the certification as safe of new lines. And from the days of canals, Parliament inherited an interest in the maximum charges which could be imposed by railways, although regulations were usually phrased in a manner that proved to make them largely ineffective. Parliament did consider extending the traditional concern with 'monopolies' and in 1844 it foreshadowed the possibility that all railways sanctioned after that date might be compulsorily acquired by the state after 21 years. (A Royal Commission in 1865–67 recommended that such an action was unnecessary and its advice was accepted.) Parliament usually had to sanction amalgamations of railway companies (since a railway company was strictly limited to those powers conferred by its original private Act, and an amending Act was required to extend them). By the 1850s, Parliament was taking a sceptical look at many proposed amalgamations and refused some, including the proposals of the largest of railway companies. *Laissez faire* in England never meant uninhibited freedom for businessmen; rather it meant freedom to act within certain constraints one of which was the unacceptability of monopolies, 'monopolies' in its everyday meaning rather than in the strict sense of elementary economics.

Thus railways were built in Britain primarily by private enterprise seeking private profit, drawing on a geographically and occupationally varied capital market and gradually evolving a national railway system. The role of the state was secondary but certainly not absent.

The concept of 'social saving'

So far we have been concerned with various aspects of the ways in which England acquired its social overhead capital between 1750 and 1860. We turn now to seek more precision to notions about the effects which social overhead capital had on the economy. For this purpose we employ the concept of the 'social saving' associated with an innovation.

Ex post cost–benefit

The social saving, for example of the railways, is measured as the difference between the actual cost of the transportation services provided by the railways and the hypothetical cost of those same services in the absence of the railways using the best available alternative source of transport services. If the prices used accurately reflect resource use, this also measures the difference in national income with and without the railways, given that the economy is not allowed to adjust to the absence of railways (by, for example, relocating economic activity so that less transport is required for a given level of total output).

The difference in the cost of specified transport by railways and by an alternative system involves more than a direct comparison of rates charged on various goods. Allowance has to be made for such things as differences in the reliability of each system for transporting goods safely, for differences in seasonal unavailability because of weather conditions, for differences in speed, for differences in the cost of trans-shipments and of supplementary haulage by another transport means such as horse-drawn wagons if the two systems differ in the amount of such services required, and perhaps for other things as well. Furthermore, the difference in transport costs cannot be equated with the difference in national income if the improved transport system induces external economies in other parts of the economy.

Equally, it is important not to double count the gain to an economy from an innovation in transport. What might appear to be distinct gains may well be different manifestations of the cheapening of transport services. For example, the formation of a railway can be expected to increase the rental value of land close to it. The change in rents is an alternative route to the measurement of the extent by which transport costs were reduced but it is not a benefit additional to a comparison of transport costs with and without the railway; to add the two would be to double count by including both a direct measure of the change in the income stream and the change in the valuation of assets resulting from the change in the income stream.

As expounded so far, the notion of social saving is quite simple. It is an analogue after the fact to the hopes underlying any projected innovation or investment project. In other words, it is the benefit half of a cost–benefit study. Indeed, it is formally no more than a particular application of the fundamental economic concept of 'opportunity cost', that the cost of anything is ultimately what must be given up to attain it. But such simplicity disappears as subtleties of interpretation are attached to estimates of a social saving. The most significant complexities are readily apparent from the definition of the concept: the use of the actual transport services in a given year, the need for 'appropriate' prices, and the need to consider external economies separately.

If a very large innovation or investment project is not undertaken then the pattern of output of a particular economy is unlikely to be the same as if it were undertaken. For example, in the absence of railways, the British economy might well have arranged production to require less transport so that although total production would have been lower than the level achieved with railways the difference would not be as great as the 'social saving'. This point has been christened the problem of 'terminal weighting'. Its significance depends on the precise question being asked. If one is concerned with the impact on growth of a particular innovation, one can define the social saving (as a measure of that impact), as the difference between the resources which the economy has to devote to some activity such as transport so as to reach a certain production pattern with and without the innovation. No bias through 'terminal weighting' is involved. But it is still open to anybody to complain that other measurements would be more in line with normal notions and to seek modifications of the social saving (usually using an estimate of the sensitivity to price of the demand for transport to try to evaluate the extent to which less transport would be required in the absence of the innovation). A second line of approach is to accept the bias imposed by terminal weighting and seek to use it in the argument being constructed. Since no adjustment which an economy is likely to make to the absence of railways would increase the gap between the level of income achieved and that which could be achieved by making no adjustment at all to the absence of railways, the 'social saving' can be interpreted as an upper bound on the effect of an innovation on income or as an upper bound to the social returns to an investment project. If one wishes merely to argue that the effects of railways were not as great as sometimes thought, then an upper bound may be sufficient. But it is unlikely that such an argument will be sufficient for all purposes; as soon as one is engaged in international comparisons one will want to go further. One then has to abandon any hope of simple solutions.

The prices which are conceptually appropriate for a social saving calculation are clear enough. In the case of railways they are the resource costs of certain transport services provided by the railways, and the resource costs of those same services by the best alternative transport means. For the railways, one needs to be concerned only about possible imperfections in the average price charged by the railway system. But for the alternative, one cannot have a direct observation. Any canals which survive railway competition can hardly be typical of a canal system required to undertake the transport services provided by the railways. (It is obvious enough that if two transport services co-exist within one market in a perfectly competitive economy, then the social saving of replacing one with the other must be zero.) On the other hand, the *charges* made by canals in an earlier era may well be far from the resource cost of canal transport in later years. One needs to have some notion of the cost function of canal transport. Only then can we form some idea of at what cost the economy could have obtained the transport services of a later year without the use of railways.

Like 'social saving' and 'social overhead capital', the concept of 'external economy' soon proves to be less simple than it first appears. Again the general idea is clear. A particular innovation such as the railways may have more impact on national income than it does on transport costs because it enables a saving in resources elsewhere in the economy than the transport sector. If the railways are directly responsible for some secondary innovation in the iron industry, cheapening iron for all uses, then the effect of the railways will be greater than the social saving. In assessing the impact of the innovation of railways, it is only external economies specifically related to the use of railways which are relevant. In assessing the returns to investment in railways, it is not so clear that all external economies flowing from the investment in railways – whether they originate in the particular innovation or in the cheapening of transport however that is achieved – should not be added to the social saving.

In either case, it is important not to confuse an external economy with the direct effects of the cheaper transport made available by railways which are measured by the social saving itself. Cheaper transport makes resources available for other purposes but that is what the social saving is designed to measure. It is any secondary innovation which may require an addition to the social saving in assessing the effects of the railways. The difficulty with such external economies is simply that they must be identified and measured.

Counterfactual analysis

It may still be surprising to some readers, especially those with a background in orthodox historical methodology as distinct from historical practice, that we should take seriously the use of counterfactual methods such as imagining a British transport system without railways. For a long time, orthodoxy recommended study of what happened, not speculation about what might have happened. But such a dictum was not, and could not, be followed. Statements of what happened inevitably imply statements about what did not happen; the proposal of causal connections immediately carries counterfactual implications which might be the most convenient means for subjecting the proposed connection to a demanding empirical test.

It must be remembered that concern with a counterfactual situation is an analytical tool for describing and analysing historical events. A counterfactual is obviously untrue in the sense that it does not directly describe reality (and some people have been concerned about whether a 'true' argument can be based on an obviously 'untrue' proposition) but counterfactuals are used in arguments not directly but as measures or effects or causal connections which are not themselves untrue. (As indeed, they have long been in various mathematical and logical arguments.) That railways did not exist in England in 1865 is obviously false. But that does not imply that it is false to say 'maintenance of 1865 levels of production without the use of railways would require a diversion to transport of 10 per cent of the 1865 national income'.

More particularly, statements about the effects of an innovation and investment project such as the railways always have counterfactual implications and it is an obvious path to greater precision of knowledge to seek to specify those counterfactual implications more closely. It is, of course, true that one can never hope to make definitive statements about counterfactual situations, but then finality is as much an illusion in historical writing as it was in Lord John Russell's speeches about parliamentary reform.

Specifying the appropriate counterfactual for assessing any proposition is often a tricky task. In our discussion of the concept of social saving, we noted the different counterfactuals required for only slightly varying aspects of the introduction of railways into the English economy. Each of these has to be separately scrutinised and assessed. But the essential defence of the use of explicit counterfactuals is that the technique has advanced our knowledge in a number of fields of economic history in the last ten to fifteen years – not by as much as the most enthusiastic proponents would claim but by enough to justify the technique itself.

The modern concern with counterfactuals should be clearly seen as a concern about the *precision* of the specification of the counterfactual situation. It is generalisations about the 'importance' or 'significance' of the railways which carry most counterfactual implications. Studies which have given most explicit attention to the counterfactual have been clearly limited in the area of their interest; the economic effect of railways, and still more the effects of railways on economic growth, constitute a much narrower field of study than their importance or significance. Those who wish to assess the effects of railways on the location of industry, or on the distribution of income (and still more on welfare) or on other aspects of history have to construct different counterfactuals, or have to rely on more traditional methods recognising that they cannot give such precise results.

The social saving of English railways in 1865

Because there has been more study of railways than of earlier innovations, and because information on railways is more readily available, we turn first to the social saving of the later innovation.

Passenger traffic (cf. Hawke 1970, 1971)

By 1865, the railways of England and Wales were providing approximately 2.2 thousand million passenger miles of transport services to the economy, about half of those being in third class travel. That represents about a sixfold increase in personal travel from the time when railways first became available. By 1865, the railways of England and Wales provided a comprehensive range of services and the number of companies and alternative routes ensured that railway prices allowed for very little surplus over the resource cost involved.

If the 1865 level of personal travel were to be sustained in the absence of railways, some travel would have been diverted to shipping (and some to canal boats), but, if only because of the inland nature of most travel, most would have had to be accommodated on coaches. The cost of coach travel fell between 1820 and 1840, partly because of competition within the coaching industry and partly because the fear or fact of railways eliminated monopoly rents, and it is probable that coach fares approached long-run resource costs in that period. Fares of 4d per passenger mile inside coaches and 2½d per passenger mile for outside travel were described as 'slightly over the mark' by a parliamentary committee in the 1840s but they were accepted as accurate by a Royal Commission in the 1860s. A sixfold increase in scale would be likely to raise the social costs of coaches (as such items as road maintenance become more burdensome), but the unamended figures are taken as the appropriate costs here.

More difficulty arises in assessing the relative comfort of coach and rail travel. In the 1840s, it was not uncommon to compare first class rail travel with inside coach travel and other classes with the outside seats of coaches. But in the 1860s, the Royal Commission compared first class rail travel with posting (i.e. the running of an individual coach between any two points, changing horses at pre-arranged 'posts' on the route) at 24d per passenger mile. And in all respects but the complete freedom from timetable constraints in posting (and that is not a marked advantage over the extremely frequent train services of the 1860s), the comparison of the Royal Commission cannot be said to have been unduly favourable to the railways of 1865.

If we adopt the comparison of the Royal Commission, then, to maintain the 1865 level of personal travel by coach transport, the economy would have had to divert resources of about £48 millions to the transport sector, or about 5.8 per cent of the UK national income. If we adopt the comparison used in the 1840s, the amount involved is about £13 millions, or about 1.6 per cent of the UK national income. We may combine these by saying that the 1865 levels would have required a diversion to transport of about 6 per cent of the UK national income, but that three-quarters of that diversion could be avoided by accepting a marked retrogression in the comfort enjoyed in travelling. (Even though there was a sixfold increase in personal travel from the 1840s to 1865, it is perhaps the change in the comfort of travel which most justifies thinking of the railways as introducing the new commodity of personal travel pleasure into the economy.) We would, of course, like to know more about the demand for travel in 1865 so that we could add further conclusions to the study of social saving. But the study of choices among the various classes of rail travel offered by individual railway companies makes it clear that the valuation of the difference between, for example, first and second class travel varied markedly among them. We have no firm basis for estimating what people in 1865 would have done about the comfort of travel had it markedly increased in price.

We do know that the average length of passenger journey in 1865 was very short – not much more than ten miles. This reflects the density of the rail network in 1865, and the success of the railways in attracting people for even short journeys. It also implies that there is no need for any significant addition to the social saving to reflect the greater speed of rail traffic.

Freight traffic (Hawke 1970: chs. III–VII)

In 1865, English railways provided approximately three thousand million ton-miles of freight transport services. The freights involved were obviously much less homogeneous than was the case with passenger services, as almost every conceivable type of commodity produced or consumed in England was represented in the freight of railways. But about two-thirds of the freight carried on railways, measured by either tons or ton-miles, consisted of minerals, mostly coal.

To maintain the 1865 level of transport services without railways would have required in particular an increased use of canals. Some traffic would have been diverted to coastal shipping and the livestock traffic of the railways could be diverted to droving (and the calculations reported here make some allowance for these alternatives) but most of the traffic must be considered as diverted to canals. In particular, railways permitted the development of *inland* coalfields when they were competitive with coastal fields; the transport from those fields could not have been provided to any significant extent by coastal shipping.

Much the weakest point in any attempt to measure the social saving of railways is our knowledge of the costs involved in such an alternative transport network. But the very limited information available does suggest that canal costs were roughly constant over increasing volume (although costs are not, of course, observable up to the volume of 1865 transport services). The costs of canals were however a much smaller fraction of the cost of shipping by canal than much of the literature would suggest. And the evidence on costs other than those associated with the maintenance of the canal bed itself – those connected with organisations running canal boats – is least satisfactory, although *a priori* expectations of constant costs in an industry of small units are not inconsistent with the scattered data which exist. (Much of the same is true of the droving alternative to the railways' livestock traffic.) These data are used to make the first calculations of the social saving on freight traffic shown in table 12.2.

The additional saving shown for meat supplies is an explicit recognition of the need for speedy transport for some freight items. In 1865, the main such item was what contemporaries referred to as 'dead meat' but which the modern tendency to euphemism would label 'fresh meat'. Even this trade was in its infancy in 1865, being mostly concerned with meat supplies to London and being markedly promoted in the mid-1860s by various animal diseases which interrupted the livestock trade. Other trades in perishable commodities, such as milk and fresh vegetables, were developed mostly after 1865 and are not separately

244

Table 12.2. *The social saving on freight in 1865*

	(1) £ million	(2) (1) as % of national income
Freight traffic		
Aggregate	14.0	1.7
Livestock and meat supplies (additional saving)	0.35–2.54	0.04–0.31
Supplementary wagon haulage		
Minerals	7.1	0.9
Other	3.5	0.4
Inventory adjustments	0–1.0	0–0.1
Total	25.0–28.1	3.0–3.4

Source: Hawke (1970: 188).

accounted for. A trade in fish was not new but the extra saving is not large enough to be significant.

Conceptually, the dead meat trade resembles the comfort of first class passenger traffic. In the absence of railways, it would probably have been replaced by a larger livestock trade rather than by an alternative fast transport service. But that replacement could not be complete. The dead meat trade permitted the removal of abattoirs from city centres and eventually enabled salesmen to take advantage of divergent price trends in different markets for particular cuts of meat. It represented a genuine addition to the services available in the economy. If one wants to eliminate that consideration from the social saving attributable to the innovation of railways one has only to deduct between 0.1 and 0.7 million pounds from the total shown in the table.

The estimated cost of the non-rail canal-dominated alternative transport system used in the table allows for the approximately 20 per cent greater distance between two points by canal than by rail. But in addition to that, a canal system required a greater amount of supplementary wagon haulage between place of production and the transport system, or between the latter and place of consumption, and this is shown separately in the table. So is an allowance for the greater speed of rail transport through its effect on inventory costs. This cannot be other than small. The average distance for which freight was transported in 1865 was only between 30 and 35 miles and although this is obviously the average of both longer and shorter distances, the difference in stock requirements because of the difference in speed of goods trains and water transport obviously cannot be large. The limited direct observations of stock levels lead to the same conclusion. Furthermore, for some commodities, especially agricultural products, stock levels are determined by seasonal production patterns, and speedier transport, while it can redistribute the holding of stocks among producers, wholesalers, retailers, and consumers, cannot affect the total level. And while the English climate is execrable, it did not make canal transport unavailable for large parts of the year as happened in some other countries. Floods and ice in winter and shortages of water in summer did occur but not usually for long periods, and there is no need for a substantial adjustment for the greater reliability of rail transport.

The table shows that the maintenance of 1865 freight transport services in the absence of English railways would have required a diversion of 3 to $3\frac{1}{2}$ per cent of the UK national income, which is equivalent to about 4 per cent of the national income of England and Wales. That can probably be extended to Britain or to the United Kingdom without significant change.

External economies (Hawke 1970: chs. VIII–XV)

It is much easier to recognise that the social saving will underestimate the effect on national income of railways if they induced 'external economies' (i.e. cost reductions in other industries over and above reduction in the cost of transport itself) than it is to identify means by which the railways made an effective addition to the resources of the economy other than by the provision of cheaper transport services. The railways did use a substantial fraction of total investment or the total labour force in certain years, but this is the cost of the railways, the means by which the social saving was achieved, rather than any gain to the economy over and above the social saving.

The item of investment which attracts most attention is the iron content of rails and there have been numerous suggestions that the demand for rails was a significant influence in the growth of the iron industry (Hobsbawm 1968). It is perfectly true that rails were a substantial fraction of the output of both blast furnaces and rolling mills, and, indeed, the traditional case is strengthened when it is noted that the demand for iron for railways was more than proportionately directed to the iron industry of South Wales and that rails used by railways in England and Wales probably accounted for 10 to 15 per cent of the output of the region's blast furnaces over the peak years 1844–51. That percentage is much less than some accounts would suggest but it is still substantial. But the industry consisted of many plants, and if mere size of output was sufficient to cheapen iron for uses other than railways – for an external economy to be exploited – then simple amalgamation of some individual plants would have sufficed to replace the innovation of railways. It is not easy to trace any connection between the specific demands of rail making and technical change in the industry. For example, among Welsh furnaces there is no obvious connection between those which were prominent suppliers of rails and those which were the early users of the hot blast technique. And, at least in the case of the Bessemer industry before 1870, a similar conclusion must be reached about the relationship between rails and the development of the steel industry. Hesitancy and the requirement of high standards of proof that steel rails were superior to iron on the part of railway companies meant that steel rails were not a large part of the output of the steel industry in the 1860s. Nor were early steel masters usually in firms that had supplied a large quantity of iron rails; the switch from iron to steel rails usually involved a switch to a new supplier.

Once this conclusion has been reached for the most likely sources of external economies, it is not surprising that it is difficult to find any in other parts of the economy. In particular, railways in England and Wales were built between existing centres of economic activity so that it is unlikely that economies arose from the relocation of industry over and above the cheaper transport available from sites close to a railway. The productivity record of railways was impressive but does not indicate that there were significant improvements in management techniques made available to other sectors; the productivity gains came mainly from improvements in the performance of assets peculiar to the railway industry. Direct scrutiny of the railways' use of management techniques in accountancy and marketing results in a similar conclusion. Changes in company law followed the logic of legal and political argument rather than simple experience with railways, and while railways had a large impact on such institutions as the stock exchange, there was no substantial increase in efficiency in other sectors of the economy that could not have occurred without them.

The study of railway problems did lead directly to the theory of imperfect competition, but the long term gain from that is problematical and it certainly had no impact on the economy in the nineteenth century! But the particular pricing policy adopted by English railways, a rather sophisticated form of discrimination among commodities and among regions, may well have had the effect of bringing into the economy certain resources which would otherwise have remained unused. The railways seem genuinely to have accepted a social responsibiity which could have had the effect of some net gain to the economy. But overall the incidence of external economies is unlikely to alter the order of magnitude of the social saving as previously calculated.

It should be emphasised that this conclusion is in no way inconsistent with the more familiar proposition that railways markedly altered the English economy in such aspects as the location of industry, the total volume of iron output, the volume of business on stock exchanges, the relative fortunes of individual businesses units, and the creation of railways towns such as Crewe, Swindon and Wolverton. What this conclusion says is that such changes were the means by which the social saving was achieved, not additional gains to national income over and above social saving. In many ways, the nature of the railway towns is symbolic; what is significant is that they did not develop industries unrelated to railways signifying gains to the non-railway sectors of the economy distinct from the provision of cheaper transport.

The returns to investment in railways (Hawke 1970: 405–8)

The social saving calculation summarised for 1865 can be repeated – with a greater degree of approximation – for each of the years 1840–70. The resulting estimates can then be combined with data on railway investment, and on the private profits of the railway companies, to determine the social rate of return on investment in English railways. The return on English railways between 1830 and 1870 is found to be of the order of 15 to 20 per cent, and it is unlikely that any alternative use of the resources involved could have earned a greater return.

We can be confident that the calculation underestimates the true social return to investment in railways. Any external economies which should be added to the social saving to obtain a measure of the effects of the railways as an innovation should also be taken into account in assessing the returns to investment in railways. But one should also consider those ways in which the railways facilitated growth in other sectors whether or not the railways were technically necessary for the change in the other sectors. The test is simply whether there were gains elsewhere facilitated by railways, rather than gains elsewhere dependent on railways. It is not important whether the cheapening of iron from a greater scale of blast furnaces depended on the existence of railways, but only whether the railway demand for iron helped ironmasters to exploit the gains from increased scale of production. Similarly, even if the efficiency of the stock exchange was not dependent on the existence of railways, if the business associated with railways shares and debentures facilitated the improvement of exchange operations for other sectors, then the social returns to railway investment should take account of those effects. There are therefore reasons for believing the calculated social rate of return to be too low.

There are, however, biases in the other direction. We have already mentioned the problem of 'terminal weighting'. There were also negative external economies, i.e. cases in which railways imposed costs on other sectors in the economy. The costs imposed on residents of cheaper housing areas in some cities (Kellett 1969) can exemplify this, although enforced slum clearance is perhaps best thought of as a redistribution of income within the society rather than as a net loss of income.

Evaluation of the net effect of unquantified elements in the social returns to railway investment must be impressionistic, but the judgement can surely be made with confidence that the social returns to investment in railways were greater than the social returns available to any other use of the investment resources. This is, of course, a judgement on the investment as a whole; it is consistent with some misallocation of resources in that certain parts of the railway investment would have been better reallocated either within the railway system or to entirely different uses. Furthermore, the calculations reported here refer to the railway system as developed up to 1865. The social gains were not obtained by one flash of inspiration in which railways were conceived but in a series of developments before and after the introduction of railways (cf. Hawke 1970: 49, 89).

The gain from earlier transport improvements

There is no study of the social saving of canals comparable with that for railways. But it is likely that its order of magnitude for freight traffic would be not dissimilar. The basis of this assertion is shown in table 12.3.

The figures in the table concern coal alone, the largest but by no means the sole freight carried by canals. The key missing information is the average distance for which coal was carried by canal, the average being calculated over the whole output of coal (that is, including the coal for which the 'lead' was zero). We exclude the coal exported from north-east England, even though some of it was probably carried by canals inland from ports in southern England after being carried there by sea. The reduction in cost attributed to canals is the difference between the costs of shipping by canal (not tolls alone) and of land transport used in the study of railways drawn on in the preceding section. It is therefore an estimate of the difference in the cost of both the developed canal system and the improved road system of the early nineteenth century.

We can do no more than guess at the likely lead on canals at the beginning of the nineteenth century. But it is more likely to be near the lower than the higher figures of the table. It has to include all coal other than exports from the north-east, and coal freight on canals was probably at least as concentrated in the north of England as was coal carried on railways in the early 1850s. This would suggest that the social saving on canals in 1800 was a smaller proportion of national income than was that of the railways in 1865. On the other hand, it may be that the contribution of coal was a smaller proportion of the total in the former case, and especially that the inventory effects were then greater (although equally there would be no saving on 'supplementary wagon haulage').

The whole exercise is conjectural, non-factual rather than 'counterfactual' (see pp. 240–41 above), but it does establish that the social saving of canals was probably of the same order of magnitude as that of railways in that it was almost certainly neither a tenth as small, nor ten times as large, relative to national income.

We have to remain even less knowledgeable about the returns to investment in canals. The volume of resources devoted to such investment was certainly less than that embodied in railways and the social saving might therefore be thought to guarantee a substantial social rate of return to the investment. But the social

Table 12.3. *Hypothetical social saving of canals 1800*

(1)	Coal output	11 m. tons.
(2)	North-east exports	2.2 m. tons
(3)	Output ton-miles	
	(a) average lead 20 miles	177 m. ton-miles
	(b) average lead 50 miles	442 m. ton-miles
	(c) average lead 100 miles	883 m. ton-miles
(4)	Reduction in cost	2.6d per ton-mile
(5)	'Social saving'	
	(a)	£1.91 m.
	(b)	£4.8 m.
	(c)	£9.6 m.
(6)	Percentage of GNP	
	(a)	1.4
	(b)	3.4
	(c)	6.9

Notes and sources:
  (1) Deane and Cole (1967: 216)
  (2) Mitchell and Deane (1962: 110) (817000 chaldron of 53 cwt.)
  (3) [(1)−(2)] × specified average distance
  (4) Hawke (1970).
  (5) (3) × (4).
  (6) 1801 GNP. GDP £140 m. at 1851–60 prices. (Feinstein 1978: 82.)

saving incorporates guesses as to the resource cost of canal and land transport. Some part of it was appropriated by the canal companies, if the contemporary allegations of monopoly pricing by canals have any substance at all. (And the reductions of tolls in response to *planned* railways indicates that they had some substance although not as much as often thought.) Some part of the social return to canals was therefore incorporated in the dividend payouts of canals, and, as we have already noted, for the canal system as a whole this was by no means remarkable.

Similarly, we have to admit to ignorance about the economic benefits of the road improvements of the eighteenth and nineteenth centuries. The cost reductions were probably proportionately smaller than those associated with canals and the volume of freight less. But it is probably best to think of the road improvements as more analogous to the passenger traffic of railways, involved most in making personal travel possible.

Social overhead capital and economic development

Britain's experience with transport between 1750 and 1860 raises several interesting questions. Perhaps the two most interesting are the way in which a gap between social and private returns to investment in transport were overcome, and the way in which the social overhead capital in the form of transport was achieved with so little government intervention. Other people might, of course, find more interest in the origins of the innovations whose exploitation has been the key feature of our analysis of transport developments.

There can be little doubt that in all the major transport improvements of the period the private returns to investors did not exhaust the social gains. There were probably differences among the various improvements with the gap being larger in the cases of railways and turnpikes than of canals, but in no case did the gap prevent the investment from being undertaken. There were, it is true, various devices by which some of the social gains from the investment were internalised. Much the most important was the regional nature of transport investment until railways were well established. Those who were the beneficiaries of the uncaptured social gains were the residents of the geographical area served by a particular canal or railway, and the same group constituted the main investors and so recipients of private returns. The coincidence could not, of course, be exact, but it was substantial enough for the social/private gap not to be a major impediment to the investment.

The same point explains why privileged positions for particular interests were relatively unimportant. There were certainly cases of privileges which in modern poor countries would probably be taken as signs of corruption. Freight charges on agricultural commodities and inputs, or on building materials for parish authorities, were sometimes held especially low. Manufacturers and others were sometimes given special consideration in the allocation of shares but generally they were content with equal treatment with other shareholders paying equal tolls and receiving equal dividends rather than offsetting these. Special tolls were more common on turnpikes than on canals. The general eighteenth-century progression towards the impersonality of property (Thompson 1975; Hay et al. 1975) applied to transport investment.

Probably even more important was the simple matter that the private return was sufficient to make transport investment an attractive proposition. Essentially, this was an implication of the wealth of even eighteenth-century Britain relative to many modern poor countries so that investment funds were not guaranteed a high price because of their scarcity. It is likely that the private returns were greater in the fast growing industries of Britain – the high levels of retained profits in many industries would certainly suggest so even when it is recognised that many canal extensions were also financed internally – but the opportunities for investment in family concerns were limited. The implication of this is not so much that investment in social overhead capital was facilitated by imperfections in the capital market as that the available pool of investment resources was much more than could flow into industry, especially given the imperfect channels to the latter.

The limited role of government is explicable in a way clearly related to the foregoing analysis. Transport investment between 1750 and 1860 called for little central direction. A localised organisation was sufficient. The organisation might be a traditional parish authority or municipal corporation, a trust, or a company. In all of these cases, a 'public' component might be identified within it, and even canal and railway companies were expected or required to pay some heed to the interests of the public as well as of their shareholders if in no other way than observing maximum charges. But because the activity was regional rather than national, the central government did not need to be involved after setting such basic rules. (Satisfaction with this arrangement might well owe something to the contemporary near-identification of the interests of the public with those of property-owners.)

That Britain could build its social overhead capital by means of regional activities was fundamentally a result of the slowness of its economic growth relative to that demanded and expected in contemporary poor countries. It is the modern goal of economic growth much faster than that achieved in eighteenth- and nineteenth-century Britain, together perhaps with a greater modern concern about regional equity, which provides the pressure for centralised planning of social overhead capital (although much else is involved in making centralised direction of the economy possible). And it is the modern rate of population growth which has brought housing into the usual classification of social overhead capital while Britain could leave it to private investment.

The slowness of British economic change also highlights the significance of a distinction between development and growth. None of the transport developments discussed here can be regarded as indispensable (although any one of them might be, as can readily be seen by a rough assessment of the social saving of nineteenth-century railways with unimproved roads of 1750 as the only alternative system). And the institutional changes historically associated with the transport changes were probably not dependent on them. The gradual evolution of trusts, through geographically-based companies, to a national capital market could have taken place under some other stimulus, but was historically associated with roads, canals and railways. In the case of England, no major sudden changes were required; there were opportunities for small steps at a time. The turnpike trust could be grafted on to the ancient system of maintaining roads; the limited liability company could be grafted on to trusts and municipal corporations. New sources of investment funds could be tapped gradually. Adaptability is much enhanced when change comes in nearly unnoticeable steps. In Britain between 1750 and 1860 the changes were often concerned with transport.

252

Conclusion

Between 1750 and 1860, the British economy exploited a sequence of innovations which made transport markedly cheaper. While no single innovation can be counted as indispensable, those innovations were of such significance that the economy would have required a substantial grant of free resources from elsewhere to compensate for their absence.

The building of improved inland transport systems was the nearest activity in Britain between 1750 and 1860 to the modern category of social overhead capital. But because England was a rich country, and because the economic growth of the period was not rapid by modern standards and there was no influential aspiration towards such rapid growth, the investment could be implemented on a regional basis by organisations with very little participation by the central government.

13

Social change and the industrial revolution

M. E. ROSE

An industrial revolution?

The British industrial revolution of the late eighteenth and early nineteenth centuries has always had its fascination for the historian interested in social change and social causation. Its earliest historians such as Arnold Toynbee (1890) and John and Barbara Hammond (1911, 1925) were more concerned with its social than with its economic effects. Later historians (Nef 1934; Clark 1953) criticised the oversimplified concept of an 'industrial revolution', arguing that economic change was far more gradual and evolutionary in its development than the dramatic term 'revolution' implied. Nevertheless, social historians have generally rallied to the defence of a concept implying fundamental change within the space of less than a century. Hobsbawm (1962: 46) has argued that 'if the sudden, qualitative and fundamental transformation which happened in or about the 1780s was not a revolution then the word has no commonsense meaning'. Perkin (1969: 1) has described the process as a 'More than Industrial Revolution' in which social causes and effects may play a more important role than a wholly economic one.

The earlier social historians of the British industrial revolution painted a catastrophic picture of the destruction of an old agrarian, co-operative, handicraft society by a new industrial, factory based, competitive one. For Toynbee, the effects of the industrial revolution proved that 'free competition may produce wealth without producing well being' (Toynbee 1890: 93). The Hammonds saw the first results as 'deplorable, for instead of creating a happier, wiser, more self respecting society, this revolution led to the degradation of large masses of people and the rapid growth of town life in which everything was sacrificed to profit' (Hammond 1925: i). Since then, much historical enquiry has been devoted to the effects of the industrial revolution upon the British people, with particular focus upon the contentious question of whether the working classes experienced a rise or a fall in their living standards (chapter 9). Whilst this debate has often generated more heat than light, it has had the effect of directing social historians towards a more quantitative approach to their research. Thus statistical methods, as well as sociological and anthropological concepts, have

253

helped to form the 'new' social history, producing work which is more complex and critical, if at times less easily readable, than that of the earlier school (Blackman & Neild 1976).

For the social historian, the study of English society during this period is complicated by the fact that the pace and nature of social change was being affected not by one, but by four 'revolutions', each closely related to the other and, at some points, inextricably interlocked. At the same time as the industrial revolution was forcing the pace of economic change, the French Revolution of 1789 and its associated ideas were stimulating a critique of the existing political system in Britain and the formation of societies agitating for reform (Brown 1918; Williams 1968). In the sphere of religion, Methodism and Evangelicalism were, from the mid-eighteenth century onwards, effecting a revolutionary change by breathing new, more passionate life into the dry bones of established religion. By the early nineteeth century, the Evangelicals, with their passionate belief in individual salvation, dominated the established Church of England. Their high minded serious approach to life deeply penetrated the higher orders of society, purging it of moral laxity and corruption and preparing the ground for the zealous social reform and rigid morality of the early Victorian era (Bradley 1976; Brown 1961). Despite its break with the Church of England, the official Methodist church remained, after the death of its founder John Wesley in 1791, fiercely loyal to the established political order and intolerant of any radical or reformist movements within its ranks. Nevertheless, Wesley's original mission to the poor was never lost sight of, and the resulting tensions between authoritarian and democratic elements brought numerous breaks with the official church of which the most important was perhaps that of the Primitive Methodists in 1812. These diverse and conflicting elements in Methodism have led to considerable debate amongst historians as to whether it exercised a quietist influence upon working people during the upheavals of industrialisation through its authoritarian structure and other-worldly teaching, or whether, particularly through the more democratic breakaway churches, it provided working people with the organisational experience and the inspiration for participation in secular reformist activity (Hammond 1925: chapter 12; Halevy 1924: part III, chapter I; Wearmouth 1937; Hobsbawm 1957; E. P. Thompson 1963: chapter 11).

Despite its relatively small membership (the 90000 Wesleyan Methodists of 1801 had increased to 358000 by 1851 when the population of England and Wales was nearly eighteen million), there seems little doubt that its cultural impact on English society was a profound one.

The fourth revolution took place in the world of the arts where the Classicism of the eighteenth century was experiencing from 1800 onwards the challenge of the Romantic Movement. Though almost impossible of exact definition Romanticism performed a similar role in the arts to that of Evangelicalism in religion, breathing emotion and individual feeling into the formal structures of classicism (Kitson Clark 1955). Deriving much of its earlier inspiration from the contemporaneous political and economic revolutions, Romanticism was to provide some of the new industrial society's strongest critics from Blake, Wordsworth and Coleridge through Carlyle to William Morris (Williams 1958).

These four revolutions alone, industrial, political, religious and artistic, were sufficient to produce profound change in the society on which they acted and in which they interacted. At a crucial stage in their development, however, Britain was involved between 1793 and 1815 in a long drawn out and strenuous war with France which further speeded up the pace of social change and placed existing institutions under powerful stress. The impact of war on society remains an area requiring more research by social historians (Marwick 1974: 6–14), and the complex business of assessing the social importance of the Revolutionary and Napoleonic wars in Britain has as yet scarcely begun. Nevertheless their role in distorting the pace and shape of social change has to be taken into account in any study of the social history of this period.

The old society and the new

Perhaps the most important change which began to take shape under the pressure of these powerful interacting forces was in the structure of society and the way in which Englishmen regarded their role in it. Pre-industrial society, as depicted by Gregory King in the late seventeenth century, was a hierarchical one of descending ranks and degrees, a mountain country which sloped down from the commanding heights of the landed aristocracy through the uplands of the gentry and the professions and the lower levels occupied by tenant farmers, tradesmen and artisans to the great low plain of the labouring poor and the swamps of pauperism, vagrancy and criminality (King 1696). Patrick Colquhoun, writing in the early nineteenth century, produced a similar map of civil society, whilst at the same time unconsciously forecasting its dissolution by depicting the basis of wealth and income upon which each group rested (Colquhoun 1814). This intricate structure was kept together by the strings of patronage held by those higher in the social scale and by the ropes of dependence which bound those lower down to those above them, the tenant farmer to his landlord or the labourer to his employer (Perkin 1969: 17–62). Alternatively, society might be viewed in terms of a series of vertical interest groups in which high and low came together in a common economic cause, as landowner and tenant farmer might in a landed interest opposing any governmental policy which appeared to favour the mercantile interest to the detriment of agriculture.

Under the stress of industrialisation and war, however, a new ordering of society began to take place. Instead of the pyramidal balance of rank and degree, or the vertical range of interest groups, there emerged the horizontal outlines of a class society. Within this structure, an upper, landed class of aristocrats, squires and parsons overlay a middle, commercial and industrial class of merchants and entrepreneurs beneath which again lay a working class of artisans, factory hands, domestic outworkers and labourers. Between these groups were no bonds of patronage and dependence, but rather barriers of mistrust and antagonism which helped to create, in the two lower groups at least, a common sense of purpose, a class consciousness, which bound the group together horizontally.

It was amongst the commercial and entrepreneurial groups that this consciousness started to form. The term 'middle class' found its first expression in a sociological sense in 1812 (Briggs 1960), after pressure groups of merchants and manufacturers had begun to form in opposition to the Orders in Council. These regulations, which prohibited all trade with France and her allies except through English ports, had been laid down by the government from 1806 onwards as a reply to Napoleon's Continental System which had attempted to prevent trade between Britain and areas of Europe under French control. Many commercial men however saw the Orders in Council as clumsy weapons of war which had done untold damage to overseas trade, not least by raising unnecessarily the hostility of the United States (Halevy 1924: 314–20). Only an ignorant aristocratic government, careless of the well-being of those engaged in manufacture and trade, could have created such havoc at the same time as ever-increasing fiscal burdens were thrust upon merchants and manufacturers. Such men increasingly felt a sense of grievance against the landowning class which claimed all the spoils of social and political power and yet took no part in the productive effort of creating wealth. Theoretical support for this view came from the writings of the economist, David Ricardo. The theory of rent, as propounded in his *Principles of Political Economy*, published in 1817, appeared to show in its popularised version, a parasitic landowning class whose ever increasing rents ate up all increases in national wealth and finally brought the economy to a static state. The economic power of the landed class seemed to the middle class observer to be buttressed by its monopoly of political power both at Westminster and in the shires where the justice of the peace reigned supreme. The Corn Law of 1815 which prohibited the import of foreign corn until the price of the English farmer's wheat reached eighty shillings a quarter, seemed tangible proof of the use of political power for naked class advantage (chapter 10). The Church of England, whose bishops and clergy were closely related to the owners of land, claimed to be the established church of the nation. Although church rates were levied on Anglicans and non-Anglicans alike, the Church used the Test and Corporation Acts to bar non-members of the church from holding public office. In addition, entry to many schools and to the universities of Oxford and Cambridge was restricted to those who subscribed to the doctrines of the established church. Such conduct added a spice of religious persecution to the grievances of the dissenting merchant or the nonconformist millowner, anxious to translate his newly-acquired economic power into social and political terms..

At the same time, the advance of industrialisation and the growing economic power of the middle classes created below them feelings of grievance and hostility. These contributed in this period to what Edward Thompson (1963) has called 'the making of the English working class'. The new industrial worker, harassed by the discipline of the factory bell and by the indiscipline of a squalid urban environment, increasingly resented the demands of an employer with whom he had little relationship except through a meagre wage payment. Equally, as Thompson as shown, those outside the new textile factories, artisans, domestic outworkers and field labourers reacted with varying degrees of hostility to the pressures of economic change which were made more grievous by wartime shortage and inflation, and by postwar slump and unemployment (E. P. Thompson 1963: chapters 7–10, 14). Corn laws, poor law reform, and savage repression of organised protest such as the Peterloo Massacre of 1819, appeared to indicate the end of the protective role exercised by the higher orders in the old hierarchical society (Perkins 1969: 183–96). The French Revolutionary ideals of liberty and equality mingled with the older ideal of the 'Free Born Englishman' in the writings of Tom Paine and William Cobbett. The economics of Ricardo appeared, as translated by the 'labour economists' of the 1820s, to indicate that labour was the sole source of wealth (Menger 1899). The alternative types of society, visualised by utopians like William Godwin and Robert Owen (Harrison 1969), helped to create an ideology for this working class. Spa Fields, Peterloo and Tolpuddle gave it its first martyrs (E. P. Thompson 1963: chapter 15). By the third decade of the nineteenth century, the three-class structure of English society was, it seemed, complete.

Urbanisation

Nowhere was this new order of society more clearly visible than in the rapidly growing industrial towns of northern and midland England. By 1851, there were sixty-three towns in England and Wales with over 20000 inhabitants; in 1801 there had been only fifteen. The most rapid period of growth occurred in the decade 1820–30 when Manchester, Birmingham, Sheffield and Leeds all experienced growth rates in excess of 40 per cent (Weber 1899: 52).

These rapidly expanding and changing communities provided the base from which the middle classes could launch their attack on landed class privilege. The first half of the nineteenth century saw the rise of a lively and influential provincial press. The columns of the *Leeds Mercury*, the *Bradford Observer*, the *Manchester Guardian* and its more radical rival, the *Manchester Examiner*, were filled with demands for the reform of institutions and the reduction of aristocratic and landed privilege in economic, political and religious spheres (Read 1961;

Fraser 1976). Opinion forming and the development of a civic and a class consciousness was also aided by the regular meeting of merchants, manufacturers and professional men in the voluntary societies which were a feature of the new towns. Economic organisations like chambers of commerce, cultural ones like literary and philosophic societies, and philanthropic ones for the relief or education of the poor, all provided regular forums for the discussion, both formal and informal, of ideals and grievances (Cullen 1975; Thackray 1974). Campaigns to resist church rates or to wrest control of local government from existing oligarchies, which culminated in the struggles for incorporation under the terms of the 1835 Municipal Reform Act, gave further cohesion to the urban middle class and fired it with the stimulus of political success (Fraser 1976; Hennock 1973).

From this firmly entrenched local base, it was possible to launch into the national struggle for parliamentary reform in the early 1830s. The Reform Act of 1832 provided a uniform borough franchise which, although it excluded most members of the working classes, gave separate parliamentary representation to expanding industrial towns; these had previously been represented only through the county in which they were situated. Parliamentary reform however proved a severe disappointment to middle class radicals. County and small borough constituencies, dominated by landowners, remained heavily overrepresented in the parliament. Aristocratic influence in government seemed little disturbed. After a burst of reform legislation, culminating in the Municipal Reform Act of 1835 which abolished the old oligarchical borough corporations and provided for the establishment of ratepayer elected town councils, the Whig ministry seemed to run out of steam and appeared careless of middle class desires. The resulting dissatisfaction led to the creation of what was perhaps the most powerful of all early nineteenth century urban, middle class pressure groups, the Anti Corn Law League. Despite its anxiety to appeal to the industrial working class and to the tenant farmer and rural labourer, the League was, as its leader Richard Cobden recognised, an urban middle class organisation which conducted its campaigns on middle class lines and was reliant on industrial and commercial wealth and organisational expertise (McCord 1958). Free trade, 'that great idol moulded in Manchester and electroplated in Birmingham', as Richard Oastler, the factory reformer, described it, proved a powerful element in the formation of an urban middle class consciousness.

If urban growth was a major factor in forcing the development of a confident, aggressive middle class, it was equally effective in stimulating a challenge from below to that middle class hegemony in the shape of an industrial working class. The wealthier classes retreated from the increasing noise and dirt of town centres to reside in the healthier suburbs. Here they could create, as in Manchester's Victoria Park, or Birmingham's Edgbaston, ghettoes protected against encroachment, legally by leases and other devices and sometimes physically by gates and fences. By contrast, the inner districts of the town became increasingly crowded with those who had come to seek employment in industrial and mercantile enterprises. Thus the town developed as a geographical expression of the new class society. Engels, in a graphic description of Manchester in 1844, portrayed the concentric circles of residence for working people, the middle and the upper bougeoisie, each sharply separated from the other, and with the main roads into the city lined with small shops so that the wealthy merchant travelling in his coach from Victoria Park or Cheetham Hill to do business in the Exchange would glimpse only the decent façade of the shopkeeper and be spared the view of the overcrowded tenements and noisome cellar dwellings which lay behind them (Engels 1845: 54–6; Marcus 1974).

As with the middle classes, however, urban concentration facilitated the growth of working class organisations, friendly societies, trade societies and political clubs, and the circulation of cheap 'unstamped' newspapers and pamphlets which were eagerly read by the more educated, politically articulate artisan or factory workers (Hollis 1970). From this base of local organisation and education came support for national pressure groups like the Ten Hours Movement for factory reform and the Anti Poor Law Movement for the repeal of the hated Poor Law Amendment act of 1834 (Ward 1962; Edsall 1971). From the 1790s on, working men had been involved in agitation for parliamentary reform, activity whicn culminated in mass meetings and demonstrations prior to the Reform Act of 1832. Disappointment at their exclusion from the franchise under this measure and anger at the Whig reforms of the early 1830s such as the Poor Law Amendment Act led to the creation of the Chartist Movement in the late 1830s. Despite its eventual failure, Chartism, with its strongest bases in urban, industrial areas, seemed proof positive of the emergence of a conscious organised working class, ready to challenge the monopoly of economic and political power exercised both by the old landed ruling class and by the new commercial middle class (Hovell 1918; Briggs 1959a; Ward 1970).

Alarmed by the increasing gulf between the classes which urbanisation was creating, members of the upper and middle classes attempted, by means of philanthropic activity often of a religious nature, to build social bridges across the widening chasm. Statistical societies investigated the educational and material condition of the poor in cities like Manchester or London (Cullen 1975). Town missions organised schemes of visiting working class homes and aimed, inspired in part by the work of the Scottish divine Thomas Chalmers, to restore the old hierarchical order of society by reviving the parochial system in inner urban areas (Owen 1965: 225–8; Young and Ashton 1956: 67–80). Concerned writers like Benjamin Disraeli, Charles Kingsley and Elizabeth Gaskel used the medium of fiction to warn their readers of the division of society into two nations (Cazamian 1973; Tillotson 1954). For some observers of the urban scene in the 1840s, however, it seemed that the warnings came too late and that the efforts at reconciliation were too feeble to prevent social catastrophe. Friedrich Engels, from the standpoint of Manchester, could confidently predict the imminence and inevitability of open class warfare (Engels 1845: 336).

Three classes or more?

Numerous explanations have been put foward by historians to explain why, despite deepening class divisions, England emerged relatively unscathed from the troubled decades of the early nineteenth century and entered a period of relative social stability, an 'age of equipoise' in mid-century (Burn 1964). The flexibility of the landed aristocracy in surrendering indefensible outworks of privilege, the institutionalisation of class conflict by channelling it through middle class pressure groups or working class trades unions, the process of liberalisation which used the widening economic and social differentials between skilled and unskilled workers to divide the working class and and bring the skilled labour aristocracy into the orbit of middle class liberalism, all these have been advanced as explanations of this relative social stability in the face of rapid social change (Kitson Clark 1962; Perkin 1969; Foster 1974). Implicit or explicit in all these explanations, however, is the realisation that English society in this period was more complex than the rather simple three class model discussed so far in this chapter can allow for. William Dodd, writing in 1847 with an American readership in mind, portrayed English society as being divided into eight classes. First came the royal family, followed by the nobility, and then by a third class 'the millionaires commonly called the vulgar rich' which contained those who had 'amassed immense wealth by manufactures, commerce, railroad speculation etc.' Fourthly came a class composed of 'clergy, professional gentlemen, merchants, tradesmen etc.' and fifthly the 'higher order of mechanics' who shared this position with shopkeepers. The sixth class consisted of 'manufacturing, agricultural and many other kinds of labourers' getting their living by 'the sweat of their brow' but without having to serve a lengthy apprenticeship to any trade. Below this large group, Dodd envisaged two further classes, one of paupers and the other of thieves, gamblers, prostitutes and similar social outcasts. Classes one and two, in Dodd's view, constituted the head of society and seven and eight the tail. The first five classes were the 'lawmakers', whilst the sixth, seventh and eighth had 'nothing to do with laws except obey' (Dodd 1847: 9–10). Such a model implies a less simple structure of society than a three class division and contains strong survivals of the old hierarchical society. Other Victorian writers with their use of the plural 'middle classes' or 'working classes' seem to have been visualising a more intricately structured society whose best pictorial representation is perhaps the painting *Work* by the Pre-Raphaelite artist, Ford Madox Brown. Thus the use of the three class model for the analysis of early-nineteenth-century English society has all the dangers of using a kitchen knife to dissect a flower. A more finely edged tool is required to reveal all the intricacies of the system.

R. S. Neale has suggested that a five class rather than a three class model may be of more value to the historian (Neale 1968). In this model, the upper class is retained at the head of the authority structure, but the middle class is split into a middle class of successful merchants, entrepreneurs and professional men lying close to the upper class and deferential towards it, and a middling class of petit bourgeois, intellectuals and artisans who have little hope of rising into the upper class and are therefore non-deferential and critical of it. Similarly, in Neale's model, the working class is divided into a group composed of industrial workers, both factory and domestic, who are collectivist and non-deferential in their attitudes, and another group consisting of agricultural and other low paid workers, domestic servants, and female workers who were deferential and dependent in their attitudes towards authotity. This model is by no means a perfect one since it seems designed largely to highlight the existence of the middling class which Neale discussed extensively to the neglect of the other groups. Nevertheless it demonstrates the need for historians to approach the social structure of early industrial society in England with a finer analytical tool.

The upper classes

A closer examination of the upper classes reveals that the activities and attitudes of some sectors of it, particularly the aristocracy, belie the simplistic idea of implacable hostility between an industrial middle class and an indolent landed one. Many landowners established close links with urban industrial society through their interests in mining or transport developments in connection with their landed estates, or through their ownership of large areas of development land in expanding industrial towns (Spring 1971; F. M. L. Thompson 1963). At the same time, commercial and industrial wealth was, as in the old society, used to acquire landed estate. Counties like Cheshire experienced the inward migration of wealthy Lancashire industrialists who were accepted into county society along with the more traditional social leaders (Lee 1963). Across the Pennines, great landowners in the West Riding of Yorkshire like Earl Fitzwilliam and Viscount Halifax preferred co-operation to conflict with the increasingly powerful industrial interests in the county's expanding manufacturing towns. The public schools, in the late eighteenth and early nineteenth centuries, had been viewed with distaste by middle class parents as bastions of privilege in which the sons of the aristocracy were schooled in indolence and vice. From the 1820s, however, under the influence of reforming headmasters, of whom the most famous was Thomas Arnold of Rugby, the schools began to emphasise higher moral ideals and standards. This more intense, moralistic educational system appealed to the wealthier industrialists, merchants and professional men. They therefore began

262

to send their sons to schools like Rugby or Winchester, or to the new public schools like Cheltenham or Rossall founded in the 1840s and 1850s on Arnoldian lines (Bamford 1967; Newsome 1961; Simon and Bradley 1975). At these institutions, boys from a wealthy commercial background mingled with the sons of aristocrats and landed gentlemen. In addition, the practice of primogeniture, whereby only the eldest son of a landowner succeeded to the family estates, meant that, as in the past, younger sons had to seek careers in the professions or in trade, thus ensuring that no rigid barrier of social caste could come between the landed and the upper middle classes. Marriage too aided the fusion of the old and new ruling classes, but the divisions between them had always been less dramatic and clear cut than Anti Corn Law propaganda had made it appear.

The middle classes

Even greater diversity is apparent when the label 'middle class' is closely scrutinised. Whilst the numbers covered by this term were relatively small, less than 5 per cent of the total population in 1851, they were richly diverse in their interests and attitudes. An income of £100 to £150 a year, the ability to employ at least one domestic servant and to maintain respectable standards of housing, food and clothing provided certain minimal material qualifications for middle class membership (Harrison 1971: 87–121; Banks 1954). Church or chapel going, a strong belief in hard work and individual self reliance coupled with a deep respect for the sanctity of family life together constituted the minimal behavioural ones. For contemporaries, the successful entrepreneur was the ideal 'middle class' type, particularly if he appeared to be a self made man whose success was the result of his own qualities of perseverance or industry. In fact, such historical research as has been carried out on entrepreneurial origins has shown that the wholly self made man coming from rags to riches was rare. Most new entrants to an industry moved from a secure if modest base in a small farming or in the merchanting branches of the trade (Payne 1974; Chapman 1967; Edwards 1967).

If the wholly self made man was something of a mythical figure, the big industrialist, William Dodd's 'millionaire' was by no means typical of the entrepreneurial group even in new, technologically advanced industries like cotton (Gatrell 1977). The small manufacturer or merchant, the factory manager, the shopkeeper or the clerk were numerically more significant within the middle class, although they are only just beginning to attract the attention of historians (Crossick 1977; Anderson 1976; Mayer 1975).

One important group which has merited some historical research has been that of the professional middle class. This expanded rapidly in this period as industrialisation made greater demands upon old professions like law, restructured others like medicine and created new ones like engineering (Reader 1966). Whilst sharing many aspects of consumption and behaviour with other middle class groups, professional men stood somewhat aloof from the entrepreneurial ideal of individual competition as a recipe for success. Indeed some members of the professional middle class became increasingly critical of a social system based on free and unrestricted competition. They saw their role as that of the disinterested expert intervening in the struggle between capital and labour in the interests of the fair and efficient functioning of the whole society. This was a role which was to bring them into conflict with other members of their class (Perkin 1969: 252–70).

The working classes

If a relatively small group in numerical terms like the middle classes contained within it such a diversity of groups, it is unlikely that the large body of manual workers would fit snugly under any such umbrella term as 'labour' or 'the working class'. Thomas Wright, a skilled worker who contributed many articles to mid-nineteenth-century periodicals under the pseudonym of 'The Journeyman Engineer', complained of those who talked of the 'working class' as if it was a uniform body of men and women (Wright 1871). His contemporary, the statistical writer Robert Dudley Baxter, found that, in terms of income distribution, manual labourers grouped naturally into 'three great classes' shown in table 13.1. The first group was composed of skilled workers in industries like instrument making, shipbuilding, printing, iron and steel manufacture, building and cabinet making. This corresponds fairly closely to the concept of a 'labour aristocracy', an élite group within the working class enjoying high wages and relative security of employment. This favourable position was maintained by exploiting the scarcity value of their skills, restricting entry to their trade by enforcing stringent apprenticeship regulations through the mechanism of well organised trade societies. Despite the undermining of craft exclusivity in some trades by the introduction of machinery or by the evasion of apprenticeship regulations by employers anxious to obtain the entry of unskilled female or juvenile workers into the trade, the labour aristocrat remained a figure of considerable importance during the industrial revolution (Chaloner 1969). Indeed, according to Hobsbawm, it was perhaps only in the 1840s and 1850s that the labour aristocracy became a recognisable feature of the industrial scene. It emerged during these decades from the mass of petty producers and small masters of preindustrial society (Hobsbawm 1964b). Industrialisation, far from destroying the labour aristocracy and forcing the skilled worker down into an undifferentiated proletariat, initially gave it greater coherence and cohesion.

Nevertheless the artisans in this period are often difficult to distinguish from small employers and tradesmen who, it might be argued, belong in social

264

Table 13.1. *Wages and earnings of the working class 1868*

	Persons	Average weekly wages (men)	Net annual earnings
1. Higher skilled labour and manufacturers	1 123 000	28s.–35s.	£56 149 000
2. Lower skilled labour and manufacturers	3 819 000	21s.–25s.	£127 921 000
3. Agriculture and unskilled labour	2 843 000	12s.–20s.	£70 659 000

Source: Baxter (1868).

classification to the lower middle class. As William Dodd recognised when he included shopkeepers along with mechanics in his fifth class, there was a considerable overlap not only in work skills and practices but also in broader social attitudes and values between tradesmen, small employers and skilled workers. A desire for education which went beyond mere reading and writing or the acquisition of occupational skills, a sense of independence bringing with it a hatred of oppression and corruption, freedom of belief which might involve a common bond of nonconformity in provincial England and of secularism in London, all helped to blur any class division between lower middle and skilled working class.

Such sharing of ideals did not involve the adoption of middle class values by the skilled worker. If he valued independence he sought it within the collective framework of the trade union, the cooperative or the friendly society, rather than in the individualism of the middle classes. Standing well within the craft and in local society usually meant more to him than a desire for getting on which might carry him out of both (Crossick 1978). Whilst conscious of the gulf separating him from the unskilled labourer, the ideals of independence from those above him and of solidarity with fellow members of his own craft, together with a degree of political education, might make him a formidable fighter for working class rights in the shape of trades union liberties or franchise reform (Harrison 1965; Tholfsen 1976). It is not surprising that artisans together with outworkers are in the centre of Edward Thompson's picture of the making of the English working class (E. P. Thompson 1963: chapter 8).

Next in Baxter's classification came those workers involved in less skilled labour and manufactures. This included those employed in a wide range of manufacturing industries together with miners, transport workers and servants. Some of those included, railway workers for example, belonged to a newly created trade, whilst others, like cotton workers, had experienced a revolutionary change in the nature and conditions of their work as a result of machine production and the spread of the factory system. Although they lacked the high earning power and craft exclusivity of the labour aristocracy, the members of this group, with the exception of servants, probably corresponded fairly closely to Neale's group of non-deferential workers, which he labelled Working Class A (Neale 1968: 23). By the middle of the nineteenth century, many of them, cotton workers and coal miners for example, were organised into trades unions and were beginning to articulate their grievances against employers or government.

Baxter's lowest class was dominated by agricultural and other general labourers, with public service workers and workers in rural industries like glove making or straw plaiting also falling into this category. Industrialisation had done little to improve the lot of this sector of the working classes. In agriculture the rural population increase of the late eighteenth and early nineteenth centuries, together with the fall in farm prices after 1815 and the extreme seasonality of labour demand in arable areas, had produced labour surpluses and low earnings which out-migration was only just beginning to ease by the mid-nineteenth century (Jones 1964a). The movement of rural workers and of Irish immigrants to urban areas produced pools of unskilled labour which were rarely fully drained even in periods of economic prosperity. Underemployment, insecurity and low earning thus characterised this sector of the working classes, who as a consequence generally proved deferential and non-militant.

Working women

It is significant that women workers constituted only about 5 per cent of Baxter's higher skilled group, whilst they were of considerable importance in the two lower groups. In the lower skilled group, for example, they constituted about 15 per cent of the total number if the maidservants and young girls in domestic service, whom Baxter included in this group, are excluded. If, however, female domestics are included, women workers then account for about 45 per cent of the group. In the lowest class of unskilled workers, women accounted for over 30 per cent of the total number, some of them like laundresses, seamstresses, milliners and furriers being amongst the lowest paid workers of this low paid category, with wages of around twelve shillings a week.

The role of women in the industrialising economy is in fact a far more complex problem than is implied by the traditional picture of the middle class wives and daughters imprisoned within the home whilst working class women flooded to the new factories. Factory employment for women was largely confined to textiles and thus regionally concentrated particularly in the cotton manufacturing areas of Lancashire and Cheshire. Even here, cotton factories did not provide long-term employment for women. The bulk of female factory operatives were teenage girls, half of whom left in their early twenties to get married (Hewitt 1958:

9–18). Whilst a working wife could prove a valuable asset to the income of a working class family, work after marriage was by no means as common as middle class reformers believed. Such reformers were anxious about the physical and moral comfort of homes where the wife and mother was away at work all day. But in Preston, a town dominated by the cotton industry, only about 26 per cent of wives living with their husbands worked in 1851, and many of these were younger women and those with few or no children to care for (Anderson 1971: 71). Thus many working class wives, like their middle class sisters, were confined to household duties in this period, and did not seek pecuniary employment. A working wife may well be an indicator of a family dwelling close to or below the poverty line.

Industrialisation in its early stages may well have reduced rather than increased the opportunities for female employment. Thus women who wished to work, or more commonly had to work to supplement meagre family incomes or to support a family where the husband was dead, incapacitated or unemployed, did not find employment easily, and often had to seek it in low-paid sweated industries or in domestic service. The latter employment expanded rapidly as middle class incomes rose in the early and mid-nineteenth century. It played a vital role in absorbing some of the surplus female labour in this period. In London in 1861, one woman in every three in the 15–24 age group was employed in domestic service (McBride 1976: 4). Thirty years earlier, in the cotton town of Todmorden, female factory operatives protested bitterly about the suggestion of some middle class reformers that women should be excluded from factories. Such a measure, they argued, would force them to seek employment in dressmaking or domestic service where they would become 'ill used, genteel little slaves' (Pinchbeck 1930: 199–200). In the early stages of the industrial revolution, there was little alternative to this fate for most women who had to seek paid employment.

Baxter's tripartite division of the working class, based as it was upon occupational and income differences, by no means fully illustrates the complex structure of the working classes in this period. Even such relatively concrete factors as wages, incomes and consumption patterns might differ widely between industry and industry, or between region and region (Hunt 1973). Less quantifiable aspects of working class behaviour, religious belief or political attitudes for example, are even less capable of being summed up in any general statement: like the Cheshire Cat, the working class is rarely visible as a complete whole in this period. More important for the historian is the recognition and understanding of such parts as are visible.

The survival of community: migration and kinship patterns

By the mid-nineteenth century the social structure of England was therefore far more complex than the three-class model of society allows for. This is indicative of the strong survival of many features of the old society. Foster, whilst admitting that the industrial revolution did have some massive social effects, points out that 'one thing not included in these effects was the coming of some altogether new and "open" industrial society. Instead what we are faced with is the breakdown of an old type of social structure, a transformation in the cultural organisation of the labour community' (Foster 1974: 41). Edward Thompson has shown that those who contributed to the making of the English working class 'did not pass, in one generation, from the peasantry to the industrial town' (E. P. Thompson 1963: 914). The factory and the large town were far from being the dominant spheres of work and life even by the mid-nineteenth century. Half the population still lived in the countryside in 1851, and another 15 per cent lived in towns with less than 20000 inhabitants (Weber 1899: 47). Agriculture still employed over 20 per cent of the occupied population, and domestic or small workshop industries based on handicraft trades like shoemaking or tailoring ran the factory based cotton industry close in terms of numbers employed (Kitson Clark 1962: 113–15). Whilst it would be wrong to ignore the fact that agrarian or handicraft work had been substantially affected in many ways by the industrial revolution, it is nevertheless essential to grasp the small-scale, local nature of much social change between 1780 and 1860.

Whilst population during this period was growing more rapidly in industrial than in rural areas and there was a constant stream of migrants from the countryside into the town, most migratory movements were of a short distance nature. A high proportion of immigrants made a journey of ten miles or less, and few came very great distances (Redford 1926). An analysis of migrants who lived in Preston in 1851 shows that over 40 per cent were less than ten miles from their place of origin, only 30 per cent were more than 30 miles away, and only 2 per cent of the sample had been born more than 100 miles from Preston (chapter 11; Anderson 1971: 37). Thus contacts with friends and relatives in their home villages may not have been entirely lost by many of the new residents of the industrial towns.

Nor did movement to the industrial towns necessarily shatter kinship links and leave newcomers friendless and alone in an anonymous environment. Anderson's detailed research into household and family structure in Preston, as revealed by the returns of the 1851 Census, has shown the tendency of people to dwell close to their kinsfolk. Family and kinship assistance remained important in the crises which affected people in early industrial society. The newly married, the unemployed, the widowed and orphaned often had little choice but to seek help from relatives, when the only alternative aids were those of patronising philanthropy and scanty poor relief (Anderson 1971: 151).

Residential and social differentiation may well have been less marked in smaller industrial towns like Preston or Chorley than in large cities like Manchester or Birmingham (Ward 1975; Warnes 1973). Even the larger cities differed considerably in their industrial and social structures. Engels saw the gap between employer and worker widening in Manchester. But in cities dominated by small craft industries, such as Sheffield or Birmingham, masters and their skilled employees or journeymen were often barely distinguishable (Briggs 1952). London, which the Hammonds saw as being 'scarcely touched by the Industrial Revolution', in fact saw many of its industries such as tanning, heavy engineering or shipbuilding destroyed by provincial competition. The effect of this was to 'accentuate its pre-industrial characteristics', leaving it deficient in semi-skilled factory occupations, but with a great mass of unskilled labour which crowded into the sweated industries of the East End (Stedman Jones 1971).

Differences in economic and social structure were reflected in differences in political attitudes and in degrees of class consciousness. Thus the extreme class consciousness of Oldham was barely reflected in Northampton and scarcely existed at all in South Shields (Foster 1968). Working class political movements functioned most effectively at local level, and achieved any national cohesion only with difficulty. The motive force for the 'Plug Plot' strike of 1842 was essentially a local one and was not imposed from above by the Chartist executive (Foster 1974). Chartism itself differed in its nature and in the degree of support for it according to the locality in which it developed (Briggs 1959a).

Local and central government

The strong provincialism of English life in this period was evidenced in the system of local government, which proved flexible in the face of the social problems created by industrialisation, urbanisation and population growth. Where existing authorities, such as antiquated courts or self-interested borough corporations proved inadequate to the task, energetic inhabitants often promoted local acts of parliament. These conferred the power of levying rates in order to finance measures of town improvement on *ad hoc* bodies of improvement commissioners, trustees and the like (Passfield and Webb 1922; Fraser 1976; Gill 1948). In this way, town centres were paved, lit and policed.

In other areas, the existing parish or township system was reformed through the establishment of a select vestry of leading inhabitants which met regularly to scrutinise the expenditure and activities of the parish officers. Full time salaried officers, like assistant overseers, were appointed in some parishes to aid the overburdened, part-time parish officials. Such reforms often brought with them greater stringency in rate expenditure, particularly in the granting of poor relief.

Workhouse tests and other policies designed to deter all but the really destitute from turning to the parish for financial aid were introduced well in advance of the Poor Law Amendment Act of 1834, which aimed at the adoption of such policies nationally under the scrutiny of the Poor Law Commission, a central authority based in London (Marshall 1968).

The idea of policies being promulgated and enforced by experts in central government was frequently regarded with hostility in the localities. Localism, the belief that the man on the spot, justice of the peace, poor law overseer or town councillor, knew what was required for his own parish or borough without being advised by Whitehall proved to be a major force in restricting the growth of any powerful centralised bureaucratic government in this period.

Indeed, the early part of this period saw the withdrawal of government from areas of control which it has traditionally exercised since the sixteenth and seventeenth centuries. In commercial policy the gradual reduction of tariffs and the removal of export and import prohibitions from the 1820s onwards culminated in the repeal of the Corn Laws in 1846 and of the Navigation Acts in 1849. This spelt the end of the old mercantilist policies whereby government regulated commerce in the interests of the nation (Imlah 1949). In social policy, the repeal of statutes which gave powers to justices of the peace to fix minimum wages or to regulate apprenticeship would seem to indicate a similar trend towards complete freedom for individual employers and employees to make their own bargains regardless of external regulation (E. P. Thompson 1963; Perkin 1969). In social as distinct from commercial policy however it was recognised that complete freedom would be an absurdity and a dangerous one at that. Concern for the material and moral conditions of the lower classes, particularly those employed in new industries and living in industrial towns, was combined with a fear of their increasing numbers and discontents. Such concern brought powerful pressures for legislation and regulation, to which governments tended to respond in an *ad hoc* fashion, dealing with each problem piecemeal as it arose rather than according to any ideological blueprint for reform.

In the sphere of factory reform, the Factory Act of 1833 appointed factory inspectors. These were responsible to the Home Secretary for ensuring that the Act's regulations with regard to the hours, working conditions and education of child factory workers were observed by the employers (Hutchins and Harrison 1903). In public health, an area of social policy in which central government was late in intervening, the 1848 Public Health Act established a General Board of Health in London to persuade local authorites to improve the sanitary condition of their districts, and to provide help and advice in overcoming the numerous problems they encountered (Frazer 1950). New centralised bodies such as these tended to create their own administrative momentum, providing a feedback mechanism by which inspectors in their reports to ministers suggested improvements and extensions to existing legislation (Perkin 1969: 330). In addition, the appointment of strong-minded and outspoken civil servants to these departments helped to further the extension of their role. Men like Edwin Chadwick at the Poor Law Commission and later at the General Board of Health, Sir James Kay Shuttleworth at the Education Department of the Privy Council, or Sir John Simon at its Medical Department after 1858, had clear ideas of the policies they wished their departments to pursue and rarely lost an opportunity to impress them on ministers or on the public (Finer 1952; Smith 1923; Lambert 1963). Far from initiating the later tradition of the anonymous neutral civil servant, they acted as 'statesmen in disguise', attempting to make and influence public policy (Kitson Clark 1959). In these attempts they were often aided by the activity of pressure groups such as the Health of Towns Association in the sphere of public health or the Ten Hours Movement for factory reform (Ward 1970; Hollis 1974). Public opinion too, if roused by a scandal such as that created by Edwin Chadwick's exposure of appalling sanitary conditions in his *Report on the Sanitary Condition of the Labouring Population* of 1842 or by the graphic descriptions of the conditions of employment of women and children in coal mines contained in the report of the Royal Commission on the Employment of Children in Mines of the same year, could prove a useful if somewhat fickle ally in pressing for the extention of government powers (Flinn 1965: introduction; Hammond 1923).

Thus, little by little, the powers of central government in matters of social policy were extended. After 1844, female workers in textile factories, as well as children and young persons, were protected by the Factory Acts. In 1867, the Acts were extended from textiles to other trades, hitherto unregulated, such as metalworking, paper and glassmaking (Hutchins and Harrison 1903:150–72). In 1866, the Sanitary Act gave central government the power to compel local authorities to carry out certain minimal sanitary functions, instead of merely relying on persuasion as hitherto. In 1875, the Public Health Act consolidated a whole mass of earlier legislation and gave England a sanitary code which was well adapted to the needs of a maturing industrial society (Frazer 1950: 114–25). Despite these advances, the role of government in the early and mid-nineteenth century remained a very limited one. There was hostility to increased taxation and suspicion of the corruption and nepotism which might flourish if too many civil service posts were created. This kept new departments small and inspectorates chronically understaffed. The Poor Law Board had a permanent staff of only forty-eight by mid-century, and twelve poor law inspectors were expected between them to visit and check on the relief policies being pursued in six hundred poor law unions (Roberts 1960: 119–20). Four inspectors and fifteen sub-inspectors had to ensure that the law was being observed in 4600 factories in England and Wales in 1845 (Djang 1942: 35). In the sphere of education, sixteen schools inspectors had the task of inspecting and reporting on 4400 schools in receipt of government grants in 1850 (Hurt 1971a: 53). Victorian parsimony and suspicion of government ensured that the Victorian administrative state, despite the efforts of some of its founders, was kept in a condition in which it could not exercise too much power. Thus much of the power and initiative in social reform in this period was exercised at local level by public authorities or by philanthropic societies. This was particularly true of two vitally important areas of social policy, education and poor relief.

In the sphere of education, private provision of schooling whether from commercial or philanthropic motives was universal. Before 1870, the only provision of schools by government, whether local or national, was in the shape of workhouse schools for the child inmates of these institutions. The major obstacle to any further government provision of education was the delicate question of religion. The Church of England claimed that as the state church it must assume responsibility for religious education in any schools provided by the state. Nonconformists were naturally hostile to any suggestion that schools financed from rates and taxes paid by them should instruct pupils in the tenets of an alien faith. Thus Parliamentary bills to provide some measure of state education were defeated in 1807, in 1820 and again in 1843. By way of compromise, the government in 1833 agreed to provide £20000 to aid the school building activities of the two major voluntary societies concerned with school provision, the Anglican National Society and the Nonconformist British and Foreign Schools Society. In 1839, the grant was increased and strings were attached. Schools receiving government grants were henceforth to do so only on condition that they agreed to be visited by a government appointed schools inspector who would report on their efficiency and advise on methods of improvement. The inspectors were controlled by the Education Department of the Privy Council headed by the energetic Dr James Kay (later Sir James Kay Shuttleworth). Under Kay's direction the Department was successful in continually increasing the educational grants, directing a good deal of money to the training and salaries of teachers. By 1860, the £20000 of 1833 had swollen to £800000, and a Royal Commission was enquiring into 'the present state of popular education in England' (Sturt 1967: 238–41).

Concern about the state of popular education increased rapidly during this period. Education was regarded as an essential medium of social control for the growing industrial populations. As well as teaching reading and writing, the schoolmaster could instil the virtues of hard work, obedience and Christian morality (Johnson 1970). 'The preservation of internal peace not less than the improvement of our national institutions depends on the education of the working classes', pronounced Dr Kay in his survey of the condition of the working classes in Manchester in 1832 (Kay 1832). The voices of those who had argued that to educate a labouring man was folly since it would make him discontented with his lot were drowned by those who cried that the safety of the state and the maintenance of Christian morality depended upon the proper education of the working classes. At the same time, politically articulate working men, many of them drawn from the artisan groups, argued the importance of education as a means of getting their fellow workers to read and think for themselves and not merely accept the dictates of government, church or employer (Harrison 1961).

There existed a strong demand for, and interest in, education from all social classes during the industrial revolution. As a result, despite the tardiness of governmental aid, large numbers of schools came into existence in this period. In 1851, census enumerators discovered a total of 44 836 day schools and 23 173 Sunday schools in England and Wales (Coleman 1972). These ranged from schools provided by the large philanthropic societies like the National Society, which by 1830 had 3670 schools with 346 000 pupils, to small dame schools and private adventure schools kept by elderly women or unemployed workmen; these were wholly dependent for their survival upon the small fees paid by pupils (Sturt 1967). At the same time, there was almost continuous enquiry by government committees and by unofficial bodies like statistical societies into the extent and efficiency of this educational provision for the working classes (Cullen 1975: 65–9). These enquiries produced great masses of statistical and literary evidence, much of it conflicting. Recent historians have used these statistics to continue the debate but without reaching any very positive conclusions about the effectiveness of working class schooling (West 1970; Hurt 1971a). Given the universality of fee paying and the difficulties of regular attendance in areas where there was demand for child labour or where older children were kept at home to mind younger brothers and sisters, a child's school life was normally brief and irregular. Thus, as is argued elsewhere, literacy rates probably rose only slowly during the industrial revolution (chapter 11). Educational opportunity was closely linked to social status and the degree of economic security enjoyed. Thus the worst areas of educational deprivation were the inner areas of the larger towns. It was here that private enterprise, commercial or philanthropic, had least effect, and where governmental intervention and universal compulsory schooling was most required in the later nineteenth century. Even after 1870, however, it was local government in the shape of the school board and the school rate rather than national government, which was given the major role in providing schooling where the voluntary system had proved inadequate.

Ranking with education as a medium of control in this industrialising society came the relief of the poor. Since the sixteenth century, each parish in England and Wales had been statutorily responsible for the relief of its destitute members. An overseer of the poor, elected annually by the parish vestry meeting, was responsible for carrying out this unwelcome task under the supervision of the local justice of the peace. By the early nineteenth century, criticism of this amateur *ad hoc* system of relief was growing. Nationally the cost of poor relief was mounting rapidly. From about £2 millions in 1754, it rose to £4 million in

1801 and was nearly £6 million by the end of the French wars in 1815. The onset of peace brought no reduction in costs, however, and expenditure rose to over £7 million in 1819. After this, it stabilised at around £5 millions, but from the mid-1820s began to rise until by 1831 it has passed the £7 million mark once more. In the face of these rising costs, increasing scrutiny and criticism was directed against the poor relief system. Much parliamentary time was spent, both in committee and debate, in examining the alleged defects of the poor law. Scores of pamphlets, many of them penned in country rectories, appeared suggesting either the total abolition of the poor law or its drastic reform (Poynter 1969). The chief object of blame was the system of local administration. Overseers had weakly given way in the face of the importunate demands of the able bodied poor. Magistrates had aided, abetted and even compelled overseers to follow the line of least resistance. Particular criticism was voiced against the allowance system under which the wages of low paid agricultural labourers were supplemented by poor relief payments to raise them to some form of subsistence level. In some counties, such payments were made according to a scale, approved by the magistrates, which varied according to the recipient's wage, the size of his family, and the price of bread. The establishment of such a scale for Berkshire in 1795 by magistrates meeting at the Pelican Inn, Speenhamland, led later historians of poor relief to refer to the 'Speenhamland system' (Oxley 1974).

Critics of the 'allowance system' were disturbed not merely by its apparent tendency to increase relief costs but also by its demoralising effect upon the poor. Allowances discouraged effort and encouraged the poor to breed recklessly, thus bringing the threat of some Malthusian population crisis even closer. Worse still, the poor increasingly came to see relief as their right, and became truculent or rebellious when it was curtailed or refused. In 1830, rioting by agricultural labourers spread across a wide area of southern and eastern England (Hobsbawm and Rudé 1969). The government fiercely suppressed the disturbances and also set up a royal commission of inquiry into the poor relief system which seemed to be fomenting discontent. The royal commission began its work in 1832 and carried out a detailed enquiry. It sent out questionnaires to parishes and then despatched assistant commissioners to enquire further into the state of the poor and methods of poor relief in various parts of England and Wales. Its report in 1834 urged greater national uniformity in poor relief methods. This, it recommended, could be achieved by reducing the autonomy of parish overseer and magistrate. Parishes should be merged into poor law unions administered by a ratepayer-elected board of guardians. The new larger local authorities should in their turn be controlled from London by a commission of experts. The task of formulating a national poor relief policy was to be the responsibility of the experts, and the royal commission recommended that any such policy ought to be based upon the principle of less eligibility. Any relief given to the able bodied poor ought to be in such form as to make their condition less desirable (or 'eligible') than that of the poorest independent labourer. The best way of achieving this, it was argued, was to make all relief to the able bodied dependent upon their entering the workhouse. There they would be subjected to a strict regime of regular hours, low diet and hard work. In this way relief costs would be reduced, incentives to independence stimulated, and only the genuinely needy given aid (Checkland and Checkland 1974). The Poor Law Amendment Act of 1834, which followed close on the heels of the royal commision's report, established a central commission of three members and empowered it to group parishes into unions and to formulate relief policy for the new local authorities. Relief costs fell, and grim new union workhouses sprang up to deter the poor from seeking aid from the poor law except in the direst extremity.

The royal commission's report of 1834 with its condemnation of the Speenhamland system exercised a powerful influence over contemporary and later historical views of the early-nineteenth-century poor law system (Checkland and Checkland 1974: 46–7). Recent research, much of it of a quantitative nature, has shown, however, that the charges against the poor law system levelled by the 1834 report will not stand up to investigation. Analysis of the massive statistical evidence, amassed by the royal commission but ignored by the authors of its report, has shown that, far from spreading across the country with alarming rapidity, the Speenhamland system was probably in decline by the early 1830s (Blaug 1963; 1964). Few of the economic and social ills of early-nineteenth-century rural England can be attributed to the maladministration of the poor law. Indeed the poor law system acted in response to economic trends rather than creating them (McCloskey 1973). During the period of the Revolutionary and Napoleonic wars, allowances and bread scales were but one of a number of devices used by overseers and magistrates to protect the poor against rapidly rising food prices. After the war, rural underemployment and low wages rather than high prices became the major problem. Poor law administrators responded with schemes like the labour rate and roundsmen systems, in an attempt to spread the burden of maintaining the unemployed more evenly over the community, as well as with allowances to supplement low wages (Baugh 1975; Huzel 1969). The Speenhamland system has been shown to be only one, and perhaps not the most important, of the poor law's responses to rural distress.

The Poor Law Amendment Act of 1834, based as it was upon false premises, was also perhaps less of a turning point than its designers intended it to be. Its framers were obsessed with the problem of rural distress, and the Act had little relevance to industrial unemployment and urban poverty. Thus the 'workhouse test was spurned by independent-minded boards of guardians in manufacturing areas where outdoor relief and, in some cases, wage allowances continued to be paid to the able bodied' (Rose 1966). Even in rural areas, where the 'principles of 1834 were thought to have been most effective, recent work has shown that, in the eastern counties at least, social policies towards rural underemployment continued little changed after 1834' (Digby 1975). Given the strength and flexibility of local administration and methods of relief, the Poor Law Amendment Act of 1834 provided only a minor disruption in the continuity of social policy. Here, as in many other areas, the pace of change was slow and responsive more to local conditions than to national legislation.

The varying pace of change in England from one locality to another, and the strong survival of many aspects and institutions of the old society meant that social change between 1780 and 1860 was often less dramatic and traumatic than has sometimes been depicted. Edward Thompson argues that 'in the 1830s, many English people felt that the structure of English capitalism had been only partly built and the roof not yet set upon the structure' (1963: 883). Economic and social developments in the late nineteenth and early twentieth centuries rather than in the late eighteenth and early nineteenth centuries, may have effected a greater disruption in the work practices and attitudes of the English people (Stearns 1975).

It would be wrong to deny that this was a period of continuous and important social change, but this change should not be oversimplified or overdramatised. The increasing use of the quantitative method in economic and social history has helped to reduce this tendency to oversimplification by putting the atypical example into its proper perspective. At the same time, the perspective must not be distorted in an attempt to view history through the wrong end of the telescope, looking in this period for the origins of the welfare state or of the labour movement. As John Foster has shown, the case for beginning investigation of social change in the 1780s or 1790s is 'not because this period marked any decisive change in social organisation but to dispose of claims that it did, claims which dangerously telescope England's very long road to fully fledged industrial capitalism and consequently obscure precisely those changes we are looking for' (Foster 1974: 9). As Kitson Clark pointed out some years ago, it is healthy for the historian to reflect on how close to the eighteenth century the England of the 1850s stood (Kitson Clark 1962: 59).

Bibliography

Place of publication is London unless otherwise stated.

Ahluwalia, M. S. 1974. Income inequality: some dimensions of the problem. In *Redistribution with Growth*, H. Chenery et al., pp. 3–37.

Albert, W. 1972. *The Turnpike Road System in England, 1663–1840*. Cambridge.

Anderson. C. A. 1966. Literacy and schooling on the development threshold: some historical cases. In *Education and economic development*, C. A. Anderson & M. J. Bowman (eds.), pp. 347–62.

Anderson, G. 1976. *Victorian Clerks*. Manchester.

Anderson, M. 1971. *Family Structure in Nineteenth Century Lancashire*. Cambridge.

1974. Urban migration in nineteenth century Lancashire; some insights into two competing hypotheses. In *Historical demography: problems and projects*, M. Drake (ed.), pp. 131–43. Milton Keynes.

Ashton, T. S. 1924. *Iron and Steel in the Industrial Revolution*. Manchester.

1948. *The Industrial Revolution 1760–1830*.

1955. *An Economic History of England: The Eighteenth Century*.

1959. *Economic Fluctuations in England 1700–1800*. Oxford.

Bairoch, P. 1976. *Commerce Extérieur et Développement Economique de L'Europe au XIXe Siècle*. Paris.

Bamford, T. W. 1967. *Rise of the public schools; a study of boys' public boarding schools in England and Wales from 1837 to the present day*.

Banks, J. A. 1954. *Prosperity and Parenthood: a study of family planning among the Victorian middle classes*.

Baugh, D. A. 1975. The cost of poor relief in south-east England 1790–1834. *Econ. Hist. Rev. 2nd Ser.*, **28**, 50–68.

Baxter, R. D. 1868. *National Income. The United Kingdom*.

Beaver, M. W. 1973. Population, infant mortality and milk. *Population Studies*, **27**, 243–54.

Becker, G. S. 1964. *Human Capital. A theoretical and empirical analysis, with special reference to education*. New York.

Berrill, K. 1960. International trade and the rate of economic growth. *Econ. Hist. Rev. 2nd Ser.*, **12**, 351–9.

Best, G. 1971. *Mid-Victorian Britain*.

Bienefeld, M. A. 1972. *Working hours in British industry: an economic history*.

Birch, A. 1967. *The Economic History of the British Iron and Steel Industry 1784–1879*.

Blackman, J. & Nield, K. 1976. Editorial. *Social History*, **1**, 1–3.

Blaug, M. 1963. The myth of the old poor law and the making of the new. *Journal of Economic History*, **23**, 151–84.

1964. The poor law report re-examined. *Journal of Economic History*, **24**, 229–45.

1975. The economics of education in English classical political economy: a re-examination. In *Essays on Adam Smith*, A. S. Skinner & T. Wilson (eds.), pp. 568–99. Oxford.

Blayo, Y. 1975. La mortalité en France de 1740 à 1829. *Population 30 Numéro Spécial*, 123–42.

Board of Agriculture, 1806. *Communications on Subjects Relative to the Husbandry and Internal Improvement of the Country*, vol. 5, pt. 1.

Bowley, A. L. 1900. *Wages in the United Kingdom in the Nineteenth Century. Notes for the Use of Students in Social and Economic Questions*. Cambridge.

1938. The change in the distribution of the national income, 1800–1913. In *Three Studies on the National Income*, A. L. Bowley & J. Stamp, pp. 61–87.

Bradley, I. C. 1976. *The Call to Seriousness: The Evangelical Impact on the Victorians*.

Braudel, F. 1974. *Capitalism and Material Life, 1400–1800*. Trans. M. Kochan.

Briggs, A. 1952. The background of the parliamentary reform movement in three English cities (1830–2). *Cambridge Historical Journal*, **10**, 293–317.

1959a. *The Age of Improvement*.

(ed.) 1959b. *Chartist Studies*.

1960. The language of 'class' in early nineteenth-century England. In *Essays in Labour History*, ed. A. Briggs & J. Saville, vol. 1, pp. 43–73.

Brooman, F. S. 1962. *Macroeconomics*.

Brown, F. K. 1961. *Fathers of the Victorians; the age of Wilberforce*. Cambridge.

Brown, P. A. 1918. *The French Revolution in English History*.

Brunborg, Helge. 1976. The inverse projection method applied to Norway, Denmark and Sweden; 1735–1974. Unpublished Manuscript of Population Studies Center of the University of Michigan.

Buckatzsch. E. J. 1951–52. The constancy of local populations and migration in England before 1800. *Population Studies*, **5**, 62–9.

Burn, W. L. 1964. *The Age of Equipoise; A Study of the Mid-Victorian Generation*.

Burnett, J. 1968. *Plenty and Want*. Harmondsworth.

Caird, J. 1852. *English Agriculture in 1850–51*.

Cardwell, D. S. L. 1971. *From Watt to Clausius: the rise of thermodynamics in the early industrial age*.

Carus-Wilson, E. M. (ed.) (1954) 1962. *Essays in Economic History*. 3 vols.

Cazamian, L. 1973. *The social novel in England, 1830–50: Dickens, Disraeli, Mrs Gaskell, Kingsley*. Trans. M. Fido.

Chalklin, C. W. 1962. The rural economy of a Kentish wealden parish, 1650–1750. *Agricultural History Review*, **10**, 29–45.

Chaloner, W. H. 1969. *The Skilled Artisan during the Industrial Revolution 1750–1850*.

Chambers, J. D. 1953. Enclosure and labour supply in the industrial revolution. *Econ. Hist. Rev. 2nd Ser.*, **5**, 319–43.

1957. *The Vale of Trent, 1670–1800*. Economic History Review, supplement 3.

1972. *Population, Economy and Society in Pre-industrial England*. Oxford.

Chambers, J. D. & Mingay, G. E. 1966. *The Agricultural Revolution, 1750–1880*.

Chapman, S. D. 1967. *The Early Factory Masters: the transition to the factory system in the Midlands Textile industry*. Newton Abbot.

1971a. The cost of power in the Industrial Revolution in Britain: the case of the textile industry. *Midland History*, **1**, 1–24.

278

(ed.) 1971b. *The History of Working Class Housing.* Newton Abbot.

(ed.) 1972. *The Cotton Industry in the Industrial Revolution.*

Chartres, J. A. 1977. Road carrying in England in the seventeenth century: myth and reality. *Econ. Hist. Rev. 2nd Ser.*, **30**, 73–94.

Checkland, S. G. 1964. *The rise of industrial society in England, 1815–85.*

Checkland, S. G. & E. O. A. (eds.) 1974. *The poor law report of 1834.* Harmondsworth.

Cherry, S. 1972. The role of a provincial hospital: the Norfolk and Norwich hospital, 1771–1880. *Population studies*, **26**, 291–306.

Churley, P. A. 1953. The Yorkshire crop returns of 1801. *Yorkshire Bulletin of Economic and Social Research*, **5**, 179–97.

Cipolla, C. M. 1969. *Literacy and Development in the West.* Harmondsworth.

Clapham, Sir J. 1926–38. *An Economic History of Modern Britain.* 3 vols. Cambridge. 1949. *A Concise Economic History of Britain...to 1750.* Cambridge.

Clark, G. N. 1953. *The Idea of the Industrial Revolution.* Glasgow.

Clarkson, L. A. 1971. *The Pre-Industrial Economy in England 1500–1750.*

Coelho, P. R. P. 1969. The British West Indies. Profit or loss to Great Britain: a quantitative investigation. PhD thesis, University of Washington, Seattle.

1973. The profitability of imperialism: the British experience in the West Indies 1768–72. *Explorations in Economic History*, **10**, 253–80.

Cole, W. A. 1958. Trends in eighteenth-century smuggling. *Econ. Hist. Rev. 2nd Ser.*, **10**, 395–410. Reprinted in *The Growth of English Overseas Trade in the Seventeenth and Eighteenth Centuries*, W. E. Minchinton (ed.), pp. 121–43. 1969.

1973. Eighteenth-century economic growth revisited. *Explorations in Economic History 2nd Series*, **10**, 327–48.

Cole, W. A. & Deane, P. 1965. The growth of national incomes. In *The Cambridge Economic History of Europe*, eds. H. J. Habakkuk & M. Postan, vol. VI, part 1, pp. 1–55. Cambridge.

Coleman, B. I. 1972. The incidence of education in mid-century. In *Nineteenth Century Society*, ed. E. A. Wrigley, pp. 397–410. Cambridge.

Coleman, D. C. 1977. *The Economy of England 1450–1750.*

Collins, E. J. T. 1969a. Harvest technology and labour supply in Britain, 1790–1870. *Econ. Hist. Rev. 2nd Ser.*, **22**, 453–73.

1969b. Labour supply and demand in European agriculture, 1800–80. In *Agrarian Change and Economic Development*, E. L. Jones & S. J. Woolf (eds.), pp. 61–94.

1976. Migrant labour in British agriculture in the nineteenth century. *Econ. Hist. Rev. 2nd Ser.*, **29**, 38–59.

Collins, E. J. T. & Jones, E. L. 1967. Sectoral advance in English Agriculture, 1850–80. *Agricultural History Review*, **15**, 65–81.

Colquhoun, P. 1814. *A treatise on the wealth, power and resources of the British empire.*

Cootner, P. H. 1963. Social overhead capital and economic growth. In *The Economics of Take-off into Sustained Growth*, W. W. Rostow (ed.), pp. 261–84.

Crafts, N. F. R. 1976. English economic growth in the eighteenth century: a re-examination of Deane and Cole's estimates. *Econ. Hist. Rev. 2nd Ser.*, **29**, 226–35.

1977a. Income elasticities of demand and the release of labour by agriculture during the British industrial revolution. *Warwick Economic Research Papers 113*. Mimeo.

1977b. Industrial revolution in England and France: some thoughts on the question 'Why was England first?' *Econ. Hist. Rev. 2nd Ser.*, **30**, 429–41.

Crossick, G. 1976. The labour aristocracy and its values. a study of mid-Victorian Kentish London, *Victorian Studies*, **19**, 301–28.

(ed.) 1977. *The lower middle class in Britain, 1870–1914.*

1978. *An Artisan Elite in Victorian Society: Kentish London, 1840–80.*

Crouzet, F. 1966. England and France in the eighteenth century: a comparative analysis of two economic growths. In *The Causes of the Industrial Revolution in England*, R. M. Hartwell (ed.), pp. 139–74. 1967.

(ed.) 1972. *Capital Formation in the Industrial Revolution.*

Cullen, L. M. 1968. *Anglo-Irish Trade 1660–1800.* Manchester.

Cullen, M. J. 1975. *The statistical movement in early Victorian Britain: the foundations of empirical social research.* Hassocks.

Dallas, K. 1974. *One Hundred Songs of Toil.*

David P. A. 1975. *Technical Choice, Innovation and Economic Growth: Essays on American and British Experience in the Nineteenth Century.*

Davis, R. 1954. English foreign trade, 1660–1700. *Econ. Hist. Rev. 2nd Ser.*, **7**, 150–66. Reprinted in *The Growth of English Overseas Trade in the Seventeenth and Eighteenth Centuries*, W. E. Minchinton (ed.), pp. 78–98. 1969.

1962a. English foreign trade, 1700–94. *Econ. Hist. Rev. 2nd Ser.*, **15**, 285–303.

1962b. *The Rise of the English Shipping Industry in the Seventeenth and Eighteenth Centuries.*

1966. The rise of protection in England, 1689–1786. *Econ. Hist. Rev. 2nd Ser.*, **19**, 306–17.

1979. *The Industrial Revolution and British Overseas Trade.* Leicester.

Davis, T. 1794. *General View of the Agriculture of the County of Wiltshire.*

Deane, P. 1955. The implications of early national income estimates for the measurement of long-term economic growth in the United Kingdom. *Economic Development and Cultural Change*, **4**, 3–38.

1957a. Contemporary estimates of national income in the second half of the nineteenth century. *Econ. Hist. Rev. 2nd Ser.*, **9**, 451–61.

1957b. The output of the British woollen industry in the eighteenth century. *Journal of Economic History*, **17**, 207–23.

1961. Capital formation in Britain before the railways age. *Economic Development and Cultural Change*, **9**, 352–68.

1965. *The First Industrial Revolution.* Cambridge.

1968. New estimates of gross national product for the United Kingdom, 1830–1914. *Review of Income and Wealth*, **14**, 95–112.

1973. The role of capital in the industrial revolution. *Explorations in Economic History*, **10**, 349–64.

Deane, P. & Cole, W. A. 1967. *British Economic Growth, 1688–1959. Trends and Structure.* 2nd edn. Cambridge.

Denison, E. F. 1962. *The Sources of Economic Growth in the United States and the Alternatives before us.* New York.

1967. *Why Growth Rates Differ: Postwar Experience in Nine Western Countries.* Washington.

De Vries, J. 1974. *The Dutch rural economy in the golden age, 1500–1700.*

Dickson, P. G. M. 1967. *The Financial Revolution in England.*

Digby, A. 1975. The labour market and the continuity of social policy after 1834: the case of the eastern counties. *Econ. Hist. Rev. 2nd Ser.*, **28**, 69–83.

Djang, T. K. 1942. *Factory Inspection in Great Britain.*

280

Dodd, W. (Pseud. An Englishman). 1847. *The labouring classes of England, especially those engaged in agriculture and manufactures*. Boston, Mass.

Drake, M. (ed.) 1969. *Population in Industrialization*.

Dupâquier, J. 1976. Les caractères originaux de l'histoire démographique française au XVIIIe siècle. *Revue d'Histoire Moderne et Contemporaine* N.S., **23**, 182–202.

Durand, J. 1974. Historical estimates of world population: an evaluation. *Analytical and Technical reports No. 10*. Population Studies Center of The University of Pennsylvania.

Eden, F. M. 1797. *The State of the Poor*, vol. 3. 1966.

Edsall, N. C. 1971. *The anti-Poor Law movement, 1834–44*. Manchester.

Edwards, M. M. 1967. *The growth of the British cotton trade, 1780–1815*. Manchester.

Ellison, T. 1886. *The Cotton Trade of Great Britain*.

Emery, F. 1976. The mechanics of innovation: clover cultivation in Wales before 1750. *Journal of Historical Geography*, **2**, 35–48.

Engels, F. 1845a. *The Condition of the Working Class in England*. Trans. W. O. Henderson & W. H. Chaloner. Oxford. 1958.

1845b. *The Condition of the Working Class in England*. Moscow. 1973.

Enke, S. 1964. *Economics for Development*.

Ernle, Lord. 1912. *English Farming Past and Present*. Reprinted 1961.

Evans, E. J. 1976. *The Contentious Tithe: The tithe problem and English agriculture, 1750–1850*.

Eversley, D. E. C. 1967. The home market and economic growth in England, 1750–80. In *Land, Labour and Population in the Industrial Revolution*, E. L. Jones & G. E. Mingay (eds.), pp. 206–59.

Feinstein, C. H. 1978. Capital formation in Great Britain. In *The Cambridge Economic History of Europe*, P. Mathias & M. M. Postnan (eds.), vol. 7, part 1, pp. 28–96. Cambridge.

Felix, D. 1956. Profit inflation and industrial growth: the historic record and contemporary analogies. *Quarterly Journal of Economics*, **70**, 441–63.

Finer, S. E. 1952. *The life and times of Sir Edwin Chadwick*.

Flinn, M. W. (ed.) 1965. *Report on the sanitary condition of the labouring population of Great Britain; by Edwin Chadwick, 1842*. Edinburgh.

1970. *British Population Growth, 1700–1850*.

1974. Trends in real wages, 1750–1850 *Econ. Hist. Rev. 2nd Ser.*, **27**, 395–413.

Floud, R. (ed.) 1974. *Essays in Quantitative Economic History*. Oxford.

Fogel, R. W. et al. 1977. The economics of mortality in North America, 1650–1910. Unpublished manuscript.

Foster, J. 1968. Nineteenth century towns – a class dimension. In *The Study of Urban History*, H. J. Dyos (ed.), pp. 281–99.

1974. *Class struggle and the Industrial Revolution; early industrial capitalism in three English towns*.

Fraser, D. 1976. *Urban politics in Victorian England; the structure of politics in Victorian cities*. Leicester.

Frazer, W. M. 1950. *A history of English public health, 1834–1939*.

Freudenberger, H. & Cummins, G. 1976. Health, work and leisure before the Industrial Revolution. *Explorations in Economic History*, **13**, 1–12.

Fussell, G. E. & Compton, M. 1939. Agricultural adjustments after the Napoleonic Wars. *Economic History*, **4**, 184–204.

Gaskin, K. 1976. An analysis of age at first marriage in Europe before 1850. Unpublished manuscript. University of Michigan, Department of Sociology.

Gatrell, V. A. C. 1977. Labour, power, and the size of firms in Lancashire cotton in the second quarter of the nineteenth century. *Econ. Hist. Rev. 2nd Ser.*, **30**, 95–139.

Gayer, A. D., Rostow, W. W & Schwartz, A. J. 1953a. *The Growth and Fluctuation of the British Economy, 1790–1850: An Historical, Statistical and Theoretical Study of Britain's Economic Development*. Oxford.

   1953b. Microfilmed data supplement to *The Growth and Fluctuation of the British Economy, 1790–1850*. Oxford.

Gerschenkron, A. 1962. Reflections on the concept of 'pre-requisites' of modern industrialization. In *Economic Backwardness in Historical Perspective*, A. Gerschenkron (ed.), pp. 31–51. Cambridge, Mass.

Gilboy, E. W. 1932. Demand as a factor in the industrial revolution. In *Facts and Factors in Economic History: Articles by Former Students of Edwin Francis Gay*, A. H. Cole et al., pp. 620–39. Cambridge, Mass.

   1934. *Wages in Eighteenth Century England*. Cambridge, Mass.

   1936. The cost of living and real wages in eighteenth-century England. *Review of Economic Statistics*, **18**, 134–43. Reprinted in *The Standard of Living in Britain in the Industrial Revolution*, A. J. Taylor (ed.), pp. 1–20. 1975.

Gill, C. 1948. Birmingham under the street commissioners, 1769–1851. *University of Birmingham Historical Journal*, **1**, 255–87.

Ginarlis, J. E. 1970. Capital formation in transport in the Industrial Revolution. Ph.D. thesis, Sheffield University.

Glass, D. V. 1965a. Gregory King's estimate of the population of England and Wales, 1695. In *Population in History*, D. V. Glass & D. E. C. Eversley (eds.), pp. 183–220.

   1965b. Population and population movements in England and Wales, 1700 to 1850. In *Population in History*, D. V. Glass & D. E. C. Eversley (eds.), pp. 221–46.

Gould, J. D. 1962. Agricultural fluctuations and the English economy in the eighteenth century. *Journal of economic History*, **22**, 313–33.

   1972. *Economic Growth in History*.

Gourvish, T. R. 1972. The cost of living in Glasgow in the early nineteenth century. *Econ. Hist. Rev. 2nd Ser.*, **25**, 65–80.

Granger, C. W. J. & Elliott, C. M. 1967. A fresh look at wheat prices and markets in the eighteenth century. *Econ. Hist. Rev. 2nd Ser.*, **20**, 257–65.

Gray, L. C. 1933. *History of Agriculture in the Southern United States to 1860*. Gloucester, Massachusetts. 1958.

Greenwood, M. J. & Thomas, L. B. 1973. Geographic labour mobility in nineteenth century England and Wales. *The Annals of Regional Science*, **7**, 90–105.

Grigg, D. 1966. *The Agricultural Revolution in South Lincolnshire*. Cambridge.

Habakkuk, H. J. 1956. Essays in bibliography and criticism. The Eighteenth Century. *Econ. Hist. Rev. 2nd Ser.*, **8**, 434–8.

   1962. *American and British technology in the nineteenth century: the search for labour-saving inventions*. Cambridge.

   1965. The economic history of modern Britain. In *Population in History*, D. V. Glass & D. C. Eversley (eds.), pp. 147–58.

Habakkuk, H. J. & Deane, P. 1963. The take-off in Britain. In *The Economics of Take-off into Sustained Growth*, W. W. Rostow (ed.), pp. 63–82.

Hadfield, C. 1955. *The Canals of Southern England*.

Hajnal, J. 1965. European marriage patterns in perspective. In *Population in History*, D. V. Glass & D. E. C. Eversley (eds.), pp. 101–43.

Halevy, E. 1924. *A History of the English People in the Nineteenth Century. Vol. I. England in 1815.* 1961.

Hammersley, G. 1973. The charcoal iron industry and its fuel, 1540–1750. *Econ. Hist. Rev. 2nd Ser.,* **26**, 593–613.

Hammond, J. L. & B. 1911. *The Village Labourer, 1760–1832.*
    1923. *Lord Shaftesbury.*
    1925. *The Town Labourer, 1760–1832.* 2nd edn.

Handley, J. E. 1953. *Scottish Farming in the Eighteenth Century.*

Harper, L. A. 1942. Mercantilism and the American revolution. *Canadian Historical Review,* **23**, 1–15.

Harrison, J. F. C. 1961. *Learning and living, 1790–1860; a study in the history of the English adult education movement.*
    1969. *Robert Owen and the Owenites in Britain and America: The Quest for the New Moral World.*
    1971. *The early Victorians, 1832–51.*

Harrison, R. J. 1965. *Before the socialists; studies in labour and politics, 1861–81.*

Hart, H. W. 1960. Some notes on coach travel, 1750–1848. *Journal of Transport History,* **4**, 146–60.

Hartwell, R. M. 1965. The causes of the industrial revolution: an essay in methodology. *Econ. Hist. Rev. 2nd Ser.,* **18**, 164–82.
    1971. *The Industrial Revolution and Economic Growth.*

Havinden, M. A. 1961. Agricultural progress in open-field Oxfordshire. *Agricultural History Review,* **9**, 73–83.

Hawke, G. R. 1970. *Railways and Economic Growth in England and Wales, 1840–70.* Oxford.
    1971. Railway passenger traffic in 1865. In *Essays on a Mature Economy: Britain after 1840,* D. N. McCloskey (ed.), pp. 367–88.

Hay, D., Linebaugh, P. & Thompson, E. P. 1975. *Albion's Fatal Tree.*

Henderson, H. C. K. 1951–52. The 1801 crop returns for Sussex. *Sussex Archaeological Collections,* **90**, 51–9.

Hennock, E. P. 1972. *Fit and proper persons: ideal and reality in nineteenth century urban government.*

Henry, L. & Blayo, Y. 1975. La population de la France de 1740 à 1860. *Population 30 Numéro Spécial,* 71–122.

Hewitt, M. 1958. *Wives and mothers in Victorian industry.*

Hicks, J. R. 1932. *The theory of wages.*
    1939. *Value and Capital.* Oxford.

Higgins, B. 1959. *Economic Development.* New York.

Higgins, J. P. P. 1971. An interim paper on the rate of capital formation in Britain, 1750–1850: Roads and waterways. Unpublished paper read to L.S.E. seminar.

Higgins, J. P. P. & Pollard, S. (eds.) 1971. *Aspects of Capital Investment in Great Britain, 1750–1850.*

Hill, C. 1967. *Reformation to Industrial Revolution.*

Hirschman, A. O. 1958. *The Strategy of Economic Development.*

Hobsbawm, E. J. 1957. Methodism and the threat of revolution in Britain. *History Today,* **7**, 115–24.

1962. *The Age of Revolution Europe 1789–1848.*

1964a. *Labouring Men.*

1964b. The labour aristocracy in nineteenth century Britain. In *Labouring Men*, by E. J. Hobsbawm, pp, 272–315.

1968. *Industry and Empire.*

Hobsbawm, E. J. & Rudé, G. 1969. *Captain Swing.*

Hoffmann, W. G. 1955. *British Industry 1700–1950.* Trans. W. O. Henderson & W. H. Chaloner. Oxford.

Hofsten, E. & Lundström, H. 1976. *Swedish Population History.* Stockholm.

Holderness, B. A. 1972. 'Open' and 'close' parishes in England in the eighteenth and nineteenth centuries. *Agricultural History Review,* **20,** 126–39.

1975. Credit in a rural community, 1660–1800. *Midland History,* **3,** 94–115.

1976. *Pre-Industrial England: Economy and Society, 1500–1750.*

Hollingsworth, T. H. 1969. *Historical Demography.*

Hollis, P. 1970. *The pauper press: a study in working class radicalism of the 1830s.*

(ed.) 1974. *Pressure from without in early Victorian England.*

Howell, M. 1918. *The Chartist movement.* Manchester.

Hudson, D. & Luckhurst, K. W. 1954. *The Royal Society of Arts 1754–1954.*

Hudson, K. 1972. *Patriotism with Profit; British Agricultural Societies in the eighteenth and nineteenth centuries.*

Hueckel, G. 1973. War and the British economy, 1793–1815: a general equilibrium analysis. *Explorations in Economic History,* **10,** 365–96.

1976. Relative prices and supply response in English agriculture during the Napoleonic wars. *Econ. Hist. Rev. 2nd Ser.,* **29,** 401–14.

Hughes, J. R. T. 1960. *Fluctuations in Trade Industry and Finance; A Study of British Economic Development 1850–60.* Oxford.

Hunt, E. H. 1973. *Regional Wage Variations in Britain, 1850–1914.* Oxford.

Hunt, H. G. 1957. The chronology of parliamentary enclosure in Leicestershire. *Econ. Hist. Rev. 2nd Ser.,* **10,** 265–72.

1959. Agricultural rent in south-east England, 1788–1825. *Agricultural History Review,* **7,** 98–108.

Hurt, J. S. 1971a. *Education in Evolution; Church, State, Society and Popular Education, 1800–70.*

1971b. Professor West on early nineteenth-century education. *Econ. Hist. Rev. 2nd Ser.,* **24,** 624–32 (reply by West, 633–42).

Hutchins, B. L. & Harrison, A. 1903. *A history of Factory Legislation.*

Huzel, J. P. 1969. Malthus, the poor law, and population in early nineteenth century England. *Econ. Hist. Rev. 2nd Ser.,* **22,** 430–52.

Hyde, C. K. 1973. The adoption of coke-smelting by the British iron industry, 1709–90. *Explorations in Economic History 2nd Series,* **10,** 397–418.

1974. Technological change in the British wrought iron industry, 1750–1815: a reinterpretation. *Econ. Hist. Rev. 2nd Ser.,* **27,** 190–206.

1977. *Technological Change and the British iron industry 1700–1870.* Princeton, NJ.

Imhof, A. E. 1976. *Aspekte der Bevölkerungsentwicklung in der Nordischen Ländern, 1720–50.* Bern.

Imlah, A. H. 1949. The fall of protection in Britain. In *Essays in history and international relations in honour of G. H. Blakeslee,* D. E. Lee & G. E. McReynolds (eds.), pp. 306–20,. Worcester, Mass.

284

1958. *Economic Elements in the Pax Britannica: Studies in British Foreign Trade in the Nineteenth Century.* Cambridge, Mass.

Ippolito, R. A. 1975. The effect of the 'agricultural depression' on industrial demand in England: 1730–50. *Economica N.S.,* **42**, 298–312.

Jackman, W. T. 1916. *The Development of Transportation in Modern England.* 2nd edn. 1962.

John, A. H. 1955. War and the English economy 1700–63. *Econ. Hist. Rev. 2nd Ser.,* **7**, 329–44.

1961. Aspects of English economic growth in the first half of the eighteenth century. *Economica N.S.,* **28**, 176–90. Reprinted in *The Growth of English Overseas Trade in the Seventeenth and Eighteenth Centuries,* W. E. Minchinton (ed.), pp. 165–83. 1969.

1965. Agricultural productivity and economic growth in England, 1700–60. *Journal of Economic History,* **25**, 19–34. Reprinted in *Agriculture and Economic Growth in England, 1650–1815,* E. L. Jones (ed.), pp. 172–93. 1967.

1967a. Agricultural productivity and economic growth in England 1700–60 (with a postscript). In *Agriculture and Economic Growth in England 1650–1815,* E. L. Jones (ed.), pp. 172–93.

1967b. Farming in wartime: 1793–1815. In *Land, Labour and Population in the Industrial Revolution; Essays Presented to J. D. Chambers,* E. L. Jones & G. L. Mingay (eds.), pp. 28–47.

1976. English agricultural improvement and grain exports, 1660–1765. In *Trade, Government and Economy in Pre-Industrial England,* D. C. Coleman & A. H. John (eds.), pp. 45–67.

Johnson, R. 1970. Educational policy and social control in early Victorian England. *Past and Present,* **49**, 96–119.

Jones, E. L. 1964a. The agricultural labour market in England 1793–1872. *Econ. Hist. Rev. 2nd Ser.,* **17**, 322–38.

1964b. *Seasons and Prices; The Role of the Weather in English Agricultural History.*

1965. Agriculture and economic growth in England 1660–1750: agricultural change *Journal of Economic History,* **25**, 1–18. Reprinted in *Agriculture and Economic Growth in England, 1650–1815,* E. L. Jones (ed.), pp. 152–71. 1967.

(ed.) 1967. *Agriculture and Economic Growth in England: 1650–1815.*

1968. *The Development of English Agriculture, 1815–73.*

1970. English and European agricultural development 1650–1750. in *The Industrial Revolution,* R. M. Hartwell (ed.), pp. 42–76. Oxford.

1974. *Agricultural and the Industrial Revolution.* New York.

Kargon, R. H. 1977. *Science in Victorian Manchester: enterprise and expertise.* Manchester.

Kay, J. P. 1832. *The moral and physical condition of the working classes employed in the cotton manufacture in Manchester.*

Kellett, J. R. 1969. *The Impact of Railways on Victorian Cities.*

Kenyon, G. H. 1955. Kirdford inventories, 1611 to 1776, with particular reference to the Weald clay farming. *Sussex Archaeological Collections,* **93**, 78–156.

Kerr, B. 1962. The Dorset agricultural labourer, 1750–1850. *Proceedings of the Dorset Natural History and Archaeological Society,* **84**, 158–77.

Keynes, J. M. 1937. Some economic consequences of a declining population. *Eugenics Review,* **29**, 13–17.

King, G. 1696. *Natural and political observations and conclusions upon the state and condition of England.* In *Estimate of the comparative strength of Great Britain 1804*, by G. Chalmers.

Kitson Clark, G. 1955. The romantic element 1830 to 1850. In *Studies in social history. A tribute to G. M. Trevelyan*, J. H. Plumb (ed.), pp. 211–39.

1959. 'Statesmen in disguise'; reflections on the history of the neutrality of the civil service. *Historical Journal*, **2**, 19–39.

1962. *The making of Victorian England.*

Krause, J. T. 1965. The changing adequacy of English Registration, 1690–1837. In *Population in History*, D. V. Glass & D. E. C. Eversley (eds.), pp. 379–93.

Kuznets, S. 1963. Underdeveloped countries and the pre-industrial phase in the advanced countries: an attempt at comparison. In *The Economics of Underdevelopment*, A. N. Agarwala & S. P. Singh (eds.), pp. 135–53. New York.

1966. *Modern economic growth: rate, structure and spread.*

1974. *Population, capital, and Growth.*

1976. Demographic aspects of the size distribution of income: an exploratory essay. *Economic Development and Cultural Change*, **25**, 1–94.

Lambert, R. 1963. *Sir John Simon, 1816–1904, and English social administration.*

Landes, D. S. 1969. *The unbound prometheus: technological change and industrial development in Western Europe from 1750 to the present.* Cambridge.

Langer, W. L. 1963. Europe's initial population explosion. *American Historical Review*, **69**, 1–17.

1975. American foods and Europe's population growth, 1750–1850. *Journal of Social History*, **8**, 51–66.

Laslett, P. & Harrison, J. 1963. Clayworth and Cogenhoe. In *Historical Essays, 1600–1750*, H. E. Bell & R. C. Ollard (eds.), pp. 157–84.

Laslett, P. & Oosterveen, K. 1973. Long-term trends in bastardy in England. *Population Studies*, **27**, 255–86.

Latham, A. J. H. 1978. *The International Economy and the Underdeveloped World 1865–1915.*

Lee, J. M. 1963. *Social leaders and public persons: a study of county government in Cheshire since 1888.* Oxford.

Lee, R. D. 1973. Population in pre-industrial England: an econometric analysis. *Quarterly Journal of Economics*, **87**, 581–607.

1974. Estimating series of vital rates and age structures from baptisms and burials: a new technique, with applications to pre-industrial England: *Population Studies*, **28**, 495–512.

1978. Models of pre-industrial population dynamics, with applications to England. In *Historical Studies of Changing Fertility*, C. Tilly (ed.), pp. 155–207. Princeton.

forthcoming. An historical perspective on economic aspects of the population explosion: the case of pre-industrial England. In *Population and Economic Change in Less Developed Countires*, R. Easterlin (ed.).

Leff, N. H. 1969. Dependency rates and savings rate. *American Economic Review*, **59**, 886–96.

Lewis. W. A. 1954. Economic development with unlimited supplies of labour. *The Manchester School of Economic and Social Studies*, **22**, 139–91.

Leveen, E. P. 1971. British slave trade suppression policies 1821–65. University of Chicago dissertation.

1975. The African supply response. *African Studies Review*, **18**, 9–28.

286

Lilley, S. 1973. Technological progress and the Industrial Revolution, 1700–1914. In *The Fontana Economic History of Europe*, C. Cipolla (ed.), vol. 3, pp. 187–254.

Little, A. J. 1976. *Deceleration in the Eighteenth-Century British Economy*.

McBride, T. 1976. *The domestic revolution: the modernisation of household service in England and France, 1820–1920*.

McClelland, P. D. 1969. The cost to America of British imperial Policy. *American Economic Review*, **59**, *Papers & Proceedings*, 370–81.

McCloskey, D. N. 1973. New perspectives on the old Poor Law. *Explorations in Economic History*, **10**, 419–36.

1975. The economics of enclosure: a market analysis. In *European Peasants and Their Markets. Essays in Agrarian Economic History*, W. N. Parker & E. L. Jones (eds.) Princeton, NJ.

McCord, N. 1958. *The Anti-Corn Law League. 1838–46*.

McCulloch, J. R. 1839: *A Statistical Account of the British Empire*, 2nd edn., vol. 1.

McCusker, J. J. 1971. The current value of English exports 1697 to 1800. *William and Mary Quarterly*, **28**, 607–28.

McKendrick, N. 1961. Josiah Wedgwood and factory discipline. *Historical Journal*, **4**, 30–55.

1974. Home demand and economic growth: a new view of the role of women and children in the Industrial Revolution. In *Historical Perspectives. Studies in English Thought and Society in Honour of J. H. Plumb*, N. McKendrick (ed.), pp. 152–210.

McKeown, T. 1976. *The Modern Rise of Population*.

McKeown, T. & Brown, R. G. 1955. Medical evidence related to population changes in the eighteenth century. *Population Studies*, **9**, 119–41.

McKeown, T., Brown, R. G. & Record, R. G. 1972. An interpretation of the modern rise of population in Europe. *Population Studies*, **26**, 345–82.

Macpherson, D. 1805. *Annals of Commerce, Manufactures, Fishing and Navigation*, vol. 4.

Maddison, A. 1967. Comparative productivity levels in the developed countries. *Banca Nazionale del Lavoro Quarterly Review*, **20**, 295–315.

Mansfield, E. 1968. *Industrial research and technological innovation: an econometric analysis*. New York.

Mantoux, P. 1964. *The Industrial Revolution in the Eighteenth Century*.

Marcus, S. 1974. *Engels, Manchester, and the working class*.

Marshall, J. D. 1968. *The Old Poor Law, 1795–1834*.

Marshall, T. H. 1929. The population problem during the Industrial Revolution. *Economic History*, **1**, 429–56. Reprinted in *Essays in Economic History*, E. M. Carus-Wilson (ed.), vol. 1, pp. 306–30. 1954. Also reprinted in *Population in History*, D. V. Glass & D. E. C. Eversley (eds.), pp. 247–68. 1965.

Marshall, W. 1705: *The Rural Economy of Norfolk*, vol. 2.

Martin, J. M. 1967. The cost of parliamentary enclosure in Warwickshire. In *Agriculture and Economic Growth in England 1650–1815*, E. L. Jones (ed.), pp. 128–51.

Marwick, A. 1974. *War and social change in the twentieth century*.

Marx, K. 1887. *Capital*, trans. S. Moore & E. Aveling; F. Engels (ed.).

Mathias, P. 1952. Agriculture and the brewing and distilling industries in the eighteenth century. *Econ. Hist. Rev. 2nd Ser.*, **5**, 249–57.

1969. *The first industrial nation: an economic history of Britain, 1700–1914*.

(ed.) 1972. *Science and Society, 1600–1900*. Cambridge

1975. Swords and ploughshares: the armed forces, medicine and public health in the late eighteenth century. In *War and Economic Development*, J. M. Winter (ed.), pp. 73–90. Cambridge.

Matthews, R. C. O. 1954. *A study in trade-cycle history: economic fluctuations in Great Britain, 1833–42*. Cambridge.

Mayer, A. 1975. The lower middle class as a historical problem. *Journal of Modern History*, **47**, 409–36.

Menger, A. 1899. *The right to the whole produce of labour. The origins and development of the theory*. Trans. M. E. Tanner.

Merton, R. K. 1970. *Science, technology and society in seventeenth-century England*. New York.

Milne, A. A. 1927. *Now We Are Six*. 1978.

Minchinton, W. E. 1969. *The Growth of English Overseas Trade in the Seventeenth and Eighteenth Centuries*.

1973. Patterns of demand 1750–1914. *The Fontana Economic History of Europe*, C. M. Cipolla (ed.), vol. 3, pp. 77–186.

Mingay, G. E. 1956. The agricultural depression 1730–50. *Econ. Hist. Rev. 2nd Ser.*, **8**, 323–38.

Mitchell, B. R. 1964. The coming of the railway and United Kingdom economic growth. *Journal of Economic History*, **24**, 315–36.

Mitchell, B. R. & Deane, P. 1962. *Abstract of British Historical Statistics*. Cambridge.

Mokyr, J. 1977. Demand vs. supply in the industrial revolution. *Journal of Economic History*, **37**, 981–1008.

Mokyr, J. & Savin, N. E. 1976. Stagflation in historical perspective: the Napoleonic Wars revisited. *Research in Economic History*, **1**, 198–259.

Mosse, G. L. 1947. The anti-League: 1844–46. *Econ. Hist. Rev. 1st Ser.*, **17**, 134–42.

Mott, R. A. 1962–63. The Newcomen engine in the eighteenth century. *Transactions of the Newcomen Society*, **35**, 69–86.

Mueller, E. 1976. The economic value of children in peasant agriculture. In *Population and Development: The Search for Selective Interventions*, R. G. Ridker (ed.), pp. 98–153. Baltimore.

Musson, A. E. 1972. *British Trade Unions 1800–75*.

Musson, A. E. & Robinson E. 1969. *Science and Technology in the Industrial Revolution*. Manchester.

Neale, R. S. 1966. The standard of living 1780–1844: a regional and class study. *Econ. Hist. Rev. 2nd Ser.*, **19**, 590–606.

1968. Class and class-consciousness in early nineteenth century England: three classes or five? *Victorian Studies*, **12**, 4–32.

Nef, J. U. 1934. The progress of technology and the growth of large scale industry in Great Britain, 1540–1640. *Econ. Hist. Rev. 1st Ser.*, **5**, 3–24.

Newsom, D. 1961. *Godliness and good learning: four studies on a Victorian ideal*.

North, D. C. 1968. Sources of productivity change in ocean shipping, 1600–1850. *Journal of Political Economy*, **76**, 953–70.

North, D. C. & Thomas, R. P. 1973. *The Rise of the Western World. A new economic history*. Cambridge.

Nurkse, R. 1960. *Problems of Capital Formation in Underdeveloped countries*. Oxford.

O'Brien, P. K. 1977. Agriculture and the Industrial Revolution. *Econ. Hist. Rev. 2nd Ser.*, **30**, 166–81.

O'Brien, P. & Keyder, C. 1978. *Economic Growth in Britain and France 1780–1914: Two Paths to the Twentieth Century*.

288

Ohlin, G. 1955. The positive and the preventive check. Unpublished Ph.D. dissertation, Department of Economics, Harvard University.

Oosterveen, K. 1974. Hawkshead (Lancs.) mobility (geographical and occupational) as shown by the reconstruction of the parish from the registers 1584–1840. *Local Population Studies*, **12**, 38–41.

Orwin, C. S. & Whetham, E. H. 1964. *History of British Agriculture, 1846–1914.*

Owen, D. 1965. *English Philanthropy 1660–1960.*

Oxley, G. W. 1974. *Poor Relief in England and Wales, 1601–1834.* Newton Abbot.

Palmer, S. H. 1977. *Economic Arithmetic: A Guide to the Sources of English Commerce, Industry, and Finance 1700–1850.* New York.

Papi, G. U. 1966. General problems of the economics of education. In *The Economics of Education*, E. A. G. Robinson & J. E. Vaizey (eds.), pp. 3–23.

Parker, W. N. 1965. The social process of agricultural improvement: sources, mechanisms and effectiveness in the United States in the 19th century. IIIrd International Conference of Economic History. Munich. Mimeographed.

Passfield, Lord & Webb, B. 1922. *Statutory Authorities for Special Purposes.*

Pawson, E. 1975. *The Turnpike Trusts of the Eighteenth Century. A Study of Innovation and Diffusion.* Oxford.

1977. *Transport and Economy: The Turnpike Roads of Eighteenth Century Britain.*

Payne, P. 1974. *British entrepreneurship in the nineteenth century.*

Pentland, H. C. 1968. Population and labour growth in Britain in the eighteenth century. In *Third International Conference of Economic History*, vol. 4, D. E. C. Eversley (ed.). pp. 157–89. Paris.

Perkin, H. 1969. *The Origins of Modern English Society, 1780–1880.*

Phelps Brown, E. H. & Hopkins, S. V. 1956. Seven centuries of the prices of consumables, compared with builders' wage rates. *Economica N.S.*, **23**, 296–314.

Philpot, G. 1975. Enclosure and population growth in eighteenth century England. *Explorations in Economic History*, **12**, 29–46.

Pinchbeck, I. 1930. *Women workers and the industrial revolution, 1750–1850.* 1969.

Pollard, S. 1958. Investment, consumption and the industrial revolution. *Econ. Hist. Rev. 2nd Ser.*, **11**, 215–26.

1968a. *The Genesis of Modern Management.* Harmondsworth.

1968b. The growth and distribution of capital in Great Britain, *c.* 1770–1870. In *Third International Conference of Economic History*, vol. 1, pp. 335–65.

Pollins, H. 1971. *Britain's Railways: An Industrial History.* Newton Abbot.

Poynter, J. R. 1969. *Society and pauperism: English ideas on poor relief, 1795–1834.*

Pressnell, L. S. 1956. *Country Banking in the Industrial Revolution.* Oxford.

Ransom, R. L. 1968. British policy and colonial growth: some implications of the burden from the navigation acts. *Journal of Economic History*, **28**, 427–35.

Razzell, P. E. 1965. Population change in 18th century England: a re-interpretation. *Econ. Hist. Rev. 2nd Ser.*, **18**, 312–32.

1972. The evaluation of baptism as a form of birth registration through cross-matching census and parish register data. *Population Studies*, **26**, 121–46.

1974. An interpretation of the modern rise of population in Europe – a critique. *Population Studies*, **28**, 5–17.

Read, D. 1961. *Press and People, 1790–1850: Opinion in Three English Cities.*

Reader, W. J. 1966. *Professional Men.*

Redford, A. 1926. *Labour Migration in England, 1800–50.* Manchester. 1964.

Reed, M. C. 1975. *Investment in Railways in Britain 1820–44.*

Reid, J. D. 1970. On navigating the navigation acts with Peter D. McClelland: comment. *American Economic Review*, **60**, 949–55.

Reinhard, M., Armengaud, A. & Dupâquier, J. 1968. *Histoire Générale de la Population Mondiale*. Paris. 3rd edn.

Richards, E. 1974. Women in the British economy since about 1700: an interpretation. *History*, **59**, 337–57.

Riden, P. 1977. The output of the British iron industry before 1870. *Econ. Hist. Rev. 2nd Ser.*, **30**, 442–59.

Roberts, D. 1960. *Victorian Origins of the Welfare State*. New Haven, Conn.

Roehl, R. 1976. French industrialization: a reconsideration. *Explorations in Economic History*, **13**, 233–81.

Rose, M. E. 1966. The allowance system under the new poor law. *Econ. Hist. Rev. 2nd Ser.*, **19**, 607–20.

1972. *The Relief of Poverty, 1834–1914*.

1976. Settlement, removal and the new poor law. In *The New Poor Law in the Nineteenth Century*, D. Fraser (ed.), pp. 25–44.

Rosenberg, N. 1960. The directions of technological change: inducement mechanisms and focusing devices. *Economic Development and Cultural Change*, **18**, 1–24.

1972. *Technology and American economic growth*. New York.

1976. *Perspective on technology*. Cambridge.

Rostow, W. W. 1956. The take-off into self-sustained growth. *Economic Journal*, **66**, 25–48.

1960. *The Stages of Economic Growth*. Cambridge.

1975. *How it all began: origins of the modern economy*.

Rousseaux, P. 1938. *Les Mouvements de Fond de l'Economie Anglaise, 1800–1913*. Brussels.

Rubinstein, W. D. 1974. Men of property: some aspects of occupation, inheritance and power among top British wealthholders. In *Elites and Power in British Society*, P. Stanworth & A. Giddens (eds.), pp. 144–69. Cambridge.

Salter, W. E. 1966. *Productivity and Technical Change*. Cambridge.

Samuel, R. 1977. The workshop of the world: steam power and hand technology in mid-Victorian Britain. *History Workshop*, **3**, 6–72.

Sandberg, L. 1974. *Lancashire in Decline*. Columbus, Ohio.

Sanderson, J. M. 1972. Literacy and social mobility in the Industrial Revolution in England. *Past and Present*, **56**, 75–104.

Sauerbeck, A. 1886. Prices of commodities and the precious metals. *Journal of the Statistical Society*, **49**, 581–648.

Schlöte, W. 1952. *British Overseas Trade from 1700 to the 1930s*. Trans. W. O. Henderson & W. H. Chaloner. Oxford.

Schofield, R. E. 1963. *The Lunar Society of Birmingham – A Social History of Provincial Science and Industry in Eighteenth Century England*. Oxford.

Schofield, R. S. 1972. 'Crisis' mortality. *Local Population Studies*, **9**, 10–22.

1973. Dimensions of illiteracy, 1750–1850. *Explorations in Economic History*, **10**, 437–54.

Schumpeter, E. B. 1960. *English Overseas Trade Statistics, 1697–1808*. Oxford.

Schwarz, L. D. 1976. Conditions of life and work in London *c*. 1770–1820, with special reference to East London. Unpublished D.Phil. thesis, University of Oxford.

1979. Income distribution and social structure in London in the late eighteenth century. *Econ. Hist. Rev. 2nd Ser.*, **32**, 250–9.

Sheridan, R. B. 1965. The wealth of Jamaica in the 18th century. *Econ. Hist. Rev. 2nd Ser.*, **18**, 292–311.

1968. The wealth of Jamaica in the 18th century: a rejoinder. *Econ. Hist. Rev. 2nd Ser.*, **21**, 46–61.

Short, T. 1767. *A comparative history of the increase and decrease of mankind.* Reprinted 1973.

Sigsworth, E. 1966. A provincial hospital in the eighteenth century and early nineteenth centuries. *The College of General Practitioners Yorkshire Faculty Journal*, 24–31.

Simon, B. & Bradley, I. 1975. *The victorian public school. Studies in the development of an educational institution.* Dublin.

Slater, G. 1906. Testimony before the Agricultural Committee. In *Report of the Tariff Commission, 3, Report of the Agricultural Committee,* 2nd edn, paras 37–40.

Slicher van Bath, B. H. 1963. *The Agrarian History of Western Europe, A.D. 500–1850.* Trans. O. Ordish.

Smelser, N. J. 1959. *Social change in the Industrial Revolution. An application of theory to the Lancashire cotton industry, 1770–1840.*

Smith, A. 1776. *An Inquiry into the Nature and Causes of the Wealth of Nations.* 1910.

Smith, F. 1923. *The life and work of Sir James Kay-Shuttleworth.*

Smith, J. H. 1962. *The Gordon's Mill Farming Club 1758–64.* Edinburgh.

Soltow, L. 1968. Long-run changes in British income inequality. *Econ. Hist. Rev. 2nd Ser.*, **21**, 17–29.

Spring, D. 1971. English landowners and nineteenth century industrialism. In *Land and Industry. The landed estate and the Industrial Revolution,* J. T Ward & R. G. Wilson (eds.), pp. 16–62. Newton Abbot.

Spring, E. 1964. The settlement of land in nineteenth-century England. *American Journal of Legal History*, **8**, 209–23.

Stearns, P. 1975. *Lives of labour: work in a maturing industrial society.*

Stedman Jones, G. 1971. *Outcast London: a study in the relationship between classes in Victorian society.* Oxford.

Stern, W. M. 1964. The bread crisis in Britain, 1795–96. *Economic N.S.* **31**, 168–87.

Stigler, G J. 1954. The early history of empirical studies of consumer behaviour. *Journal of Political Economy*, **62**, 95–113.

Stone, L. 1969. Literacy and education in England, 1640–1900. *Past and Present*, **42**, 69–139.

Sturgess, R. W. 1967. The agricultural revolution on the English clays: a rejoinder. *Agricultural History Review*, **15**, 82–7.

Sturt, M. 1967. *The education of the people. A history of primary education in England and Wales in the nineteenth century.*

Taylor, A. J. (ed.) 1975. *The Standard of Living in Britain in the Industrial Revolution.*

Thackray, A. 1974. Natural knowledge in cultural context: the Manchester model. *American Historical Review*, **79**, 672–709.

Thirsk, J. 1957. *English Peasant Farming; the Agrarian History of Lincolnshire from Tudor to Recent Times.*

1970. Seventeenth-century agriculture and social change. *Agricultural History Review* **18** Supplement, 148–77.

Tholfsen, T. R. 1976. *Working class radicalism in mid-Victorian England.*

Thomas, D. 1963. *Agriculture in Wales During the Napoleonic Wars.* Cardiff.

Thomas, K. 1964. Work and leisure in pre-industrial society. *Past and Present*, **29**, 50–62.

Thomas, R. P. 1965. A quantitative approach to the study of the effects of British imperial policy upon colonial welfare: some preliminary findings. *Journal of Economic History*, **25**, 615–38.

1968. The sugar colonies of the old empire: profit or loss for Great Britain? *Econ. Hist. Rev. 2nd Ser.*, **21**, 30–45.

Thomis, M. I. 1970. *The Luddites: machine-breaking in Regency England*. Newton Abbot.

1974. *The town labourer in the industrial revolution*.

Thompson, A. 1973. *The Dynamics of the Industrial Revolution*.

Thompson, E. P. 1963. *The making of the English working class*. Harmondsworth, 1970.

1967. Time, work-discipline, and industrial capitalism. *Past and Present*, **38**, 56–97.

1975. *Whigs and Hunters*.

Thompson, F. M. L. 1963. *English Landed Society in the Nineteenth Century*.

Thompson, R. J. 1907. An enquiry into the rent of agricultural land in England and Wales during the nineteenth century. *Journal of the Royal Statistical Society*, **70**, 587–625.

Tillotson, K. 1954. *Novels of the Eighteen Forties*. Oxford.

Timmer, C. P. 1969. The turnip, the new husbandry and the English agricultural revolution. *Quarterly Journal of Economics*, **83**, 375–95.

Toynbee, A. 1890. *Lectures on the Industrial Revolution of the eighteenth century in England*. 3rd edn.

Tranter, N. L. 1967. Population and social structure in a Bedfordshire parish: the Cardington listing of Inhabitants, 1782. *Population Studies*, **21**, 261–82.

1973a. *Population Since the Industrial Revolution: The Case of England and Wales*.

1973b. The social structure of a Bedfordshire parish in the mid-nineteenth century. *International Review of Social History*, **18**, 90–106.

Tucker, R. S. 1936. Real wages of artisans in London, 1729–1935. *Journal of the American Statistical Association*, **31**, 73–84. Reprinted in *The Standard of Living In Britain in the Industrial Revolution*, A. J. Taylor (ed.), pp. 21–35. 1975.

Turner, H. A. 1962. *Trade union growth, structure, and policy: a comparative study of the cotton unions*.

van der Woude, A. M. 1972. Het Noorderkwartier. *Afdeling Agrarische Geschiedenis Bijdragen*, **16**, vol. 1.

von Tunzelmann, G. N. 1977. Trends in real wages, revisited. Unpublished.

1978. *Steam power and British industrialization to 1860*. Oxford.

1979. Trends in real wages, 1750–1850, revisited. *Econ. Hist. Rev. 2nd Ser.*, **32**, 33–49.

Walton, G. M. 1971. The new economic history and the burdens of the navigation acts. *Econ. Hist. Rev. 2nd Ser.*, **24**, 533–42.

Ward, D. 1975. Victorian cities; how modern? *Journal of Historical Geography*, **1**, 135–51.

Ward, J. R. 1974. *The Finance of Canal Building in Eighteenth-Century England*.

Ward, J. T. 1962. *The Factory Movement, 1830–50*.

(ed.) 1970. *Popular Movements, c. 1830–50*.

Warnes, A. M. 1973. Residential patterns in an emerging industrial town. *Institute of British Geographers. Special Publications*, **5**, 169–89.

Watson, J. A. S. 1928. Bakewell's legacy. *Journal of the Royal Agricultural Society of England*, **89**, 22–32.

Wearmouth, R. F. 1937. *Methodism and the Working Class Movements of England, 1800–50*.

Weber, A. F. 1899. *The growth of cities in the nineteenth century*. New York.

Webster, C. 1975. *The great instauration: science, medicine, and reform 1626–60*.

1976. Changing perspectives in the history of education. *Oxford Review of Education*, **2**, 201–13.

West. E. G. 1970. Resource allocation and growth in early nineteenth-century British education. *Econ. Hist. Rev. 2nd Ser.*, **23**, 68–95.,

1971., The interpretation of early nineteenth-century education statistics. *Econ. Hist. Rev. 2nd Ser.*, **24**, 633–42.

1975. *Education and the Industrial Revolution.*

1978. Literacy and the Industrial Revolution. *Econ. Hist. Rev. 2nd Ser.*, **31**, 369–83.

Whitehead, D. 1964. History to scale? The British economy in the 18th century. *Business Archives and History*, **4**, 72–83.

1970. The English industrial revolution as an example of growth. *The Industrial Revolution*, R. M. Hartwell (ed.) , pp. 3–27. Oxford.

Wilkinson, R. G. 1973. Poverty and progress. An ecological model of economic development.

Williams, E. 1944. *Capitalism and Slavery*. Chapel Hill, North Carolina.

Williams, G. 1968. *Artisans and sansculottes. Popular movements in France and Britain during the French Revolution.*

Williams, M. 1970. The enclosure and reclamation of wasteland in England and Wales in the eighteenth and nineteenth centuries. *Transactions of the Institute of British Geographers*, **51**, 55–69.

Williams, R. 1958. *Culture and Society, 1780–1950.*

Williamson, J. G. 1979. Two Centuries of British income inequality: reconstructing the past from tax assessment data, 1708–1919. University of Wisconsin (Madison), graduate program in economic history, discussion paper series, April 1979.

Wilson, C. 1965. *England's Apprenticeship 1603–1763.*

Wood, G. H. 1899. The course of average wages betweem 1790 and 1860. *Economic Journal*, **9**, 588–92.

1910. *The History of Wages in the Cotton Trade During the Past Hundred Years.*

Woodward, J. 1974. *To do the sick no Harm: a study of the British Voluntary Hospital System to 1875.*

World Bank. 1974. *Population Policies and Economic Development*. Baltimore.

Wright, T. (Pseud. The Journeyman Engineer). 1871. *Our New Masters.*

Wrigley, E. A. 1966. Family limitation in pre-industrial England. *Econ. Hist. Rev. 2nd Ser.*, **19**, 82–109.

1967. A simple model of London's importance in Changing English Society and Economy 1650–1750: *Past and Present*, **37**, 44–70.

1969. *Population and History.*

1975. Baptism coverage in early nineteenth century England: the Colyton area. *Population Studies*, **29**, 299–316.

1976a. Rickman's Parish Register Returns of 1801. Unpublished manuscript.

1976b. Age at Marriage in Early Modern England. Unpublished manuscript of the Cambridge Group for the History of Population and Social Structure.

Young, A. 1804. *A General View of the Agriculture of the County of Norfolk.*

Young, A. F. & Ashton, E. T. 1956. *British social work in the nineteenth century.*

Youngson, A. J. 1959. *Possibilities of Economic Progress*. Cambridge.

1967. *Overhead Capital: A Study of Development Economics*. Edinburgh.

Index and glossary

absolute advantage
Greater efficiency than someone else. For example, Britain had an absolute advantage in both agriculture and manufacturing in the nineteenth century. Absolute advantage is irrelevant, however, to the question of what Britain should have specialised in doing: comparative advantage (q.v.) is relevant. Cf. Vol. 2, p. 65.

accelerator
The dependence of investment on consumption, as the building of petrol stations depends on the amount of petrol sold. The 'acceleration' refers to the speeding up of flow it causes in an underemployed economy: a rise in investment in one industry causes a rise in income earned in others by the 'multiplier' (q.v.), which then causes still more investment (to service the consumption out of the new income), accelerating the rise in income. Cf. Vol. 2, p. 37.

accounting methods, agricultural, 83
accumulation of capital
Cf. capital accumulation
age-specific rate
The frequency of some event at a specific age. The age-specific death rate, for instance, is the deaths per 1000 people of age 1 year; similar rates can be calculated for those aged 2 years, 10–15 years, 60–70 years etc. Marriage, birth and other rates are also used. Cf. Vol. 1, p. 23; Vol. 2, p. 145.
fertility, 19
mortality, 19
age structure
The proportion of people at each age. In a rapidly growing population, for example, there will be many more children than old people, and the age structure will look, if plotted on a graph, like a triangle with a large base; there will be a high proportion at ages 1 year, 2 years, etc. Cf. Vol. 1, p. 22; Vol. 2, p. 149.

aggregate demand
Cf. demand, aggregate
aggregate production function
The relation of outputs to inputs for the entire economy, considering income as a whole to be one good.
Agricultural Labourers, Friendly Society of, 201
agriculture, 3, 17, Ch. 4 passim, Ch. 10 passim, 217
Board of Agriculture, 81
capital, 4, 128
changes in livestock, 186–7
exports, 39
impact of railway, 243
imports, 39
labour costs, 189
labour force, 198–201, 205–6, 265, 273
productivity, 49, 62, 116
technical change, 46, 56, 62, 74, 132, 149, 184–94, 199–203
American colonies, 43–4, 90
Anderson, M., 267
Anne, Queen, 70
Anti-Corn Law League, 258
Anti-Poor Law Movement, 259
appreciation
Of a currency; a rise in its value relative to other currencies. Cf. depreciation.
apprenticeship, 263, 269
aristocracy, 256, 260, 261
Aristotle, 5
Arkwright, Richard, 5, 111, 146
Arnold, Thomas, 261
Ashby, Lord, 148
Ashton, T. S., 13, 54, 109, 160
Atlantic economy
The economy of Europe and North America, viewed as surrounding the Atlantic and constituting by virtue of cheap transport across it one economy. In this view, which is associated especially with the work of Brinley Thomas, national boundaries in the nineteenth century are not necessarily important economic boundaries. Cf. Vol. 2, p. 160.

collective bargaining
The laws, customs, and civilized conventions for handling disputes between employers and unionized employees, especially disputes over the agreed conditions under which the workers shall in future supply labour.
Greater relative efficiency than someone else. 'Relative' here means 'relative to the other things one could do'. Thus, Britain had a comparative advantage in manufacturing in the 19th century, even when (by the end of the century) other countries could do some manufacturing better absolutely: relative to the other uses to which British men and machines could be put (e.g., agriculture), Britain was wise to use them for manufacturing. The mother can do both the washing up and the cooking better than the children, but one does not on that account leave everything to mother. Contrast 'absolute advantage'. Cf. Vol. 2, p. 65.
competitive markets
Markets undistorted by monopoly, that is, by concentrations of power among either buyers or sellers.
complementary factor
An input that helps another to be useful. Petrol and automobiles are complementary.
consols
British government *consol*idated stock. Consols were promises to pay lenders to government a low rate of interest forever. Cf. Vol. 2, p. 43.
constant elasticity form
A choice of mathematical equation such that the *elasticity* is constant. The elasticity is constant when it appears as an exponent. For example, $Q = DP^{-e}$ is a constant elasticity form for a demand curve. The form $Q = D + eP$ is not.
constant price
See current price

constant returns to scale
A constancy in the cost of a good as its production enlarges. Cf. economies of scale, diminishing returns.
consumer demand
The demand for goods by British households as distinct from British firms, the British government, or foreigners.
consumer price index
A number measuring prices in general facing consumers. Cf. base-year prices, cost-of-living index (identical to the consumer price index).
consumers' surplus
The excess of what consumers are willing to pay at most for something over what they actually pay. Those consumers who in 1816 actually paid 30 shillings for a yard of cotton gray cloth would have been willing, if pressed, to pay the same amount in 1830. In fact, however, they only had to pay 9 shillings, earning therefore at least 21 shillings of consumers' surplus. Cf. Vol. 2, p. 196.
consumption function
The relation between expenditure on home consumption (as distinct from saving, taxes, and imports) and total income. If the consumption function has a steep slope, nearly all new income is spent, and becomes someone else's income. If it is flat, then little is spent. The flatter the slope (called the marginal propensity to consume, q.v.) the smaller therefore will be the 'multiplier' effects (q.v.) of a given stimulus to income. Cf. Vol. 2, p. 340.
consumption good
A thing, such as a television or a load of bread, purchased to satisfy human desire now, as distinct from an investment good (q.v.) purchased to make consumption goods later, and not for its direct, present satisfaction of desire.
correlation coefficient
A measure of how closely one number varies with another, as price might vary with quantity. A coefficient of $+1\cdot0$ means perfect direct variation, one of $-1\cdot0$ perfect inverse variation. When two series have no relation (either direct or inverse) their correlation coefficient is near zero. The notation for a correlation

298

correlation coefficient (*cont.*)
coefficient is *R*, whence '*R* squared' or R^2: the square of *R* turns out to be the proportion of the variance (q.v.) in one series explained by the other. Strictly speaking, the explanation must be a straight line (cf. regression).

cost–benefit analysis, 238
An assessment using economics of the desirability of some project, such as a railway. The railway has costs, smoke pollution as well as the conventional costs such as engines, that may require the use of economic methods. And it has benefits that may require their use as well: the total benefit, for example, is what consumers are willing to pay, not merely what they actually pay, and the method of demand curves must be used to assess the willingness to pay. Cf. consumers' surplus, social savings, Vol. 1, p. 238.

cost, at constant factor
See national income at factor cost

cost curve, cost function
The expenditure to produce various different amounts of a good. What 'the' expenditure is depends on what definition one has in mind: of 'total' cost (all the expenditures to produce the amount produced), 'average' cost (total cost per unit produced), or 'marginal' cost (the increase in total cost from producing one more unit). The total cost of producing a million yards of cotton gray cloth might be 6 million shillings; this would imply an average cost of 6 shillings a yard. But if it were difficult to expand production the marginal cost might be higher, say 10 shillings a yard.

cost-of-living index
A measure of the prices of consumer goals, such as food, housing, health care, clothes, and so forth.

cost-push inflation
A rise in prices caused by rises in costs, such as oil prices or trade union wages. The existence of such inflation is disputed among economists, as is its opposite, demand-pull inflation.

cotton industry
consumption of cotton, 2
exports, 39, 100
investment, 118, 133, 138, 142
labour force, 59, 207, 221, 264
machinery, 5
technical change, 12, 62, 108–15, 123, 145–6, 151–4, 158

counterfactual, 12, 41, 96, 165–6, 176, 240
An event contrary to actual fact, though perhaps possible. 'British income would have been 10 per cent lower in 1865 had the railway never been invented' is a counterfactual: the railway was in actual fact invented, and the counterfactual makes an assertion about what the world would have been like if it had not. Statements of cause, such as that the railway caused 10 per cent of British national income in 1865, are said to entail counterfactuals. Consequently, analytical economic history of the sort pursued in this book, which wishes to make causal statements, uses counterfactuals. Cf. Vol. !, p. 240.

covariance
A measure of how closely two things vary together. Over the 19th century, for example, British national income and exports have positive, large covariance, which is to say that when exports were high so was income. Like correlation (q.v.), to which covariance is related mathematically, covariance does not imply the two things are causally connected, or causally connected in one direction.

Crafts, N. F. R., 49, 64

credit creation, credit multiplier, money multiplier
The lending of banks to businesses and so forth, especially the loans that banks make beyond the money they have in their vaults to back up the loans. Cf. bank credit.

Crompton, Samuel, 5, 111, 145–6
Cromwell, Thomas, 19

cross-section
Of facts, given in person-to-person form, or place-to-place; in contrast with time series, which is year-to-year. The general average price of flats in Britain in 1914, 1915, 1916 and so forth is a time series; the price of flats in 30 towns in 1914 is a cross-section. Cf. Vol. 2, p. 129.

crowding-out
The view that investment by the government in dams, roads, housing, and so forth would merely push aside private investment, not increase the nation's investment. Cf. Vol. 2, p. 249, 250, 414

Cumberland, 190
Cummings, G., 220

current account
The statement of, say, Britain's foreign trade in goods and services. Contrast the capital account (the trade in loans) and the monetary account (the trade in money). Your own current account consists of the goods and services you sell and the goods and services you buy: a plumber exports plumbing services but imports food, housing, haircuts and so forth. Changes in his loans or his bank balance outstanding are other accounts. Cf. balance of payments, balance of trade.

current prices vs. constant prices
'Current-price' refers to valuing, say, national product in this year's prices, by simply adding up every good produced. 'Constant-price' values goods produced at the prices of some base year (q.v.), the better to compare output or income free of the effects of more inflation.
cycle, business, 121, 122, 152, 170
cyclical unemployment
Men out of work because of a depression. It is identical to demand-deficient unemployment, distinct from frictional employment, q.v. Cf. unemployment, full employment.

Darby, Abraham, 5, 152
Darwin, Erasmus, 80
Davis, R., 87, 88, 99
Davy, Humphry, 197
Deane, P., 1–9, 13, 14, 17, 21, 28, 38, 43, 44, 46, 47, 48, 50, 51, 58, 63, 64, 70, 87, 89, 104, 107, 153, 167, 170, 174, 206, 207, 218, 220
dear money
See cheap money
debt redemption
Paying back loans.
deficit financing
The act of financing government expenditure partially through borrowing from the public, rather than taxing it.
deflation
(1) A condition of low aggregate demand (q.v.).
(2) A fall in prices, said sometimes to result from (1).
deflator
The index of prices used to express incomes earned in one year in terms of the prices of another year (the base year). The verb 'deflation', is the use of such a price index. Cf. consumer price index, base-year prices.
Defoe, Daniel, 70, 103
demand, Ch. 3 passim
demand, aggregate, 13, 61
The total demand for all goods and services in the economy. Its actual level will be identical to national income (q.v.). Its planned level depends on the consumption and investment plans of households, government, and firms, because consumption, government spending, and investment is what income can be used for. Aggregate demand in this second, planned sense is what drives the Keynesian model (q.v.) of the determination of the national income.
demand-curve, 101
The amounts of a commodity that people wish to buy at various different prices per unit of

it. At a low price of labour, for example, businesses and other buyers of labour would like to buy much of it. Whether or not their wish is fulfilled depends on the supply curve (q.v.).
demand-deficient unemployment
Men out of work because the society does not wish to buy all of what it produces. Distinguish frictional unemployment, i.e., men out of work temporarily while moving from a job society does not now want to a job it does want. Identical to cyclical unemployment.
demand, effective, 13
Equilibrium (q.v.), aggregate demand (q.v.). It is, in other words, the national income, being the amount of spending by households, governments, and firms that they were able to effect.
demand for labour
The number of people businesses wish to hire at some wage. The lower the wage the larger the number demanded.
demand management
The government's attempt to keep the society's spending at the level of full employment (q.v.), neither too high nor too low, by manipulating its own expenditures. Since its expenditures are part of aggregate demand (q.v.), the attempt may theoretically achieve success. See full employment, surplus, fiscal policy, budget deficit.
demand-pull inflation
A rise in prices generally in the economy due to the society's desire to buy more than it has. Contrast cost-push inflation, cf. deflation.
demographic crisis, subsistence crisis, 25
Overpopulation relative to the amount of land available for agriculture, and the misery that results. Cf. Vol. 1, p. 25.
demographic transition
The move experienced by all European countries through the 18th, 19th and 20th centuries from a roughly stable population brought about by high birth rates matched with equally high death rates to a roughly stable population brought about by low birth rates matched with equally low death rates. Cf. Vol. 2, p. 242.
dependency ratio
the ratio of those who do not work for money, i.e., normally children, old people and some married women, to those who work.
deposits, deposit liabilities, demand deposits
Cheque-drawing privileges; your chequing account.
depreciation, replacement investment
(1) The wearing-out of capital; (2) expenditure to replace the worn-out capital; (3) the fund

depreciation, replacement investment (*cont.*) accumulated to allow for the expenditure to replace the worn-out capital. The three need not be identical. Depreciation is subtracted from 'gross' income to get 'net' income because a fund used to maintain capital is not available for satisfying present wants.

depreciation, currency
Of a currency, a fall in its value relative to other currencies.
Contrast appreciation, a rise in value.
Contrast also devaluation, which entails some intent.

Derbyshire, 189, 193

devaluation
A fall in the value of a currency relative to another, with the connotation that the fall was intended and arranged (if not necessarily desired) by a nation's government. Contrast depreciation, which connotes an unintended fall in value.

deviation from trend, absolute and relative
Of a time-series i.e., a statistic for a series of years. Cases in which the statistics are higher or lower than a *trend*, i.e., higher or lower than what might be expected from a line fitted through the points. A harvest failure in 1816, for example, would be a deviation from the trend of the wheat crop 1800 to 1820. The absolute deviation is the number of bushels below the 1800–20 trend that the crop fell; the relative deviation is the percentage fall. Cf. Vol. 2, p. 29–31.

differentials
Usually in reference to wages, differences between wages from one job to another or from one place to another. If the higher wage is compensation for worse conditions or higher skills, the differentials have no tendency to disappear, and are called 'compensating' or 'equalizing'.

diminishing returns, 3, 10, 12, 17, 59, 62, 107–8
The fall in the amount of additional output as additional doses of input are applied. The nation's agriculture is subject to diminishing returns as more workers and capital apply themselves to the fixed amount of land. Output does not fall: it merely rises less than it did from previous doses. Cf. Vol. 1, p. 107.

direct investment
An investment in one's own company by contrast with investment in the bonds of other companies ('portfolio investment'). Cunard Lines, Ltd. investing in port facilities for itself in Quebec would be an example of direct investment; investing in Canadian Pacific Railway bonds would be indirect or portfolio investment. Cf. Vol. 2, p. 73.

direct tax
Levied on the people on whom it is believed or intended to fall, such as the income tax. The distinction between direct and indirect taxes, however, 'is practically relegated to the mind of the legislator. What he proposes should be borne by the original payer is called a direct tax, what he intends to be borne by someone else than the original taxpayer is called indirect. Unfortunately, the intention of the legislator is not equivalent to the actual result' (E. R. A. Seligman, *On the Shifting and Incidence of Taxation*, 1982, p.183). Cf. indirect tax.

discounted value, discounted present value, present value
The amount by which one down-values income earned in the future relative to income earned today. If the interest rate were 10 per cent, for example, one would down-value a pound earned next year to 90P relative to a pound earned today: the discounted value would be 10 per cent below the money value.

discount rate, market rate of discount
The percentage reduction of the price of a short-term IOU (e.g., a 90 day bill) now below its value when it falls due later. For example, a bill worth 100.00 pounds 90 days from now might sell for 99.00 pounds today. The rate is usually expressed as the annual percentage interest rate one would earn on buying such a bill for 99 pounds and holding it to maturity [Approximately $(12/3) \times (£1/£99) = 4$ per cent; more exactly, allowing for compounding, 3.67 per cent].

discounting
See rediscounting

diseconomies of (managerial) scale
Rises in cost as an enterprise becomes too big for the abilities of its managers to manage. Cf. economies of scale.

disposable income
National income (q.v.) minus personal taxes plus subsidies and payments of interest on the government debt. It is the income available in someone's bank account or pocket for spending or saving, the government having taken its share of the product earlier.

Disraeli, Benjamin, 259

distribution
of agricultural goods, 69
of income, 4, 29, 50, 57–9, 137, 145, 164
(1) By size: the frequency of rich and poor.
(2) Functional: how income is allotted to labour, to land and to capital.

Elizabeth I, Queen, 161
employment, Ch. 11 passim
  agricultural, 3
  full, 3, 15–16
  industrial, 3
  unemployment, 170
enclosure, 71, 72, 74, 83–4, 117
  Parliamentary, 5, 56, 62, 83, 184
  Literally, the fencing of new farms. Historically, it was the reorganization of traditional
  agriculture in England, beginning as early as
  the 14th century and climaxing in the 'Parliamentary' enclosures of the late 18th century.
  It created modern farms out of so-called
  'open' fields (q.v.), i.e., traditional holdings
  scattered about the village and subject to
  common grazing.
endogenous
  Caused inside the system being analysed. The
  price of housing is endogenous to the market
  for housing.
  Contrast exogenous; cf. Vol. 1, p. 35.
Engels, Friedrich, 175, 209, 260–8
Engel's Law, 30
  'The poorer a family, the greater the proportion of its total expenditure that must be
  devoted to the provision of food', as Ernst
  Engel (not Friedrich Engels) put it in 1857. Cf.
  Vol. 2, p. 132; income elasticity of demand.
engineering
  civil, 149, 225
  mechanical, 37, 150, 151, 156, 202, 263
England, Church of, 106
Enke, S., 228
entrepreneurship, 76–8, 118, 120, 142, 152–3,
  204, 219
  Managerial skill; or, especially as used by
  Joseph Schumpeter and other theorists of
  capitalism in the early 20th century, *unusual*
  managerial skill combined with a willingness
  to take risks and a perspicacity about the
  future. From the French word meaning
  simply 'contractor'.
equilibrium
  A much-used term in economics, meaning a
  condition in which no forces of self-interest,
  arithmetic, or whatever tend to change the
  situation. If the gap between urban and rural
  wages is an equilibrium, for instance, there is
  no natural tendency for it to disappear. A ball
  at the bottom of a bowl is in equilibrium.
equilibrium growth path for capital
  The way capital would pile up in an economy
  if it grew neither too fast nor too slow (in the
  opinion of those supplying and demanding it).
equilibrium level of interest rate
  The return on borrowing or lending that

makes the amount people wish to borrow
equal to the amount (other) people wish to
lend.
equilibrium wage
  The payment to workers that makes the
  amount of hours workers as a whole wish to
  supply equal to the amount buyers of labour
  (owners of cotton mills, buyers of haircuts,
  students at university) wish to buy. Cf. Vol.
  2, p. 269.
equity
  (1) Titles of ownership; stock certificates.
  (2) The value of ownership in a company; the
  right of ownership.
equity interest
  The value of a company. Both words are here
  used in uncommon senses: 'equity' to mean
  'the value of ownership' (as in the phrase, 'I
  have £2000 of equity in my house left after the
  mortgage is subtracted from the price of the
  house'); 'interest' to mean 'legally recognized
  concern or right'.
Eversley, D. E. C., 145
ex ante
  The anticipated value; or from the point of
  view of before the event; or planned. For
  example, *ex ante* profits in a venture are
  always high – for why else would one embark
  on it? *Ex post*, alas, they may be low.
ex post
  The realized value, or from the point of view
  of after the event, or attained. See *ex ante*.
excess capacity
  The amount less that one produces when
  producing less than one can. The British
  economy in 1933 had excess capacity, with
  workers out of work and factories idle.
excess demand
  (1) In microeconomics, a situation in a
  market in which the amount people wish to
  buy is at the existing price larger than the
  amount (other) people wish to sell.
  (2) In macroeconomics, a condition in which
  aggregate demand (q.v., that is, what people
  wish to spend) is larger than aggregate supply
  (i.e., what they plan currently to produce).
exchange rate
  The value of one country's money in terms of
  another, such as $4.86 per pound sterling (the
  rate during much of the past two centuries).
  An exchange rate is 'fixed' if the government
  of one of the countries is willing to buy and
  sell its currency at the fixed price, in the same
  way as it might fix the price of wheat.
exogenous
  Caused outside the system being analysed.
  The weather (except smog) is exogenous to the

exogeneous (*cont.*)
  economy: it may cause things in the economy but is not in turn caused by them. The price of housing, in contrast, *is* caused inside the economy. Cf. autonomous spending; contrast endogenous; cf. Vol. 1, p. 35.

expected, expectation, expected value
  Statistically speaking, the average of what one anticipates. If one anticipated that the profits on new cotton spindles, say, could be 4, 6, or 8 per cent, each equally likely, then the expected value would be 6 per cent.

expected lifetime income
  One's anticipated income over one's remaining life. The concept is useful because decisions by income earners depend presumably on their expected lifetime income, not merely the income they happen to have this year. A surgeon, for example, would be sensible to buy more than he earns early in his career, in anticipation of high income later. Identical to permanent income.

expenditure tax
  Taxes imposed only on the amounts people spend, as distinct from taxes on income, which tax what they save out of the income as well as what they spend. A tax on food would be an expenditure tax, on all income an income tax, on income from bonds a savings tax.

exponential growth
  Growth at a constant percentage rate per year, in the manner of compound interest. A straight line upward sloping on an ordinary graph against time has a falling percentage rate of growth, because the constant absolute rise per year is applied to a larger and larger base. An exponential curve would have to be curving up steeper and steeper to maintain the same rate.

exports, Ch. 3 passim, 14–15, 38, 44, 67, Ch. 5 passim, 104, 140, 145
  See Volume 2, Chapter 3, 'Foreign Trade, Competition and the Expanding International Economy', for discussion of Exports after 1800.

externalities, external effects, external economies or diseconomies, 84, 239, 245
  Effects you did not directly pay for, such as the pain of smoke in your eye from the local factory or the pleasure of the council's flower garden. The weeds that spread from your neighbour's ill-kept plot in the village fields to your plot is a 'negative' (i.e., bad) externality. The quickening of trade that spreads from the new railway to your business is a positive (i.e., good) externality. An alternative terminology is that external economies are good, external diseconomies are bad. Whatever terminology is used, the key idea is the external nature of the event, that is, outside your own control and not directly affected by your activities. Contrast internal economies of scale. Cf. Vol. 1, p. 239, 245.

factor, factor of production
  One of the inputs into making things, especially the tripartite division into the inputs land, labour and capital.

factor endowments
  The inputs a nation has at its disposal, including labour, machinery, buildings, and skills as well as coal, climate, and soil. Cf. classical vs. Heckscher–Ohlin.

factor income distribution
  The incomes to each of the three classical 'factors' of productions, i.e., labour, land, and capital. Cf. Vol. 2, p. 122. It is also called the functional distribution of income.

factor shares, 6–7, 28
  The fractions of income going to labour, capital, land and other inputs. Cf. Vol. 2, p. 176.

factory, 37, 109, Ch. 8 passim, 219, 253, 257, 265
  Factory Acts, 165, 176, 179, 221, 269–70

family, 47, 165, 200, 267–8
  family reconstitution, 19, 26, 27
    A technique for deriving demographic statistics such as birth rates, marriage rates, and death rates from family trees, the family trees having been 'reconstituted' from various sources like orange juice from concentrate.

Feinstein, C. H., 4, 72, 172
fens, 107
fertiliser, 188, 196, 197
fertility, 26–7, 31–2, 35, 165–6, 177, 205, 209, 212
final goods
  Goods used for consumption, investment, government spending, or exports, i.e., not used merely to make other goods. Contrast intermediate goods, compare aggregate demand.

Finland, 31
fiscal policy
  The plans by government for its own taxing and spending, which may achieve goals such as full employment, growth and stable prices. Cf. Monetary policy, demand management, full employment surplus.

fish, 68, 244
Fitzwilliam, Earl, 261
fixed capital
  Capital that cannot be varied in amount quickly to suit circumstances; opposite, therefore, of 'working capital', 'variable capital',

gold devices
    The exploitation by the Bank of England of details in the market for gold in order to encourage or discourage the flow of gold into Britain, especially in the late 19th century. For instance, though legally bound to pay out English gold coins (sovereigns) for Bank of England notes at a fixed rate, the Bank could pay out foreign coins at whatever rate it could get. Cf. Vol. 2, p. 45.

gold exchange standard
    The system of valuing paper currencies at fixed amounts of gold or of other currencies whose value is fixed in terms of gold. Thus, the currency of a small country might be backed by reserve holdings of gold or of sterling or dollars.

gold reserve
    The holdings of gold by the Bank of England available to maintain the gold value of British paper money. Cf. Vol. 2, p. 45; official reserves.

gold standard
    The system of valuing paper currencies (pounds, dollars, francs) at fixed amounts of gold. Being fixed to gold they are fixed (within limits of transport cost called 'gold points') to each other. The gold standard, then, amounted to a system of fixed exchange rates. Britain was on gold from 1819 to 1914 and from 1925 to 1931. From 1872 to 1931 or 1933 enough other countries were on gold to justify calling it a system. Cf. Vol. 2, p. 43.

goodwill
    The reputation, trademark, employee morale, good collection of managers, or other distinctive feature of a firm. As an accounting idea it makes cost equal revenue when revenue is high: if revenue exceeds costs the excess can be called the income of goodwill. As an economic idea it serves a similar function, and is called 'entrepreneurial income'.

Gorden's Mill Farming Club, 82

government, 268–73
    agriculture, 85
    debt
        Bonds, or IOUs, issued by government. Cf. budget deficit, consols.
    expenditure, 14–15, 135–6, 170
        For purposes of reckoning the national income, the purchases by the government of goods and services valued by consumers. Transfers of income that are not purchases of goods are not part of government spending in this sense: allowances under the Poor Law are not part of spending, nor under some conventions are interest pay-

ments on past government borrowings. Under some conventions of measuring national income, indeed, the provision of roads and police are taken to be depreciation, and are therefore, not included in net income.

factory, legislation, 165, 179
    hostility to, 120
    local, 258, 268–73
    loans, 160
    poor relief, 179
    trade policy, 87, 93, 227, Vol. 2, Ch. 3
    transport policy, 227, 237, 251–2

grain, 92
    exports of, 39, 92
    import of, 92

Grand Junction Railway, 236

Grand National Consolidated Trades Union, 201

grass crops, 78

Great Central Railway, 235

Great Depression
    (1) The business slump of the 1930s which was in Britain a continuation of a slump in the 1920s.
    (2) In an obsolete and exploded but still widely used sense, the slow growth of 1873–96 – which was not in fact slow real growth but merely a fall in prices. Cf. Vol. 2, chapter 1.

Great Northern Railway, 235

gross
    In economic terminology, 'inclusive of something', distinguished from 'net'. Thus gross exports of shipping services from Britain are all British sales of shipping services to foreigners, whereas net exports are all British sales to foreigners minus sales by foreigners to Britain.

gross barter terms of trade
    The ratio of the amount of exports a country gains from trade to the amount of exports it must sacrifice to acquire the imports. The concept was introduced by the American economist Frank Taussig (1859–1940) to allow for tribute payment and immigrants' remittances home as an element in trade. It has proven unsuccessful, and most modern studies focus attention on the net barter terms, simply called *the* terms of trade (q.v.).

gross domestic fixed capital formation
    The expenditure to produce (to 'form') new machinery, buildings, and other slow-to-adjust assets ('fixed capital') located at home ('domestic', as opposed to foreign), and including ('gross of') replacements of worn-out capital as well as entirely new capital.

human capital (*cont.*)
such as buildings and machines. Like them it is a result of costly investment and yields returns in the future. Cf. capital.
Hyde, C. K., 147, 151–3

illegitimacy, 27
imports, Ch. 3 passim, Ch. 5 passim, Vol. 2, Ch. 3
food, 3, 67, 184, 195, 201, 216, 256
income effect
The virtual increase in the income of consumers that takes place when a price of something they buy falls. The fall in the price of grain in the late 19th century, for example, had two effects on the consumption of grain: by the 'substitution' effect, cheaper grain was substituted for other goods, increasing the amount of grain consumed; by the income effect, less grain was consumed, for richer people (made richer by the price fall) buy proportionately less grain. Cf. Engel's Law; Vol. 2, p. 331.
income elasticity of demand, 47, 49, 56
How sensitive the demand for some particular product is to changes in the incomes of demanders. If a 10 per cent rise in income, for example, causes a 5 per cent rise in the quantity of food demanded, then food is said to have an income elasticity of 5/10 (or 1/2). Cf. Vol. 2, p. 121. Cf. elasticity.
income elasticity of expenditure
How sensitive expenditure (i.e., non-savings) is to a rise of income. If expenditure rose in proportion to income the elasticity would be 1·0; if less than in proportion, less than 1·0. Cf. consumption function, propensity to consume.
India, 145, 213
indirect tax
Levied 'on' the goods, such as a tax on petrol levied on the station owner, 'in the expectation and intention [as Mill put it] that he shall indemnify himself at the expense of another', i.e., the motorist. Thus are import duties, excises, sales taxes, and so forth distinguished from 'direct' taxes, such as the income tax or the land tax. Cf. direct tax.
industry, Ch. 3 passim, Ch. 8 passim
and foreign trade, 102
demand for, 31
domestic, 70
investment in, 4
labour supply, 205
inflation
A sustained rise in money prices. The rise in one price – say, food – is not inflation, for it

may represent merely a growing scarcity of food relative to other goods. Inflation is a growing scarcity of all goods relative to money. Cf. cost-push inflation.
inflationary finance
The support of government by the printing of money, as distinct from taxing or borrowing from the public. Cf. budget deficit, government debt, balanced budget, fiscal policy, demand management.
inflationary gap
An excess of desired expenditure in the nation over the capacity to produce it. In the Keynesian theory the gap is the cause of inflation.
informal empire
The nations tied to Britain by commerce and foreign policy, especially in Latin America; 'the empire of free trade' as distinct from the literal empire in Canada, India, and so forth. Cf. Vol. 2, p. 71.
informational cost
Expense incurred in finding information, as for example the time spent looking up this definition. The cost of discovering the market price is an informational cost, which will be high across high barriers of distance and culture. Cf. adjustment costs.
infrastructure
The capital and the institutions needed for an economy to work well: good roads, fair and fast courts of law, honest (or predictably corrupt) government, and the like.
input–output analysis
The use of input–output tables (q.v.) to reckon what flows among industries might be in various hypothetical circumstances.
input–output table
An array of the flows of goods around the economy. One column in such an array might be, for example, the steel industry. The steel output is produced by other industries putting in coal, iron ore, railways, machinery, oil, electricity, paper, and so forth. One row in such an array might also be steel. The steel output is distributed to the machinery industry (which in turn sells machinery back to steel) to construction, to shipbuilding, to railways and so forth. The table includes only intermediate goods, i.e., goods used to make goods.
intermediate goods
Goods used to make goods, as distinct from 'final' goods (q.v.). Steel ingots, railway freight, jet fuel, computer services are all examples. Cf. input–output table.

Keynesian (*cont.*)
attack, advocated the use of government spending and other active policy to offset the cycle of boom and bust. See multiplier, foreign trade multiplier, accelerator, full employment, consumption function, aggregate demand, autonomous spending, demand management, demand-deficient unemployment, budget deficit, full employment surplus, demand-pull inflation, Harrod–Domar model, excess capacity, fiscal policies; contrast monetarism.

Kingsley, Charles, 259

King, Gregory, 18, 46, 64, 69, 70, 71, 220, 255

Kitson Clark, G., 275

Kuznets, S., 8–9, 70

Kuznets cycle, long swing
Variations in the rate of growth of some 20 years' duration from peak to peak, discovered by Simon Kuznets. They have been connected to periodic waves in migration, population growth, housebuilding, technological change, and frontier settlement. An alternative view is that they do not exist, i.e., that they are statistical artifacts created by random variation in the 'real' (roughly 10-year) business cycle. See Vol. 2, p. 33.

labour force, 28–31, 138, Ch. 11 passim
agricultural, 154, 189–92, 198–201
distribution of, 164
female and child, 146, 162, 165, 176, 200, 205, 207, 221, 265
in foreign trade, 90
industrial, 154
participation in, 29, 58, 176, 178–9, 205, 209–10
political views, 257, 261
skilled, 263
All workers for money income. Housewives, who do not work for money income, are not part of the labour force, as are not people who do not work, at all, such as small children.

labour intensive
Using much labour relative to other inputs, especially capital. A blacksmith's forge is a labour-intensive way to make nails compared with a fully-automated nail mill.

labour-saving innovations, labour-augmenting innovations
Improvements in knowledge of how to do things that reduce the amount of labour especially. The assembly line is an example, as are machine tools (saving on skilled hand labour). Labour-saving is not the same thing as technical progress or productivity change generally, because there is more than labour used to make things – capital, land, and materials are used and saved as well. See productivity, labour productivity, biased technical progress.

lace industry, 146

Lancashire,
cotton industry in, 111
female labour in, 265
literacy in, 224
population of, 106
railway investment in, 236
upper class in, 261
wages in, 124

land-intensive
Using much land relative to capital or, especially, labour. Wool was a land-intensive product relative to wheat in the 19th century, for example; and agriculture as a whole is obviously land-intensive relative to manufacturing.

land–labour ratio
The quotient of the acreage of agricultural land available and the number of workers available to work it. In an economy with little capital, such as pre-industrial England, the ratio falls as population increases, and workers are impoverished relative to landlords. Cf. Malthusian trap.

Landes, D. S., 146, 151

landlords, 75–8, 103, 107, 118–19, 132, 188, 192–4, 199, 255–6, 259, 261

Lawes, J. B., 197

leakage of purchasing power
The income saved or spent on imports that does not directly cause production and employment here at home here and now. It 'leaks' out, which is to say that it is unstimulative, not useless. See multiplier.

learning-by-doing
The teaching of the best teacher, experience. In other words, it is the improvement in making steel, cotton cloth, or whatever that comes with practice. Learning by doing has become a popular way in economics of summarizing one source of productivity change (q.v.) a source that amounts to economies of scale (q.v.). Cf. Vol. 2, p. 71.

leasehold, 188

leather industry, 39

Leblanc process, 149

Leeds and Liverpool Canal, 234

Leeds, growth of, 106, 257

leisure, 171

leisure preference, 50, 51, 58
The taste, whether great or large, for activities other than working in the market, such as

312

mixed farming, 79, 80, 85, 186, 189, 190, 191,
193, 196, 197, 202
mobility
labour, 216–18, 224, 226, 265
population, 216
Movement of resources from one employment
to another. If owners of capital have mobility
their capital will earn the same return everywhere, for they will move it if it does not. If
land is not mobile, as it is not, then land will
not earn the same return everywhere.
Mokyr, J., 13, 144, 153
monetarism
The macroeconomic theory, associated especially with the American economist Milton
Friedman, claiming that the money supply
(q.v.) is a prime mover of the level of prices
and of income. Cf. quantity theory of money,
monetary policy, high-powered money. Contrast Keynesian.
monetary policy
The plans by governments for changing the
amounts of money in order to affect unemployment and inflation. Cf. fiscal policy, central
bank, Bank rate, money supply, high-powered
money.
money, high-powered,
See high-powered money
money market
All exchanges of which the rate of interest is
the price, that is, all borrowing and lending.
Sometimes the term is specialized to mean all
such exchanges for short periods (such as 3
months) among banks, governments, and
large enterprises.
money supply, money stock
The sum of all means of payment, such as
coin, banknotes, chequing accounts, and
easily cashable savings accounts. Cf. high-
powered money, bank credit, credit creation,
monetary policy.
monopoly, 237
monopsony
'One buyer', as monopoly means 'one seller':
The single coal company in a northern village
might be a monopsonist in buying labour.
Morris, William, 255
mortality, 23–6, 32, 35, 165–6, 177, 205, 209,
212–16
infant, 212–13
mortgage market, 73, 75
All borrowing and lending on the security of
houses and land: if the borrower cannot pay
the agreed interest he forfeits the house to the
lender (usually a building society or the like).
moving average
An average over several years, called

'moving' because as years pass the earlier
years are dropped from the average and the
mid-year of the average moves. It is a crude
way of smoothing out jumps in a series of, say,
wheat prices to reveal the underlying trend.
multilateral settlement
The usual pattern of buying and selling among
all countries. The word 'settlement' arises
from the notion that all must in the end settle
up, paying for purchases from country *Y* with
receipts from *X* and *Z*. Britain's large deficit
in trade with the United States around 1910,
for example, was made up in the multilateral
settlement by a surplus with India, which in
turn ran a surplus with the Continent, which
in turn ran a surplus with the United States.
Multilaterally – i.e., looking at it from many
sides – the accounts balance. Cf. Vol. 2, p. 67.
multiplier, 13, 15, 42–3, 45
The ratio in which new expenditure in an
underemployed economy results in a larger
rise of income. New exports of steel in 1933,
for example, would have earned steelworkers
and owners in South Wales more income,
which they would spend on, say, bread and
housing, thereby giving more income to bread
bakers and housebuilders. The multiple effects
eventually die out, killed by 'leakages' (q.v.)
that do not cause higher British income (e.g.,
imports or saving). But the flow of income is
permanently higher than it was before, at least
if the initial rise or expenditure is permanent.
Cf. consumption function, accelerator,
Keynesian.
money, Cf. credit creation
Municipal Reform Act, 1835, 258
Musson, A. E., 148, 150

national debt
The loans owed by the state. 'National' is a
misnomer, because it is not all loans in the
nation but only those owed by the state. The
chief source of such indebtedness since the
18th century has been the exigencies of war.
national income, national product, national
value added
The sum of the value of everything produced
for the nation, taking care not to count the
value of, say, coal twice, once when it is mined
and again when it is burned to make iron.
National income is the sum of every income
earned in the nation: workers, capitalists,
landlords, bureaucrats. As a first approximation it is equal to national product, for the cost
of producing things is someone's income. The
taxes on things, such as sales tax on bread,
however, make for a difference between what

national income, national product, national
value added (*cont.*)
is paid ('at market prices') and what is earned
('at factor costs'). The national income at
factor cost, then, is rather lower than national
product (which itself may be lowered by removing depreciation; cf. gross national product). The national value added is the sum of
all values added. The value added by each firm
is the value of the labour and capital it uses,
that is, the value of its goods in excess of its
purchases from other industries. The sum of
all these will be the value of labour and
capital, i.e., national income.
National Society, 271–2
natural price of labour, 32
The wage that would result in the long run if
the number of labourers always increased (by
birth) when they grew to some degree prosperous. Cf. Iron Law of Wages; Mathusian
trap. Cf. Vol. 1, p. 32.
natural rate of growth
In the Harrod–Domar model (q.v.) the percentage rate at which income would grow if it
grew in accord with growing population.
natural rate of unemployment
The percentage of people out of work in
normal times, such as people between jobs. It
is, therefore, the lowest possible rate of unemployment. Identical to frictional unemployment. Cf. Vol. 2, p. 273.
Navigation Acts, 92, 94
effects on America, 95–7
effects on Britain, 96–9
repeal of, 269
A set of acts of Parliament from the 1660s
through the 18th century meant to reserve the
foreign trade of Britain and its colonies for
British subjects. In particular, they protected
the British shipping industry against European competition, protected other industries
at home from colonial competition, and compelled the colonies to trade through British
ports. Cf. Vol. 1, p. 94.
Neale, R. S., 261, 265
neo-classical economics
The modern orthodoxy in economics, as distinct from classical economics (q.v.) before it
and modern Marxian, institutionalist, or
Austrian economics. It emphasizes mathematics in method and profit-maximizing in
substance. In its simplest and most characteristic form it treats as given the technology,
taste and resources of an economy, turning its
attention to how these interact. The various
schools may be distinguished by their respective forefathers: those of neo-classical economics are Adam Smith and his intellectual
grandson, Alfred Marshall. Cf. Marshallian,
classical economics.
net investment
All investment minus the investment in depreciation. That is to say, it is the investment
that results during a year in a net increase –
allowing for replacement as it wears out – of
the stock of capital.
net national product
Cf. gross national product. Briefly, it is what
the nation makes excluding that used to repair
old machines and buildings.
net output
Cf. value added.
net overseas assets
The value of what foreigners owe Britain
subtracting out what Britain owes them.
new husbandry, 79, 191
The system of agriculture introduced in England from the 16th to the 18th century (there
is controversy about precisely when) involving
the use of grasses, turnips, and other novelties.
Cf. Norfolk rotation, mixed farming, Vol. 1,
p. 79.
new issues
Fresh IOUs, as distinct from ones made in the
past and now being traded.
New York, 106
Newcastle, 92
Newcomen engine, 156–7
nonconformity, 18–19, 106
non-pecuniary benefits
Cf. externalities. Briefly, good things that
happen to you for which you do not pay, such
as the pleasure from a neighbour's garden
(presuming that you did not pay more to buy
your house on account of his garden).
Norfolk, 86, 201
Norfolk rotation, 82
A pattern of alternation of crops on a field,
initiated in Norfolk in the 17th century and
before that in Holland on the Continent,
which replaced with crops of turnips and
clover the nitrogen removed from the soil
by crops of wheat and barley. The older
rotation was simply wheat, barley, fallow;
the Norfolk was wheat, turnips, barley,
clover (with no fallow). Cf. new husbandry,
mixed farming.
normal profits
The return to the owners of a business just
necessary to keep the industry at its best size
(namely the size at which supply equals
demand). A sudden rise in demand for coal

partial equilibrium analysis
Economic thinking that takes one small sector of the economy in isolation, on the argument (sometimes true, sometimes false) that the more remote consequences of a change in question by way of other parts of the economy are unimportant. The other members of the pair is 'general equilibrium analysis'.
participation rate, 29
The percentage of a group who work in the market instead of at home. It is most commonly applied to women, whose rate has varied markedly from one time or social class to another. See labour force.
patent, 5
An exclusive right to use or sell one's invention.
Peel, Sir Robert, 165, 176
Perkin, H., 175, 253
permanent income
The income one can count on having, contrasted with 'transitory' income (which includes any unusual unexpected rise or fall in income). The 'permanent income hypothesis' is the notion that the amount people consume (i.e., the amount they do not save) is dependent on their permanent not their transitory income. Identical to expected lifetime income. Cf. relative income hypothesis, transitory/windfall income, Vol. 2, p. 130.
Peterloo Massacre, 164, 257
piece rates
Wages paid by what the worker produces (shirt-collars attached, tons of coal mined) rather than by the hour.
ploughback of capital
Using the earning from a business investment to make more investments, rather then distributing the earnings as profits. Identical to retained earnings. See Vol. 2, p. 270.
Poor Law, 71, 217, 257, 272–5
Amendment Act, 1834, 259, 269, 274, 275
Royal Commission on, 1832–4, 269, 270, 273
Speenhamland System, 273–4
population, Ch. 2 passim, Ch. 11 passim
1700–1800, 2, 10, 12, Ch. 2 passim, 46, 107
1780–1860, 103, 105–8, 144, 177, Ch. 11 passim
age structure, 22
demand from, 46, 144
distribution, 177, 267
living standards, Ch. 9 passim
portfolio investment
Lending in exchange for IOUs such as bonds. Contrast direct investment, equity; see Vol. 2, p. 73.

potato, 32, 215
pottery industry, 39, 59, 145
power loom, 146
present value, Cf. discounted present value
Preston, 107, 217, 218, 266–8
price–cost squeeze
A term in man-in-the-street economics meaning a fall in profits.
price deflated return
The interest rate earned per year minus the relevant inflation rate per year. A loan to the government in 1800 that earned 6% by 1801 would really earn only 2% if inflation in the meantime had been 4% because the pounds in which the government repaid £106 for every £100 borrowed would be worth 4% less.
prices
food, 2, 46, 137, 182–8, 192–6, 202
land, 132
price elasticity of demand, See elasticity
primary goods, primary sector
Those coming 'earliest' in the stages of production. It is therefore another word for both 'investment' goods, i.e., goods such as bricks, coal, iron used to build machinery and buildings; and for agricultural goods on the idea that agriculture is fundamental. Carrying on, 'secondary' goods are manufactured commodities, such as cloth, glass, processed food, and so forth. 'Tertiary' goods are not goods at all but services, such as barbering and teaching. The sequence from raw materials and agriculture through commodities to human services is in this view a progression from primary to tertiary. Cf. Vol. 2, p. 138.
primary producing areas
Areas such as America and Australia and Africa that produced in the 19th century 'primary' goods (q.v.), i.e., raw materials for Europe's machines.
private return
Rewards from a project that come directly to the investors in the project, by contrast with the more comprehensive returns that include any benefits (subtracting any hurts) that come to people other than those who invested. The profits from a railway line, for example, would be private returns; the rise in the rent of my land when the railway ran by it would have to be added to measure 'social' returns (q.v.).
process innovation
The introduction of a new way of making an old thing, as distinct from the introduction of a new thing ('product' innovation).
producers' surplus
The excess of what producers are actually paid

real income
Formally, money income expressed in the prices of some year, removing therefore the objection in comparisons of income in say, 1800 and 1850, that a pound in 1800 did not buy the same amount as a pound in 1850. Cf. base-period prices

real national income, real output
The nation's income (or production because what it produced accrues as someone's income) brought back to the £s of some particular year, such as 1913. The result allows income to be compared from year to year even if prices have changed between them.

real per capita consumption
The consumption part of the nation's real national income (q.v.) per head, in real terms, i.e., eliminating inflation. The other parts are investment, government spending, and exports.

real vs. money wages
Money wages are the pay packet in money; real wages express its purchasing power in the prices of some other year. Cf. Vol. 2, p. 54.

rediscounting, discounting
The purchase of IOUs before they are due, giving the original holder money immediately and giving the holder in due course the interest to be earned by holding them. The Bank of England, for example, commonly rediscounted bills (i.e., short term IOUs) for the banks. The banks had themselves bought the bills (discounted them), and the Bank bought the bills in turn from them (rediscounted the bills).

redistribution of income
A shift in who gets what as pay or other earnings.

re-exports
Goods imported into Britain and then immediately exported abroad without further processing. Under the Navigation Acts (q.v.) Britain was by law endowed with a large re-export trade of products from the colonies bound for foreign countries.

Reform Act, 1832, 104, 178, 258–9

regression analysis, regression equation, curve fitting
Techniques for fitting straight lines through a scatter of points. In finding the straight line that would best summarize the relationship during 1921–38 between consumption and income, for instance, one is said to 'regress consumption on income', i.e., fit a straight line through points on a graph of annual consumption and income from these years. The simplest and by far the most widely used of the

techniques is called 'least squares' or 'ordinary least squares'. The result will be, as it is (roughly) in Vol. 2, p. 342, eq. 1, an equation for a straight line, such as Consumption in £ million at 1938 prices equals £277 million plus 0·44 times income in £ million at 1938 prices. Symbolically, the equation is in general $C = \alpha + \beta Y$. The actual numerical result says that the line that best fits the scatter of combinations of consumption and income is a constant (£277 million) plus 44 per cent of whatever income happens to be. The 'slope' or 'slope coefficient' or 'regression coefficient' or 'beta' is in this case 0.44. Consumption here is called the 'dependent' variable, income the 'independent' variable, in accord with the notion that consumption is dependent on income. The technique generalizes easily to more than one independent variable, in which case it is called 'multiple regression' and amounts to fitting a plane (rather than a line) though points in space (rather than through points on a plane surface). In multiple regression the coefficient 'on' (i.e., multiplying) each independent variable measures the way each by itself influences the dependent variable. The equation fitted in the case mentioned above (Vol. 2, p. 342, eq. 1) was in fact Consumption = 277 + (0·44) Income + (0·47) Consumption Last Year, which is a multiple regression of this year's consumption on this year's income and last year's consumption. It says that for a given consumption last year each £ of income raised consumption by £0.44; and for a given income each £ of consumption last year raised consumption this year by £0·47. The technique generalizes with rather more difficulty to more than one dependent variable, in which case it is called 'simultaneous equation estimation'.

regressive taxes
Taxes whose burden falls on the poor, such as taxes on food, are said to be 'regressive' relative to 'progressive' taxes such as those on mink coats and yachts.

Reinhard, M., 215

relative income hypothesis
The notion that one's consumption (as distinct from savings) depends on one's relative economic position, not absolute wealth. According to the hypothesis, the poor will save little (i.e., consume virtually all their income) even though they are in absolute terms as wealthy as, say, the high-saving middle class of a much poorer country. Cf. permanent income hypothesis; Vol. 2, p. 130.

relative price
  As distinct from 'nominal' or 'money' or 'absolute' prices, the price of one good in terms of another good, rather than in terms of money. If farm labour earns 16 shillings a week when wheat sells for 8 shillings a bushel, then the price of a week of labour relative to a bushel of wheat is 2·0 bushels per week. Note the units: they are physical, not money, units. Relative prices are determined by the real effectiveness of the economy, whereas money prices are determined by relative prices and by the dearness of money. Cf. Vol. 2, p. 410.

rent, economic rent, pure rent
  The return to specialized factors of production in an industry, i.e., those factors used in that industry alone. Agricultural land with no use outside of agriculture is the classic example. A coal seam is another. Economic rent need not correspond exactly to the amount earned in 'rent' in the ordinary sense of weekly rent for a flat, or even yearly rent for land. For definitions in slightly different terms, cf. economic rent, producer's surplus.

rents, 6, 7, 84, 103
rentier
  The receiver of rent, from French (and pronounced as French). Often with an unfavourable connotation, it means the receiver of income without labour, as the owner of government bonds, for example, or the owner of urban land.

replacement investment
  Cf. depreciation. Briefly, it is the new machinery and buildings installed when the old wear out.

residual, the, 6, 7, 139, 155, 158
  A name for 'total factor productivity' (q.v., under productivity) emphasizing its character as what rise of output is left over to explain after the rise of inputs has explained what it can.

Restoration, 1660, 74, 75, 83, 85
retail price index, cost-of-living index
  The average of prices in shops, as distinct from prices at the warehouses '(wholesale price index') or in the economy generally ('GNP deflator'). Cf. base-year price.

retirement, age of, 221
Ricardo, David, 10, 11, 103, 107, 256–7
  Ricardian Theory
  Any idea associated with David Ricardo (1772–1823), the great English economist who brought the system of Adam Smith to a high degree of logical refinement. The chief of these ideas, and the one usually meant when 'Ricardian' is used without further qualification, is the theory of rent (q.v.), namely, the idea that the demand for something available in limited supply (such as well-located land) determines its price.

Richards, E., 207
Richman, John, 18, 19, 20, 28
risk-adjusted, risk premium, risk differentials
  In the capital market, the allowance for risk in the annual return on an IOU. The return to common stock in the UK, for example, was well above the return to Indian railway bonds, but the higher return required the greater taking of risk in holding stocks: 'risk-adjusted', in other words, one might conclude that the returns were the same. In the labour market, the differentials are additional rewards necessary to induce people to enter hazardous occupations, such as coal-mining or lending to unreliable governments.

river transport, 231
road transport, 134, 160, 228, 230–4, 242, 249–50
Roberts, Richard, 154
Robinson, E., 148, 150
romanticism, 254
Romney, Lord, 81
Rosenberg, N., 153, 154
Rossall School, 262
Rostow, W. W., 105, 135, 148, 156, 157, 169
Rothamsted Experimental Station, 197
Royal Agricultural College, 197
Royal Agricultural Society of England, 196
Royal College of Veterinary Surgeons, 197
Royal Society, 82, 148, 149, 150
Royal Society of Arts, 82
Rubinstein, W. D., 178
Rugby School, 262
Russell, J. C., 48
Russell, Lord John, 241
Russia,
  population growth in, 213
  wheat imports from, 194

Salford,
  growth of, 107
Samuel, R., 160
Sanitary Act (1866), 270
Sanitary Condition of the Labouring Population, Royal Commission on (1842), 270
Savin, N. E., 153
savings, *see* consumption, investment
  Abstention from consumption. Any income a person or a nation does not consume in a year but sets aside to yield future consumption is called 'saving'.

savings functions
Statements of what things savings (i.e., expenditures other than on goods and services) desired by people depend on. The most obvious thing is income: a rich man saves more in total, and perhaps even more as a percentage of his income, than does a poor man. Another thing on which savings depend on is the interest rate earned on the savings accounts, bonds, stocks, etc. into which savings are put: if interest (after tax and risk) is high, people wish to save more.

savings ratio, savings rate
The ratio of abstention from consumption to all income; that is, the percent of all income today set aside to produce income tomorrow.

scale, economies of, *see* economies of scale

Schofield, R. S., 223, 224

Schwartz, A. J., 169

science, 148, 149

Scotland,
agriculture, 68, 82
demographic history of, 17
harvest labour from, 190
mixed farming in, 195

search theory
The economics of finding the best deal, the logic of which has only recently been explored seriously. Its main significance is that it offers a rationale for conditions otherwise outside the traditional economic models of man. A condition of ignorance about who exactly will pay the highest price for one's product may be the best one can do, in view of the high costs of search. A condition of unemployment, likewise, may be the best one can do, in view of the high costs of search.

secondary sector, *see* primary, tertiary

secular stagnation
A view associated in particular with the American Keynesian economist Alvin Hansen in the late 1930s and early 1940s that modern capitalism had exhausted its ability to grow. Circa 1940 the view was quite plausible, considering the recent experience of the Great Depression (q.v.) and a sharp fall in the growth rate of the population associated with the demographic transition (q.v.).

service sector, 110

Settlement, Act of, 71, 217
A law of 1662, in effect with varying force for a century and a half after, that allowed local authorities to expel a newcomer to the parish within 40 days of his arrival if he seemed likely to become destitute. Theoretically a great obstacle to the mobility of working people, its practical effect is in doubt.

Shakespeare, William, 264

sheep, 69, 79, 81

Sheffield,
growth of, 106, 257
social structure in, 268

Sheridan, R. B., 97, 98

shipping, 108, 109, 116, 157
coastal, 243, 248
costs of, 93
merchant, 92, 94, 134
regulation of, 94

short-run cost curve
The expenditure of a company or person to supply something before they have been permitted to adjust their affairs to supply it cheapest. For instance, the short run cost curve of steel shows what additional steel will cost if no new plants, iron mines, or marketing arrangements are permitted. In the long run the cost will be lower, for new plants will be built to service the additional quantity demanded. Cf. cost.

Simon, Sir John, 270

Sinclair, Sir John, 17

skill, 222–5, 263

slave trade, 99, 100, 156

Slicher Van Bath, B. H., 215

smallpox, 32, 214

Smeaton, John, 150

Smiles, Samuel, 153

Smith, Adam, 41, 54, 74, 97, 99, 103, 122

smuggling, 44, 53, 55

social change, Ch. 13 passim

social class, 255, 256

social history, 'new', 254

social mobility, 178

social opportunity costs
The value of alternatives sacrificed by some decision, viewed from the entire society's point of view. A decision to pay one's rent of £100 on a farm, for example, costs the private opportunity cost of the money: one cannot buy that £100-worth of goods. From the social point of view however, the opportunity cost is zero, because the landlord gains what you lose. There is no real sacrifice entailed in using the land, for (let us suppose) it has no alternative use outside agriculture. Cf. rent, opportunity cost.

social overhead capital, 73, 74
Capital used by the whole society, especially in circumstances in which expenditure on it is large and the ability to charge for its use is small: roads, dams, schools, the diplomatic corps, etc. Cf. Vol. 1, p. 227; Vol. 2, p. 73.

social rate of return
The rate of return on a project earned by the

320

social rate of return (*cont.*)
entire society, rather than by one group of beneficiaries. The social rate of return to the building of canals, for example, is not merely the return from fares to the owners of the canals (5%, say) but also the return to shippers and landowners not captured by the canal owners (an additional 4%, say) for a social rate of return of 9% per year. See private return; and Vol. 1, p. 99; Vol. 2, p. 88.

social savings
The benefit from a project, measured to include all benefits over the entire society, The annual social savings divided by the opportunity costs (q.v.) of the investment would be the social rate of return (q.v.). For purposes of economic history the leading example of calculating social savings is R. W. Fogel's in *Railroads and American Economic Growth* (1964). Cf. Vol. 1, p. 99, 237–48; Vol. 2, p. 88.

Soltow, L. 172
Somerset Levels, 107
South Sea Bubble
A speculative mania of 1720, unimportant in itself but important for the long-lasting hostility to dealings in shares of companies that it evoked.
South Shields, 268
Spa Fields Riot, 257
Spain, 36, 44, 96, 102
specialised factors of production
Inputs that are used in one industry alone. Skilled miners or, still more, the coal seams themselves are highly specialised factors of production. They receive the above-normal or below-normal returns to the industry, being unwilling and unable to move in and out of the industry in response to good and bad times. Cf. rent.
specie payments
Giving gold or silver ('specie') in exchange for paper currency. When specie payments are made on demand at a fixed ratio of so much gold or silver per pound or dollar the currency may be said to be 'backed' by specie or to be on a specie standard. Cf. Gold standard, gold reserves, official reserves.
Staffordshire, 107
standard deviation
A measure of variability; the square root of variance (q.v.). Cf. coefficient of variation.
standard-of-living index
A measure of the incomes of ordinary people reckoned in real terms. Cf. real per capita consumption, real income.

staple products
(1) Basic industries, or industries on which the prosperity of the nation was and is thought to depend, such as coal and cotton. Cf. Vol. 2, Ch. 13.
(2) Raw materials. The phrase is used in connection with the 'staples theory' of economic growth, which alleges that the enrichment of some countries (notably the 'new' frontier countries especially Canada and Australia) has depended on exports of raw materials. Cf. primary products.

statistics
economic, 129, 140
in social history, 253, 275
medical, 214
nutritional, 216
social, 259, 272
steam engine, 5, 11, 12, 108, 109, 115, 116, 133, 142, 149, 150, 151, 152, 153, 155–8, 162, 202, 219
steel industry, 246
stockbuilding, inventory investment
Adding to inventories. If shoemakers increase their inventories of unprocessed leather or unsold shoes, then stockbuilding has occurred.
Stockton and Darlington Railway, 112, 235
strict settlement
In English law, a device by which the heir to a property cannot dispose of it, or is in some other way restricted in his use of it, for the advantage of future heirs. The family line was thus protected against the greed or foolishness of any one member but likewise was prevented from taking advantage of novel opportunities for enrichment. Cf. Vol. 1, p. 75.
strikes, 153, 154, 179
supply curve
The amounts of a commodity forthcoming at various different prices for it. At a low wage, for example, the supply curve of labour will yield a small amount of labour (measured in hours, say), at a high wage a large amount. Cf. elasticity, demand curve.
supply elasticity, elasticity of supply
The sensitivity with which the amount supplied responds to changes in price. If some buyer of wheat offered a little more than the going market price, for example, sellers would rush in to service him. He would face a very high elasticity of supply. On the other hand, if the world as a whole offered a higher price for wheat, very little more would be forthcoming: the world as a whole faces a quite *in*elastic supply of wheat. Cf. elasticity.

supply price
The payment that will induce suppliers of milk, labour, and bonds to supply milk, labour and bonds.

Sussex, 84
swede, 80–1
Sweden, 24
Swindon, 246

take-off
The aerodynamic metaphor used by W. W. Rostow in a book in 1959 to describe the onset of economic growth. According to Rostow's chronology, Britain's take-off was in the late 18th century.

tariff, 93, 182, 193, 195, 202, 256, 259, Vol. 2, Ch. 3.

taxation, 14, 15, 74, 93, 170, 175

technical change, technological change, 3, 8, 10–11, 59–60, 108–10, 117, 123, 138, 142, Ch. 8 passim, 155, 185, 199–200, 222

in agriculture, 66, 74, 77–8
An alteration, normally an improvement, in ways of making goods and providing services. Cf. productivity change. The two terms are often used interchangeably, although technical change may be applied to a single small change while technological change implies a wider range of changes.

Ten Hours Act, 1847, 165
Ten Hours Movement, 259–70

terms of trade, Ch. 3 passim
The price of exports divided by the price of imports. More generally, it is the price of what a country buys relative to what it sells. For example, your wages (the price of your exports) divided by the prices you face in the market (the price of your imports) are your personal terms of trade. Since 'exports' are not a single good with a meaningful price of £3 per cubic yard, say, the value of the terms of trade in one year has no meaning. But a comparison of heights between the terms of trade in say 1880 and 1913 for Britain does have meaning. For example, an 'improvement in the terms of trade' would entail a rise in the price of exports relative to the price of imports; in the case mentioned the ratio rose 16 per cent. In the technical literature of economics this concept is called the net barter terms of trade. (Cf. gross barter terms of trade). Cf. Vol. 2, p. 54.

tertiary sector, 12, 18, 24, 136, 138, 244
The service portion of the economy. That it is third reflects the view that agriculture and other fruits of the earth are primary, lending this admirable quality to related industries, such as steel. Services in this (untenable) view border on superfluous. Cf. primary, secondary, Vol. 2, p. 138.

Test and Corporation Acts, 256

textile industry, 87, 103, 108, 111, 122, 123, 146, 158, 161, 205, 206, 215, 224

Thomas, R. P., 96, 97, 98
Thomis, M. I., 161
Thompson, A., 87
Thompson, E. P., 257, 264, 267, 275

time series
Of facts, given in, e.g., year-to-year or month-to-month form; in contrast with cross-section, which is person-to-person or place-to-place. Income of the nation in 1860, 1861, 1862, and so forth is a time series; the incomes of 100 blast furnacemen in 1860 is a cross-section (q.v.).

tithes, 83, 84

tobacco trade, 93

Todmorden,
female employment in, 266

Tolpuddle martyrs, 201, 257

total vs. variable costs
Total costs are all cost, whereas variable costs are only those costs that vary with output. 'Fixed' costs (such as the site rent of a ship or the mortgage payment on the purchase of machinery) do not vary with output and are the other element. Cf. cost.

Toynbee, Arnold, 253

trade
colonial, 43
foreign, 2–4, 13, 15, 38–45, 53, 55, 74, Ch. 5 passim, 103, 105, 121, 145, 178, 182, 195, 227, 256, Vol. 2, Ch. 3 passim
gains from, Cf. gains from trade, consumer surplus

trade unions, 179–80, 201, 259, 264

transactions costs
Expenses of doing business, such as the expense of finding someone to do it with, of negotiating a deal, and of making sure the deal is carried out.

transactions demand
The desire to hold money to spend, at once, as distinct from holding it for a rainy day or as an investment.

transitory/windfall income
The part of income that is not one's long-run, expected ('permanent') income. Simple Keynesian theory (q.v.) asserts that the amount spent on consumption depends on this income, not permanent income. Simple Friedmanite theory asserts that it depends on